HUMAN–ROBOT INTERACTION IN LAW AND ITS NARRATIVES

Robots are with us, but law and legal systems are not ready for them. This book identifies the issues posed by human–robot interactions in substantive law, procedural law, and law's narratives, and suggests how to address them. When human–robot interaction results in harm, who or what is responsible? Part I addresses substantive law, including the issues raised by attempts to impose criminal liability on different actors. When robots perceive aspects of an alleged crime, can they be called as a sort of witness? Part II addresses procedural issues raised by human–robot interactions, including evidentiary problems arising out of data generated by robots monitoring humans, and issues of reliability and privacy. Beyond the standard fare of substantive and procedural law, and in view of the conceptual quandaries posed by robots, Part III offers chapters on narrative and rhetoric, suggesting different ways to understand human–robot interactions and how to develop coherent frameworks to do that. This title is available as Open Access on Cambridge Core.

SABINE GLESS is Professor of Criminal Law at the University of Basel, Switzerland. Her research focuses on criminal justice issues related to the digitization of our living environment, as well as on human rights in transnational criminal law. As a member of editorial boards of journals and as a delegate in science funding committees, she particularly aims to promote interdisciplinary research on law and new technology.

HELENA WHALEN-BRIDGE is Associate Professor at the Faculty of Law, National University of Singapore. A recipient of multiple competitive research grants, her research interests include legal ethics and access to justice, legal narrative, and legal education. Her research in narrative was awarded the 2019 Teresa Godwin Phelps Award for Scholarship in Legal Communication, and she is the recipient of NUS Teaching Excellence Awards.

HUMAN–ROBOT INTERACTION IN LAW AND ITS NARRATIVES

Legal Blame, Procedure, and Criminal Law

Edited by

SABINE GLESS

University of Basel, Switzerland

HELENA WHALEN-BRIDGE

National University of Singapore

CAMBRIDGE
UNIVERSITY PRESS

CAMBRIDGE
UNIVERSITY PRESS

Shaftesbury Road, Cambridge CB2 8EA, United Kingdom

One Liberty Plaza, 20th Floor, New York, NY 10006, USA

477 Williamstown Road, Port Melbourne, VIC 3207, Australia

314–321, 3rd Floor, Plot 3, Splendor Forum, Jasola District Centre, New Delhi – 110025, India

103 Penang Road, #05–06/07, Visioncrest Commercial, Singapore 238467

Cambridge University Press is part of Cambridge University Press & Assessment, a department of the University of Cambridge.

We share the University's mission to contribute to society through the pursuit of education, learning and research at the highest international levels of excellence.

www.cambridge.org
Information on this title: www.cambridge.org/9781009431484

DOI: 10.1017/9781009431453

First published 2024
First paperback edition 2025

A catalogue record for this publication is available from the British Library

ISBN 978-1-009-43150-7 Hardback
ISBN 978-1-009-43148-4 Paperback

This book is dedicated to Kate Claghorn and Hilda Geiringer, who contributed significantly to the understanding of statistics in central ways that paved the way for others who invented robots, and who each managed, against the odds and despite the challenges of their individual lives, to become a member of the scientific community.

CONTENTS

CONTRIBUTORS

Editors

SABINE GLESS is Professor of Law at the University of Basel, Switzerland. Her research focuses on international and European criminal law, as well as criminal justice issues related to the digitalization of our living environment. As a member of editorial boards of journals and as a delegate in science funding committees, she particularly aims to promote interdisciplinary research on law and new technology.

HELENA WHALEN-BRIDGE is Associate Professor of Law at the National University of Singapore. A recipient of multiple competitive research grants, her research interests include legal ethics and access to justice, legal narrative, and legal education. Her research in narrative was awarded the 2019 Teresa Godwin Phelps Award for Scholarship in Legal Communication, and she is the recipient of NUS Teaching Excellence Awards.

Contributors

JÖRG ARNOLD is Deputy Director and Head of Science of the Zurich Science Institute (FOR) in Switzerland. He studied Physics at ETH Zurich and specialized in road traffic accident reconstruction. He has published several articles on technology and digitalization in the context of law, especially in connection with road traffic accidents, criminal law, and modern cars.

SARA SUN BEALE is the Charles L. B. Lowndes Professor of Law at Duke University, USA. Her research interests include the federal government's role in the criminal justice system, the laws defining federal crimes, and various issues of criminal procedure, including prosecutorial discretion.

She has been active in law reform efforts related to the federal government's role in criminal justice matters.

MARTA BO is a researcher at the Dutch Asser Institute, Associate Senior Researcher at the Stockholm International Peace Research Institute (SIPRI), and Research Fellow at the Graduate Institute for International and Development Studies (Geneva, Switzerland). Her research focuses on emerging military technologies, autonomous weapons systems and their compliance with international criminal and humanitarian law.

BART CUSTERS is Professor of Law and Data Science and Director of eLaw, the Center for Law and Digital Technologies at Leiden University, the Netherlands. He has a background in both law and physics and is an expert in the area of law and digital technologies, including profiling, big data, privacy, discrimination, cybercrime, technology in policing, and artificial intelligence.

JANNEKE DE SNAIJER is a PhD student at the University of Basel, Switzerland. Her research focuses on criminal law and her PhD research investigates the applicability of the trust principle to human–robot interaction. She works and teaches at the University of Basel at the chair of Professor Dr. Sabine Gless.

JEANNE GAAKEER is Professor of Jurisprudence: Hermeneutical and Narrative Foundations at the Erasmus School of Law, Rotterdam, the Netherlands. Her research focuses on the meaning of narrativity to legal practice, especially judicial decision-making. She also serves as a Justice in the Criminal Law section of the Appellate Court of The Hague. She is co-founder, with Greta Olson (Giessen University), of the European Network for Law and Literature.

DAVID GRAY is the Jacob A. France Professor of Law at the University of Maryland, Francis King Carey School of Law, USA, where he teaches criminal law, criminal procedure, evidence, international criminal law, and jurisprudence. His research focuses on criminal law, criminal procedure, constitutional theory, and transitional justice. In 2019, he was named University Researcher of the Year in recognition of his scholarly contributions.

TATJANA HÖRNLE is the Director of the Department of Criminal Law, Max Planck Institute for the Study of Crime, Security and Law in Freiburg, Germany, and Honorary Professor at the Humboldt University in Berlin, Germany. Her research focuses on the foundations of criminal law, including theories of punishment, theories of criminalization, questions of attribution to the perpetrator, such as the justification of an accusation of guilt, and the role of the victim, as well as sexual criminal law.

HAYLEY LAWRENCE is an associate attorney at Gibson Dunn, USA. She received her Juris Doctor and Master of Laws (LLM) from Duke Law School in 2021. She served as Editor-in-Chief of the *Duke Journal of Constitutional Law & Public Policy* and received the Class of 2021 Intellectual Curiosity Award. She clerked for the Honorable Robin L. Rosenberg of the US District Court for the Southern District of Florida.

ERIN E. MURPHY is the Norman Dorsen Professor of Civil Liberties at New York University School of Law, USA. Her research focuses on technology in the criminal justice system, with a particular emphasis on forensic evidence. She is an internationally recognized expert in forensic DNA typing. In addition, she served as the Associate Reporter for the American Law Institute's project to revise Article 213 of the Model Penal Code, the law of sexual assault.

FRODE HELMICH PEDERSEN is Professor of Nordic Literature at the Department of Linguistic, Literary and Aesthetic Studies at the University of Bergen, Norway. He has written numerous articles and commentaries on literature, criticism, and social issues, and has been a member of the editorial boards of the journals *Prosopopeia*, *Vagant*, and *Vinduet*. In 2021, he was named literary critic of the year by the Norwegian Critics' Association.

ANDREA ROTH is Professor of Law at the University of Berkeley, USA. Her research focuses on how pedigreed concepts of criminal procedure and evidentiary law work in an era of science-based prosecutions. In 2021, she was appointed Chair of the Legal Resource Task Group of the National Institute of Standards and Technology's Organization of Scientific Area Committees. She is also an elected member of the American Law Institute.

EMILY SILVERMAN, a Senior Researcher at the Max Plank Institute for the Study of Crime, Security and Law in Freiburg, Germany, holds a JD from the University of California, Berkeley, School of Law and an LLM from the University of Freiburg. Her current research focuses on the role of artificial intelligence in the administration of criminal justice. She has received grants from the German Academic Exchange Service (DAAD) and the Max Planck Society.

LONNEKE STEVENS is Professor of Law at the Vrije Universiteit Amsterdam, the Netherlands. After her PhD, she worked as a criminal lawyer in Amsterdam and as an associate professor. Since February 2016, she has been a full Professor of Criminal Law and Criminal Procedure in the Department of Criminal Law and Criminology. Her recent research focuses on the topics of evidence in criminal law and the standardization of detection in the digital age.

THOMAS WEIGEND is Emeritus Professor of Law at the University of Köln, Germany. He was Professor of Criminal Law and Criminal Procedure from 1986 to 2016, Head of the Institute of Foreign and International Criminal Law, and Dean of the Faculty of Law from 2009 to 2011. He is a co-editor of the *Zeitschrift für die gesamte Strafrechtswissenschaft* (ZStW). Until 2015, he was Head of the Criminal Law section of the Society for Comparative Law.

FOREWORD

Robots are not humans: they are "mere" machines that do as we tell them. They have no "will," no "consciousness" and no autonomy in the sense that humans do. As with dolls and diaries, we may be tempted to attribute a kind of agency to them, "recognizing" their inner mind, believing they understand our language and share our zest for life. As in the case of dolls and diaries, they may trigger our imagination and help us to generate new ideas while interacting with them, though, as with dolls and diaries, we need to emancipate ourselves from naïve beliefs in them being capable of suffering humiliation or joy. It is hard to steer free from, on the one hand, the attribution of human agency to lifeless contraptions that execute complex, mathematically informed programs and, on the other hand, the idea that they are mere tools like hammers, mechanical cars or newspapers. Unlike previous technologies, robots that thrive on machine learning can anticipate our behaviors and – depending on their program – pre-empt us by tweaking the choice architecture that channels our action potential. In that sense, robots are agents, though with "mindless minds."

This is a new chapter in the history of the relationship with our environment. We must learn to deal with the fact that these new types of agents can diminish or enhance our own agency, based on upstream design decisions taken by engineers who are keen on modeling our user behavior, hoping to make their machines ever more effective in steering us in the direction chosen by whoever pays for their design. As data-driven design is fundamentally probabilistic, whoever develops, provides, or deploys these robots takes the risk of harm due to errors, misuse, or unforeseen behaviors, and such risk-taking raises notable questions of guilt, wrongfulness and causality.

The release of ChatGPT has demonstrated how fluent our robot parrots have become and how easily they can convince us of the salience of their output. The release of large language models also reminds us of the extent to which these models succumb to producing what Harry Frankfurt coined as "bullshit." Frankfurt distinguished bullshit from lying, explaining that whoever lies still cares about the truth, whereas those who bullshit have no interest in the truth, only in serving their own interests. Machines have no interests, not even in the truth. In that sense, their hallucinations are beyond both lying and bullshit. But when discussing criminal liability, the law of evidence, and criminal procedure, it is important to remember that even if positive law could very well attribute legal personhood to robots, there cannot be moral personhood for systems incapable of anything beyond the execution of – possibly highly complex and sophisticated – instructions.

The lack of moral personhood of robots highlights the well-known issues about who should be made liable for the harm caused by the potentially unpredictable behavior of these systems. These issues, in turn, confront us with the difference between criminal law, private law, and administrative and constitutional law. Whereas the attribution of private law liability to an AI system could at some point make sense, provided that those who took the risk of harming or diminishing others are not left off the hook, the attribution of criminal law liability is another matter. Blaming a system that has no intentionality in the sense of Brentano, i.e., intentionality as awareness of the world, would disrupt the foundational framework that has informed criminal law in constitutional democracies. Data-driven robots process data that serve as a proxy for the world they need to navigate, but they have no own stake in that world and no way of sensing, thinking, and acting as we do (which may raise some red flags regarding some of the definitions proposed in this volume). They have been programmed to model the distribution of the data, whether based on examples (supervised learning), on pattern recognition (unsupervised learning), or on goals defined in a way that a machine can execute (reinforcement learning). In the latter case, their output can be further "aligned" with the intended outcome by way of prompt engineering (reinforcement learning with human feedback). None of this, however, makes them aware of their environment. They can only process the data they are being trained on, following the mathematics that defines their model construction. The ingenuity, imagination, and novelty of their operations and output is the result of human investment; it is the developers, providers, deployers, and end-users who create, shape, and reconfigure robotic systems.

This edited volume takes the challenge of mindless, data-driven agency seriously, seeking to reconsider key tenets of substantive and procedural criminal law. Moreover, this volume reaches beyond an inquiry into the fitness of doctrinal intricacies that were developed for another era, where law was text-driven if anything. The final part devotes keen attention to how we can explain to ourselves what the role of robots can and should be in the context of constitutional democracies and how this implicates the criminal law. All this engages the pivotal question of what world we want to live in, share, and reconstruct, turning the volume into a crucial intervention in the debate on how criminal law should respond to the integration of robots in everyday life. With a star line-up of authors, coming from a diversity of perspectives to scrutinize the same pressing issue, the reader will find themselves both enlightened and perplexed, on the verge of a better understanding of the complex underlying issues and real-world challenges posed by the design and the deployment of data-driven robots.

Professor Dr. Mireille Hildebrandt

ACKNOWLEDGMENTS

The editors wish to thank contributing authors, including Janneke de Snaijer, who throughout the project provided invaluable logistical and thoughtful organizational support. The editors also thank the NUS Law research students who helped edit and format chapter text and footnotes, Stanley Wei Siang Woo, Teo Gi Sing, Jared Sim Yu Hern, and Reesa Chua. Anonymous reviewers provided valuable feedback which we are very grateful for. Joe Ng of Cambridge University Press has been of great assistance in bringing the book to publication. The editors would also like to thank Georg and John for their ongoing contributions and support.

To better envision a world with human–robot interactions, we enlisted Bartosz Mamak to work with authors and produce an illustration to accompany the chapters. Thanks to Kamil Mamak, a post-doctoral researcher at the Department of Practical Philosophy at the University of Helsińki and an Assistant Professor of Criminal Law at Jagiellonian University, we were able to bridge multidisciplinary gaps and language challenges. We are grateful to the artist and the authors for working together in a non-traditional way to include visual expressions of key concepts offered by the book, and to the artist for the book cover.

This research project carried on through challenges posed by COVID-19, and we conducted many discussions online. We also had support from Daniel Seng and the National University of Singapore Centre for Technology, Robotics, Artificial Intelligence & the Law (TRAIL). At the end of the project, we held a hybrid session at the University of Basel, a conference at the Council of Europe, and an art exhibition of book illustrations at the Druckraum (Warteck, Basel). The editors wish to thank Clement Bailly, Carlo Chiaromonte, Marcel Mayer, Rosy Mürner, and Martin Thüring for their assistance.

The research project has been funded by the Swiss National Science Foundation for several years and the book is made possible by their generous support for open access publications. The complex application and reporting process has been administered by Claudine Abt with great care, for which we want to express our warmest thanks. This research was also supported by the Ministry of Education, Singapore, under the Academic Research Funds Tier 1 Grant R-241-000-185-11. We wish to thank both institutions for the ongoing support.

TABLE OF CASES

Council of Europe

European Union

Germany

Netherlands

Norway

Switzerland

United Kingdom

United States

TABLE OF STATUTES

Austria

Germany

Greece

The Netherlands

Norway

Singapore

Switzerland

United Kingdom

United States

International

TABLE OF COUNCIL OF EUROPE INSTRUMENTS

TABLE OF OTHER COUNCIL OF EUROPE MATERIALS

TABLE OF EUROPEAN UNION INSTRUMENTS

Charters

Decisions

Directives

Regulations

TABLE OF OTHER EUROPEAN UNION MATERIALS

TABLE OF OTHER MATERIALS

International

Germany

Switzerland

ABBREVIATIONS

AAVE	African American Vernacular English
ADR	alternative dispute resolution
ADS	automated driving system
AI	artificial intelligence
AIG	American International Group
AOT	Advanced Osteotomy Tools
API	First Additional Protocol to the Geneva Conventions
A*STAR	Agency for Science, Technology and Research
ATR	autonomous or automatic target recognition
AV	autonomous vehicle
AW	autonomous weapon
BCG	Boston Consulting Group
CARLO	Cold Ablation Robot-guided Laser Osteotome
CARTS	Committee on Autonomous Road Transport for Singapore
CCR	corporate criminal responsibility/criminal responsibility of corporations
CCTV	closed-circuit television
CEN	*Comité Européen de Normalisation* (European Committee for Standardization)
CENELEC	European Committee for Electrotechnical Standardization
CEO	Chief Executive Officer
CJEU	Court of Justice of the European Union
COMPAS	Correctional Offender Management Profiling for Alternative Sanctions
CCP	Code of Criminal Procedure
CrimPC	Criminal Procedure Code
CSLI	cell site location information
DNA	deoxyribonucleic acid
DSSAD	Data Storage System for Automated Driving
ECHR	European Convention on Human Rights
ECLI	European Case Law Identifier
ECtHR	European Court of Human Rights

EDR	Event Data Recorder
ENFSI	European Network of Forensic Science Institutes
ESI	electronically stored information
ETSI	European Telecommunications Standards Institute
EU	European Union
FISA	Foreign Intelligence Surveillance Act
FMH	Code of Conduct of the Swiss Medical Association
GAO	Government Accountability Office
GDPR	General Data Protection Regulation
GPS	Global Positioning System
HCDR	historical call data records
HMI	human–machine interface
HRI	human–robot interactions
ICC	International Criminal Court
ICL	international criminal law
IEEE	Institute of Electrical and Electronic Engineers
IHL	international humanitarian law
IoT	Internet of Things
IP	internet protocol
IRS	Internal Revenue Service
ISO	International Organization for Standardization
IT	information technology
LAPD	Los Angeles Police Department
LED	Law Enforcement Directive
LTA	Land Transport Authority
MedBG	Medical Professions Act
MHC	meaningful human control
ML	machine learning
MoT	Ministry of Transport (Singapore)
MPC	Model Penal Code
MRT	Mass Rapid Transit
NFI	Netherlands Forensic Institute
NHTSA	National Highway Traffic Safety Administration (US)
NTSB	National Transportation Safety Board
NTU	Nanyang Technological University
NTUC	National Trades Union Congress
NUS	National University of Singapore
NYPD	New York Police Department
OBD	On-Board Diagnostics
OEDR	Object and Event Detection and Response
RFID	radio frequency identification
RISC	*Recidive inschattings schalen*

robo-witness	robot witness
Rome Statute	Rome Statute of the International Criminal Court
SAVI	Singapore Autonomous Vehicle Initiative
SCC	Swiss Criminal Code
SDV	self-driving vehicle
SMRT	Singapore Mass Rapid Transport
STAR	Smart Tissue Autonomous Robot
StGB	*Strafgesetzbuch* (German Criminal Code)
TPA	Therapeutic Products Act
UK	United Kingdom
UN	United Nations
UNECE	UN Economic Commission for Europe
UNIDIR	UN Institute for Disarmament Research
US	United States
USA	United States of America
VIN	vehicle identification number
VIPER	Video Interactive Patrol Enhancement Response
VPN	virtual private network
Wjsg	Justice and Prosecution Data Act (*Wet justitiële en strafvorderlijke gegevens*)
Wpg	The Police Data Act (*Wet politiegegevens*)

Introduction

SABINE GLESS AND HELENA WHALEN-BRIDGE

Chatbots and search systems provide us with access to essential information. Automobiles and driving assistants share steering wheels with human drivers on public roads. Robot vacuums navigate and map our homes. These examples illustrate how robots play a central role in our daily lives, often in ways that we no longer question. This book examines the regulation of some of these human–robot interactions.

The book uses the term "robot," rather than a concept such as AI system, in order to focus on the common understanding of a robot as an automated machine that can execute specific tasks with speed and precision but with little or no human intervention, as it is partly this degree of autonomy that raises issues in human–robot interactions. Our working definition of robot is broad, and it embraces the description in Sara Sun Beale and Hayley Lawrence's chapter, that of an "engineered machine that senses, thinks, and acts," as well as the definition offered in Chapter 8 by Emily Silverman, Jörg Arnold, and Sabine Gless, who refer to a system "capable of sensing information in their environment, processing it, and ultimately deciding autonomously whether and how to respond." Definitions for the new generations of robots to come are now part of the regulation negotiations regarding the use of the complex technologies referred to collectively as artificial intelligence (AI), e.g., in the EU AI Act, which proposes that AI is "software that is developed with one or more of [certain] approaches and techniques ... and can, for a given set of human-defined objectives, generate outputs such as content, predictions, recommendations, or decisions influencing the environments they interact with." The degree to which a robot functions independently can of course vary, as Janneke de Snaijer discusses in her chapter on medical robots. However, such discrepancies do not interfere with the common understanding of a robot as a gadget capable of carrying out a complex series of actions automatically.

Robots are commonplace in many of our activities, but when harm is brought about in human–robot interaction, who or what is responsible? When robots perceive aspects of an alleged crime, can they be called as a sort of witness? How do courts explain the role of the new actor in a legal case? Despite the central role that robots play in our activities, law is tailored to human actors, and legal systems seem little prepared for robots. This volume addresses some of the questions raised by the need to acknowledge the appearance of robots in the legal context. The volume comprises three Parts, each with its own more detailed introduction. Part I addresses substantive law, including the issues raised by attempts to impose criminal liability when human–robot interaction causes harm, or to specifically exclude such responsibility for the use of certain AI systems. Part II addresses procedural issues, such as evidentiary problems arising from using data generated by robots monitoring humans during cooperation, and issues of reliability and privacy. How should we understand robots, and how do legal authorities conceptualize this actor and explain it to the public? Beyond the standard fare of substantive and procedural law, and given the conceptual quandaries posed by robots, Part III includes chapters on narrative and rhetoric. To assist readers in envisioning the new issues raised in different contexts, most chapters are also accompanied by illustrations of chapter themes, provided by the team of Kamil and Bartosz Mamak, and developed jointly with chapter authors.

Robots are here, even if we don't notice some of them, and they pose a host of issues for society and the justice system. This volume is offered in order to suggest ways to frame the relevant questions and think about the answers. But much more needs to be done, and there is considerable room for future contributions.

PART I

Human–Robot Interactions and Substantive Law

1

The Challenges of Human–Robot Interaction for Substantive Criminal Law

Mapping the Field

TATJANA HÖRNLE*

I Mapping the Field: Preliminary Remarks

Technological innovations are likely to increase the frequency of human–robot interactions in many areas of social and economic relations and humans' private lives. Criminal law theory and legal policy should not ignore these innovations. Although the main challenge is to design civil, administrative, and soft law instruments to prevent harm in human–robot interactions and to compensate victims, the developments will also have some impact on substantive criminal law. Criminal laws[1] should be scrutinized and, if necessary, amendments and adaptations recommended, taking the two dimensions of criminal law and criminal law theory, the preventive and the retrospective, into account.

The prevention of accidents is obviously one of the issues that needs to be addressed, and regulatory offenses in the criminal law could contribute to this end. Regulatory offenses are part of a larger legal toolbox that can be called upon to prevent risks and harms caused by malfunctioning technological innovations and unforeseen outcomes of their interactions with human users (see Section II.A). In addition to the risk of accidents, some forms of human–robot interaction, such as automated weapon systems and sex robots, are also criticized for other reasons, which invites the

* I would like to thank Emily Silverman for improving the language of this chapter.

[1] The category "criminal law" is used here in a wide sense, encompassing all norms that prohibit conduct and prescribe sanctions for noncompliance. Details and distinctions, e.g., between criminal offenses in a narrow sense and administrative offenses (*Ordnungswidrigkeiten*) in German law, are not discussed here. They will, however, play a role once prohibitions are seriously considered, and then, notions such as proportionality or *ultima ratio* become relevant and the kind and seriousness of potential sanctions need more thought.

question of whether these types of robots should be banned (Section II.B). If we turn to the second, retrospective dimension of criminal law, the major question, again, is liability for accidents. Under what conditions can humans who constructed, programmed, supervised, or used a robot be held criminally liable for harmful outcomes caused by the robot (Section III.A)? Other questions are whether existing criminal laws can be applied to humans who commit crimes with robots as tools (Section III.B), how dilemmatic situations should be evaluated (Section III.C), and whether self-defense against robots is possible (Section III.D). From the perspective of criminal law theory, the scope of inquiry should be even wider and extend beyond questions of criminal liability of humans for harmful events involving robots. Might it someday be possible for robots to incur criminal liability (Section III.E)? Could robots be victims of crime (Section III.F)? And, as robots become increasingly involved in the day-to-day life of humans and become subject to legal responsibility, might this also have a long-term impact on how human–human interactions are understood (Section IV)?

The purpose of this introductory chapter is to map the field in order to structure current and future discussions about human–robot interactions as topics for substantive criminal law. Marta Bo, Janneke de Snaijer, and Thomas Weigend analyze some of these issues in more depth in their chapters. Before we turn to the mapping exercise, the term "robot" deserves some attention,[2] including delineation from the broader concept of artificial intelligence (AI). Per the Introduction to the volume, which references the EU AI Act, AI is "software that is developed with one or more of [certain] approaches and techniques … and can, for a given set of human-defined objectives, generate outputs such as content, predictions, recommendations, or decisions influencing the environments they interact with."[3] The consequences of the growing use of information technology (IT) and AI are discussed in many areas of law and legal policy.[4] In the field of criminal justice, AI systems can be utilized at the pre-trial and sentencing stages as well

[2] See also Monika Simmler & Nora Markwalder, "Guilty Robots? Rethinking the Nature of Culpability and Legal Personhood in an Age of Artificial Intelligence" (2019) 30:1 *Criminal Law Forum* 1 ["Guilty Robots"] at 5–6.

[3] European Union, European Commission, Proposal for a Regulation of the European Parliament and of the Council Laying Down Harmonised Rules on Artificial Intelligence and Amending Certain Union Legislative Acts, COM/2021/206 final (Brussels, Belgium: European Commission, April 21, 2021).

[4] See e.g., Horst Eidenmüller & Gerhard Wagner, *Law by Algorithm* (Heidelberg, Germany: Mohr Siebeck, 2021) [*Law by Algorithm*].

as for making decisions about parole, to provide information on the risk of reoffending.[5] Whether these systems analyze information more accurately and comprehensively than humans, and the degree to which programs based on machine learning inherit biases, are issues under discussion.[6] The purpose of this volume is not to examine the relevance of these new technologies to criminal law and criminal justice in general; the focus is somewhat narrower. Robots are the subject. Entities that are called robots can be based on machine learning techniques and AI, technologies already in use today, but they also have another crucial feature. They are designed to perform actions in the real word[7] and thus must usually be embodied as physical objects. It is primarily this ability to interact physically with environments, objects, and the bodies of humans that calls for safeguards.

II The Preventive Perspective: Regulating Human–Robot Interactions

II.A Preventing Accidents

Regulation is necessary to prevent accidents caused by malfunctioning robots and unforeseen interactive effects. Some of these rules might need to be backed up by sanctions. It is almost impossible to say much more on a general level about potential accidents and what should be prohibited or regulated to minimize the risk of harm, as a more detailed analysis would require covering a vast area. The exact nature of important "dos and don'ts" that might warrant enforcement by criminal laws obviously depends on the kinds of activities that robots perform, e.g., in manufacturing, transportation, healthcare, households, and warfare, and the potential risks involved. The more complex a robot's task, the more that can go wrong. The kind and size of potential harm depends, among other things,

[5] For such instruments, see Sheldon Zhang, Robert Roberts, & David Farabee, "An Analysis of Prisoner Reentry and Parole Risk Using COMPAS and Traditional Criminal History Measures" (2014) 60:2 *Crime and Delinquency* 167; Carolyn McKay, "Predicting Risk in Criminal Procedure: Actuarial Tools, Algorithms, AI and Judicial Decision-Making" (2020) 32:1 *Current Issues in Criminal Justice* 22; Lucia Sommerer, *Personenbezogenes Predictive Policing* (Baden-Baden, Germany: Nomos, 2020).

[6] See e.g., Solon Barocas & Andrew Selbst, "Big Data's Disparate Impact" (2016) 104:3 *California Law Review* 671; Richard Berk, Hoda Heidari, Shahin Jabbari *et al.*, "Fairness in Criminal Justice Task Assessments: The State of the Art" (2017) 50:1 *Sociological Methods & Research* 3; John Kleinberg, Himabindu Lakkaraju, Jens Ludwig *et al.*, "Human Decisions and Machine Predictions" (2018) 133:1 *Quarterly Journal of Economics* 237.

[7] See Erico Guizzo, "What Is a Robot?" *IEEE* (August 1, 2018), https://robots.ieee.org/learn/what-is-a-robot/.

on the physical properties of robots, such as weight and speed, the frequency with which they encounter the general public, and the closeness of their operations to human bodies. Autonomous vehicles and surgical robots, e.g., require tighter regulation than robot vacuum cleaners.

The task of developing proper regulations for potentially dangerous human–robot interaction is challenging. It begins with the need to determine the entity to whom rules and prohibitions are addressed: manufacturers; programmers; those who rely on robots as tools, such as owners or users; third parties who happen to encounter robots, e.g., in the case of automated cars, other road users; or malevolent intruders who, e.g., hack computer systems or otherwise manipulate the robot's functions. Another question is who can – and who should – develop legal standards. Not only legislatures, but also criminal and civil courts can and do contribute to rule-setting. Their rulings, however, generally target a specific case. Systematic and comprehensive regulation seems to call for legislative action. But before considering the enactment of new laws, attention should be paid to existing criminal laws, i.e., general prohibitions that protect human life, bodily integrity, property, etc. These prohibitions can be applied to some human failures that involve robots, but due to their unspecific wording and broad scope, they do not give sufficient guidance for our scenarios. More specific norms of conduct, norms tailored to the production, programming, and use of robots, would certainly be preferable. This leads again to the question of what institution is best situated to develop these norms of conduct. This task requires constant attention to and monitoring of rapid technological developments and emerging trends in robotics. Ultimately, traditional modes of regulation by means of laws might not be ideally suited to respond effectively to emerging technologies. Another major difficulty is that regulations in domestic laws do not make much sense for products circulating in global markets. This may prompt efforts to harmonize national laws.[8] As an alternative, soft law in the form of standards and guidelines proposed by the private sector or regulatory agencies might be a way to achieve faster and perhaps also more universal agreement among the producers and users of robots.[9]

For legal scholars and legal policy, the upshot is that we should probably not expect too much from substantive criminal law as an instrument

[8] See *Feasibility Study of a Future Council or Europe Instrument on Artificial Intelligence and Criminal Law* (European Committee on Crime Problems, September 4, 2020).

[9] Gary Marchant & Brad Allenby, "Soft Law: New Tools for Governing Emerging Technologies" (2017) 73:2 *Bulletin of the Atomic Scientists* 108; Ryan Hagemann, Jennifer Huddleston, & Adam Thierer, "Soft Law for Hard Problems: The Governance of Emerging

to control the use of new technologies. Effective and comprehensive regulation to prevent harm arising out of human–robot interactions, and the difficult task of balancing societal interest in the services provided by robots against the risks involved, do not belong to the core competencies of criminal law.

II.B Beyond Accidents

Beyond the prevention of accidents, other concerns might call for criminal prohibitions. If there are calls to suppress certain conduct rather than to regulate it, the criminal law is a logical choice. Strict prohibitions would make sense if one were to fundamentally object to the creation of AI and autonomous robots, in part because the long-term consequences for humankind might be serious,[10] although it may be too late for that in some instances. A more selective approach would be to demand not a categorical decision against all research in the field of AI and the production of advanced robots in general, but rather efforts to suspend research[11] or to stop the production of some kinds of robots. An example of the latter approach would be prohibiting devices that apply deadly force against humans, such as remotely controlled or automated weapons systems, addressed in this volume by Marta Bo.[12] Not only is the possibility of accidents a particularly serious concern in this area, but also the reliability of target identification, the precision of application, and the control of access are of utmost importance. Even if autonomous weapon systems work as intended, they might in the long run increase the death toll in wars, and ethical doubts regarding war might grow if the humans responsible for aggressive military operations do not face personal risks.[13]

Technologies in an Uncertain Future" (2018) 17:1 *Colorado Technology Law Journal* 37; Anna Thaler, *Values and Ethical Principles for AI and Robotics: A Qualitative Content Analysis of EU Soft Law Initiatives* (Hamburg, Germany: Verlag Dr. Kovač, 2021).

10 See, for possible future risks, Nick Bostrom, *Superintelligence: Paths, Dangers, Strategies* (New York, NY: Oxford University Press, 2014).

11 For a proposal signed by prominent AI researchers and entrepreneurs, see "Pause Giant AI Experiments: An Open Letter," *Future of Life*, https://futureoflife.org/open-letter/pause-giant-ai-experiments/.

12 See Chapter 2 in this volume; see also: Jai Galliot, *Military Robots: Mapping the Moral Landscape* (Abingdon, UK: Routledge, 2017); Paul Springer, *Outsourcing War to Machines: The Military Robotics Revolution* (Santa Barbara, CA: Praeger, 2018); Paul Scharre, *Army of None: Autonomous Weapons and the Future of War* (New York, NY: W.W. Norton & Company, 2018) [*Army of None*].

13 For an overview of the ethical issues, see Nehal Bhuta, Susanne Beck, Robin Geis *et al.* (eds.), *Autonomous Weapons Systems: Law, Ethics, Policy* (Cambridge, UK: Cambridge University Press, 2016); *Army of None*, note 12 above, at 271–296.

Arguments that point to the risk of remote harm are often based on moral concerns. This is most evident in the discussions about sex robots. Should sex robots in general or, more particularly, sex robots that imitate stereotypical characteristics of female prostitutes, be banned?[14] The proposition of such prohibitions would need to be supported by strong empirical and normative arguments, including explanations as to why sex robots are more problematic than sex dolls, whether it is plausible to expect such robots to have negative effects on a sizable number of persons, why sexual activity involving humans and robots is morally objectionable, and even if convincing arguments of this kind could be made, why the state should engage in the enforcement of norms regarding sexual morality.

For legal theorists, it is also interesting to ask whether, at some point, policy debates will no longer focus solely on remote harms to other human beings, collective human concerns such as gender equality, or human values and morals, but will instead expand to include the interests or rights of individual robots as well. Take the example of sex robots. Could calls to prohibit sexual interactions between humans and robots refer to the dignity of the robot and its right to dignity? Might we experience a re-emergence of debates about slavery? At present, it would certainly be premature to claim that humans and robots should be treated as equivalent, but discussions about these issues have already begun.[15] As long as robots are distinguishable from humans in several dimensions, such as bodies, social competence, and emotional expressivity, it is unlikely that the rights humans grant one another will be extended to them. As long as there are no truly humanoid robots, i.e., robots that resemble humans in all or most physiological and psychological dimensions,[16] tremendous cognitive abilities alone are unlikely to trigger widespread demands for equal treatment such as the recognition of robots' rights. For the purpose

[14] Campaign against Sex Robots website, https://campaignagainstsexrobots.org/; Oliver Bendel, "Love Dolls and Sex Robots in Unproven and Unexplored Fields of Application" (2020) 12:1 *Paladyn, Journal of Behavioral Robotics* 1.

[15] See e.g., Phil McNally & Sohail Inayatullah, "The Rights of Robots: Technology, Culture and Law in the 21st Century" (1988) 20:2 *Futures* 119; Mark Coeckelbergh, "Robot Rights? Towards a Social-Relational Justification of Moral Consideration" (2010) 12:3 *Ethics and Information Technology* 209; David Gunkel, *Robot Rights* (Cambridge, MA: MIT Press, 2018); Henry Shevlin, "How Could We Know When a Robot Was a Moral Patient?" (2021) 30:3 *Cambridge Quarterly of Healthcare Ethics* 459; John Danaher, "What Matters for Moral Status: Behavioural or Cognitive Equivalence?" (2021) 30:3 *Cambridge Quarterly of Healthcare Ethics* 472.

[16] See, for an example from fiction, Ian McEwan, *Machines Like Me* (London, UK: Penguin Books, 2019).

of this introductory chapter, it must suffice to point out that thinking in this direction would also be relevant to debates concerning the need to criminalize selected conduct in order to protect the interests of robots.

III The Retrospective Perspective: Applying Criminal Law to Human–Robot Interactions

The harmful outcomes of human–robot interactions not only provide an impetus to consider creating preventive regulation. Harmful outcomes can also give rise to criminal investigations and, ultimately, to proceedings against the humans involved. The criminal liability of robots is also discussed below.

III.A Human Liability for Unforeseen Accidents

III.A.1 Manufacturers and Programmers

If humans have been injured or killed through interaction with a robot, if property has been damaged, or if other legally protected rights have been disregarded, questions of criminal liability will arise. It could, of course, be argued that the more pressing issue is effective compensation, a goal achievable by means of tort law and mandatory insurance, perhaps in combination with the legal construct of robots as "electronic persons" with their own assets.[17] Serious accidents, however, are also likely to engage criminal justice officials who need to clarify whether a human suspect or, depending on the legal system, a corporation has committed a criminal offense.

The first group of potential defendants could be those who built and programmed the robot. If the applicable criminal law does not include a strict liability regulatory offense, criminal liability will depend on the applicability of general norms, such as those governing negligent or reckless conduct. The challenges for prosecutors and courts are manifold, and they include establishing causality, attributing outcomes to acts and

[17] See, for the idea of an electronic person, European Union, The European Parliament, Resolution of February 16, 2017 with Recommendations to the Commission on Civil Law Rules on Robotics (2015/2103(INL)), OJ 2015 C 252 (EU: Official Journal of the European Union, 2017) at No. 59(f); Susanne Beck, "Intelligent Agents and Criminal Law – Negligence, Diffusion of Liability and Electronic Personhood" (2016) 86:4 *Robotics and Autonomous Systems* 138 ["Intelligent Agents"] at 141–142; Jacob Turner, "Legal Personality for AI" in Jacob Turner, *Robot Rules* (London, UK: Palgrave, 2018) ["Legal Personality for AI"] 173; *Law by Algorithm*, note 4 above, at 103–126.

omissions, and specifying the standard of care that applied to the defendant's conduct.[18] Determining the appropriate standard of care requires knowledge of what could have been done better on the technical level. In addition, difficult, wide-ranging normative considerations are relevant. How much caution do societies require, and how much caution may they require when innovative products such as robots are introduced?[19] As a general rule, standards of care should not be so strict as to have a chilling effect on progress, since manufacturers and programmers can relieve humans of manual, tiresome, and tedious work, robots can compensate for the lack of qualified employees in many areas, and the overall effect of robot use can be beneficial to the public, e.g., by reducing traffic accidents once the stage of automated driving has been reached. Such fundamental issues of social utility should be one criterion when determining the standards of care upon which the criminal liability of manufacturers and programmers are predicated.[20]

Marta Bo focuses on the criminal liability of programmers in Chapter 2, "Are Programmers in or out of Control? The Individual Criminal Responsibility of Programmers of Autonomous Weapons and Self-Driving Cars." She asks whether programmers could be accused of crimes against persons if automated cars or automated weapons cause harm to humans or if the charge of indiscriminate attacks against civilians can be made. She describes the challenges facing programmers of automated vehicles and autonomous weapons and discusses factors that can undermine their control over outcomes. She then turns her attention to legal assessments, including criteria such as *actus reus*, the causal nexus between programming and harm caused by automated vehicles and autonomous weapons, and negligence standards. Bo concludes that it is possible to use criminal law criteria for imputation to test whether programmers had "meaningful human control."

An obvious challenge for criminal law assessment is to determine the degree to which, in the case of machine learning, programmers can foresee developments in a robot's behavior. If the path from the original algorithm to the robot's actual conduct cannot be reconstructed, it might be worth considering whether the mere act of exposing humans to encounters with a somewhat unpredictable and thus potentially dangerous robot

[18] See "Intelligent Agents", note 17 above, at 139.

[19] See, for the notion of "admissible risk," "Intelligent Agents", note 17 above, at 141.

[20] Sabine Gless, Emily Silverman, & Thomas Weigend, "If Robots Cause Harm, Who is to Blame? Self-Driving Cars and Criminal Liability" (2016) 19:3 *New Criminal Law Review* 412 ["If Robots Cause Harm"] at 433–434.

could, without more, be labeled criminally negligent. While this might be a reasonable approach when such robots first appear on the market, the question of whether it would be a good long-term solution merits careful consideration. It seems preferable to focus on strict criteria for licensing self-learning robots, and on civil law remedies such as compensation that do not require proof of individual negligence, and abandon the idea of criminal punishment of humans just for developing and marketing robots with self-learning features.

III.A.2 Supervisors and Users

Humans who are involved in a robot's course of action in an active cooperative or supervisory way could, if an accident occurs, incur criminal liability for recklessness or negligence. Again, for prosecutors and courts, a frequent problem will be to identify the causes of an accident and the various roles of the numerous persons involved in the production and use of the robot. A "diffusion of responsibility"[21] is almost impossible to avoid. Also, the question will arise as to what can realistically be expected of humans when they supervise and use robots equipped with AI and machine learning technology. How can they keep up with self-learning robots if the decision-making processes of such robots are no longer understandable and their behavior hard to predict?[22]

In Chapter 3, "Trusting Robots: Limiting Due Diligence Obligations in Robot-Assisted Surgery under Swiss Criminal Law," Janneke de Snaijer describes one area where human individuals might be held criminally liable as a consequence of using robots. She focuses on the potential and the challenges of robot-assisted surgery. The chapter introduces readers to a technology already in use in operating rooms: that of automated robots helping surgeons achieve greater surgical precision. These robots can perform limited tasks independently, but are not fully autonomous. De Snaijer concentrates primarily on criminal liability for negligence, which depends on how the demands of due diligence are defined. She describes general rules of Swiss criminal law doctrine that provide some guidelines for requirements of due diligence. The major problem she identifies is how much trust surgeons should be allowed to place in the functioning of the robots with which they cooperate. Concluding that

[21] Susanne Beck, "Google Cars, Software Agents, Autonomous Weapons Systems – New Challenges for Criminal Law?" in Eric Hilgendorf & Uwe Seidel (eds.), *Robotics, Autonomics, and the Law* (Baden-Baden, Germany: Nomos, 2017) 227 ["Google Cars"] at 245.

[22] Ibid. at 243.

Swiss law holds surgeons accountable for robots' actions to an unreasonable degree, she diagnoses contradictory standards in that surgeons are held responsible but required by law to use new technology to improve the quality of surgery.

In other contexts, robots are given the task of monitoring those who use them, e.g., by detecting fatigue or alcohol consumption, and, if need be, issuing warnings. Under such circumstances, a human who fails to heed a warning and causes an accident may face criminal liability. Presuming negligence in such cases might have the effect of establishing a higher standard for humans carrying out an activity while under the surveillance of a robot than for humans carrying out the same activity without the surveillance function. It might also mean that the threshold for assuming recklessness, or, under German law, conditional intent,[23] will be lowered. An interesting question is the degree to which courts will allow leeway for human psychology, including perhaps a human disinclination to be bossed around by a machine.

III.A.3 Corporate Liability

In many cases, it will not be possible or very difficult to trace harm caused by a device based on artificial intelligence to the wrongful conduct of an individual human being who acted in the role of programmer, manufacturer, supervisor, or user. Thomas Weigend starts Chapter 4, entitled "Forms of Robot Liability: Criminal Robots and Corporate Criminal Responsibility," with the diagnosis of a "responsibility gap." He then examines the option of holding robots criminally liable before going a step further and considering the introduction of corporate criminal responsibility for the harmful actions of robots. Weigend begins with the controversial discussion of whether corporations should be punished for crimes committed by employees. He then develops the idea that the rationales used to justify the far-reaching attribution of employee conduct to corporations could be applied to the conduct of robots as well. He contends that criminal liability should be limited to cases in which humans acting on behalf of the corporation were (at a minimum) negligent regarding the designing, programming, or controlling of robots.

[23] See, for the notion of conditional intent in German criminal law: Michael Bohlander, *Principles of German Criminal Law* (Oxford, UK: Hart, 2009) [*German Criminal Law*] at 63–67; Tatjana Hörnle & Rita Vavra, "Criminal Law" in Joachim Zekoll & Gerhard Wagner (eds.), *Introduction to German Law*, 3rd ed. (Philadelphia, PA: Wolters Kluwer, 2019) ["Criminal Law"] 503 at 509.

III.B Human Liability for the Use of a Robot with the Intent to Commit a Crime

Robots can be purposefully used to commit crimes, e.g., to spy on other persons.[24] If the accused human intentionally designed, manipulated, used, or abused a robot to commit a crime, he or she can be held criminally liable for the outcome.[25] The crucial point in such cases is that the human who employs the robot uses it as a tool.[26] If perpetrators pursue their criminal goals with the use of a tool, it does not matter whether the tool is of the traditional, merely mechanical kind, such as a gun, or whether it has some features of intelligence, such as an automated weapon that is, e.g., reprogrammed for a criminal purpose.

While this is clearly the case for many criminal offenses, particularly those that focus on outcomes such as causing the death of another person, the situation with regard to other criminal offenses is not so clear. It will not always be obvious that a robot will be able to fulfil the definitional elements of all offenses. It could, e.g., be argued that sexual offenses that require bodily contact between offender and victim cannot be committed if the offender causes a robot to touch another person in a sexual way. In such cases, it is a matter of interpretation if wrongdoing requires the physical involvement of the human offender's body. I would answer this particular question in the negative, because the crucial point is the penetration of the victim's body. However, answers must be developed for different crimes separately, based on the legal terminology used and the kind of interest protected.

III.C Human Liability for Foreseen but Unavoidable Harm

In the situation of an unsolvable, tragic dilemma, in which there is no alternative harmless action, a robot might injure humans as part of a planned course of action. The most frequently discussed examples of these dilemmas involve automated cars in traffic scenarios in which all available options, such as staying on track or altering course, will lead to a crash with human victims.[27] If such events have been anticipated by human programmers, the question

[24] See, for the potential of service robots to be used this way, "Google Cars", note 21 above, at 231.

[25] "Legal Personality for AI", note 17 above, at 118; "If Robots Cause Harm", note 20 above, at 425.

[26] For a discussion of characterization of robots as a tool, see Chapter 13 in this volume.

[27] For this dilemma, see Dietmar Hübner & Lucie White, "Crash Algorithms for Autonomous Cars: How the Trolley Problem Can Move Us beyond Harm Minimisation" (2018) 21:3 *Ethical Theory and Moral Practice* 685; Rob Lawlor, "The Ethics of Automated

arises of whether they could perhaps be held criminally liable, should the dilemmatic situation in fact occur. When human drivers in a comparable dilemma knowingly injure others to save their own lives or the lives of their loved ones, criminal law systems recognize defenses that acknowledge the psychological and normative forces of strong fear, the will to survive, and personal attachments.[28] The rationale of such defenses does not apply, however, if a programmer, who is not in acute distress, decides that the automated car should always safeguard passengers inside the vehicle, and thus chooses the course that will lead to the death of humans outside the car.

If a human driver has to choose between swerving to save the lives of two persons on the road directly in front of the car, thus hitting and killing a single person on the sidewalk, or staying the course, thus hitting and killing both persons on the road, criminal law doctrine does not provide clear-cut answers. Under German doctrine, which displays a built-in aversion to utilitarian reasoning, the human driver who kills one person to save two would risk criminal punishment.[29] Whether this would change once the assessment shifts from the human driver at the wheel of the car at the crucial moment to the vehicle's programmer is an interesting question. German law is shaped by a strong preference for remaining passive, i.e., one may not become active in order to save the greater number of lives, but for the programmer, this phenomenological difference dissolves completely. At the time the automated car or other robot is manufactured, it is simply a decision between programming option A or programming option B for dilemmatic situations.[30]

Vehicles: Why Self-Driving Cars Should Not Swerve in Dilemma Cases" (2021) 28:1 *Res Publica* 193; and Chapter 15 in this volume.

[28] See *Strafgesetzbuch* (German Criminal Code) (StGB), Germany (November 13, 1998 (Federal Law Gazette I, p. 3322), as amended by Art. 2 of the Act of June 19, 2019 (Federal Law Gazette I, p. 844)) [StGB], §35 (excusing necessity); and David Ormerod & Karl Laird, *Smith, Hogan, and Ormerod's Criminal Law*, 15th ed. (New York, NY: Oxford University Press, 2018) at 364–367 for the "duress of circumstances" doctrine in English law.

[29] See StGB, note 28 above, §34; from the viewpoint of legal philosophy, Ivó Coca Vila, "Self-Driving Cars in Dilemmatic Situations: An Approach Based on the Theory of Justification in Criminal Law" (2018) 12:1 *Criminal Law and Philosophy* 59 at 64–66; see for a more critical perspective on the anti-utilitarian German stance, Eric Hilgendorf, "Automated Driving and the Law" in Eric Hilgendorf & Uwe Seidel (eds.), *Robotics, Autonomics, and the Law* (Baden-Baden, Germany: Nomos, 2017) 171 at 190; and for an empirical analysis that shows the human preference for saving the greater number of humans, Anja Faulhaber, Anke Dittmer, Felix Blind *et al.*, "Human Decisions in Moral Dilemmas Are Largely Described by Utilitarianism: Virtual Car Driving Study Provides Guidelines for Autonomous Driving Vehicles" (2019) 25:2 *Science and Engineering Ethics* 399.

[30] Tatjana Hörnle & Wolfgang Wohlers, "The Trolley Problem Reloaded. Wie sind autonome Fahrzeuge für Leben-gegen-Leben-Dilemmata zu programmieren?" (The Trolley

III.D Self-Defense against Robots

If a human faces imminent danger of being injured or otherwise harmed by a robot, and the human knowingly or purposefully damages or destroys that robot, the question arises as to whether this situation is covered by a justificatory defense. In some cases, a necessity/lesser evil defense could be raised successfully if the danger is substantial. In other cases, it could be questioned if a lesser evil defense would be applicable, e.g., if someone shoots down a very expensive drone to prevent it from taking pictures.[31] Under such circumstances, another justificatory defense might be that of self-defense. In German criminal law, self-defense does not require a proportionality test.[32] In the case of an unlawful attack, it is permissible to destroy valuable objects even if the protected interest might be of comparatively minor importance. The crucial question in the drone case is whether an "unlawful attack"[33] or "unlawful force by another person"[34] requires that the attacker is a human being.

III.E Criminal Liability of Robots

In the realm of civil liability, robots could be treated as legal persons, and this status could be combined with the duty of producers or owners to endow robots with sufficient funds to compensate potential accident victims.[35] A different question is whether a case could also be

Problem Reloaded. How Should Autonomous Vehicles Be Programmed for the Case of a Life-against-Life Dilemma?) (2018) 165:1 *Goltdammer's Archiv für Strafrecht* 12 at 23–24; Thomas Weigend, "Notstandsrecht für Selbstfahrende Autos?" (Emergency Law for Self-Driving Cars?) (2017) 10 *Zeitschrift für Internationale Strafrechtdogmatik* 599.

[31] Regarding questions of self-defense, see Michael Froomkin & Zak Colangelo, "Self-Defense against Robots and Drones" (2015) 48:1 *Connecticut Law Review* 1; Severin Löffler, "Rechtswidrigkeit der Abwehr von Drohnen über privaten Wohngrundstücken" (Lawfulness of Defense against Drones above Private Property) in Susanne Beck, Carsten Kusche, & Brian Valerius (eds.), *Digitalisierung, Automatisierung, KI und Recht* (Baden-Baden, Germany: Nomos, 2020) 329.

[32] *German Criminal Law*, note 23 above, at 104.

[33] StGB, note 28 above, §32; "Google Cars", note 21 above, at 236 and 242; Wolfgang Mitsch, "Roboter und Notwehr" (Robots and Self-Defense) in Susanne Beck, Carsten Kusche, & Brian Valerius (eds.), *Digitalisierung, Automatisierung, KI und Recht* (Baden-Baden, Germany: Nomos, 2020) 365.

[34] American Law Institute, Model Penal Code: Official Draft and Explanatory Notes: Complete Text of Model Penal Code as Adopted at the 1962 Annual Meeting of the American Law Institute at Washington, DC, 24 May 1962 (Philadelphia, PA: American Law Institute, 1985), §3.04(1).

[35] See the citations stated in note 17 above.

made for the capacity of robots to incur criminal liability.[36] This is a highly contested proposal and a fascinating topic for criminal law theorists. Holding robots criminally liable would not be compatible with traditional features of criminal law: its focus on human agency and the notion of personal guilt, i.e., *Schuld*, which is particularly prominent in German criminal law doctrine. Many criminal law theorists defend these features as essential to the very idea of criminal law and thus reject the idea of permitting criminal proceedings against robots. But this is at best a weak argument. Criminal law doctrine is not set in stone; it has adapted to changes in the real world in the past and can be expected to do so again in the future.

The crucial question is whether there are additional principled objections to subjecting robots to criminal liability. Scholars typically examine the degree to which the abilities of robots are similar to those of humans[37] and ask whether robots fulfil the requirements of personhood, which is defined by means of concepts such as autonomy and free will.[38] These positions could be described as status-centered, anthropocentric, and essentialist. Traditional concepts of personhood rely on ontological claims about what humans are and the characteristics of humans *qua* humans. As possible alternatives, notions such as autonomy and personhood could also be described in a more constructivist manner, as the products of social attribution,[39] and it is worth considering whether the criminal liability of robots could at least be constructed for a limited subsection of criminal law, i.e., strict liability regulatory offenses, for legal systems that recognize such offenses.[40]

Instead of exploring the degree of a robot's human-ness or personhood, the alternative is to focus on the functions of criminal proceedings and punishments. In this context, the crucial question is whether some goals of criminal punishment practices could be achieved if norms of conduct

[36] See, for the argument that the categories of *actus reus* and *mens rea* could also be applied to robots, Gabriel Hallevy, *When Robots Kill* (Boston, MA: Northeastern University Press, 2013).

[37] Lawrence Solum, "Legal Personhood for Artificial Intelligences" (1992) 70:4 *North Carolina Law Review* 1231 ["Legal Personhood"] at 1255–1280.

[38] "Legal Personality for AI", note 17 above, at 416–417; see Chapter 15 in this volume.

[39] See Gunther Teubner, "Rights of Non-Humans? Electronic Agents and Animals as New Actors in Politics and Law" (2006) 33:4 *Journal of Law & Society* 497; "Guilty Robots", note 2 above, at 13–21.

[40] See Mireille Hildebrandt, "Criminal Liability and 'Smart' Environments" in Antony Duff & Stuart Green (eds.), *Philosophical Foundations of Criminal Law* (New York, NY: Oxford University Press, 2011) 507 ["Criminal Liability"] at 525–526.

were explicitly addressed to robots and if defendants were not humans but robots. As we will see, it makes sense to distinguish between the preventive functions of criminal law, such as deterrence, and the expressive meaning of criminal punishment.

The purpose of deterring agents is probably not easily transferrable from humans to robots. Deterring someone presupposes that the receiver of the message is actually aware of a norm of conduct but is inclined not to comply with it, because other incentives seem more attractive or other personal motives and emotions guide his or her decision-making. AI will probably not be prone to the kind of multi-layered, sometimes blatantly irrational type of decision-making practiced by humans. For robots, the point is to identify the right course of conduct, not to avoid being sidetracked by greed and emotions. But preventive reasoning could, perhaps, be brought to bear on the humans involved in the creation of robots who might be indirectly influenced. They might be effectively driven toward higher standards of care in order to avoid public condemnation of their products' behavior.[41]

In addition to their potentially preventive effects, criminal law responses have expressive features. They communicate that certain kinds of wrongful conduct deserve blame, and more specifically they reassure crime victims that they were indeed wronged by the other party to the interaction, and not that they themselves made a mistake or simply suffered a stroke of bad luck.[42] Some of the communicative and expressive features of criminal punishment might retain their functions, and address the needs of victims, if robots were the addressees of penal censure.[43] Even if robots will not for a long time, if ever, be capable of feeling remorse as an emotional state, the practice of assigning blame could persist with some modifications.[44] It might suffice if robots had the cognitive capacity to understand what their environment labels as right and wrong and the reasons behind these judgments, and if they adapted their behavior to norms of conduct. Communication would be possible with smart robots that

[41] Ying Hu, "Robot Criminals" (2019) 52:2 *University of Michigan Journal of Law Reform* 487 ["Robot Criminals"] at 508–510.

[42] Tatjana Hörnle, "The Role of Victims' Rights in Punishment Theories" in Antje du Bois-Pedain & Anthony Bottoms (eds.), *Penal Censure: Engagements Within and Beyond Desert Theory* (London, UK: Hart, 2019) 207.

[43] "Guilty Robots", note 2 above, at 21–28.

[44] See "Robot Criminals", note 41 above, at 504–507; Karsten Gaede, *Künstliche Intelligenz – Rechte und Strafen für Roboter?* (Artificial Intelligences – Rights and Criminal Punishment for Robots?) (Baden-Baden, Germany: Nomos, 2019) [*Künstliche Intelligenz*] at 64.

are capable of explaining the choices they have made.[45] In their ability to respond and to modify parameters for future decision-making, advanced robots are distinguishable from others not held criminally liable, e.g., animals, young children, and persons with severe mental illness.

Admittedly, criminal justice responses to the wrongful behavior of robots cannot be the same as the responses to delinquent humans. It is difficult, e.g., to conceive of a "hard treatment" component of criminal punishment[46] that would apply to robots, and such a component, if conceived, might well be difficult to enforce.[47] It could, however, be argued that punishment in the traditional sense is not necessary. For an entirely rational being, the message that conduct X is wrongful and thus prohibited, and the integration of this message into its future decision-making, would be sufficient. The next question would be if blaming robots and eliciting responses could provide some comfort to human victims and thus fulfil their emotional needs. It is conceivable that a formal, solemn procedure might serve some of the functions that traditional criminal trials fulfil, at least in the theoretical model, but study would be required to determine whether empathy or at least the potential for empathy are prerequisites for calling a perpetrator to account. Criminal law theorists have argued that robots could only be held criminally liable if they were able to understand emotional states such as suffering.[48] In my view, a deeply shared understanding of what it means, emotionally, to be hurt is not necessarily essential for the communicative message delivered to victims who have been harmed by a robot.

Another question, however, is whether a merely communicative "criminal trial," without the hard treatment component of sanctions, would be so unlike criminal punishment practices as we know them that the general human public would consider it pointless and not worth the effort, or even a travesty. This question moves the inquiry beyond criminal law theory. Answers would require empirical insight into the feasibility and acceptance of formal, censuring communication with robots. If designing procedures with imperfect similarities to traditional criminal trials would make sense, the question of criminal codes for robots should perhaps also be addressed.[49]

[45] "Robot Criminals", note 41 above, at 499.

[46] For the distinction between blame and hard treatment, see Andrew von Hirsch, *Censure and Sanctions* (Oxford, UK: Clarendon, 1993) at 9–14.

[47] *Künstliche Intelligenz*, note 44 above, at 66–69.

[48] "Criminal Liability", note 40 above, at 530–531.

[49] "Robot Criminals", note 41 above, at 500–503.

III.F Robots as Victims of Crime

Another area that might require more attention in the future is the interpretation of criminal laws if the victim of the crime is not a human, as assumed by the legislators when they passed the law, but a robot. Crimes against personality rights, e.g., might lead to interesting questions. Might it be a criminal offense to record spoken words, a criminal offense under §201 of the *Strafgesetzbuch* (German Criminal Code), if the speaker is a robot rather than a human being? Thinking in this direction would require considering whether advanced robots should be afforded constitutional and other rights[50] and, should such a discussion gain seriousness, which rights these would be.

IV The Long-Term Perspective: General Effects on Substantive Criminal Law

The discussion in Section III above referred to criminal investigations undertaken after a specific human–robot interaction has caused or threatened to cause harm. From the perspective of criminal law theory, another possible development could be worth further observation. Over time, the assessment of human conduct, in general, might change, and perhaps we will begin to assess human–human interactions in a somewhat different light, once humanoid robots based on AI become part of our daily lives. At present, criminal laws and criminal justice systems are to different degrees quite tolerant with regard to the irrational features of human decision-making and human behavior. This is particularly true of German criminal law where, e.g., the fact that an offender has consumed drugs or alcohol can be a basis for considerable mitigation of punishment,[51] and offenders who are inclined to not consider possible negative outcomes of their highly risky behavior receive only a very lenient punishment or no punishment at all.[52] This tolerance of human imperfections might shrink if the more rational, de-emotionalized version of decision-making by AI has an effect on our expectations regarding careful behavior. At present, this is merely a hypothesis; it remains to be seen whether the willingness of criminal courts to accommodate human deficiencies really will decrease in the long term.

[50] For a discussion about the legal rights of robots, see "Legal Personhood", note 37 above.

[51] StGB, note 28 above, §21; *German Criminal Law*, note 23 above, at 135.

[52] The definition of conditional intent requires the defendant to be aware of the risk and to accept it: see *German Criminal Law*, note 23 above, at 63–67; "Criminal Law", note 23 above, at 509.

ERROR
OK

2

Are Programmers in or out of Control?

The Individual Criminal Responsibility of Programmers of Autonomous Weapons and Self-Driving Cars

MARTA BO*

I Introduction

In March 2018, a Volvo XC90 vehicle that was being used to test Uber's emerging automated vehicle technology killed a pedestrian crossing a road in Tempe, Arizona.[1] At the time of the incident, the vehicle was in "autonomous mode" and the vehicle's safety driver, Rafaela Vasquez, was allegedly streaming television onto their mobile device.[2] In November 2019, the National Transportation Safety Board found that many factors contributed to the fatal incident, including failings from both the vehicle's safety driver and the programmer of the autonomous system, Uber.[3] Despite Vasquez later being charged with negligent manslaughter

* I am grateful for the helpful discussions within the DILEMA team at the Asser Institute and the feedback received on an earlier draft during the author workshop within the SNSF project "Human–Robot Interaction in Law and its Narratives: Legal Blame, Criminal Law, and Procedure." I thank James Patrick Sexton for his invaluable research assistance and for helping me improve earlier drafts of this chapter. All errors remain mine.

1 Sam Levin & Julia Carrie Wong, "Self-Driving Uber Kills Arizona Woman in First Fatal Crash Involving Pedestrian," *The Guardian* (March 19, 2018), www.theguardian.com/technology/2018/mar/19/uber-self-driving-car-kills-woman-arizona-tempe ["Self-Driving Uber"]; see also Chapters 6 and 15 in this volume.

2 Lucia Binding, "Arizona Uber Driver Was 'Streaming The Voice' Moments Before Fatal Crash," *Sky News* (June 22, 2018), https://news.sky.com/story/arizona-uber-driver-was-streaming-the-voice-moments-before-fatal-crash-11413233. In this chapter, I will use interchangeably the terms "driver," "occupant," "operator," and "user."

3 *Highway Accident Report: Collision between Vehicle Controlled by Developmental Automated Driving System and Pedestrian Tempe, Arizona March 18, 2018* (National Transportation Safety Board, 2019), www.ntsb.gov/investigations/AccidentReports/Reports/HAR1903.pdf.

in relation to the incident,[4] criminal investigations into Uber were discontinued in March 2019.[5] This instance is particularly emblematic of the current tendency to consider responsibility for actions and decisions of autonomous vehicles (AVs) as lying primarily with users of these systems, and not programmers or developers.[6]

In the military realm, similar issues have arisen. For example, it is alleged that in 2020 an autonomous drone system, the *STM Kargu-2*, may have been used during active hostilities in Libya,[7] and that such autonomous weapons (AWs) were programmed to attack targets without requiring data connectivity between the operator and the use of force.[8] Although AW technologies have not yet been widely used by militaries, for several years, governments, civil society, and academics have debated their legal position, highlighting the importance of retaining "meaningful human control" (MHC) in decision-making processes to prevent potential "responsibility gaps."[9] When debating MHC over AWs as well as responsibility issues, users or deployers are more often scrutinized than programmers,[10] the latter being considered too far removed from the effects

4 *State of Arizona* v. *Rafael Stuart Vasquez*, Indictment 785 GJ 251, Superior Court of the State of Arizona in and for the County of Maricopa (August 27, 2020), www.maricopacountyattorney.org/DocumentCenter/View/1724/Rafael-Vasquez-GJ-Indictment [*State of Arizona*].

5 "Uber 'Not Criminally Liable' for Self-Driving Death," *BBC News* (March 6, 2019), www.bbc.com/news/technology-47468391.

6 Manufacturers of AVs often include responsibility clauses in their contracts with end-users; however, practice may vary: see Keri Grieman, "Hard Drive Crash: An Examination of Liability for Self-Driving Vehicles" (2018) 9:3 *Journal of Intellectual Property, Information Technology and E-Commerce Law* 294 ["Hard Drive Crash"] at para. 29.

7 Letter dated March 8, 2021 from the Panel of Experts on Libya established pursuant to resolution 1973 (2011) addressed to the President of the Security Council (United Nations Security Council, 8 March 2021) S/2021/229, at paras 63–64.

8 Ibid. at para. 63.

9 See Filippo Santoni de Sio & Jeroen van den Hoven, "Meaningful Human Control over Autonomous Systems: A Philosophical Account" (2018) 5 *Frontiers in Robotics and AI* 1 ["MHC over Autonomous Systems"] at 10; "Killer Robots and the Concept of Meaningful Human Control: Memorandum to Convention on Conventional Weapons (CCW) Delegates" (Human Rights Watch, 2016), www.hrw.org/news/2016/04/11/killer-robots-and-concept-meaningful-human-control; "Artificial Intelligence and Machine Learning in Armed Conflict: A Human-Centred Approach" (International Committee of the Red Cross, 2019), www.icrc.org/en/document/artificial-intelligence-and-machine-learning-armed-conflict-human-centred-approach.

10 Berenice Boutin & Taylor Woodcock, "Aspects of Realizing (Meaningful) Human Control: Legal Perspective" in Robin Geiß & Henning Lahmann (eds.), *Research Handbook on Warfare and Artificial Intelligence* (Cheltenham, UK: Edward Elgar, 2024) 9 ["Realizing MHC"] at 2–10.

of AWs. However, programmers' responsibility increasingly features in policy and legal discussions, leaving many interpretative questions open.[11]

To fill this gap in the current debates, this chapter seeks to clarify the role of programmers, understood simply here as a person who writes programmes that give instructions to computers, in crimes committed with and not by AVs and AWs ("AV- and AW-related crimes"). As artificial intelligence (AI) systems cannot provide the elements required by criminal law, i.e. the *mens rea*, the mental element, and the *actus reus*, the conduct element, including its causally connected consequence,[12] the criminal responsibility of programmers will be considered in terms of direct responsibility for commission of crimes, i.e., as perpetrators or co-perpetrators,[13] rather than vicarious or joint responsibility for crimes committed by AI. Programmers could, e.g., be held responsible on the basis of participatory modes of responsibility, such as aiding or assisting users in perpetrating a crime. Despite their potential relevance, participatory modes of responsibility under national and international criminal law (ICL) are not analyzed in this chapter, as that would require a separate analysis of their *actus reus* and *mens rea* standards. Finally, it must be acknowledged that as used in this chapter, the term "programmer" is a simplification. The development of AVs and AWs entails the involvement of numerous actors, internal and external to tech companies, such as developers, programmers, data labelers, component manufacturers, software developers, and manufacturers. These distinctions might entail difficulties in individualizing responsibility and/or a distribution of

[11] Marta Bo, Laura Bruun, & Vincent Boulanin, *Retaining Human Responsibility in the Development and Use of Autonomous Weapon Systems: On Accountability for Violations of International Humanitarian Law Involving AWS* (Stockholm, Sweden: Stockholm International Peace Research Institute, 2022) at 38 and 39.

[12] See Thomas C. King, Nikkita Aggarwal, Mariarosaria Taddeo *et al.*, "Artificial Intelligence Crime: An Interdisciplinary Analysis of Foreseeable Threats and Solutions" (2020) 26:2 *Science and Engineering Ethics* 89 at 95; see *contra* the work of Gabriel Hallevy, "The Criminal Liability of Artificial Intelligence Entities: From Science Fiction to Legal Social Control" (2010) 4:2 *Akron Intellectual Property Journal* 171; see Chapter 4 in this volume.

[13] Direct commission or principal responsibility under international criminal law also includes joint commission and co-perpetration: Gerhard Werle & Florian Jessberger, *Principles of International Criminal Law* (New York, NY: Oxford University Press, 2020) at paras. 623–659. Co-perpetration as a form of principal responsibility in German criminal law is founded on the concept of "control over whether and how the offense is carried out": Thomas Weigend, "Germany" in Kevin Jon Heller & Markus D. Dubber (eds.), *The Handbook of Comparative Criminal Law* (Redwood City, CA: Stanford University Press, 2011) 252 ["Germany"] at 265 and 266. There is no similar "co-perpetration" mode of liability in the United States.

criminal responsibility, which could be captured by participatory modes of responsibility.[14]

This chapter will examine the criminal responsibility of programmers through two examples, AVs and AWs. While there are some fundamental differences between AVs and AWs, there are also striking similarities. Regarding differences, AVs are a means of transport, implying the presence of people onboard, which will not necessarily be a feature of AWs. As for similarities, both AVs and AWs depend on object recognition technology.[15] Central to this chapter is the point that both AVs and AWs can be the source of incidents resulting in harm to individuals; AWs are intended to kill, are inherently dangerous, and can miss their intended target, and while AVs are not designed to kill, they can cause death by accident. Both may unintentionally result in unlawful harmful incidents.

The legal focus regarding the use of AVs is on crimes against persons under national criminal law, e.g., manslaughter and negligent homicide, and regarding the use of AWs, on crimes against persons under ICL, i.e., war crimes against civilians, such as those found in the Rome Statute of the International Criminal Court ("Rome Statute")[16] and in the First Additional Protocol to the Geneva Conventions (AP I).[17] A core issue is whether programmers could fulfil the *actus reus*, including the requirement of causation, of these crimes. Given the temporal and spatial gap between programmer conduct and the injury, as well as other possibly intervening causes, a core challenge in ascribing criminal responsibility lies in determining a causal link between programmers' conduct and AV- and AW-related crimes. To determine causation, it is necessary to delve into the technical aspects of AVs and AWs, and consider when and which of their associated risks can or cannot be, in principle, imputable to a programmer.[18] Adopting a preliminary categorization of AV- and AW-related risks based on programmers' alleged control or lack of it over the behavior

[14] See Chapter 4 in this volume.

[15] See Sections II and III.

[16] United Nations, Rome Statute of the International Criminal Court, 2187 UNTS 3 (adopted July 17, 1998, entered into force July 1, 2002) (Rome, Italy: United Nations, 1998) [Rome Statute].

[17] United Nations, Protocol Additional to the Geneva Conventions of 12 August 1949 and Relating to the Protection of Victims of International Armed Conflicts, 1125 UNTS 3 (signed June 8, 1977, entered into force December 7, 1978) (Geneva, Switzerland: United Nations, 1977) [AP I].

[18] Some theories of causation recognize that causation in law is a matter of imputation, i.e., a matter of imputing a result to a criminal conduct: Paul K. Ryu, "Causation in Criminal Law" (1958) 106:6 *University of Pennsylvania Law Review* 773 ["Causation in Criminal Law"] at 785, 795, and 796.

and/or effects of AVs and AWs, Sections II and III consider the different risks and incidents entailed by the use of AVs and AWs. Section IV turns to the elements of AV- and AW-related crimes, focusing on causation tests and touching on *mens rea*. Drawing from this analysis, Section V turns to a notion of MHC over AVs and AWs that incorporates requirements for the ascription of criminal responsibility and, in particular, causation criteria to determine under which conditions programmers exercise causal control over the unlawful behavior and/or effects of AVs and AWs.

II Risks Posed by AVs and Programmer Control

Without seeking to identify all possible causes of AV-related incidents, Section II begins by identifying several risks associated with AVs: algorithms, data, users, vehicular communication technology, hacking, and the behavior of bystanders. Some of these risks are also applicable to AWs.[19]

In order to demarcate a programmer's criminal responsibility, it is crucial to determine whether they ultimately had control over relevant behavior and effects, e.g., navigation and possible consequences of AVs. Thus, the following sections make a preliminary classification of risks on the basis of the programmers' alleged control over them. While a notion of MHC encompassing the requirement of causality in criminal law will be developed in Section V, it is important to anticipate that a fundamental threshold for establishing the required causal nexus between conduct and harm is whether a programmer could understand and foresee a certain risk, and whether the risk that materialized was within the scope of the programmer's "functional obligations."[20]

II.A Are Programmers in Control of Algorithm and Data-Related Risks in AVs?

Before turning to the risks and failures that might lie in algorithm design and thus potentially under programmer control, this section describes the tasks required when producing an AV, and then reviews some of the rules that need to be coded to achieve this end.

The main task of AVs is navigation, which can be understood as the AV's behavior as well as the algorithm's effect. Navigation on roads is mostly

[19] In the context of AVs, the responsibility of manufacturers and programmers might overlap; see "Hard Drive Crash", note 6 above, at para. 29.

[20] See Sections IV and V.

premised on rules-based behavior requiring knowledge of traffic rules and the ability to interpret and react to uncertainty. In AVs, automated tasks include the identification and classification of objects usually encountered while driving, such as vehicles, traffic signs, traffic lights, and road lining.[21] Furthermore, "situational awareness and interpretation"[22] is also being automated. AVs should be able "to distinguish between ordinary pedestrians (merely to be avoided) and police officers giving direction," and conform to social habits and rules by, e.g., "interpret[ing] gestures by or eye contact with human traffic participants."[23] Finally, there is an element of prediction: AVs should have the capability to anticipate the behavior of human traffic participants.[24]

In AV design, the question of whether traffic rules can be accurately embedded in algorithms, and if so who is responsible for translating these rules into algorithms, becomes relevant in determining the accuracy of the algorithm design as well as attributing potential criminal responsibility. For example, are only programmers involved, or are lawyers and/or manufactures also involved? While some traffic rules are relatively precise and consist of specific obligations, e.g., a speed limit represents an obligation not to exceed that speed,[25] there are also several open-textured and context-dependent traffic norms, e.g., regulations requiring drivers to drive carefully.[26]

AV incidents might stem from a failure of the AI to identify objects or correctly classify them. For example, the first widely reported incident involving an AV in May 2016 was allegedly caused by the vehicle sensor system's failure to distinguish a large white truck crossing the road from the bright spring sky.[27] Incidents may also arise due to failures to correctly

[21] Henry Prakken, "On the Problem of Making Autonomous Vehicles Conform to Traffic Law" (2017) 25:3 *Artificial Intelligence and Law* 341 ["Making Autonomous Vehicles"] at 353.

[22] Ibid.

[23] Ibid. at 354.

[24] Ibid.

[25] See Prakken's analysis of Dutch traffic laws which could be extended to other similar European systems by analogy: "Making Autonomous Vehicles", note 21 above, at 345, 346, and 360. However, Prakken also provides an overview of open-textured and vague norms in Dutch traffic law: ibid. at 347 and 348.

[26] "Making Autonomous Vehicles", note 21 above, at 347 and 348. See the open-textured traffic rules in the *Straßenverkehrsgesetz* (Swiss Traffic Code) (StVG), SR 741.01 (as of January 1, 2020), Arts. 4, 26, and 31, www.admin.ch/opc/de/classified-compilation/19580266/index.html.

[27] Danny Yadron & Dan Tynan, "Tesla Driver Dies in First Fatal Crash While Using Autopilot Mode," *The Guardian* (July 1, 2016), www.theguardian.com/technology/2016/jun/30/tesla-autopilot-death-self-driving-car-elon-musk.

interpret or predict the behavior of others or traffic conditions, which may sometimes be interlinked with or compounded by problems of detection and sensing.[28] In turn, mistakes in both object identification and prediction might occur as a result of faulty algorithm design and/or derived from flawed data. In the former case, *prima vista*, if mistakes in object identification and/or prediction occur due to an inadequate algorithm design, the criminal responsibility of programmers could be engaged.

In relation to the latter, the increasing and almost dominant use of machine learning (ML) algorithms in AVs[29] means that issues of algorithms and data are interrelated. The performance of algorithms has become heavily dependent on the quality of data. A multitude of different algorithms are used in AVs for different purposes, with supervised and unsupervised learning-based algorithms often complementing one another. Supervised learning, in which an algorithm is fed instructions on how to interpret the input data, relies on a fully labeled dataset. Within AVs, the supervised learning models are usually: (1) "classification" or "pattern recognition algorithms," which process a given set of data into classes and help to recognize categories of objects in real time, such as street signs; and (2) "regression," which is usually employed for predicting events.[30] In cases of supervised learning, mistakes can arise from incorrect data annotation instead of a faulty algorithm design per se. If incidents do occur,[31] the programmer arguably would not be able to foresee those risks and be considered in control of the subsequent navigation decisions.

Other issues may arise with unsupervised learning[32] where an ML algorithm receives unlabeled data and programmers "describe the desired behaviour and teach the system to perform well and generalise to new

[28] See e.g., the accident involving a Tesla Model 3 which hit a Ford Explorer pickup truck, killing one passenger: Neal E. Boudette, "Tesla Says Autopilot Makes Its Cars Safer. Crash Victims Say It Kills," *The New York Times* (July 5, 2021), www.nytimes.com/2021/07/05/business/tesla-autopilot-lawsuits-safety.html.

[29] "How Machine Learning Algorithms Made Self Driving Cars Possible?" *upGrad Blog* (November 18, 2019), www.upgrad.com/blog/how-machine-learning-algorithms-made-self-driving-cars-possible/.

[30] See Mindy Support, "How Machine Learning in Automotive Makes Self-Driving Cars a Reality," *Mindy News Blog* (February 12, 2020), https://mindy-support.com/news-post/how-machine-learning-in-automotive-makes-self-driving-cars-a-reality/.

[31] See ibid.

[32] See "What Does Unsupervised Learning Have in Store for Self-Driving Cars?" *intellias* (August 22, 2019), intellias.com/what-does-unsupervised-learning-have-in-store-for-self-driving-cars/.

environments through learning."[33] Data can be provided in the phase of simulating and testing, but also during the use itself by the end-user. Within such methods, "deep learning" is increasingly used to improve navigation in AVs. Deep learning is a form of unsupervised learning that "automatically extracts features and patterns from raw data [such as real-time data] and predicts or acts based on some reward function."[34] When an incident occurs due to deep learning techniques using real data, it must be assessed whether the programmer could have foreseen that specific risk and the resulting harm, or whether it derived, e.g., from an unforeseeable interaction with the environment.

II.B Programmer or User: Who Is in Control of AVs?

As shown in the March 2018 Uber incident,[35] incidents can also derive from failures of the user to regain control of the AV, with some AV manufacturers attempting to shift the responsibility for ultimately failing to avoid collisions onto the AVs' occupants.[36] However, there are serious concerns as to whether an AV's user, who depending on the level of automation is essentially in an oversight role, is cognitively in the position to regain control of the vehicle. This problem is also known as automation bias,[37] a cognitive phenomenon in human–machine interaction, in which complacency, decrease of attention, and overreliance on the technology might impair the human ability to oversee, intervene, and override the system if needed.

Faulty human–machine interface (HMI) design, i.e., the technology which connects an autonomous system to the human, such as a dashboard or interface, could cause the inaction of the driver in the first place. In these instances, the driver could be relieved from criminal responsibility. Arguably, HMIs do not belong to programmers' functional obligations and therefore fall outside of a programmer's control.

[33] Sampo Kuutti, Richard Bowden, Yaochu Jin *et al.*, "A Survey of Deep Learning Applications to Autonomous Vehicle Control" (2021) 22:2 *Institute of Electrical and Electronics Engineers Transactions on Intelligent Transportation Systems* 712 at 713.

[34] Abhishek Gupta, Alagan Anpalagan, Ling Guan *et al.*, "Deep Learning for Object Detection and Scene Perception in Self-Driving Cars: Survey, Challenges, and Open Issues" (2021) 10:10 *Array* 1 at 8.

[35] See "Self-Driving Uber", note 1 above.

[36] See "Hard Drive Crash", note 6 above.

[37] Kathleen L. Mosier & Linda J. Skitka, "Human Decision Makers and Automated Decision Aids: Made for Each Other?" in Raja Parasuraman & Mustapha Mouloua (eds.), *Automation and Human Performance: Theory and Applications* (Boca Raton, FL: CRC Press, 1996) 201 at 203–210.

There are phases other than actual driving where a user could gain control of an AV's decisions. Introducing ethics settings into the design of AVs may ensure control over a range of morally significant outcomes, including trolley-problem-like decisions.[38] Such settings may be mandatorily introduced by manufacturers with no possibility for users to intervene and/or customize them, or they may be customizable by users.[39] Customizable ethics settings allow users "to manage different forms of failure by making autonomous vehicles follow [their] decisions" and their intention.[40]

II.C Are Some AV-Related Risks Out of Programmer Control?

There are a group of risks and failures that could be considered outside of programmer control. These include communications failures, hacking of the AV by outside parties, and unforeseeable bystander behavior. One of the next steps predicted in the field of vehicle automation is the development of software enabling AVs to communicate with one another and to share real-time data gathered from their sensors and computer systems.[41] This means that a single AV "will no longer make decisions based on information from just its own sensors and cameras, but it will also have information from other cars."[42] Failures in vehicular communication technologies[43] or inaccurate data collected by other AVs cannot be attributed to a single programmer, as they might fall beyond their responsibilities and functions, and also beyond their control.

Hacking could also cause AV incidents. For example, "placing stickers on traffic signs and street surfaces can cause self-driving cars to ignore speed restrictions and swerve headlong into oncoming traffic."[44] Here,

[38] See Sadjad Soltanzadeh, Jai Galliott, & Natalia Jevglevskaja, "Customizable Ethics Settings for Building Resilience and Narrowing the Responsibility Gap: Case Studies in the Socio-Ethical Engineering of Autonomous Systems" (2020) 26:5 *Science and Engineering Ethics* 2693 ["Customizable Ethics"] at 2696.

[39] Ibid. at 2705.

[40] Ibid. at 2697.

[41] Kim Harel, "Self-Driving Cars Must Be Able to Communicate with Each Other," *Aarhus University Department of Electrical and Computer Engineering: News* (June 2, 2021), https://ece.au.dk/en/currently/news/show/artikel/self-driving-cars-must-be-able-to-communicate-with-each-other/.

[42] Ibid.

[43] See, on this topic, M. Nadeem Ahangar, Qasim Z. Ahmed, Fahd A. Kahn *et al.*, "A Survey of Autonomous Vehicles: Enabling Communication Technologies and Challenges" (2021) 21:3 *Sensors* 706.

[44] Keith J. Hayward & Matthijs M. Maas, "Artificial Intelligence and Crime: A Primer for Criminologists" (2021) 17:2 *Crime Media Culture* 209 at 216.

the criminal responsibility of a programmer could depend on whether the attack could have been foreseen and whether the programmer should have created safeguards against it. However, the complexity of AI systems could make them more difficult to defend from attacks and more vulnerable to interference.[45]

Finally, imagine an AV that correctly follows traffic rules, but hits a pedestrian who unforeseeably slipped and fell onto the road. Such unforeseeable behavior of a bystander is relevant in criminal law cases on vehicular homicide, as it will break the causal nexus between the programmer and the harmful outcome.[46] In the present case, it must be determined which unusual behavior should be foreseen at the stage of programming, and whether standards of foreseeability in AVs should be higher for human victims.

III Risks Posed by AWs and Programmer Control

While not providing a comprehensive overview of the risks inherent in AWs, Section III follows the structure of Section II by addressing some risks, including algorithms, data, users, communication technology, hacking and interference, and the unforeseeable behavior of individuals in war, and by distinguishing risks based on their causes and programmers' level of control over them. While some risks cannot be predicted, the "development of the weapon, the testing and legal review of that weapon, and th[e] system's previous track record"[47] could provide information about the risks involved in the deployment of AWs. Some risks could be understood and foreseen by the programmer and therefore be considered under their control.

III.A Are Programmers in Control of Algorithm and Data-Related Risks in AWs?

Autonomous drones provide an example of one of the most likely applications of autonomy within the military domain,[48] and this example will be

[45] Matthew Caldwell, Jerone T. A. Andrews, Thomas Tanay *et al.*, "AI-Enabled Future Crime" (2020) 9:1 *Crime Science* 14 at 22.

[46] See Section IV.

[47] Arthur Holland Michel, *Known Unknowns: Data Issues and Military Autonomous Systems* (Geneva, Switzerland: UN Institute for Disarmament Research, 2021) [*Known Unknowns*] at 10.

[48] Merel Ekelhof & Giacomo Persi Paoli, *Swarm Robotics: Technical and Operational Overview of the Next Generation of Autonomous Systems* (Geneva, Switzerland: United Nations Institute for Disarmament Research, 2020) at 51.

used to highlight the increasingly autonomous tasks in AWs. This section will address the rules to be programmed, and identify where some risks might lie in the phase of algorithm design.

The two main tasks being automated in autonomous drones are: (1) navigation, which is less problematic than on roads and a relatively straightforward rule-based behavior, i.e., they must simply avoid obstacles while in flight; and (2) weapon release, which is much more complex as "ambiguity and uncertainty are high when it comes to the use of force and weapon release, bringing this task in the realm of expertise-based behaviours."[49] Within the latter, target identification is the most important function because it is crucial to ensure compliance with the international humanitarian law (IHL) principle of distinction, the violation of which could also cause individual criminal responsibility for war crimes. The principle of distinction establishes that belligerents and those executing attacks must distinguish at all times between civilians and combatants, and not target civilians.[50] In target identification, the two main automated tasks are: (1) object identification and classification on the basis of pattern recognition;[51] and (2) prediction, e.g., predicting that someone is surrendering, or based on the analysis of patterns of behavior, predicting that someone is a lawful target.[52]

Some of the problems in the algorithm design phase may derive from translating the open-textured and context-dependent[53] rules of IHL,[54] such as the principle of distinction, into algorithms, and from incorporating programmer knowledge and expert-based rules,[55] such as those needed to analyze patterns of behavior in targeted strikes and translate them into code.

There are some differences compared with the algorithm design phase in AVs. Due to the relatively niche and context-specific nature of IHL,

[49] Andree-Anne Melancon, "What's Wrong with Drones? Automatization and Target Selection" (2020) 31:4 *Small Wars and Insurgencies* 801 ["What's Wrong"] at 806.

[50] The principle of distinction is enshrined in AP I, note 17 above, at Art. 48, with accompanying rules at Arts. 51 and 52.

[51] Ashley Deeks, "Coding the Law of Armed Conflict: First Steps" in Matthew C. Waxman & Thomas W. Oakley (eds.), *The Future Law of Armed Conflict* (New York, NY: Oxford University Press, 2022) 41 ["First Steps"]; "What's Wrong", note 49 above, at 12 and 13.

[52] E.g., autonomous drones equipped with autonomous or automatic target recognition (ATR) software to be employed for targeted killings of alleged terrorists.

[53] "First Steps", note 51 above, at 53.

[54] On the challenges, see Alan L. Schuller, "Artificial Intelligence Effecting Human Decisions to Kill: The Challenge of Linking Numerically Quantifiable Goals to IHL Compliance" (2019) 15:1–2 *Journal of Law and Policy for the Information Society* 105.

[55] "What's Wrong", note 49 above, at 14–16.

compared to traffic law which is more widely understood by programmers, programming IHL might require a stronger collaboration with outside expertise, i.e., military lawyers and operators.

However, similar observations to AVs can be made in relation to supervised and unsupervised learning algorithms. *Prima vista*, if harm results from mistakes in object identification and prediction based on an inadequate algorithm design, the criminal responsibility of the programmer(s) could be engaged. Depending on the foreseeability of such data failures to the programmer and the involvement of third parties in data labeling, and assuming mistakes could not be foreseen, criminal responsibility might not be attributable to programmers. Also similar to AVs, the increasing use of deep learning methods in AWs makes the performance of algorithms dependent on both the availability and accuracy of data. Low quality and incorrect data, missing data, and/or discrepancies between real and training data may be conducive to the misidentification of targets.[56] When unsupervised learning is used in algorithm design, environmental conditions and armed conflict-related conditions, e.g., smoke, camouflage, and concealment, may inhibit the collection of accurate data.[57] As with AVs, programmers of AWs may at some point gain sufficient knowledge and experience regarding the robustness of data and unsupervised machine learning that would subject them to due diligence obligations, but the chapter assumes that programmers have not reached that stage yet. In the case of supervised learning, errors in data may lie in a human-generated data feed,[58] and incorrect data labeling could lead to mistakes and incidents that might be attributable to someone, but not to programmers.

III.B Programmer or User: Who Is in Control of AWs?

The relationship between programmers and users of AWs presents different challenges than AVs. In light of current trends in AW development, arguably toward human–machine interaction rather than full autonomy of the weapons system, the debate has focused on the degree of control that militaries must retain over the weapon release functions of AWs.

[56] See *Known Unknowns*, note 47 above, at 4; Joshua Hughes, "The Law of Armed Conflict Issues Created by Programming Automatic Target Recognition Systems Using Deep Learning Methods" (2018) 21 *Yearbook of International Humanitarian Law* 99 at 106 and 107.

[57] *Known Unknowns*, note 47 above, at 6.

[58] *Known Unknowns*, note 47 above, at 4.

However, control can be shared and distributed among programmers and users in different phases, from the design phase to deployment. As noted above, AI engineering in the military domain might require a strong collaboration between programmers and military lawyers in order to accurately code IHL rules in algorithms.[59] Those arguing for the albeit debated introduction of ethics settings in AWs maintain that ethics settings would "enable humans to exert more control over the outcomes of weapon use [and] make the distribution of responsibilities [between manufacturers and users] more transparent."[60]

Finally, given their complexity, programmers of AWs might be more involved than programmers of AVs in the use of AWs and in the targeting process, e.g., being required to update the system or implement some modifications to the weapon target parameters before or during the operation.[61] In these situations, it must be evaluated to what extent a programmer could foresee a certain risk entailed in the deployment and use of an AW in relation to a specific attack rather than just its use in the abstract.

III.C Are Some AW-Related Risks Out of Programmer Control?

In the context of armed conflict, it is highly likely that AWs will be subject to interference and attacks by enemy forces. A UN Institute for Disarmament Research (UNIDIR) report lists several pertinent examples: (1) signal jamming could "block systems from receiving certain data inputs (especially navigation data)"; (2) hacking, such as "spoofing" attacks, might "replace an autonomous system's real incoming data feed with a fake feed containing incorrect or false data"; (3) "input" attacks could "change a sensed object or data source in such a way as to generate a failure," e.g., enemy forces "may seek to confound an autonomous system by disguising a target"; and (4) "adversarial examples" or "evasion," which are attacks that "involve adding subtle artefacts to an input datum that result in catastrophic interpretation error by the machine."[62] In such situations, the issue of criminal responsibility for programmers will depend on the modalities of the adversarial interference, whether it could have been foreseen, and whether the AW could have been protected from foreseeable types of attacks.

59 "First Steps", note 51 above, at 53 and 54.

60 "Customizable Ethics", note 38 above, at 2704 and 2705.

61 Military targeting must be intended as encompassing more than critical functions of weapon release.

62 *Known Unknowns*, note 47 above, at 7.

Similar to the AV context, failures of communication technology, caused by signal jamming or by failures of communication systems between a human operator and the AI system or among connected AI systems, may lead to incidents that could not be imputed to a programmer.

Finally, conflict environments are likely to drift constantly as "[g]roups engage in unpredictable behaviour to deceive or surprise the adversary and continually adjust (and sometimes radically overhaul) their tactics and strategies to gain an edge."[63] The continuously changing and unforeseeable behavior of opposing belligerents and the tactics of enemy forces can lead to "data drift," whereby changes that are difficult to foresee can lead to a weapon system's failure without it being imputable to a programmer.[64]

IV AV-Related Crimes on the Road and AW-Related War Crimes on the Battlefield

The following section will distil the legal ingredients of crimes against persons resulting from failures in the use of AVs and AWs. The key question is whether the *actus reus*, i.e., the prohibited conduct, including its resulting harm, could ever be performed by programmers of AVs and AWs. The analysis suggests that save for war crimes under the Rome Statute, which prohibit a conduct, the crimes under examination on the road and the battlefield are currently formulated as result crimes, in that they require the causation of harm such as death or injuries. In relation to crimes of conduct, the central question is whether programmers controlled the behavior of an AV or an AW, e.g., the AW's launching of an indiscriminate attack against civilians. In relation to crimes of result, the central question is whether programmers exercise causal control over a chain of events leading to a prohibited result, e.g., death, that must occur in addition to the prohibited conduct. Do programmers exercise causal control over the behavior and the effects of AVs and AWs? Establishing causation of crimes of conduct presents differences compared with crimes of result in light of the causal gap that characterizes the latter.[65] However, this difference is irrelevant in the context of crimes committed with the intermediation

[63] *Known Unknowns*, note 47 above, at 9.

[64] Ibid.

[65] Crimes of conduct "rest on an immediate connection between the harmful action and the relevant harm"; crimes of result "are characterized by a [special and temporal] causal gap between action and consequence": George P. Fletcher, *Basic Concepts of Criminal Law* (New York, NY: Oxford University Press, 1998) [*Basic Concepts*] at 61.

of AI since, be they of conduct or result, they always present a causal gap between a programmer's conduct and the unlawful behavior or effect of an AV and AW. Thus, the issue is whether a causal nexus exists between a programmer's conduct and either the behavior (in the case of crimes of conduct) or the effects (in the case of crimes of result) of AVs and AWs. Sections IV.A and IV.B will describe the *actus reus* of AV- and AW-related crimes, while Section IV.C will turn to the question of causation. While the central question of this chapter concerns the *actus reus*, at the end of this section, I will also make some remarks on *mens rea* and the relevance of risk-taking and negligence in this debate.

IV.A Actus Reus *in AV-Related Crimes*

This section focuses on the domestic criminal offenses of negligent homicide and manslaughter in order to assess whether the *actus reus* of AV-related crimes could be performed by a programmer. It does not address traffic and road violations generally,[66] nor the specific offense of vehicular homicide.[67]

Given the increasing use of AVs and pending AV-related criminal cases in the United States,[68] it seems appropriate to take the Model Penal Code (MPC) as an example of common law legislation.[69] According to the MPC, the *actus reus* of manslaughter consists of "killing for which the person is reckless about *causing* death."[70] Negligent homicide concerns instances where a "person is not aware of a substantial risk that a death will *result* from his or her conduct, but should have been aware of such a risk."[71]

While national criminal law frameworks differ considerably, there are similarities regarding causation which are relevant here. Taking Germany as a representative example of civil law traditions, the *Strafgesetzbuch*

[66] See, on this topic, "Making Autonomous Vehicles", note 21 above.

[67] While the United States' Model Penal Code does not contain a provision dealing with vehicular homicide, legislations in certain domestic systems envisage it.

[68] See *State of Arizona*, note 4 above.

[69] American Law Institute, Model Penal Code: Official Draft and Explanatory Notes: Complete Text of Model Penal Code as Adopted at the 1962 Annual Meeting of the American Law Institute at Washington, DC, May 24, 1962 (Philadelphia, PA: American Law Institute, 1985) [Model Penal Code].

[70] Ibid., §2.13(1)(b); see Paul H. Robinson, "United States" in Kevin Jon Heller & Markus Dubber (eds.), *The Handbook of Comparative Criminal Law* (Redwood City, CA: Stanford University Press, 2011) ["United States"] 563 at 585 (emphasis added).

[71] Ibid. (emphasis added).

(German Criminal Code) (StGB) distinguishes two forms of intentional homicide: murder[72] and manslaughter.[73] Willingly taking the risk of causing death is sufficient for manslaughter.[74] Negligent homicide is proscribed separately,[75] and the *actus reus* consists of causing the death of a person through negligence.[76]

These are crimes of result, where the harm consists of the death of a person. While programmer conduct may be remote with regard to AV incidents, some decisions taken by AV programmers at an early stage of development could decisively impact the navigation behavior of an AV that results in a death. In other words, it is conceivable that a faulty algorithm designed by a programmer could cause a fatal road accident. The question then becomes what is the threshold of causal control exercised by programmers over an AV's unlawful behavior of navigation and its unlawful effects such as a human death.

IV.B Actus Reus *in AW-Related War Crimes*

This section addresses AW-related war crimes and whether programmers could perform the required *actus reus*. Since the *actus reus* would most likely stem from an AW's failure to distinguish between civilian and military targets, the war crime of indiscriminate attacks, which criminalizes violations of the aforementioned IHL rule of distinction,[77] takes on central importance.[78] The war crime of indiscriminate attacks refers inter alia to an attack that strikes military objectives and civilians or civilian objects without distinction. This can occur as a result of the use of weapons that are incapable of being directed at a specific military objective or accurately distinguishing between civilians and civilian

[72] *Strafgesetzbuch* (German Criminal Code), Germany (November 13, 1998 (Federal Law Gazette I, p. 3322), as amended by Art. 2 of the Act of June 19, 2019 (Federal Law Gazette I, p. 844)) [StGB], §211(1) (emphasis added).

[73] Under German criminal law, manslaughter is the intentional killing of another person without aggravating circumstances: StGB, note 72 above, §212.

[74] "Germany", note 13 above, at 262.

[75] StGB, note 72 above, §222.

[76] "Germany", note 13 above, at 263.

[77] For the underlying IHL, see AP I, note 17 above, Art. 51(4)(a); see also Jean-Marie Henckaerts & Louise Doswald-Beck, *Customary International Humanitarian Law, vol. 1: Rules* (New York, NY: Cambridge University Press, 2005), Rule 12, at 40.

[78] See Marta Bo, "Autonomous Weapons and the Responsibility Gap in Light of the Mens Rea of the War Crime of Attacking Civilians in the ICC Statute" (2021) 19:2 *Journal of International Criminal Justice* 275 ["Autonomous Weapons"] at 282–285.

objects and military objectives; these weapons are known as inherently indiscriminate weapons.[79]

While this war crime is neither specifically codified in the Rome Statute nor in AP I, it has been subsumed[80] under the war crime of directing attacks against civilians. Under AP I, the *actus reus* of the crime is defined in terms of causing death or injury.[81] In crimes of result with AWs, a causal nexus between the effects resulting from the deployment of an AW and a programmer's conduct must be established. Under the Rome Statute, the war crime is formulated as a conduct crime, proscribing the *actus reus* as the "directing of an attack" against civilians.[82] A causal nexus must be established between the unlawful AW's behavior and/or the attack and the programmer's conduct.[83] Under both frameworks, the question is whether programmers exercised causal control over the behavior and/or effects, e.g., death or attack, of an AW.

A final issue relates to the required nexus with an armed conflict. The Rome Statute requires that the conduct must take place "in the context of and was associated with" an armed conflict.[84] However, while undoubtedly there is a temporal and physical distance between programmer conduct and the armed conflict, it is conceivable that programmers may program AW software or upgrade it during an armed conflict. In certain instances, it could be argued that programmer control continues

[79] Knut Dörmann, *Elements of War Crimes under the Rome Statute of the International Criminal Court: Sources and Commentary* (Cambridge, UK: Cambridge University Press, 2003) [*Elements of War Crimes*] at 131 and 132; it is worth noting that programmers may have a greater role and responsibility, particularly when it comes to inherently indiscriminate weapons.

[80] Both by the ICC and the International Criminal Tribunal for the former Yugoslavia. The latter interpreted violations of Art. 3 of its Statute, relevant to unlawful attack charges, by resorting to AP I, note 17 above, Art. 85(3); See "Autonomous Weapons", note 78 above, at 283 and 284.

[81] AP I, note 17 above, Art. 85(3), the *actus reus* of the war crime of willfully launching attacks against civilians contains the requirement that an attack against civilians causes "death or serious injury to body or health."

[82] Rome Statute, note 16 above, Arts. 8(2)(b)(i) and 8(2)(e)(i).

[83] Moreover, under the Rome Statute, an attack could be considered as a result; Albin Eser, "Mental Elements – Mistake of Fact and Mistake of Law" in Antonio Cassese, Paola Gaeta, & John R.W.D. Jones (eds.), *The Rome Statute of the International Criminal Court: A Commentary* (New York, NY: Oxford University Press, 2002) 889 at 911.

[84] Element 4 of the elements of the crime at Rome Statute, note 16 above, Art. 8(2)(b)(i). As elaborated by the International Tribunal for the former Yugoslavia, the law of war crimes applies "from the initiation of … an armed conflict and extend beyond the cessation of hostilities until a general conclusion of peace is reached"; *Elements of War Crimes*, note 79 above, at 19–20.

even after the completion of the act of programming, when the effects of their decisions materialize in the behavior and/or effects of AWs in armed conflict. Programmers can be said to exercise a form of control over the behavior and/or effects of AWs that begins with the act of programming and continues thereafter.

IV.C The Causal Nexus between Programming and AV- and AW-Related Crimes

A crucial aspect of programmer criminal responsibility is the causal control they exercise over the behavior and/or effects of AVs and AWs. The assessment of causation refers to the conditions under which an AV's and AW's unlawful behavior and/or effects should be deemed the result of programmer conduct for purposes of holding them criminally responsible.

Causality is a complex topic. In common law and civil law countries, several tests to establish causation have been put forward. Due to difficulties in establishing a uniform test for causation, it has been argued that determining conditions for causation are "ultimately a matter of legal policy."[85] But this does not render the formulation of causality tests in the relevant criminal provisions completely beyond reach. While a comprehensive analysis of these theories is beyond the scope of this chapter, for the purposes of establishing when programmers exercise causal control, some theories are more aligned with the policy objectives pursued by the suppression of AV- and AW-related crimes.

First, in common law and civil law countries, the "but-for"/*conditio sine qua non* test is the dominant test for establishing physical causation, and it is intended as a relationship of physical cause and effect.[86] In the language of MPC §2.03(1)(a), the conduct must be "an antecedent but for which the result in question would not have occurred." The "but for" test works satisfactorily in cases of straightforward cause and effect, e.g., pointing a loaded gun toward the chest of another person and pulling the trigger. However, AV- and AW-related crimes are characterized by a temporal and physical gap between programmer conduct and the behavior

[85] "Causation in Criminal Law", note 18 above, at 785; see *contra Basic Concepts*, note 65 above, at 63 and 66.

[86] See "Causation in Criminal Law", note 18 above, at 787; also described as "empirical causality," which refers to the "metaphysical [and deterministic] question of cause and effect"; Marjolein Cupido, "Causation in International Crimes Cases: (Re)Conceptualizing the Causal Linkage" (2021) 32:1 *Criminal Law Forum* 1, ["International Crimes"] at 24.

and effect of AVs and AWs. They involve complex interactions between AVs and AWs and humans, including programmers, data providers and labelers, users, etc. AI itself is also a factor that could intervene in the causal chain. The problem of causation in these cases must thus be framed in a way that reflects the relevance of intervening and superseding causal forces which may break the causal nexus between a programmer's conduct and AV- and AW-related crime.

Both civil law and common law systems have adopted several theories to overcome the shortcomings[87] and correct the potential over-inclusiveness[88] of the "but-for" test, in complex cases involving numerous necessary conditions. Some of these theories include elements of foreseeability in the causality test.

The MPC adopts the "proximate cause test," which "differentiates among the many possible 'but for' causal forces, identifying some as 'necessary conditions' – necessary for the result to occur but not its direct 'cause' – and recognising others as the 'direct' or 'proximate' cause of the result."[89] The relationship is "direct" when the result is foreseeable and as such "this theory introduces an element of culpability into the law of causation."[90]

German theories about adequacy assert that whether a certain factor can be considered a cause of a certain effect depends on "whether conditions of that type do, generally, in the light of experience, produce effects of that nature."[91] These theories, which are not applied in their pure form in criminal law, include assessments that resemble a culpability assessment. They bring elements of foreseeability and culpability into the causality test, and in particular, a probability and possibility judgment regarding the actions of the accused.[92] However, these theories leave unresolved the different knowledge perspectives, i.e., objective, subjective, or mixed, on which the foreseeability assessment is to be based.[93]

Other causation theories include an element of understandability, awareness, or foreseeability of risks. In the MPC, the "harm-within-the risk" theory considers that causation in reckless and negligent crimes is

[87] "Causation in Criminal Law", note 18 above, at 787.

[88] Ibid.

[89] Arthur Leavens, "A Causation Approach to Criminal Omissions" (1988) 76 *California Law Review* 547 ["Causation Approach"] at 564.

[90] "Causation in Criminal Law", note 18 above, at 789.

[91] Ibid. at 791.

[92] Ibid. at 792.

[93] Ibid. at 795.

in principle established when the result was within the "risk of which the actor is aware or … of which he should be aware."[94] In German criminal law, some theories describe causation in terms of the creation or aggravation of risk and limit causation to the unlawful risks that the violated criminal law provision intended to prevent.[95]

In response to the drawbacks of these theories, the teleological theory of causation holds that in all cases involving a so-called intervening independent causal force, the criterion should be whether the intervening causal force was "produced by 'chance' or was rather imputable to the criminal act in issue."[96] Someone would be responsible for the result if their actions contributed in any manner to the intervening factor. What matters is the accused's control over the criminal conduct and whether the intervening factor was connected in a but/for sense to their criminal act,[97] thus falling within their control.

In ICL, a conceptualization of causation that goes beyond the physical relation between acts and effects is more embryonic. However, it has been suggested that theories drawn from national criminal law systems, such as risk-taking and linking causation to culpability, and thus to foreseeability, should inform a theory of causation in ICL.[98] It has also been suggested that causality should entail an evaluation of the functional obligations of an actor and their area of operation in the economic sphere. According to this theory, causation is "connected to an individual's control and scope of influence" and is limited to "dangers that he creates through his activity and has the power to avoid."[99] As applied in the context of international crimes, which have a collective dimension, these theories could usefully be employed in the context of AV and AW development, which is collective by nature and is characterized by a distribution of responsibilities.

Programmers in some instances will cause harm through omission, notably by failing to avert a particular harmful risk when they are under a

[94] Model Penal Code, note 69 above, §2.03(3); §2.03(2) and (3) formulate several exceptions to the general proximity standard in cases of intervening and superseding causal forces.

[95] Among the "but-for" conditions that are *not* considered attributable are: "[a] consequence that the perpetrator has caused … if that act did not unjustifiably increase a risk"; "[a] consequence was not one to be averted by the rule the perpetrator violated"; and "if a voluntary act of risk taking on the part of the victim or a third person intervened." For details, see "Germany", note 13 above, at 268. See also "International Crimes", note 86 above, at 26 and 27.

[96] "Causation in Criminal Law", note 18 above, at 797.

[97] Ibid. at 798.

[98] "International Crimes", note 86 above, at 43–47.

[99] "International Crimes", note 86 above, at 41.

legal duty to prevent harmful events of that type ("commission by omission").[100] In these cases, the establishment of causation will be hypothetical as there is no physical cause-effect relationship between an omission and the proscribed result.[101] Other instances concern whether negligence on the side of the programmers, via, e.g., a lack of instructions and warnings, have contributed to and caused the omission, constituting a failure to intervene on behalf of the user. Such omissions amount to negligence, i.e., violations of positive duties of care,[102] and since it belongs to *mens rea*, will be addressed in the following section.

IV.D Criminal Negligence: Programming AVs and AWs

In light of the integration of culpability assessments in causation tests, an assessment of programmers' criminal responsibility would be incomplete without addressing *mens rea* issues. In relation to *mens rea*, while intentionally and knowingly programming an AV or AW to commit crimes falls squarely under these prohibitions, in both these contexts, the most expected and problematic issue is the unintended commission of these crimes, i.e., cases in which the programmer did not design the AI system to commit an offense, but harm nevertheless arises during its use.[103] In such situations, programmers had no intention to commit an offense, but still might incur criminal liability for risks that they should have known and foreseen. To define the scope of criminal responsibility for unintended harm, it is crucial to determine which risks can be known and foreseen by an AV or AW programmer.

There are important differences in the *mens rea* requirements of AV- and AW-related crimes. Under domestic criminal law, the standards of recklessness and negligence apply to the AV-related crimes of manslaughter and negligent homicide. While "[a] person acts 'recklessly' with regard to a result if he or she *consciously disregards a substantial risk* that his or

[100] StGB, note 72 above, §13.

[101] On causation in criminal omissions, see Graham Hughes, "Criminal Omissions" (1958) 67:4 *Yale Law Journal* 590 at 627–631. Causation in "commission by omission" is strictly connected with duties to act and duty to prevent a certain harm: see George Fletcher, *Rethinking Criminal Law* (New York, NY: Oxford University Press, 2000) at 606; "Causation Approach", note 89 above, at 562.

[102] See Marta Bo, "Criminal Responsibility by Omission for Failures to Stop Autonomous Weapon Systems" (2023) 21:5 *Journal of International Criminal Justice* 1057.

[103] See also Sabine Gless, Emily Silverman, & Thomas Weigend, "If Robots Cause Harm, Who Is to Blame? Self-Driving Cars and Criminal Liability" (2016) 19:3 *New Criminal Law Review* 412 at 425.

her conduct will cause the result; he or she acts only 'negligently' if he or she is *unaware of the substantial risk but should have perceived it*."[104] The MPC provides that "criminal homicide constitutes manslaughter when it is committed recklessly."[105] In the StGB, *dolus eventualis*, i.e., willingly taking the risk of causing death, would encompass situations covered by recklessness and is sufficient for manslaughter.[106] For negligent homicide,[107] one of the prerequisites is that the perpetrator can foresee the risk to a protected interest.[108]

Risk-based *mentes reae* are subject to more dispute in ICL. The International Tribunal for the former Yugoslavia accepted that recklessness could be a sufficient *mens rea* for the war crime of indiscriminate attacks under Article 85(3)(a) of AP I.[109] However, whether recklessness and *dolus eventualis* could be sufficient to ascribe criminal responsibility for war crimes within the framework of the Rome Statute remains debated.[110]

Unlike incidents with AVs, incidents in war resulting from a programmer's negligence cannot give rise to their criminal responsibility. Where applicable, recklessness and *dolus eventualis*, which entail understandability and foreseeability of risks of developing inherently indiscriminate AWs, become crucial to attribute responsibility to programmers in scenarios where programmers foresaw and took some risks. Excluding these mental elements would amount to ruling out the criminal responsibility of programmers in most expected instances of war crimes.

V Developing an International Criminal Law-Infused Notion of Meaningful Human Control over AVs and AWs that Incorporates *Mens Rea* and Causation Requirements

This section considers a notion of MHC applicable to AVs and AWs that is based on criminal law and that could function as a criminal

104 "United States", note 70 above, at 575 (emphasis added); see also Guyora Binder, "Homicide" in Markus Dubber & Tatjana Hörnle (eds.), *The Oxford Handbook of Criminal Law* (New York, NY: Oxford University Press, 2014) 702 at 719: "Negligent manslaughter now usually requires objective foreseeability of death, rather than the simple violation of a duty of care."

105 Model Penal Code, note 69 above, §2.13(1)(b).

106 "Germany", note 13 above, at 262.

107 StGB, note 72 above, §222.

108 "Germany", note 13 above, at 263.

109 See the case law quoted in "Autonomous Weapons", note 78 above, at 293.

110 "Autonomous Weapons", note 78 above, at 286–294.

responsibility "anchor" or "attractor."[111] This is not the first attempt to develop a conception of control applicable to both AVs and AWs. Studies on MHC over AWs and moral responsibility of AWs[112] have been extended to AVs.[113] In their view, MHC should entail an element of traceability entailing that "*one human agent in the design history* or use context involved in designing, programming, operating and deploying the autonomous system … *understands or is in the position to understand the possible effects* in the world of the use of this system."[114] Traceability requires that someone in the design or use understands the capabilities of the AI system and its effects.

In line with these studies, it is argued here that programmers may decide and control how both traffic law and IHL are embedded in the respective algorithms, how AI systems see and move, and how they react to changes in the environment. McFarland and McCormack affirm that programmers may exercise control not only over an abstract range of behavior, but also in relation to specific behavior and effects of AWs.[115] Against this background, this chapter contends that programmer control begins at the initial stage of the AI development process and continues into the use phase, extending to the behavior and effects of AVs and AWs.

Assuming programmer control over certain AV- and AW-related unlawful behavior and effects, how can MHC be conceptualized so as to ensure that criminal responsibility is traced back to programmers when warranted? The foregoing discussion of causality in the context of AV- and AW-related crimes suggests that theories of causation that go beyond deterministic cause-and-effect assessments are particularly amenable to developing a theory of MHC that could ensure responsibility. These theories either link causation to *mens rea* standards or

111 Daniele Amoroso & Guglielmo Tamburrini, "Autonomous Weapons Systems and Meaningful Human Control: Ethical and Legal Issues" (2020) 1 *Current Robotics Reports* 187 at 189.

112 "MHC over Autonomous Systems", note 9 above, at 6–9.

113 Simeon C. Calvert, Daniel Heikoop, Giulio Mecacci *et al.*, "A Human Centric Framework for the Analysis of Automated Driving Systems Based on Meaningful Human Control" (2020) 21:3 *Theoretical Issues in Ergonomics Science* 478 ["Human Centric Framework"] at 490–492.

114 "MHC over Autonomous Systems", note 9 above, at 9; "Human Centric Framework", note 113 above, at 490 and 491 (emphasis added).

115 Tim McFarland & Tim McCormack, "Mind the Gap: Can Developers of Autonomous Weapons Systems Be Liable for War Crimes?" (2014) 90 *International Law Studies* 361 at 366.

describe it in terms of the aggravation of risk. In either case, the ability to understand the capabilities of AI systems and their effects, and foreseeability of risks, are required. Considering these theories of causation in view of recent studies on MHC over AVs and AWs, the MHC's requirement of traceability arguably translates into the requirement of foreseeability of risks.[116] Because of the distribution of responsibilities in the context of AV and AW programming, causation theories introducing the notion of function-related risks are needed to limit programmers' criminal responsibility to those risks within their respective obligations and thus their sphere of influence and control. According to these theories, the risks that a programmer is obliged to prevent and that relate to their functional obligations, i.e., their function-related risks, could be considered causally imputable in principle.[117]

VI Conclusion

AVs and AWs are complex systems. Their programming implies a distribution of responsibilities and obligations within tech companies, and between them and manufacturers, third parties, and users, which makes it difficult to identify who may be responsible for harm stemming from their use. Despite the temporal and spatial gap between the programming phase and crimes, the responsibility of programmers in the commission of crimes should not be discarded. Indeed, crucial decisions on the behavior and effects of AVs and AWs are taken in the programming phase. While a more detailed case-by-case analysis is needed, this chapter has mapped out how programmers of AVs and AWs might be in control of certain AV- and AW-related risks and therefore criminally responsible for AV- and AW-related crimes.

This chapter has shown that the assessment of causation as a threshold for establishing whether an *actus reus* was committed may converge on the criteria of understandability and foreseeability of risks of unlawful behavior and/or effects of AVs and AWs. Those risks which fall within programmers' functional obligations and sphere of influence can be considered under their control and imputable to them.

116 The anticipation of data issues is central to the above-mentioned UNIDIR report relating to data failures in AWs; see *Known Unknowns*, note 47 above, at 13 and 14.

117 See Boutin and Woodcock arguing for the need to ensure MHC in the pre-deployment phase: "Realizing MHC", note 10 above.

Following this analysis, a notion of MHC applicable to programmers of AVs and AWs based on requirements for the imputation of criminal responsibility can be developed. It may function as a responsibility anchor in so far as it helps trace back responsibility to the individuals that could understand and foresee the risk of a crime being committed with an AV or AW.

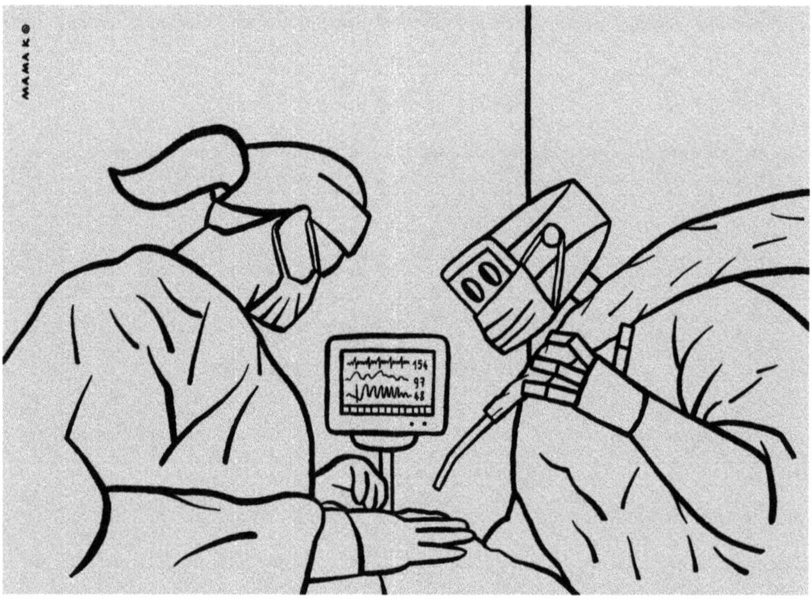
MAMA K ©
154
97
68

3

Trusting Robots

Limiting Due Diligence Obligations in Robot-Assisted Surgery under Swiss Criminal Law

JANNEKE DE SNAIJER*

I Introduction

Surgeons have been using automated tools in the operating room for several decades. Even more robots will support surgeons in the future, and at some point, surgery may be completely delegated to robots. This level of delegation is currently fictional and robots remain mostly under the command of the human surgeon. But some robots are already making discrete decisions on their own, based on the combined functioning of programming and sensors, and in some situations, surgeons rely on a robot's recommendation as the basis for their directions to the robot.

This chapter discusses the legal responsibility of human surgeons working with surgical robots under Swiss law, including robots who notify surgeons about a patient's condition so the surgeon can take a particular action. Unlike other jurisdictions, negligence and related duties of care are defined in Switzerland not only by civil law,[1] but by criminal law as well.[2] This chapter focuses on the surgeon's individual criminal responsibility for negligence,[3] which is assessed under the general concept of Article 12,

* The author owes great thanks for the outstanding support regarding this chapter to Prof. Dr. Sabine Gless and Assoc. Prof. Helena Whalen-Bridge.

1 *Entscheid des Bundesgerichts* (Decision of the Swiss Federal Court) BGE 133 III 121 E. 3.1; BGE 115 Ib 175 E. 2b; BGE 139 III 252 E. 1.5; BGE 133 III 121 E. 3.1 (the abbreviation for the Swiss Federal Court is BGE, and cases are cited by volume and starting page; all decisions are available online at: www.bger.ch).

2 See e.g., Christopher Geth, *Strafrecht Allgemeiner Teil* (Criminal Law General Part) (Basel, Switzerland: Helbing Lichtenhahn Verlag, 2021) [*Strafrecht Allgemeiner Teil*] at 170. Regarding the civil responsibility of a doctor, see Lisa Blechschmitt, *Die straf- und zivilrechtliche Haftung des Arztes beim Einsatz roboterassistierter Chirurgie* (The Criminal and Civil Liability of Physicians When Using Robot-Assisted Surgery) (Baden-Baden, Germany: Nomos, 2017).

3 *Strafgesetzbuch* (Swiss Criminal Code), SR 311.0 (as amended January 23, 2023) [SCC], Art. 12, para. 3, www.fedlex.admin.ch/eli/cc/54/757_781_799/en. Negligence differs from

paragraph 3 of the Criminal Code of Switzerland ("SCC").[4] Under the SCC, the surgeon is required to carry out a medical surgery in accordance with state-of-the-art due diligence.

In the general context of task sharing among humans, which includes surgeons working in a team, a principle of trust (*Vertrauensgrundsatz*) applies. The principle of trust allows team members to have a legitimate expectation that each participant will act with due diligence. The principle of trust also means that participants are for the most part only responsible for their own actions, which limit their obligations of due diligence. However, when the participant is a robot, even though the surgeon delegates tasks to the robot and relies on it in a manner similar to human participants, the principle of trust does not apply and the surgeon is responsible for what the robot does. Neither statutes nor cases clearly state an application or rejection of the traditional principle of trust to robots. However, at this point, the principle has only been applied to humans, and it is safe to assume that it does not apply to robots, mainly because a robot is currently not capable of criminal responsibility under Swiss law.[5] Application of the principle of trust to robots together with a corresponding limitation on the surgeon's liability would therefore create a responsibility gap.[6]

In view of the important role robots play in a surgical team, one would expect governing regulation to apply traditional principles to the division of work between human surgeons and robots, but the use of surgical robots has not led to any relevant changes, or the introduction of special care regulations that either limit the surgeon's responsibility or allocate it among other actors. This chapter explores an approach to limiting the surgeon's criminal liability when tasks are delegated to robots. As the SCC does not provide guidance regarding the duties of care when a robot is used, other law must be consulted. The chapter argues that the principle of trust (*Vertrauensgrundsatz*) should be applied to limit the due diligence expected from a surgeon interacting with a robot. Incorporating and handling robots in surgery are becoming more integral to effective surgery due to specialization arising from division of labor among humans and robots, and the increase in more precise and quicker medical-technical solutions for

intentional action under Art. 12, para. 2, according to which someone intentionally commits a crime or misdemeanor if they carry out the act with knowledge and will.

4 SCC, note 3 above, Art. 12, para. 3.

5 Regarding the ongoing discussion of an e-personhood for robots, see e.g., Martin Zobl & Michael Lysakowski, "E-Persönlichkeit für Algorithmen?" (E-Personhood for Algorithms?) (2019) 1 *Digma* 42.

6 See Chapter 15 in this volume.

patients. Surgeons must rely to some degree on the expertise of the robots they use, and therefore surgeons who make use of promising robots in their operating room should be subject to a valid and practical approach to due diligence which does not unreasonably expand their liability. While the chapter addresses the need to limit the surgeon's liability when working with robots, chapter length does not allow for analysis of related issues such as the connection to permissible risk, i.e., once the surgical robot is established in society, the possible risks are accepted because its benefits outweigh the risks. The chapter does not address other related issues, such as situations in which a hospital instructs surgeons to use robots, issues arising from the patient's perspective, or the liability of the manufacturer, except for situations where the robot does not perform as it should or simply fails to function.[7]

The chapter proceeds by articulating the relevant concept of a robot (Section II). A discussion of due diligence (Section III) explains the duties of care and the principle of trust when a surgeon works without a robot (Section III.B), which is followed by a discussion of duties of care when a surgeon works with a robot (Section III.C). The chapter addresses in detail the due diligence expected when a surgical robot asks the human to take a certain action (Section III.C.3). Moving to a potential approach that restricts a surgeon's criminal liability to appropriate limits, the chapter explores the principle of trust as it could apply to robots (Section III.D), and suggests an approach that applies and calibrates the principle of trust based on whether the robot has been certified (Section III.E). The chapter applies these legal principles to the first stage of surgical robots, which are still dependent on commands from humans to take action and do not contain complete self-learning components. The conclusion (Section IV) looks to the future and shares some brief suggestions about how to deal with likely developments in autonomous surgical robots.

II Terminology: Robots in Surgery

A standardized definition of a robot does not exist.[8] There is some agreement that a robot is a mechanical object.[9] In 1920, Karel Capek characterized the

[7] See Section III in this chapter, and Chapter 4 in this volume.

[8] Neil Richards & William Smart, "How Should the Law Think about Robots?" in Ryan Calo, A. Michael Froomkin, & Ian Kerr (eds.), *Robot Law* (Cheltenham, UK: Edward Elgar, 2016) 3 ["Think about Robots"].

[9] Melinda Florina Müller, "Roboter und Recht" (Robots and Law) (2014) 5 *Aktuelle Juristische Praxis* 595; Isabelle Wildhaber & Melinda Florina Lohmann, "Roboterrecht – eine Einleitung" (Robotlaw – An Introduction) (2017) 2 *Aktuelle Juristische Praxis* 135.

term "*robota*" (slavish, slave labor)[10] by his story about artificial slaves who take over humankind.[11] Thereafter, the term was used in countless other works.[12] The modern use of robot includes the requirement that a robot has sensors to "sense," processors to "think," and actuating elements to "act."[13] Under this definition, pure software, which does not interact physically with the world, does not count as a robot.[14] In general, robots are partly intelligent, adaptive machines that extend the human ability to act in the world.[15]

Traditionally, robots are divided into industrial and service robots. A distinction is also made between professional service robots such as restaurant robots, and service robots for private use such as robot vacuums.[16] The robots considered in this chapter come under the category of service robots, which primarily provide services for humans as opposed to industrial processes. Among other things, professional service robots can interact with both unskilled and skilled personnel, as in the case of a service robot at a restaurant, or with exclusively skilled personnel, as with a surgeon in an operating room.

In discussions of robots and legal responsibility, the terms "agents" or "autonomous systems"[17] are increasingly used almost interchangeably with the term robot. To avoid definitional problems, only the term "robot" will be used in the chapter. However, the chapter does distinguish between autonomous and automated robots, and only addresses automated robots over which the surgeon exercises some control, not fully autonomous robots. Fully autonomous robots would have significantly increased autonomy and their own decision-making ability, whereas automated robots primarily execute predetermined movement patterns.[18]

10 Susanne Beck, "Grundlegende Fragen zum Umgang mit der Robotik" (Basic Questions about the Use of Robotics) (2009) 6 *Juristische Rundschau* 225.

11 Thomas Christaller, Michael Decker, M. Joachim Gilsbach *et al.*, *Robotik* (Robotics) (Berlin, Germany: Springer, 2001) [*Robotik*] at 18; Karel Capek, "R.U.R." (play written in 1920, and premiered in Prague in 1922).

12 See e.g., Isaac Asimov, *The Complete Robot* (London, UK: Harper Collins, 1983).

13 George Bekey, *Autonomous Robots: From Biological Inspiration to Implementation and Control* (Cambridge, MA: MIT Press, 2005) 2.

14 See also George A. Bekey, "Current Trends in Robotics" in Patrick Lin, Keith Abney, & George Bekey (eds.), *Robot Ethics* (Cambridge, MA: MIT Press, 2012) 17; "Think about Robots", note 8 above, at 6: "… our definition excludes wholly software-based artificial intelligences that exert no agency in the physical world."

15 *Robotik*, note 11 above, at 5.

16 IFR-Website (International Federation of Robotics), https://ifr.org/.

17 More often for programs and artificial intelligence, not necessarily only for robots.

18 Using the example of driving, Daimler, "Information on Daimler AG," www.daimler.com/innovation/case/autonomous/rechtlicher-rahmen.html; Aleks Attanasio,

Fully autonomous robots that do not require human direction are not covered in this chapter because innovations in the field of surgery have not yet reached this stage,[19] although the conclusion will share some initial observations regarding how to approach the liability issues raised by autonomous robots.

III Legal Principles Regarding Due Diligence and Cooperation

Generally applicable principles of law regarding due diligence and cooperation are found in Swiss criminal law. Humans must act with due diligence, and if they do not, they can be liable for negligence. According to Swiss criminal law, any person is liable for lack of care if he or she fails to exercise the duty of care required by the circumstances and commensurate with personal capabilities.[20] But while it is a ubiquitous principle that humans bear responsibility for their own behavior, we normally do not bear responsibility for someone else's conduct. We must consider the consequences of our own behavior and prevent harm to others, but we are not our brother's or sister's keeper. The scope of liability can change if we share responsibilities, such as risk-prone work, with others.[21] And whether we are acting alone or in cooperation with others, we must be careful, depending on the circumstances and our personal capabilities.

Bruno Scaglioni, Elena De Momi *et al.*, "Autonomy in Surgical Robotics" (2021) 4 *Annual Review of Control, Robotics, and Autonomous Systems* 651, www.annualreviews.org/doi/abs/10.1146/annurev-control-062420-090543?casa_token=6SiJq_gdMesAAAAA:ykrIDELrN9BO1-Z63N2jcLiZ8ggbiPnLyTp4n65jy5LMz_Ov-Wko-hlyWeBQTAjVVOyHQnqjV94VSg.

19 Examples from different areas: Rolf H. Weber, "Automatisierte Entscheidungen: Perspektive Grundrechte" (Automated Decisions: Fundamental Rights Perspective) (2020) 1 *SZW* 18, section III; *Atlas der Automatisierung, Automatisierte Entscheidungen und Teilhabe in Deutschland* (Atlas of Automation, Automated Decisions and Participation in Germany) (AlgorithmWatch, 2019) 26, https://atlas.algorithmwatch.org/wpcontent/uploads/2019/04/Atlas_of_Automation_by_AlgorithmWatch.pdf. For definitions of autonomy in robotic-assisted surgery, see Guang-Zhong Yang, James Cambias, Kevin Cleary *et al.*, "Medical Robotics – Regulatory, Ethical and Legal Considerations for Increasing Levels of Autonomy" (2017) 2:4 *Science Robotics* 2.

20 SCC, note 3 above, Art. 12, para. 3.

21 See, for a detailed analysis, Nathalia Bautista Pizzaro, *Das erlaubte Vertrauen im Strafrecht* (The Permissible Trust in Criminal Law), Strafrecht Studien vol. 77 (Zurich, Switzerland and Baden-Baden, Germany: Nomos, 2017).

III.A Basic Rules with Examples Regarding the Due Diligence of Surgeons

Unlike other jurisdictions, Swiss law explicitly defines the basic rule determining criminal negligence. In Article 12, paragraph 3 of the SCC, a "person commits a felony or misdemeanour through negligence if he fails to consider or disregards the consequences of his conduct due to a culpable lack of care. A lack of care is culpable if the person fails to exercise the care that is incumbent on him in the circumstances and commensurate with his personal capabilities."[22]

Determining a person's precise due diligence obligations can be a complex endeavor. In Swiss criminal law a myriad of due diligence rules underpin negligence and are used to specify the relevant obligations, including legal norms, private regulations, and a catch-all-clause, dubbed the risk principle (*Gefahrensatz*).[23] The risk principle establishes that everyone has to behave in a reasonable way that minimizes threats to the relevant legal interest as best as possible.[24] For example, a surgeon must take all reasonable possible precautions to avoid increasing a pre-existing danger to the patient.[25]

To apply the risk principle, the maximum permissible risk must be determined.[26] For this purpose, the general risk range must first be determined, and this range is limited by human skill;[27] no one can be reproached for not being able to prevent the risk in spite of doing everything humanly possible (*ultra posse nemo tenetur*).[28] The risk range is

22 SCC, note 3 above, Art. 12, para. 3.

23 Andreas Donatsch, Stefan Heimgartner, Berhard Isenring *et al.* (eds.), *Kommentar zum Schweizerischen Strafgesetzbuch* (Commentary on the Swiss Criminal Code), 20th ed. (Zürich: Orell Fussli, 2018) [*Schweizerischen Strafgesetzbuch*], at Art. 12 Note 15.

24 Andreas Donatsch, *Sorgfaltsbemessung und Erfolg beim Fahrlässigkeitsdelikt* (Due Diligence and Success in the Crime of Negligence) (Zürich, Switzerland: Schulthess Verlag, 1987) [*Sorgfaltsbemessung*] at 117.

25 See Günther Stratenwerth, *Schweizerisches Strafrecht* (Swiss Criminal Law), *Allgemeiner Teil I: Die Straftat*, 4th ed. (Bern, Switzerland: Stampli, 2011) [*Schweizerisches Strafrecht*] at s. 16 N 9.

26 *Sorgfaltsbemessung*, note 24 above, at 128; Andreas Donatsch & Brigitte Tag, *Strafrecht I* (Criminal Law I), 9th ed. (Zürich, Switzerland: Schulthess Verlag, 2013) [*Strafrecht I*] at 343; BGE 90 IV 11, BGE 116 IV 308, BGE 117 IV 61, BGE 118 IV 133, BGE 121 IV 14, BGE 129 IV 121; for the permitted risk in the context of autonomous vehicles, see also Nadine Zurkinden, "Strafrecht und selbstfahrende Autos – ein Beitrag zum erlaubten Risiko" (Criminal Law and Self-driving Cars – A Contribution to the Permitted Risk) (2016) 3 *Recht* 144 ["Selbstfahrende Autos"].

27 *Sorgfaltsbemessung*, note 24 above, at 156.

28 Ibid. at 144; *Schweizerisches Strafrecht*, note 25 above, at s. 16 N 10; BGE 127 IV 44, BGE 130 IV 14.

therefore limited by society's understanding of the permissible risk, and by the abilities possessed by a capable, psychologically, and physically normal person; no superhuman performance is expected.[29] However, if a person's ability is lower than what is required in a situation, the performed activity should be refrained from.[30] In the context of medical personnel, a surgeon who is not familiar with the use of robots may not perform such an operation.

As the law does not list the exact duties of care of a surgeon, it is left to the courts to specify in more detail the content and scope of the medical duties of care based on the relevant statutes and regulations. In that respect, it is not of significance whether the treatment is governed by public or private law.[31]

III.B Due Diligence Standards Specific to Surgeons

Swiss criminal law is applied in the medical field, and every healthcare professional who hurts a patient intentionally or with criminal negligence can be liable.[32] Surgery is an activity that is, in principle, hazardous, and a surgeon may be prosecuted if he or she, consciously or unconsciously,[33] neglects a duty of care.[34] According to the Swiss Federal Supreme Court, the duty of care when applying conventional methods of treatment is based on "the circumstances of the individual case, i.e., the type of intervention or treatment, the associated risks, the discretionary scope and time

[29] *Sorgfaltsbemessung*, note 24 above, at 130, 146, and 154; *Strafrecht I*, note 26 above, at 345.

[30] *Sorgfaltsbemessung*, note 24 above, at 154; Marcel Alexander Niggli & St. Maeder, "Article 12" in Marcel Alexander Niggli & Hans Wiprächtiger (eds.), *Basler Kommentar, Strafrecht I* (Basel Commentary Criminal Law), 3rd ed. (Basel, Switzerland: Helbing Lichtenhahn Verlag, 2013) at N 102; BGE 73 IV 180, BGE 80 IV 49, BGE 106 IV 264, BGE 106 IV 312, BGE 135 IV 70 et seq.

[31] BGE 139 III 252 E. 1.5; BGE 133 III 121 E. 3.1; BGE 115 Ib 175 E. 2b; The general duties of physicians and hospitals are not considered here; for details of the contractual relationships between patient and physician or patient and hospital, see Walter Fellmann, "Arzt und das Rechtsverhältnis zum Patienten" (Doctor and the Legal Relationship with the Patient) in Moritz Kuhn & Thomas Poledna (eds.), *Arztrecht in der Praxis*, 2nd ed. (Zürich, Switzerland: Schulthess Verlag, 2007) 103 ["Rechtsverhältnis zum Patienten"] at 106.

[32] Anna Petrig & Nadine Zurkinden, *Swiss Criminal Law* (Zürich, Switzerland: Dike Verlag, 2015) [*Swiss Criminal Law*] at 108.

[33] Ibid. "Consciously" means that the person disregards the consequences of his or her behavior through a violation of duty of care. The person has considered it possible that it might succeed, but hopes that it will not. Unconsciously, a person acts if he has not considered the possibility of success occurring at all, although he should have noticed it. Both are treated equally in Swiss law.

[34] *Swiss Criminal Law*, note 32 above, at 108.

available to the physician in the individual case, as well as his objectively expected education and ability to perform."[35]

This reference of the Swiss Federal Supreme Court to the educational background and efficiency of the physician does not indicate that the standard is entirely subjective. Rather, the physician should be assessed according to the knowledge and skills assumed to be available to representatives of his specialty at the time the measures are taken.[36] This objective approach creates an ongoing obligation for the further education of surgeons.

Part of a surgeon's obligation is that they owe the patient a regime of treatment that complies with the generally recognized state of medical art (*lex artis*),[37] determined at the time of treatment. *Lex artis* is the guiding principle for establishing due diligence in an individual case in Swiss criminal law.[38] It encompasses the entire medical procedure, from the examination, diagnosis, therapeutic decision, and implementation of the

[35] BGE 133 III 121 E. 3.1; BGE 120 II 248 E.2c.

[36] However, successful treatment is not owed (BGE 133 III 121 E.3.1). Generally accepted and valid principles of medical science are: professional treatment and reasonable care. Thomas Gächter & Dania Tremp, "Arzt und seine Grundrecht" (Doctor and His Fundamental Right) in Moritz Kuhn & Thomas Poledna (eds.), *Arztrecht in der Praxis*, 2nd ed. (Zürich, Switzerland: Schulthess Verlag, 2007) 7; "Rechtsverhältnis zum Patienten", note 31 above, at 120.

[37] Gunther Arzt, "Die Aufklärungspflicht des Arztes aus strafrechtlicher Sicht" (The Physician's Duty to Inform from a Criminal Law Perspective) in Wolfgang Wiegand (ed.), *Arzt und Recht, Berner Tage für die juristische Praxis* (Bern, Switzerland: Stampli, 1985) 52 at Diskussion 73. Wiegand stated as late as 1985 that, according to the Swiss Federal Supreme Court, the exercise of the medical profession requires a certain boldness, which lawyers must never restrict. In 1987, however, the Swiss Federal Supreme Court corrected these earlier cited decisions and stated in BGE 113 II 429, 432 E.3a that limiting "… the liability of doctors to severe violations of the duty of care … is not supported by the law." See also BGE 116 II 519, 521 E. 3: "According to the most recent case law of the Swiss Federal Supreme Court, the liability of physicians is not limited to severe violations of the medical art."

[38] See BGE 134 IV 175, E. 3.2, 177 et seq.; 130 IV 7, E. 3.3, 11 et seq.; 120 Ib 411, E. 4a, 412 et seq.; 113 II 429, E. 3a, 431 et seq.; 66 II 34, 35 et seq.; 64 II 200, E. 4a, 205 f; Antoine Roggo & Daniel Staffelbach, "Offenbarung von Behandlungsfehlern/Verletzung der ärztlichen Sorgfaltspflicht, Plädoyer für konstruktive Kommunikation" (Disclosure of Treatment Errors/Violation of the Medical Duty of Care, Plea for Constructive Communication) (2006) 4 *Aktuelle Juristische Praxis/PJA* 407; Moritz Kuhn, "Artz und Haftung aus Kunst- bzw. Behandlungsfehlern" (Physician and Liability Arising from Malpractice or Medical Malpractice) in Moritz Kuhn & Thomas Poledna (eds.), *Arztrecht in der Praxis*, 2nd ed. (Zürich, Switzerland: Schulthess Verlag, 2007) 601 ["Artz und Haftung"] at 601 and 669. Depending on the success of the offense, (negligent) bodily injury offenses are mainly considered after SCC, note 3 above, Arts. 122, 123, 125, or 126; BGE 134 IV 175 et seq.; BGE 130 IV 7 et seq.

treatment, and in the case of surgeons from preparing the operation to aftercare.[39] The standard is therefore not what is individually possible and reasonable, but the care required according to medical indications and best practice.[40] A failure to meet this medical standard leads to a breach of duty of care. Legal regulation, such as the standards of the Medical Professions Act ("MedBG"),[41] especially Article 40 lit. a, may be used to determine the respective state of medical art. Together, the regulatory provisions provide for the careful and conscientious practice of the medical profession.[42]

Doctors must also observe and not exceed the limits of their own competence. A surgeon must recognize when they are not able to perform a surgery and need to consult a specialist. This obligation includes the duty to cooperate with other medical personnel, because performing an operation without the required expertise is a breach of duty of care in itself.[43] As with other areas of medical care, the surgeon's obligations do not exceed the human ability to foresee events and to influence them in a constructive way.[44]

If there are no legal standards for an area of medical practice, courts may refer to guidelines from medical organizations.[45] In practice, courts usually refer to the private guidelines of the Swiss Academy of Medical Sciences[46] and the Code of Conduct of the Swiss Medical Association ("FMH").[47] Additionally, general duties derived from court decisions,

[39] Ulrich Schroth, "Die strafrechtliche Verantwortlichkeit des Arztes bei Behandlungsfehlern" (The Criminal Liability of the Physician in Cases of Medical Malpractice) in Claus Roxin & Ulrich Schroth (eds.), *Handbuch des Medizinstrafrechts*, 4th ed. (Stuttgart, Germany: Richard Boorberg Verlag, 2010) 125 ["Strafrechtliche Verantwortlichkeit"]; Brigitte Tag, "Strafrecht im Arztalltag" (Criminal Law in the Everyday Life of a Doctor) in Moritz Kuhn & Thomas Poledna (eds.), *Arztrecht in der Praxis*, 2nd ed. (Zürich, Switzerland: Schulthess Verlag, 2007) 669 ["Strafrecht im Arztalltag"] at 685.

[40] "Rechtsverhältnis zum Patienten", note 31 above, at 121.

[41] *Bundesgesetz über die universitären Medizinalberufe* (Medical Professions Act), Switzerland, SR 811.11 (with effect from June 23, 2006), www.fedlex.admin.ch/eli/cc/2007/537/de.

[42] "Rechtsverhältnis zum Patienten", note 31 above, at 124.

[43] "Strafrecht im Arztalltag", note 39 above, at 669.

[44] *Schweizerischen Strafgesetzbuch*, note 23 above, at s. 12 N 20.

[45] BGE 130 IV 7, E. 3.3, 11 et seq. It is stated in the "Botschaft zum MedBG (*Medizinalberufegesetz*)" that the code of conduct of the FMH can be used for the interpretation of the open law.

[46] Swiss Academy of Medical Sciences, (SAMWASSM), www.samw.ch/en.html; for the Project on Artificial Intelligence, see www.samw.ch/de/Projekte/Uebersicht-der-Projekte/Kuenstliche-Intelligenz.html.

[47] FMH Homepage, https://fmh.ch/.

such as "practising the art of medicine according to recognized principles of medical science and humanity," can be used in a secondary way to articulate a doctor's specific due diligence obligation.[48]

III.C Due Diligence of a Surgeon in Robot-Assisted Surgery

New technologies have long been making appearances in operating rooms. *Arthrobot* assisted for the first time in 1983; responding to voice command, the robot was able to immobilize patients by holding them steady during orthopedic surgery.[49] *Arthrobots* are still in use today.[50]

The introduction of robots to surgery accomplishes two main aims: (1) they perform more accurate medical procedures; and (2) they enable minimally invasive surgeries, which in turn increases surgeon efficacy and patient comfort by providing a faster recovery. A doctor is, generally, not responsible for the dangers and risks that are inherent in every medical action and in the illness itself.[51] However, the surgeon's obligation of due diligence applies when using a robot. The chapter argues that the precise standards of care should differ, depending on whether the surgeon has control of the robot's actions or whether the robot reacts independently in the environment, and depending on the extent of the surgeon's control, including the ability to intervene in a procedure.[52]

The next section introduces and explains the functioning of several examples of surgical robots. These robots qualify as medical devices under Swiss law,[53] and as such are subject to statutes governing medical devices. Medical devices are defined as instruments, equipment,

[48] BGE 130 IV 7, E. 3.3, 11 et seq.; *Strafrecht Allgemeiner Teil*, note 2 above, at 160.

[49] Olga Lechky, "World's First Surgical Robot in B.C.," *The Medical Post* (November 12, 1985), www.brianday.ca/imagez/1051_28738.pdf.

[50] See e.g., Alex Nemiroski, Yanina Y. Shevchenko, Adam A. Stokes *et al.*, "Arthrobots" (2017) 4:3 *Soft Robotics* 183.

[51] "Artz und Haftung", note 38 above, at 601.

[52] See also Jan-Philipp Günther, *Roboter und rechtliche Verantwortung* (Robots and Legal Responsibility) (Munich, Germany: Herbert Utz Verlag, 2016) [*Rechtliche Verantwortung*].

[53] Federal Act on Medicinal Products and Medical Devices, Therapeutic Products Act, TPA, Switzerland, SR 812.21 (as amended January 1, 2022), www.fedlex.admin.ch/eli/cc/2001/422/en [TPA]; and the Medical Devices Ordinance, Switzerland, SR 812.213 (as amended August 1, 2020), www.fedlex.admin.ch/eli/cc/2001/520/en [MedDO] specify the classification as a medical device. According to Swiss law, the classification as a medical device does not depend on whether or not it acts directly on the human body: only the purpose is relevant (judgment of the Swiss Federal Administrative Court C-669/2016 of September 17, 2018, E.5.1.2; judgment of the Swiss Federal Court 2A.504/2000 of February 28, 2001, E.3).

software, and other objects intended for medical use.[54] Users of medical devices must take all measures required by the state of the art in science and technology to ensure that they pose no additional risk. The *lex artis* for treatment incorporating robots under Swiss criminal law requires users to apply technical aids *lege artis* and operate them correctly. For example, when the robot is used again at a later time, its functionality and correct reprocessing must be checked.[55] A surgeon does not have to be a trained technician, but he or she must have knowledge of the technology used, similar to the way that a driver must "know" a car, but need not be a mechanic.

On its own, the concept of *lex artis* does not imply specific obligations, and the specific parameters of the obligations must be determined based on individual circumstances. According to Article 45, paragraph 1 of the Therapeutic Products Act (TPA), a medical device must not endanger the health of patients when used as intended. If a technical application becomes standard in the field, falling below or not complying with the standard (*lex artis*) is classified as a careless action.[56] Lack of knowledge of the technology, as well as a lack of control over a device during an operation, leads to an assumption of liability ("*Übernahmeverschulden*").[57]

A final aspect of the surgeon's obligations regarding surgical robots is that a patient must always be informed[58] about the robot before an operation, and the duty of documentation[59] must be complied with. Although the precise due diligence obligations of surgeons always depend on the circumstances of individual cases, the typical duties of care regarding two different kinds of robots that incorporate elements of remote-control, and the situation in which a robot provides a warning to the surgeon, are outlined below.

54 MedDO, note 53 above, Art. 1.

55 TPA, note 53 above, Art. 49; MedDO, note 53 above, Art. 19, para. 1 and Art. 20, para. 1.

56 Monika Gattiker, "Arzt und Medizinprodukte" (Phycisian and Medical Devices) in Moritz Kuhn & Thomas Poledna (eds.), *Arztrecht in der Praxis*, 2nd ed. (Zürich, Switzerland: Schulthess Verlag, 2007) 495.

57 Ibid.

58 Iris Herzog-Zwitter, "Die Aufklärungspflichtverletzung und ihre Folgen" (The Breach of the Duty of Disclosure and its Consequences) (2010) *HAVE* 316 at 318. On the duty of information, see in general, Walter Fellmann, "Aufklärung von Patienten und Haftung des Arztes" (Information of Patients and Liability of the Physician) in Bernhard Rütsche (ed.), *Medizinprodukte: Regulierung und Haftung* (Bern, Switzerland: Stampfli, 2013) 171; BGE 119 II 456 = Pra 1995 Nr. 72 E.2c.

59 BGE 141 III 363 E.5.1.

III.C.1 Remote-Controlled Robots

The kind of medical robots prevalent today are remote-controlled robots, also referred to as telemanipulation systems in medical literature. They are controlled completely and remotely by the individual surgeon,[60] usually from a short distance away via the use of joysticks. An example of a remote-controlled robot, *DaVinci*, was developed by the company *Intuitive*, and it is primarily used in the fields of urology and gynecology. *DaVinci* does not decide what maneuver to carry out; it is completely controlled by the surgeon, who works from an ergonomic 3D console using joysticks and foot pedals.[61] The surgeon's commands are thus translated directly into actions by the robot. In this case, the robot makes it possible for the surgeon to make smaller incisions and achieve greater precision.

What is the due diligence obligation of a surgeon making use of remote-controlled robots? Remote-controlled robots such as the *DaVinci*, which have no independence and are not capable of learning, do not present any ambiguities in the law. If injury has occurred, the general Swiss criminal law of liability for negligence holds the surgeon responsible. The robot's arms are considered to be an extension of the surgeon's hands, who remains in complete control of the operation.[62] In fact, the surgeon has always needed tools such as scalpels to operate. Today, thanks to technological progress, the tool has simply become more sophisticated. The surgeon's duties of care remain the same with a remote-controlled robot as without, and can be stated as follows:[63] the surgeon must know how the robot works and be able to operate it. Imposing full liability on the surgeon is appropriate here, as the surgeon is in complete control of the robot.

According to Dr. med. Stephan Bauer, a surgeon needs training with *DaVinci* to work the robot, including at least 15 operations with the console control to become familiar with the robot, and 50 more to be able to operate it correctly.[64] The surgeon must also attend follow-up training and

60 Azad Shademan, Ryan S. Decker, Justin D. Opfermann *et al.*, "Supervised Autonomous Robotic Soft Tissue Surgery" (2016) 8:337 *Science Translational Medicine* 1 ["Soft Tissue Surgery"].

61 Intuitive, "Da Vinci," www.intuitive.com/en-us/products-and-services/da-vinci.

62 *Rechtliche Verantwortung*, note 52 above, at 255f.

63 See Jonela Hoxhaj, *Quo vadis Medizintechnikhaftung?: Arzt-, Krankenhaus- und Herstellerhaftung für den Einsatz von Medizinprodukten* (Quo vadis Medical Technology Liability?) (Frankfurt, Germany: Peter Lang Verlag, 2000) at 85.

64 Hirslanden, Profile of Dr. med. Stephan Bauer, www.hirslanden.ch/de/corporate/aerzte/1/dr-med-stephan-bauer.html; Martina Bortolani, "Dr. Robotnik, übernehmen Sie!" (Dr. Robotnik, Take Over!) *Blick* (July 3, 2016), www.blick.ch/life/gesundheit/medizin/wenn-die-maschine-operiert-dr-robotnik-uebernehmen-sie-id5213024.html.

regular education in order to fulfil his or her duty of care. This degree of training is not currently specified in any medical organization's guideline, but it is usually recommended by the manufacturer. The surgeon must also be able to instruct and supervise his or her surgical team sufficiently, and should not use a remote-controlled robot if there is insufficient knowledge of the type of operation it will be used in. Lastly, the surgeon must be able to complete the operation without the robot. These principles are basic aspects of any kind of medical due diligence in Switzerland, and they must apply in any kind of modern medicine such as the use of surgical robots.[65]

Medical doctors who do not fulfil the duty of care and supervision for a remote-controlled robot can be held criminally responsible to the same degree as if the doctor made use of a scalpel directly on a patient's body. If, however, injury occurs due to a malfunction of the robot, such as movements that do not comply with the surgeon's instructions or a complete failure during the operation, the manufacturer,[66] or the person responsible for ensuring the regular maintenance of the device,[67] could be held criminally responsible.

III.C.2 Independent Surgical Robots

Some surgical robots in use today have dual capabilities. These robots are pre-programmed by the responsible surgeon in advance and carry out programming without further instruction from the surgeon, but they can also perform certain tasks independently, based on the combined functioning of their sensors and their general programming. Initially the surgeon plans and programs the motion sequences of the robot in advance, and the robot carries out those steps, but the robot may have the ability to act without instruction from the surgeon. These robots are referred to here as "independent robots," to indicate that their abilities are not limited to remote-controlled actions, and to distinguish them from fully autonomous robots capable of learning.

65 Execution of the Swiss Federal Court on telemedicine: BGE 116 II 519, E.3. This decision is a civil law decision, but no reasons are apparent why these principles should not also apply to the criminal law assessment.

66 Sabine Gless, "Strafrechtliche Produkthaftung" (Criminal Product Liability) (2013) 2 *Recht* 54 ["Strafrechtliche Produkthaftung"] at 56: A manufacturer must bring a product onto the market that is free from defects according to the state of the art in science and technology. See also Chapter 2 in this volume.

67 "Strafrechtliche Produkthaftung", note 66 above, at 54: Infringement of the duty to inspect and monitor.

An example of an independent robot with dual capabilities is Smart Tissue Autonomous Robot (STAR),[68] which carries out pre-programmed instructions from the surgeon, but which can also automatically stitch soft tissue. Using force and motion sensors and cameras, it is able to react to unexpected tissue movements while functioning.[69] In 60 percent of cases, it does not require human assistance to do this stitching, while in the other cases, it only needs minimal amounts of input from the surgeon.[70] Although the stitching currently requires more time than the traditional technique by a human, it delivers better results.[71] Another example, Cold Ablation Robot-guided Laser Osteotome (CARLO),[72] is able to cut bones independently after receiving the surgeon's instructions, but it can also use sensors to check whether the operation is going smoothly.[73] According to the manufacturer Advanced Osteotomy Tools (AOT),[74] CARLO is thus the "world's first medical, tactile robot that can cut bone … with cold laser technology. The device allows the surgeon to perform bone operations with unprecedented precision, and in freely defined, curved and functional sectional configurations, which are not achievable with conventional instruments."[75] In summary, CARLO's lasers open up new possibilities in bone surgery.

Independent robots have the advantage of extreme precision, and they have no human deficits such as fatigue, stress, or distraction. Among other benefits, use of these robots decreases the duration of hospitalization, as well as the risks of infection and pain for the patient, because the

[68] Star Automation, "Cartesian Robots – Es-II Series" (Smart Tissue Autonomous Robot), www.star-europe.com/en/prodotti/robot-cartesiani-serie-es-ii-4.

[69] "Soft Tissue Surgery", note 60 above.

[70] Star Automation, "Robot cartesiani serie Es-II," www.star-europe.com/es-ii/; Nicola von Lutterotti, "Der Roboter übernimmt" (The Robot Takes Over), *Neue Burcher Beitung* (May 16, 2016), www.nzz.ch/wissenschaft/medizin/intelligente-medizinaltechnik-der-roboter-uebernimmt-ld.82237?reduced=true.

[71] Werner Pluta, "Operationsroboter übertrifft menschliche Kollegen" (Surgical Robot Outperforms Human Colleagues), *Golem.de* (May 9, 2016), www.golem.de/news/robotik-operationsroboter-uebertrifft-menschliche-kollegen-1605-120779.html.

[72] See AOT, "CARLO,"https://aot.swiss/carlo/ ["CARLO"].

[73] Santina Russo & Noemi Lea Landolt, "Der überflüssige Chirurg: Schon bald sägen Roboter unsere Schädel auf" (The Superfluous Surgeon: Robots Will Soon Be Sawing Open Our Skulls), *Aargauer Zeitung* (April 23, 2016), www.aargauerzeitung.ch/leben/der-ueberfluessige-chirurg-schon-bald-saegen-roboter-unsere-schaedel-auf-ld.1550792. www.aargauerzeitung.ch/leben/der-uberflussige-chirurg-schon-bald-sagen-roboter-unsere-schadel-auf-ld.1550792

[74] "CARLO", note 72 above.

[75] Ibid.

incision and the injury to the tissue is minimal. When independent robots function as intended, surgery time is usually shortened, accidents due to hand trembling of the surgeon are reduced, and improved 3D visualization can be guaranteed.

As noted above, a surgeon is fully responsible for injury caused by a remote-controlled robot, in part because the surgeon has full control over the robot, which can be viewed as an extension of the surgeon's own hands. What are a surgeon's due diligence obligations when using an independent surgical robot? When independent surgical robots use their ability to make decisions on their own, should criminal responsibility be transferred to, or at least shared with, say, the manufacturer, particularly in cases where it was not possible for the surgeon to foresee the possible injury?

To the extent that independent robots are remote-controlled, i.e., simply carrying out the surgeon's instructions, surgeons must continuously comply with the duties of care that apply when using a remote-controlled robot, including the accurate operation, control, and maintenance of the robot. A surgeon's obligations regarding a careful operation while using an independent robot include, prior to the operation, the correct definition of the surgical plan and the programming of the robot. The surgeon must also write an operation protocol, disinfect the area, and make the first incision.[76] In addition, further duties arise under Swiss law because of the independence of the robot in carrying out the instructions the surgeon provided earlier, i.e., non-contemporaneous instructions.[77] During the operation, the surgeon must observe and monitor the movements of the robot so that he can intervene at any time if he or she realizes harm may occur. According to the manufacturer AOT,[78] CARLO "allows the surgeon full control over this … osteotomy device at any time." This standard of supervision is appropriate, because the surgeon's supervision is needed to prevent injury, but as reviewed below, there are limits to what can be expected of a surgeon supervising a robot.

Even if a surgeon complies with the obligations to take precautions and carry out surveillance of the surgery while it is ongoing, a surgical robot may still make a mistake, e.g., cutting away healthy tissue. If it is established that a cautious and careful surgeon in the same position would not have been able to regain control of the robot and avoid the injury, the surgeon is deemed to have not violated his or her duty of care or acted in

[76] "Rechtsverhältnis zum Patienten", note 31 above, at 103.

[77] See also *Rechtliche Verantwortung*, note 52 above, at 255f.

[78] "CARLO", note 72 above.

a criminally negligent manner.[79] If this occurs, no criminal charges will be brought against the surgeon. This standard is also appropriate, because proper supervision could not have prevented the injury.

III.C.3 Due Diligence after a Robot Warning

Per the principle *lex artis*, a surgeon using any kind of surgical robot is required to be knowledgeable regarding the functionality of the robot, including the emergency and safety functions, and the messages and warning functions.[80] A human surgeon using a robot for surgery cannot blindly trust the technology, and current law requires the surgeon to supervise and check whether or not their intervention is required and whether a change of plan is necessary. In the event that the robot fails, or issues a warning signal, the human must complete the surgery without the assistance of the robot. If the robot issues an alert, the human surgeon must always be capable of checking whether such notification is correct and react adequately.[81] If the human surgeon is not capable of taking over, Swiss law imposes liability according to a sort of organizational negligence, the "*Übernahmeverschulden*," which is the principle that if a person assumed a task that he cannot handle properly, and harm is caused, the surgeon acted negligently.[82] If an alert is ignored because the surgeon does not understand its significance or is not monitoring adequately, the surgeon also acts in a criminally negligent manner.

If the surgeon perceives the robot's alert, but assesses that the robot advice is wrong, the surgeon may override it. There is a saying in Switzerland that also applies to a surgeon who relies on a surgical robot, although not completely: "Trust is good, verification is better." In a clearly established cooperation between a surgeon and a robot, if the surgeon decides not to follow an alert from the robot, the surgeon does need a valid justification. For example, if CARLO notifies the surgeon that the bone

[79] Sabine Gless & Thomas Weigend, "Intelligente Agenten und das Strafrecht" (Intelligent Agents and Criminal Law) (2014) 126:3 *ZStW* 561; Nora Markwalder & Monika Simmler, "Roboterstrafrecht, zur strafrechtlichen Verantwortlichkeit von Robotern und künstlicher Intelligenz" (Robot Criminal Law) (2017) 2 *Aktuelle Juristische Praxis* 177. In the context of autonomous cars, see "Selbstfahrende Autos", note 26 above; Alexander Schorro, "Autonomes Fahren – erweiterte strafrechtliche Verantwortlichkeit des Fahrzeughalters?" (Autonomous Driving – Extended Criminal Liability of the Vehicle Owner?) (2017) 1 *ZStrR* 81, and regarding self-driving cars, see Chapters 2 and 4 in this volume.

[80] See also *Rechtliche Verantwortung*, note 52 above, at 255f.

[81] Regarding robot testimony, see Chapters 6 and 8 in this volume.

[82] A more detailed description can be found under Section III.A.

cannot be cut in a certain way and the surgeon decides to proceed anyway, there would need to be a documented justification for his or her decision to overrule the robot.

While the current requirement of surgeon supervision of robots is justified generally, the law needs some adjustment. There must be a limit to a surgeon's obligation to constantly monitor and question robot alerts, because otherwise a surgeon–robot cooperation would be unworkably inefficient. It would also result in unjustifiable legal obligations, based on a superhuman expectation that the surgeon monitors every second of the robot's action. Surgeons are considered to be the "guarantors of supervision,"[83] which means that they are expected to control everything that the robot does. But when it is suitably established that robots perform more accurately than the average human medical professional in the field, the human must be allowed to step out of the process to some degree. For example, a surgeon would always need to go through the whole operating plan to be sure that robots such as STAR or CARLO are functioning properly. However, this obligation to double-check the robot should not apply to every minute movement the robot makes, as an obligation like this would be contrary to the purpose of innovative technology such as surgical robots, which were invented precisely for the purposes of greater accuracy and time-saving.

Additionally, when it is established that a surgical robot performs consistently without engaging in unacceptable mistakes, there will be a point where it would be wiser for the surgeon to not second-guess the robot, and in the case of a warning or alert, follow its directions. In fact, ignoring the directions of a surgical robot, which is part of the medical state of the art and acts correctly to an acceptable degree, is likely to lead to negligent, if not intentional, liability.

III.D Limiting the Surgeon's Due Diligence Obligations regarding Surgical Robots through the Principle of Trust (Vertrauensgrundsatz)*?*

The surgeon's obligation of supervision currently imposes excessive amounts of liability for the use of surgical robots, because, as discussed above, while surgeons rightfully have obligations to monitor the robot, they should not be required to check every movement the robot makes before it proceeds. The chapter argues that in the context of robot

[83] "Strafrecht im Arztalltag", note 39 above, at 692.

supervision, variations of the principle of trust (*Vertrauensgrundsatz*) should apply to limit the surgeon's criminal liability.

When a surgeon works with human team members, the legitimate expectation is that individuals are responsible only for their own conduct and not that of others. The principle of trust is a foundational legal concept, one that enables effective cooperation by identifying spheres of responsibility and limiting the duties of due diligence to those spheres. It relieves individuals from having to evaluate the risk-taking of every individual in the team in every situation, and allows for the effective division of expertise and labor. The principle of trust was developed in the context of road traffic regulation, but it has widespread relevance and is applied today in medical law as well as other areas.[84]

The principle of trust has limits and does not provide a *carte blanche* justifying all actions. If there are concrete indications that trust is unjustified, one must analyze and address that situation.[85] An example regarding surgical robots might be the *DaVinci*[86] robot. It has been in use for a long time, but if a skilled surgeon notices that the robot is defective, the surgeon must intervene and correct the defect.

The limitations of due diligence arising out of the principle of trust are well established in medical law, an environment where many participants work together based on a division of expertise and labor. In an operating room, several different kinds of specialists are normally at work, such as anesthesiologists, surgeons, and surgical nurses. The principle of trust in this environment limits responsibility to an individual's own area of expertise and work.[87]

[84] For an overview, see Matthias Richard Heierli & Jörg Rehberg, *Die Bedeutung des Vertrauensprinzips im Strassenverkehr und für das Fahrlässigkeitsdelikt* (The Significance of the Principle of Trust in Road Traffic and for the Crime of Negligence) (Zürich, Switzerland: Schulthess Juristische Medien, 1996); from road traffic law: BGE 129 IV 282, 286; BGE 115 IV 239, 240; René Schaffhauser, *Grundriss des schweizerischen Strassenverkehrsrechts* (Outline of the Swiss Road Traffic Law), Band I: *Grundlagen, Verkehrszulassung und Verkehrsregeln*, 2nd ed. (Bern, Switzerland: Stampfli, 2002) at N 441.

[85] See "Strafrechtliche Verantwortlichkeit", note 39 above, at 135; "Strafrecht im Arztalltag", note 39 above, at 692; on the principle of trust in general, BGE 125 IV 83, E. 2, 87 et seq.; BGE 120 IV 300, E.3; BGE 118 IV 277, E.4.

[86] A more detailed description can be found under Section III.C.1.

[87] See "Strafrechtliche Verantwortlichkeit", note 39 above, at 135; "Strafrecht im Arztalltag", note 39 above, at 692; Hans Wiprächtiger, "'Kriminalisierung' der ärztlichen Tätigkeit? Die Strafbarkeit des Arztfehlers in der bundesgerichtlichen Rechtsprechung" ("Criminalization" of Medical Practice? The Criminal Liability of Medical Malpractice in Federal Court Jurisprudence) in Andreas Donatsch, Felix Blocher, & Annemarie Hubschmid Volz (eds.), *Strafrecht und Medizin: Tagungsband des Instruktionskurses der*

One way of understanding the division of labor in surgery is that the primary area is the actual task, i.e., the operation, and the secondary area is supervisory, i.e., being alert to and addressing the misconduct of others.[88] Supervisory responsibility can be imposed horizontally (surgeon–surgeon) or vertically (surgeon–nurse), depending on the position a person occupies in the operating room. An example of the horizontal division of labor in the medical context would be if several doctors are assigned equal and joint control, with all having an obligation to coordinate the operation and monitor one another. If an error is detected, an intervention must take place, and if no error is detected, the competence of the other person can be trusted.[89] With vertical division of labor, a delegation to surgical staff such as assistants or nursing professionals requires supervisory activities such as selection, instruction, and monitoring. The important point here is that whether supervision is horizontal or vertical, the applicability of the principle of trust is not predicated upon constant control.[90]

So far, the principle of trust has only been applied to the behavior of human beings. This chapter argues that the principle of trust should be applied to surgical robots, when *lex artis* requires it. First, as a general principle, delegation of certain activities must be permitted. Surgeons cannot perform an operation on their own, as this would, in itself, be a mistake in treatment.[91] Second, regarding robots in particular, given the degree to which surgical robots offer better surgical treatment, surgeons should use them as part of the expected standard of medical treatment.

But can robots, even certified robots, be equated with another human in terms of trustworthiness? Should a surgeon trust the functioning of a robot, and in what situations is trust warranted? The chapter argues that a variation of the principle of trust should be applied to a surgeon's use of surgical robots. Specifically, an exception to the non-application of the principle of trust for robots should be created for robots that have been certified by competent authority as safe, referred to here as certification-based

Schweizerischen Kriminalistischen Gesellschaft vom 26./27. Oktober 2006 in Flims (Bern, Switzerland: Stampfli, 2007) 61 at 82; on the principle of trust in general, see BGE 125 IV 83, E. 2, 87 et seq.; BGE 120 IV 300, E.3; BGE 118 IV 277, E.4.

88 See Hanspeter Kuhn, Gian Andrea Rusca, & Simon Stettler, "Rechtsfragen der Arztpraxis" (Legal Issues of the Medical Practice) in Moritz Kuhn & Thomas Poledna (eds.), *Arztrecht in der Praxis*, 2nd ed. (Zürich, Switzerland: Schulthess Verlag, 2007) 265 at 287.

89 See "Strafrecht im Arztalltag", note 39 above, at 693.

90 See also "Strafrechtliche Verantwortlichkeit", note 39 above, at 139; "Strafrecht im Arztalltag", note 39 above, at 694.

91 "Strafrecht im Arztalltag", note 39 above, at 669.

trust. Before and until the certification is awarded, the principle of mistrust (*Misstrauensgrundsatz*) should apply. This approach would also impose greater responsibility on the surgeon if, e.g., the robot used by the surgeon was still in a trial phase, or had a lower level of approval from the relevant authorities.[92]

The concept of certified-based trust is supported by the principle of permissible risk. It is a fact that people die in the operating room, because medical and surgical procedures are associated with a certain degree of risk to health or life, but in Switzerland, this is included in the permissible risk.[93] There is no reason why this level of acceptable risk should not apply to surgical robots. According to Olaf Dössel:[94]

> [t]rust in technology is well founded if (a) the manufacturer has professionally designed, constructed and operated the machinery, (b) safety and reliability play an important role, (c) the inevitable long-term fatigue has been taken into account, and (d) the boundary conditions of the manufacturer remain within the framework established when the machinery was designed.

A certification-based trust approach is also consistent with other current practices, e.g., cooperating with newcomers in a field always requires a higher duty of care. When the reliability and safety of surgical robots becomes sufficiently established in practice, the principle of trust should then be applied, to establish the surgeon's due diligence obligations within the correct parameters.

III.E Certified for Trust

This chapter argues that surgeons working with surgical robots can develop a legitimate expectation of trust consistent with principles of due diligence if the robot they use is certified. This approach to surgeon liability places increased importance on the process of the medical device certification, which is discussed further here.

[92] For more on the topic, see e.g., Michael Isler, "Off Label Use von Medizinprodukten" (Off Label Use of Medical Devices) (2018) 2 *LSR* 79.

[93] The theory of "de facto control" is used primarily to determine the indirect actors and accomplices; see e.g., *Schweizerisches Strafrecht*, note 25 above, at s. 13 N 11.

[94] Olaf Dössel, "Vertrauen in die Technikwissenschaften, Vertrauen in die Medizintechnik?!" (Trust in Engineering Sciences, Trust in Medical Technology?!) (2013) *Berlin-Brandenburgische Akademie der Wissenschaften* 75, https://edoc.bbaw.de/files/2207/13_Debatte13_Doessel.pdf ["Vertrauen in die Technikwissenschaften"].

Certification of medical devices is a well-developed area. In addition to the TPA[95] and the Medical Devices Ordinance,[96] other standards apply, including Swiss laws and ordinances, international treaties, European directives, and other international requirements.[97] These standards define the safety standards for the production and distribution of medical devices.[98]

Swiss law requires that manufacturers keep up with the current state of scientific and technical knowledge, and comply with applicable standards when distributing the robot.[99] Manufacturers of surgical robots must successfully complete a conformity assessment procedure in Switzerland.

A robot with a CE-certification can be placed on the market in Switzerland and throughout the European Union.[100] A CE-certification mark means that a product has been "assessed by the manufacturer and deemed to meet EU safety, health and environmental protection requirements."[101] For the robot to be used in an operating room in Switzerland, a CE-certification[102] must be issued by an independent certification body.[103] After introducing the robot to the market, the manufacturer remains obliged to check its product.[104]

This chapter argues that a surgeon's due diligence obligations when using a surgical robot should be limited by a principle of trust, and that

95 TPA, note 53 above.

96 MedDO, note 53 above.

97 See European Union, The European Parliament, & The Council of the European Union Regulation, Regulation (EU) 2017/745 of the European Parliament and of the Council of 5 April 2017 on Medical Devices, Amending Directive 2001/83/EC, Regulation (EC) No 178/2002 and Regulation (EC) No 1223/2009 and Repealing Council Directives 90/385/EEC and 93/42/EEC, OJ 2017 L 117 (EU: Official Journal of the European Union, 2017).

98 Relevant are ISO 13485:2016; ISO IEC 80601-2-78:2019-07.

99 "Strafrechtliche Produkthaftung", note 66 above, at 56.

100 See *Abkommen zwischen der Schweizerischen Eidgenossenschaft und der Europäischen Gemeinschaft über gegenseitige Anerkennung von Konformitätsbewertungen* (Agreement between Switzerland and the European Union on mutual recognition in relation to conformity assessment, June 21, 1999), SR 0.946.526.81, www.fedlex.admin.ch/eli/cc/2002/276/de.

101 For a brief overview of CE-certification, see https://europa.eu/youreurope/business/product-requirements/labels-markings/ce-marking/index_en.htm.

102 See MedDO, note 53 above, Arts. 8, 9, and 10; SwissMedic, "Aktuell," www.swissmedic.ch/md.

103 Unlike medicinal products, medical devices do not need to be subject to official approval. Swissmedic's focus in the area of medical devices is, therefore, on efficient market surveillance: Swissmedic, "Medizinprodukte," www.swissmedic.ch/swissmedic/de/home/medizinprodukte.html. For the CE-certification in Switzerland, the various conformity assessment bodies are monitored by Swissmedic.

104 "Strafrechtliche Produkthaftung", note 66 above, at 59; see Chapter 4 in this volume.

the principle should apply when the robot is certified. A certification-based trust approach is consistent with Dössel's suggestion that trust in technology is well-founded if, inter alia, the manufacturer has professionally designed, constructed, and operated the machinery.[105] It is currently not an accepted point of law that the CE-certification is a sufficient basis for the user to trust the robot and not be held criminally responsible, but the chapter suggests that as a detailed, well-established standard, the CE-certification is an example of a certification that could form the basis of application of the principle of trust.

If the principle of certification-based trust is adopted, the surgeon would still retain other due diligence obligations, including the duty to inform patients about the risks involved in a robot's use.[106] This particular duty will likely become increasingly important over time, as the performance range of surgical robots increases.

IV Conclusion

Today, *lex artis* requires surgeons to ensure the performance of the robot assistant and comply with its safety functions. The human surgeon must maintain the robot's functionality and monitor it during a medical operation and be ready to take over if needed. Requiring surgeons to supervise the robots they use is a sound position, but surgeons should not be expected to monitor the robot's every micro-movement, as that would interfere with the functioning of surgical robots and the benefits to patients. However, under current Swiss law, the surgeon is liable for all possible injury, unless the robot's movements do not comply with the surgeon's instructions or there is a complete failure of the robot during the operation.

Surgeons working with surgical robots are therefore accountable for robotic action to an unreasonable degree, even though the robot is used to enhance the quality of medical services. Thus, a strange picture emerges in

105 "Vertrauen in die Technikwissenschaften", note 94 above.

106 On consent to the procedure, see Philippe Weissenberger, *Die Einwilligung des Verletzten bei den Delikten gegen Leib und Leben* (The Consent of the Injured Person in the Case of Offenses against Life and Limb) (Bern, Switzerland: Stampfli, 1996) at 145. Concerning the obligation to monitor the product after market entry, see "Strafrechtliche Produkthaftung", note 66 above, at 60. Concerning the responsibility of the manufacturer and the operator in the field of autonomous cars, see Sabine Gless & Ruth Janal, "Hochautomatisiertes und autonomes Autofahren – Risiko und rechtliche Verantwortung" (Highly Automated and Autonomous Driving – Risk and Legal Responsibility) (2016) 10 *Juristische Rundschau* 561.

Swiss criminal law. In a field where robotics drive inventions that promise to make surgery safer, surgeons who use robots run a high risk of criminal liability if the robot inflicts injury. Conversely, if the surgeon does not rely on new technology and performs an operation alone which could generally be better and more safely performed by a robot, the surgeon could also be liable. This contradictory state of affairs requires regulatory reform, with a likely candidate being the application of a certification-based trust that limits the surgeon's liability to appropriate limits.

This chapter has addressed issues raised by the robots being used today in operating rooms, including remote-control and independent surgical robots. The chapter has not addressed more advanced, self-learning robots. Given that the law already requires reform regarding today's robots, even larger legal issues will be raised when it becomes necessary to determine who is responsible in the event of injury by autonomous robots,[107] those capable of learning and making decisions. In this context, it will be more difficult to determine whether the malfunction was due to the original programming, subsequent robot "training,"[108] or other environmental factors.[109] Surgeons may also find that robots capable of learning may act in unpredictable ways, making harm unavoidable even with surgeon supervision. In the case of unpredictable robot action, a surgeon should arguably be able to rely on the technology and avoid criminal negligence, provided it has a CE-certification. Ever-increasing amounts of due diligence, such as constant monitoring, are not desired with today's or tomorrow's robots, because the robot is supposed to relieve the surgeon's workload and should be considered competent to do so if it is certified.

[107] See e.g., Cade Metz, "The Robot Surgeon Will See You Now," *The New York Times* (April 30, 2021), www.nytimes.com/2021/04/30/technology/robot-surgery-surgeon.html; James Martin, Bruno Scaglioni, Joseph C. Norton *et al.*, "Enabling the Future of Colonoscopy with Intelligent and Autonomous Magnetic Manipulation" (2020) 2:10 *Nature Machine Intelligence* 595.

[108] See Andreas Matthias, *Automaten als Träger von Rechten* (Automatic Machines as Bearers of Rights), Dissertation, 2nd ed. (Berlin, Germany: Logos Verlag Berlin, 2010) at 25.

[109] Susanne Beck, "Roboter und Cyborgs" (Robots and Cyborgs) in Susanne Beck (ed.), *Jenseits von Mensch und Maschine* (Baden-Baden, Germany: Nomos, 2012) 9.

4

Forms of Robot Liability

Criminal Robots and Corporate Criminal Responsibility

THOMAS WEIGEND

I The Responsibility Gap

The use of artificial intelligence (AI) makes our lives easier in many ways. Search engines, driver's assistance systems in cars, and robots that clean the house on their own are just three examples of devices that we have become reliant on, and there will undoubtedly be many more variants of AI accompanying us in our daily lives in the near future. Yet, these normally benevolent AI-driven devices can suddenly turn into dangerous instruments: self-driving cars may cause fatal accidents, navigation software may mislead human drivers and land them in dangerous situations, and a household robot may leave the home on its own and create risks for pedestrians and drivers on the street. One cannot help but agree with the pessimistic prediction that "[a]s robotics and artificial intelligence (AI) systems increasingly integrate into our society, they will do bad things."[1] If a robot's[2] malfunctioning can be proved to be the result of inadequate programming[3] or testing, civil and even criminal liability of the human being responsible for manufacturing or controlling the device can provide an adequate solution – *if* it is possible to identify an individual who can be blamed for being reckless or negligent in producing, coding, or training the robot.

1 Mark A. Lemley & Bryan Casey, "Remedies for Robots" (2019) 86:5 *University of Chicago Law Review* 1311 ["Remedies for Robots"] at 1313. For a brief overview of applications of AI and the legal issues related to them, see Eric Hilgendorf, "Modern Technology and Legal Compliance" in Eric Hilgendorf & Maria Kaiafa-Gbandi (eds.), *Compliance Measures and Their Role in Greek and German Law* (Athens: Π.Ν. ΣΑΚΚΟΥΛΑΣ, 2017) 21 at 27–33. For problems associated with controlling self-driving cars, see Chapter 15 in this volume.

2 Although I am aware that the terms "AI device" and "robot" have slightly different connotations, I use them interchangeably in this chapter.

3 On the liability of programmers, see Chapter 2 in this volume.

But two factors make it unlikely that an AI device's harmful action can always be traced back to the fault of an individual human actor. First, many persons, often belonging to different entities, contribute to getting the final product ready for action; if something goes wrong, it is difficult to even identify the source of malfunctioning, let alone an individual who culpably caused the defect. Second, many AI devices are designed to learn from experience and to optimize their ability to reach the goals set for them by collecting data and drawing "their own conclusions."[4] This self-teaching function of AI devices greatly enhances their functionality, but also turns them, at least to some extent, into black boxes whose decision-making and actions can be neither predicted nor completely explained after the fact. Robots can react in unforeseeable ways, even if their human manufacturers and handlers did everything they could to avoid harm.[5] It can be argued that putting a device into the hands of the public without being able to predict exactly how it will perform constitutes a basis for liability, but among other issues it is not clear whether this liability ought to be criminal liability.

This chapter considers two novel ways of imposing liability for harm caused by robots: holding robots themselves responsible for their actions, and corporate criminal responsibility (CCR). It will be argued that it is at present neither conceptually coherent nor practically feasible to subject robots to criminal punishment, but that it is in principle possible to extend the scope of corporate responsibility, including criminal responsibility if recognized in the relevant jurisdiction, to harm caused by robots controlled by corporations and operating for their benefit.

II Robots as Criminals?

To resolve the perceived responsibility gap in the operation of robots, one suggestion has been to grant legal personhood to AI devices, which could make them liable for the harm they bring about. The issue of recognizing

4 For an interesting example of the logical but dysfunctional learning process of a drone, see "Remedies for Robots", note 1 above, at 1313: A drone was trained to stay within a certain circle and to head toward the center. If the drone left the circle, it was shut off and someone picked it up on the ground and carried it back into the circle. The drone thus "learned" to leave the circle whenever it got close to the margin, because it could then rely on being carried back into the circle.

5 See Mihailis E. Diamantis, "Algorithms Acting Badly: A Solution from Corporate Law" (2021) 89:4 *George Washington Law Review* 801 ["Algorithms Acting Badly"] at 821–822; Sabine Gless, Emily Silverman, & Thomas Weigend, "If Robots Cause Harm, Who Is to Blame?" (2016) 19:3 *New Criminal Law Review* 415 ["If Robots Cause Harm"] at 426–428.

E-persons was discussed within the European Union when the European Parliament presented this option.[6] The idea has not been taken up, however, in the EU Commission's 2021 Proposal for an Artificial Intelligence Act,[7] which mainly relies on strictly regulating the marketing of certain AI devices and holding manufacturers and users responsible for harm caused by them. Although the notion of imprisoning, fining, or otherwise punishing AI devices must appear futuristic,[8] some scholars favor the idea of extending criminal liability to robots, and the debate about this idea has reached a high intellectual level.[9] According to recent empirical research, the notion of punishing robots is supported by a fairly large percentage of the general population, even though many people are aware that the normal purposes of punishment cannot be achieved with regard to AI devices.[10]

II.A Approximating the Responsibilities of Machines and Legal Persons

As robots can be made to look and act more and more like humans, the idea of approximating their movements to human acts becomes more plausible – which might pave the way to attributing the notion of *actus*

[6] European Union, European Parliament, Committee on Legal Affairs, Report with Recommendations to the Commission on Civil Law Rules on Robotics, 2015/2103(INL) (Strasbourg, France: European Parliament, January 27, 2017) at 8, www.europarl.europa.eu/doceo/document/A-8-2017-0005_EN.pdf. For a brief account of the ensuing discussion, see Anat Lior, "AI Entities as AI Agents: Artificial Intelligence Liability and the AI Respondeat Superior Analogy" (2020) 46:5 *Mitchell Hamline Law Review* 1043 ["AI Entities"] at 1067–1069. See also Roman I. Dremliuga, Alexey Yu Mamychev, O. A. Dremliuga *et al.*, "Artificial Intelligence as a Subject of Law: Pros and Cons" (2019) VII:1 *Revista Dilemas Contemporáneos: Educación, Política y Valores* 1 at 9–12.

[7] European Union, European Commission, Proposal for a Regulation of the European Parliament and of the Council Laying Down Harmonised Rules on Artificial Intelligence and Amending Certain Union Legislative Acts, COM/2021/206 final (Brussels, Belgium: European Commission, April 21, 2021).

[8] See e.g., "Algorithms Acting Badly", note 5 above, at 807; "AI Entities", note 6 above, at 1070–1071.

[9] See Ying Hu, "Robot Criminals" (2019) 52:2 *Michigan Journal of Law Reform* 487 at 491; Gabriel Hallevy, *Liability for Crimes Involving Artificial Intelligence Systems* (Cham, Switzerland: Springer, 2015); Gabriel Hallevy, "The Criminal Liability of Artificial Intelligence Entities – from Science Fiction to Legal Social Control" (2010) 4:2 *Akron Intellectual Property Journal* 171. For a discussion, see "If Robots Cause Harm", note 5 above, at 415–422.

[10] Gabriel Lima, Meeyoung Cha, Chihyung Jeon *et al.*, "The Conflict between People's Urge to Punish AI and Legal Systems" (2021) 8 *Frontiers in Robotics and AI* Article 756242.

reus to robots' activities. By the same token, robots' ways of processing information and turning it into a motive for getting active may approach the notion of *mens rea*. The law might, as Ryan Abbott and Alex Sarch have argued, "deem some AIs to possess the functional equivalent of sufficient reasoning and decision-making abilities to manifest insufficient regard" of others' protected interests.[11]

Probably the most sophisticated argument to date in favor of robots' criminal responsibility has been advanced by Monika Simmler and Nora Markwalder.[12] These authors reject as ideologically based any link between the recognition of human free will and the ascription of culpability;[13] they instead subscribe to a strictly functionalist theory of criminal law that bases criminal responsibility on an "attribution of freedom as a social fact."[14] In such a system, the law is free to "adopt a concept of personhood that depends on the respective agent's capacity to disappoint normative expectations."[15] The essential question then becomes "whether robots can destabilize norms due to the capacities attributed to them and due to their personhood and if they produce a conflict that requires a reaction of criminal law."[16] The authors think that this is a probable scenario in a foreseeable future: robots could be "experienced as 'equals' in the sense that they are constituted as addressees of normative expectations in social interaction like humans or corporate entities are today."[17] It would then be a secondary question in what symbolic way society's disapproval of robots' acts were to be expressed. It might well make sense to *convict* an AI device of a crime – even if it lacks the sensory, intellectual, and moral sensibility of feeling the impact of any traditional punishment.[18] Since the future is notoriously difficult to foresee, this concept of robots' criminal responsibility can hardly be disproved, however unlikely it may appear today that humans could have normative expectations of robots and

[11] Ryan Abbott & Alex Sarch, "Punishing Artificial Intelligence: Legal Fiction or Science Fiction" (2019) 53:1 *UC Davis Law Review* 323 ["Punishing Artificial Intelligence"] at 357.

[12] Monika Simmler & Nora Markwalder, "Guilty Robots? – Rethinking the Nature of Culpability and Legal Personhood in an Age of Artificial Intelligence" (2019) 30:1 *Criminal Law Forum* 1 ["Guilty Robots"].

[13] Ibid. at 16: "Idealistic philosophy cannot obscure the fact that the attribution of capacity to reflect, of consciousness, and of other capacities is just that – an attribution – and not cognizable and legally meaningful due to ontological circumstances."

[14] Ibid. at 15.

[15] Ibid. at 17.

[16] Ibid. at 25.

[17] Ibid. at 30.

[18] Cf. "Punishing Artificial Intelligence", note 11 above, at 365–367.

that disappointment of these expectations would call for the imposition of sanctions. However, in the brave new functional world envisioned by these authors, the term "criminal sanctions" appears rather old-fashioned, because it relies on concepts more relevant to human beings, such as censure, moral blame, and retribution (see Section II.B).

One recurring argument in favor of imposing criminal responsibility on AI devices is the asserted parallel to the criminal responsibility of corporations (CCR).[19] CCR will be discussed in more detail in the following section of this chapter, but it is addressed briefly here because calls for the criminal responsibility of corporations and of robots are reactions to a similar dilemma. In each case, it is difficult to trace responsibility for causing harm to an individual person. If, e.g., cars produced by a large manufacturing firm are defective and cause fatal accidents, it is safe to say that something must have gone wrong in the processes of designing, testing, or manufacturing the relevant type of car. But it may be impossible to identify the person(s) responsible for causing the defect, especially since the companies involved are unlikely to actively assist in the police investigation of the case. As we have seen, harm caused by robots leads to similar problems concerning the identification of responsible humans in the background. Regarding commercial firms, the introduction of CCR, which has spread from the United States to many other jurisdictions,[20] has helped to resolve the problem of the diffusion of responsibility by making corporations criminally liable for any fault of their officers or even – under the *respondeat superior* doctrine – of their employees. The main goals of CCR are to obtain redress for victims and give corporations a strong incentive to improve their compliance with relevant legal rules. If criminal liability is imposed on the corporation whenever it can be proved that one of its employees must have caused the harm, it can be expected that corporations will do everything in their power to properly select, train, and supervise their personnel. The legal trick that leads to this desired result is to treat corporations as or like responsible subjects under criminal law, even though everyone knows that a corporation is a mere product of legal rules and therefore cannot physically act, cannot form an intent,

[19] See e.g., Federico Mazzacuva, "The Impact of AI on Corporate Criminal Liability: Algorithmic Misconduct in the Prism of Derivative and Holistic Theories" (2021) 92:1 *Revue Internationale de Droit Pénal* 143 ["Impact of AI"] at 146–147; "Punishing Artificial Intelligence", note 11 above, at 357; "Guilty Robots", note 12 above, at 18–19 and 27–28.

[20] For a comparative overview, see Francisco Javier Bedecarratz Scholz, *Rechtsvergleichende Studien zur Strafbarkeit juristischer Personen* (Comparative Studies on the Punishability of Legal Persons) (Zurich, Switzerland: Dike Verlag (in cooperation with Nomos), 2016).

and cannot understand what it means to be punished. If applying this fiction to corporations has beneficial effects,[21] why should this approach not be used for robots as well?

II.B Critical Differences

However attractive that idea sounds, one cannot help but note that there exist significant differences between corporations and AI devices. Regarding the basic requirements of criminal responsibility, robots at their present stage of development cannot make free decisions, whereas corporations can do so through their statutory organs.[22] At the level of sanctioning, corporations can – through their management – be deterred from committing further offenses, they can compensate victims, and they can improve their operation and become better corporate citizens. Robots have none of these abilities,[23] although it is conceivable that their performance can be improved through reprogramming, retraining, and special supervision. The imposition of retributive criminal sanctions on robots would presuppose, however, that they can in some way feel punished and can link the consequences visited upon them to some prior malfeasance on their part. Today's robots lack this key feature of punishability, although their grandchildren may well be imbued with the required sensitivity to moral blame.

The differences between legal persons and robots do not necessarily preclude the future possibility of treating robots as criminal offenders. But the fact that corporations, although they are not human beings, can be recognized as subjects of the criminal law does not per se lend sufficient plausibility to the idea of granting the same status to today's robots.

There may, however, be another way of establishing criminal responsibility for robots' harmful actions: corporations that use AI devices and/or benefit from their services could be held responsible for the harm they cause. To make this argument, one would have to show that: (1) corporate responsibility as such is a legitimate feature of the law; and (2) corporations can be held responsible for robots as well as for their human agents.

[21] For counterarguments, see text on notes 28–32 below.

[22] Nora Osmani, "The Complexity of Criminal Liability of AI Systems" (2020) 14:1 *Masaryk University Journal of Law and Technology* 53 ["Criminal Liability of AI"] at 61; Dafni Lima, "Could AI Agents Be Held Criminally Liable: Artificial Intelligence and the Challenges for Criminal Law" (2018) 69:3 *South Carolina Law Review* 677 ["AI Agents"] at 682–683.

[23] Vikram R. Bhargava & Manuel Velasquez, "Is Corporate Responsibility Relevant to Artificial Intelligence Responsibility?" (2019) 17:3 *Georgetown Journal of Law and Public Policy* 829 at 836.

III Corporate Criminal Responsibility for Robots

III.A Should There Be Corporate Criminal Responsibility?

Before we investigate this option, we should reflect on the legitimacy of the general concept of CCR. If that concept is ethically or legally doubtful or even indefensible, we should certainly refrain from extending its reach from holding corporations responsible for the acts of their human employees to holding them responsible for their robots.

Two sets of theories have been developed for justifying the imposition of criminal responsibility of legal persons for the harmful acts of their managers and employees. One approach regards certain decision-makers within the corporation as its alter ego and therefore proposes that acts of these persons are attributed to the corporation; the other approach targets the corporation itself and bases its responsibility on its criminogenic or improper self-organization.[24] These two theories are not mutually exclusive. For example, Austrian law combines both approaches: its statute on the responsibility of corporations imposes criminal liability on a corporation if a member of its management or its control board committed a criminal offense on the corporation's behalf or in violation of its obligations, or if an employee unlawfully committed a criminal offense and the management could have prevented or rendered significantly more difficult the perpetration by applying due diligence.[25]

Whereas in the United States CCR has been recognized for more than a century,[26] its acceptance in Europe has been more hesitant.[27] In Germany, a draft law on corporate responsibility with semi-criminal

24 For an overview, see Celia Wells, "Corporate Criminal Responsibility" in Stephen Tully (ed.), *Research Handbook on Corporate Legal Responsibility* (Cheltenham, UK: Edward Elgar, 2005) 147.

25 *Verbandsverantwortlichkeitsgesetz* (Corporate Responsibility Act), Austria (as amended on May 20, 2016), § 3.

26 The seminal Supreme Court decision in favor of CCR was *New York Central & Hudson River Railroad Co.* v. *United States*, 212 U.S. 481 (1909). "Algorithms Acting Badly", note 5 above, at 817, correctly observes that today there is great public support in the United States for a broad version of CCR, so that an effort at legislative reform would be a "non-starter." For a report on the present practice of CCR in the United States, see Elisa Hoven & Thomas Weigend, "Praxis und Probleme des Verbandsstrafrechts in den USA" (Practice and Problems of Corporate Criminal Liability in the US) (2018) 130:1 *Zeitschrift für die gesamte Strafrechtswissenschaft* 213.

27 For a brief overview, see Bernd Schünemann & Luis Greco, "Vorbemerkungen zu §§ 25 para 21" in Gabriele Cirener, Henning Radtke, Ruth Rissing-van Saan *et al.* (eds.), *Strafgesetzbuch. Leipziger Kommentar* (Penal Code, Leipzig Commentary), vol. 2, 13th ed. (Berlin, Germany: De Gruyter, 2021).

features failed in 2021 due to internal dissent within the coalition government of the time.[28] Critics claim that CCR violates fundamental principles of criminal law.[29] They maintain that a corporation cannot be a subject of criminal law because it can neither act nor make moral judgments.[30] Moreover, a fine imposed on a corporation is said to be unfair because it does not punish the corporation itself, but its shareholders, creditors, and employees, who cannot be blamed for the faults of managers.[31]

It can hardly be denied that CCR is a product of crime-preventive pragmatism rather than of theoretically consistent legal thinking. The attribution of managers' and/or employees' harmful acts to the corporation, cloaked with sham historical dignity by the Latin phrase *respondeat superior*, is difficult to justify because it leads to a duplication of responsibility for the same crime.[32] It is doubtful, moreover, whether the moral blame

[28] See Germany, Bundesrat, Entwurf eines Gesetzes zur Stärkung der Integrität in der Wirtschaft (Draft Law on the Strengthening of Integrity in the Economy), Bundesratsdrucksache 440/20 (Germany: Bundesrat, August 7, 2020). The draft was not voted on before the parliamentary period ended in the fall of 2021.

[29] For critical assessments, see Ulfrid Neumann, "Zur (Un)Vereinbarkeit des Verbandsstrafrechts mit Grundprinzipien des tradierten Individualstrafrechts" (On the (In-)Compatibility of Corporate Criminal Law with Basic Principles of Traditional Criminal Law for Individuals) in Marianne Johanna Lehmkuhl & Wolfgang Wohlers (eds.), *Unternehmensstrafrecht* (Basel, Switzerland: Helbing Lichtenhahn Verlag, 2020) 49; Frauke Rostalski, "Neben der Spur: Verbandssanktionengesetzgebung auf Abwegen" (Off the Track: Legislation on Corporate Criminal Liability Going Off the Road) (2020) 73:29 *Neue Juristische Wochenschrift* 2087; Uwe Murmann, "Unternehmensstrafrecht" (Corporate Criminal Law) in Kai Ambos & Stefanie Bock (eds.), *Aktuelle und grundsätzliche Fragen des Wirtschaftsstrafrechts* (Berlin, Germany: Duncker & Humblot, 2019) 57; Franziska Mulch, *Strafe und andere staatliche Maßnahmen gegenüber juristischen Personen* (Punishment and Other State Measures against Legal Persons) (Berlin, Germany: Duncker & Humblot, 2017); Friedrich von Freier, "Zurück hinter die Aufklärung: Zur Wiedereinführung von Verbandsstrafen" (Back Behind Enlightenment: On the Re-Introduction of Criminal Punishment for Corporations) (2009) 156 *Goltdammer's Archiv für Strafrecht* 98; Arbeitsgruppe Strafbarkeit juristischer Personen, "Bericht" (Working Group Punishability of Legal Persons, "Report") in Michael Hettinger (ed.), *Reform des Sanktionenrechts*, vol. 3 (Baden-Baden, Germany: Nomos, 2002) 7. For an overview of the recent German discussion, see Thomas Weigend, "Corporate Responsibility in Germany" in Khalid Ghanayem & Yuval Shany (eds.), *The Quest for Core Values in the Application of Legal Norms: Essays in Honor of Mordechai Kremnitzer* (Cham, Switzerland: Springer, 2021) 103.

[30] "AI Agents", note 22 above, at 688.

[31] Mihailis E. Diamantis, "The Law's Missing Account of Corporate Character" (2019) 17:3 *Georgetown Journal of Law and Public Policy* 865 at 880.

[32] See Charlotte Schmitt-Leonardy, "Originäre Verbandsschuld oder Zurechnungsmodell?" (Culpability of the Corporation or Imputation Model?) in Martin Henssler, Elisa Hoven, Michael Kubiciel *et al.* (eds.), *Grundfragen eines modernen Verbandsstrafrechts* (Baden-Baden, Germany: Nomos, 2017) 71.

inherent in criminal punishment can adequately be addressed to a legal person, an entity that has no conscience and cannot feel guilt.[33] An alternative basis for CCR could be a strictly functional approach to criminal law which links the responsibility of corporations to the empirical and/or normative expectation that they abide by the legal norms applying to their scope of activities.[34]

There exists an insoluble conflict between the pragmatic and political interest in nudging corporations toward legal compliance and the theoretical problems of extending the criminal law beyond natural persons. It is thus ultimately a policy question whether a state chooses to limit the liability of corporations for faults of their employees to tort law, extends it to criminal law, or places it somewhere in between,[35] as has been done in Germany.[36] In what follows, I assume that the criminal law version of CCR has been chosen. In that case, the further policy question arises as to whether CCR should include criminal responsibility for harm caused by AI devices used by the corporation.

III.B Legitimacy of CCR for Robots

As we have seen, retroactively identifying the fault of an individual human actor can be as difficult when an AI device was used as when some unknown employee of a corporation may have made a mistake.[37] The problem of allocating responsibility for robot action is further exacerbated by the black box element in self-teaching robots used on behalf of a corporation.[38]

[33] On these and other problematic aspects of CCR, see Thomas Weigend, "Societas delinquere non potest? A German Perspective" (2008) 6:5 *Journal of International Criminal Justice* 927. For ways of dealing with corporate misconduct outside the criminal law, see Charlotte Schmitt-Leonardy, *Unternehmenskriminalität ohne Strafrecht?* (Corporate Crime without Criminal Law?) (Heidelberg, Germany: C. F. Müller Verlag, 2013).

[34] As to that approach, see notes 12–18 above.

[35] See the strong argument in favor of "a softer version of the State's powers to prohibit and punish" in "AI Agents", note 22 above, at 696. The author plausibly warns that an overextension of criminal sanctions might "weaken our perception of what criminal law is and what it has the power to do."

[36] German law presently permits the imposition of administrative fines on corporations if their leading managers committed criminal offenses or culpably failed to prevent such offenses committed by employees; see *Gesetz über Ordnungswidrigkeiten* (Law on Administrative Infractions), of February 19, 1987, Germany, Bundesgesetzblatt 1987 I, 602, §§ 30, 130.

[37] See text at note 19 above.

[38] If the law treats robots like humans, CCR could be applied directly to robots' malfeasance. See e.g., the Michigan statute discussed by Clint W. Westbrook, "The Google Made Me Do It. The Complexity of Criminal Liability in the Age of Autonomous Vehicles"

It could be argued that the responsibility gap can be closed by treating the robot as a mere device employed by a human handler, which would turn the issue of a robot's harmful action into a regular instance of corporate liability. But even assuming that the doctrine of *respondeat superior* provides a sufficient basis for holding a corporation liable for faults of its employees, extending that doctrine to AI devices employed by humans would raise additional doubts about a corporation's responsibility. It may neither be known how the robot's harmful action came about nor whether there was a human at fault,[39] nor whether the company could have avoided the employee's potential malfeasance.[40] It is therefore unlikely that many cases of harm caused by an AI device could be traced back to recklessness or criminal negligence on the part of a human employee for whom the corporation can be made responsible.

Effectively bridging the responsibility gap would therefore require the more radical step of treating a company's robots like its employees, with the consequence of linking CCR directly to the robot's malfeasance. This step could set into motion CCR's beneficial compliance mechanism: if the robot's fault is transferred by law to the company that employs it, that company will have a strong incentive to design, program, and constantly monitor its robots to make sure that they function properly.

How would a corporation's direct responsibility for actions of its robots square with the general theories on CCR?[41] The alter ego-type liability model based on a transfer of the responsibility of employees to the corporation is not well suited to accommodating activities of robots because their actions lack the quality of blameworthy human decision-making.[42] Transfer of liability would work only if the mere existence of harmful

(2017) 2017:1 *Michigan State Law Review* 97 ["Google Made Me Do It"]. Michigan Compiled Laws s. 257.665(5), introduced in 2016, declares that an automated driving system is the driver or operator of a vehicle "for purposes of determining conformance to any applicable traffic or motor vehicle laws." From that legal provision, the author concludes that "manufacturers should be held liable for AV-caused crimes where their products are shown to be culpable for certain criminal acts and harm caused thereby" ("Google Made Me Do It," at 126), i.e., if a failure in hardware or software caused the infraction (ibid. at 133).

[39] "Criminal Liability of AI", note 22 above, at 62–63 correctly notes that strict liability for any malfeasance of a robot would place too heavy a burden on its individual programmers, designers, and distributors, eventually hampering the development of new technology.

[40] The cause of the harm could also lie in the robot's self-programming. As pointed out in "Algorithms Acting Badly", note 5 above, at 819–820, humans are increasingly absent from the process of writing code, with algorithms themselves writing most of the code for sophisticated programs.

[41] See text at notes 24–25 above.

[42] See "Impact of AI", note 19 above, at 148–149 and 153.

activity on the part of an employee or robot would be sufficient to trigger CCR, i.e., in an absolute liability model. Such a model would address the difficulties raised by corporations using robots in situations where the robot's behavior is unpredictable; however, it is difficult to reconcile absolute liability with European concepts of criminal justice. A more promising approach to justifying CCR for robots relates to the corporation's overall spirit of lawlessness and/or its inherently defective organization as grounds for holding it responsible.[43] It is this theory that might provide an explanation for the corporation's liability for the harmful acts of its robots; if a corporation uses AI devices, but fails to make sure that they operate properly, or uses a robot when it cannot predict that the robot will act safely, there is good reason to impose sanctions on the corporation for this deficiency in its internal organization. This is true even where such AI devices contain elements of self-teaching. Who but the corporation that employs them should be able to properly limit and supervise this self-teaching function?

In this context, an analogy has been discussed between a corporation's liability for robots and a parent's or animal owner's liability for harm caused by children or domestic animals.[44] Even though the reactions of a small child or a dog cannot be completely predicted, it is only fair to hold the parent or dog owner responsible for harm that could have been avoided by training and supervising the child or the animal so as to minimize the risks emanating from them.[45] Similar considerations suggest a corporation's liability for its robots, at least where it can be shown that the robot had a recognizable propensity to cause harm. By imposing penalties on corporations in such cases, the state can effectively induce companies to program, train, and supervise AI devices so as to avoid harm.[46] Moreover, if there is insufficient liability for harm by robots, business firms might be tempted to escape traditional CCR by replacing human employees by robots.[47]

[43] See Kurt Schmoller, "'Verbandsschuld' als funktionsanaloges Gegenstück zur Schuld des Individualstrafrechts" ('Corporate Culpability' as a Functional Analogue to Culpability in Criminal Law for Individual Persons) in Marianne Johanna Lehmkuhl & Wolfgang Wohlers (eds.), *Unternehmensstrafrecht* (Basel, Switzerland: Helbing Lichtenhahn Verlag, 2020) 67.

[44] "AI Entities", note 6 above, at 1064–1066. Liability would normally be in tort law, but could also extend to criminal law, e.g., where an unsupervised dog bites a person.

[45] *Accord*, "Algorithms Acting Badly", note 5 above, at 809, 816, and 829 (claiming that "algorithmic action is corporate action"); "Criminal Liability of AI", note 22 above, at 71–72; "AI Entities", note 6 above, at 1067 and 1071 (arguing for treating robots as "agents").

[46] "Algorithms Acting Badly", note 5 above, at 831.

[47] Ibid. at 811.

III.C Regulating and Limiting Robot CCR

Before embracing an extension of CCR from employees to robots, however, a counterargument needs to be considered. The increased deployment of AI devices is by and large a beneficial development, saving not only cost, but also human labor in areas where such labor is not necessarily satisfying for the worker, as in conveyor-belt mechanical manufacturing. Robots do have inherent risks, but commercial interests will provide strong incentives for their companies to control these risks. Adding criminal responsibility might produce an over-reaction, inhibiting the use and further development of AI devices and thus stifling progress. An alternative to CCR for robot malfunction may be for society to accept certain risks associated with the widespread use of AI devices and to restrict liability to providing compensation for harm through insurance.[48] These considerations do not necessarily preclude the introduction of a special regime of corporate liability for robots, but they counsel restraint. Strict criminal liability for robotic faults would have a chilling effect on the development of robotic solutions and therefore does not recommend itself as an adequate solution.

Legislatures should therefore limit CCR for robots to instances where human agents of the corporation were at least negligent with regard to designing, programming, and controlling robots.[49] Only if that condition is fulfilled can it be said that the corporation deserves to be punished because it failed to organize its operation so as to minimize the risk of harm to others. Potential control over the robot by a human agent of the corporation is thus a necessary condition for the corporation's criminal liability. Mihailis E. Diamantis plausibly explains that "control" in the context of algorithms means "the power to design the algorithm in the first place, the power to pull the plug on the algorithm, the power to modify it, and the power to override the algorithm's decisions."[50] But holding

[48] Cf. "AI Agents", note 22 above, at 694: "Not everything can be foreseen, prevented, or contained, and in everyday life there are several instances where no one is to blame – much more be held criminally liable – for an undesirable outcome … Not everything can or should be regulated under criminal law."

[49] Cf. "Algorithms Acting Badly", note 5 above, at 836; Dominik Schmidt & Christian Schäfer, "Es ist schuld?! – Strafrechtliche Verantwortlichkeit beim Einsatz autonomer Systeme im Rahmen unternehmerischer Tätigkeiten" (It's Its Fault?! – Criminal Responsibility in Connection with Employing Autonomous Systems in the Context of Entrepreneurial Activities) (2021) 10:11 *Neue Zeitschrift für Wirtschaftsstrafrecht* 413 at 420; "AI Agents", note 22 above, at 693.

[50] "Algorithms Acting Badly", note 5 above, at 835.

every company that has any of these types of control liable for any harm that the robot causes, Diamantis continues, would draw the net wider than "sound policy or fairness would dictate."[51] He therefore suggests limiting liability for algorithms to companies which not only control a robot, but also benefit from its activities.[52] The combination of these factors is in fact perfectly in line with the requirements of traditional CCR, where liability presupposes that the corporation had a duty to supervise the employee who committed the relevant fault and that the employee's activity or culpable passivity was meant to benefit the corporation.

This approach appropriately limits CCR to corporations that benefit from the employment of AI devices. Even so, liability should not be strict in the sense that a corporation is subject to punishment whenever any of its robots causes harm and no human actor responsible for its malfunction can be identified.[53] In line with the model of CCR that is based on a dysfunctional organization of the corporation, criminal liability should require a fault on the part of the corporation that has a bearing on the robot's harmful activity.[54] This corporate fault can consist, e.g., in a lack of proper training or oversight of the robot, or in an unmonitored self-teaching process of the AI device.[55] There should in any event be proof that the corporation was at least negligent concerning its obligation to do everything in its power to prevent robots that work for its benefit from causing harm to others. In other words, CCR for robots is proper only where it can be shown that the corporation could, with proper diligence, have avoided the harm. This model of liability could be adopted even in jurisdictions that require some fault on the part of managers for CCR, because the task of properly training and supervising robots is so important that it should be organized on the management level.

Corporate responsibility for harm caused by robots differs from CCR for activities of humans and therefore should be regulated separately by statute. The law needs to determine under what conditions a corporation is to be held responsible for robot malfeasance. The primary issue that needs to be addressed is the necessary link between a corporation and

[51] Ibid. at 836.

[52] Ibid. at 844; "Criminal Liability of AI", note 22 above, at 69 also emphasizes the importance of the "benefit" element.

[53] *Accord*, "Criminal Liability of AI", note 22 above, at 693.

[54] For a similar concept in CCR, see *Strafgesetzbuch* (Swiss Criminal Code), SR 311.0 (as amended January 23, 2023), Art. 102, para. 2.

[55] For an overview of potential fault of human beings in connection with robots, see Chapter 1 in this volume.

an AI device. Taking an automated car as an example, there are several candidates for potential liability for its harmful operation: the firm that designed the car, the manufacturing company, the programmer of the software, the seller, and the owner of the car, if that is a corporation. If it can be proved that the malfunctioning of the car was caused by an agent of one of these companies, e.g., the programmer was reckless in installing defective software, that company will be liable under the normal CCR rules of the relevant jurisdiction. Special "Robot CCR" will come into play only if the car's aberration cannot be traced to a particular human source, for example, if the reason for the malfunction remains inexplicable even to experts, if there was a concurrence of several causes, or if the harmful event resulted from the car's unforeseeable defective self-teaching. In any of these instances, it must be determined which of the corporate entities identified above should be held responsible.

IV Conclusion

We have found that robots can at present not be subject to criminal punishment and cannot trigger criminal liability of corporations under traditional rules of CCR for human agents. Even if the reach of the criminal law is extended beyond natural persons to corporations, the differences between corporations and robots are so great that a legal analogy between them cannot be drawn. But it is in principle possible to extend the scope of corporate responsibility, including criminal responsibility if recognized in the relevant jurisdiction, to harm caused by AI devices controlled by corporations and operating for their benefit. Given the general social utility of using robots, however, corporate liability for harm caused by them should not be unlimited, but should at least require an element of negligence in programming, testing, or supervising the robot.

PART II

Human–Robot Interactions and Procedural Law

5

Introduction to Human–Robot Interaction and Procedural Issues in Criminal Justice

SABINE GLESS*

I Mapping the Field

Legal procedure determines how legal problems are processed. Many areas of procedure also raise issues of rights, which are established by substantive law and overarching principles, and allocated in the process of dispute resolution. More broadly, legal procedure reflects how authorities can impose a conflict settlement when the individuals involved are unable to do so.

Criminal procedure is an example of legal processing that has evolved over time and developed special characteristics. The state asks the alleged victim to stand back and allow the people to prosecute an individual's wrongdoing. The state also grants the defendant rights when accused by the people. However, new developments are demanding that criminal procedure adapt in order to maintain its unique characteristics. Adjustments may have to be made as artificial intelligence (AI)[1] robots enter criminal investigations and courtrooms.

In Chapter 6, Sara Sun Beale and Hayley Lawrence describe these developments, and using previous research into human–robot interaction,[2] they explain how the manner in which these developments are framed

* I wish to thank Red Preston for the careful language editing and valuable advice.

1 For a definition of AI, see the EU AI Act, Proposal for a Regulation of the European Parliament and of the Council Laying Down Harmonised Rules on Artificial Intelligence and Amending Certain Union Legislative Acts Brussels, 21.4.2021 COM(2021) 206 final 2021/0106 (COD), Art. 3(1) [Artificial Intelligence Act], "software that is developed with one or more of [certain] approaches and techniques … and can, for a given set of human-defined objectives, generate outputs such as content, predictions, recommendations, or decisions influencing the environments they interact with."

2 Kate Darling, "'Who's Johnny?': Anthropomorphic Framing in Human–Robot Interaction, Integration, and Policy" in Patrick Lin, Keith Abney, & Ryan Jenkins (eds.), *Robot Ethics 2.0: From Autonomous Cars to Artificial Intelligence* (New York, NY: Oxford University Press, 2017) 173.

is crucial. For example, human responses to AI-generated evidence will present unique challenges to the accuracy of litigation. The authors argue that traditional trial techniques must be adapted and new approaches developed, such as new testimonial safeguards, a finding that also appears in other chapters (see Section II.B). Beale and Lawrence suggest that forums beyond criminal courts could be designed as sandboxes to learn more about the basics of AI-enhanced fact-finding.

If we define criminal procedural law broadly to include all rules that regulate an inquiry into whether a violation of criminal law has occurred, then the relevance of new developments such as a "Robo-Judge" become even clearer (see Section II.D). Our broad definition of criminal procedure includes, e.g., surveillance techniques enabled by human–robot interaction, as well as the use of data generated by AI systems for criminal investigation and prosecution or fact-finding in court. This Introduction to Part II of the volume will not address the details of other areas such as sentencing, risk assessment, or punishment, which form part of the sanction regime after a verdict is rendered, but relevant discussions will be referred to briefly (Section II.D).

II The Spectrum of Procedural Issues

AI systems play a role in several areas of criminal procedure. The use of AI tools in forensics or predictive analysis reflects a policy decision to utilize new technology. Other areas are affected simply by human–robot cooperation in everyday life, because law enforcement or criminal investigations today make use of data recorded in everyday activities. This accessible data pool is growing quickly as more robots constantly monitor humans. For example, a modern car records manifold data on its user, including infotainment and braking characteristics.[3] During automated driving, driving assistants such as lane-keeping assistants or drowsiness-detection systems monitor drivers to ensure they are ready to respond to a take-over request if required.[4] If an accident occurs, this kind of alert could be used in legal proceedings in various ways.

[3] See Nhien-An Le-Khac, Daniel Jacobs, John Nijhoff *et al.*, "Smart Vehicle Forensics: Challenges and Case Study" (2020) 109 *Future Generation Computer System* 500 ["Smart Vehicle"].

[4] Sabine Gless, Xuan Di, & Emily Silverman, "Ca(r)veat Emptor: Crowdsourcing Data to Challenge the Testimony of In-Car Technology" (2022) 62:3 *Jurimetrics* 285 ["Ca(r)veat Emptor"] at 286.

II.A *Using AI to Detect Crime and Predictive Policing*

In classic criminal procedural codes, criminal proceedings start with the suspicion that a crime has occurred, and possibly that a specific person is culpable of committing it. From a legal point of view, this suspicion is crucial. Only if such a supposition exists may the government use the intrusive measures characteristic of criminal investigations, which in turn entitle the defendant to make use of special defense rights.

The use of AI systems and human–robot interactions have created new challenges to this traditional understanding of suspicion. AI-driven analysis of data can be used to generate suspicion via predictive policing,[5] natural language-based analysis of tax documents,[6] retrospective analysis of GPS locations stored in smartphones,[7] or even more vague data profiling of certain groups.[8] In all of these cases, AI systems create a suspicion which allows the authorities to investigate and possibly prosecute a crime, one that would not have come to the government's attention previously.[9]

Today, surveillance systems and predictive policing tools are the most prominently debated examples of human–robot interaction in criminal proceedings. These tools aim to protect public safety and fight crime, but there are issues of privacy, over-policing, and potentially discrimination.

Broader criminal justice issues connected to these AI systems arise from the fact that these tools are normally trained via machine learning methods. Human bias, already present in the criminal justice system, can be reinforced by biased training data, insufficiently calibrated machine learning, or both. This can result in ineffective predictive tools which

[5] Athina Sachoulidou, "Going Beyond the 'Common Suspects': To Be Presumed Innocent in the Era of Algorithms, Big Data and Artificial Intelligence" (2023) *Artificial Intelligence and Law* ["Going Beyond"] at section 2.1.

[6] Aaron Calafato, Christian Colombo, & Gordon J. Pace, "A Controlled Natural Language for Tax Fraud Detection," paper delivered at the International Workshop on Controlled Natural Language (2016).

[7] Jason Moore, Ibrahim Baggili, & Frank Breitinger, "Find Me If You Can: Mobile GPS Mapping Applications Forensic Analysis & SNAVP the Open Source, Modular, Extensible Parser" (2017) 12:1 *Journal of Digital Forensics, Security and Law* 15 at 25.

[8] Karolina Kremens & Wojciech Jasinski, "Editorial of Dossier 'Admissibility of Evidence in Criminal Process. Between the Establishment of the Truth, Human Rights and the Efficiency of Proceedings'" (2021) 7:1 *Revista Brasileira de Direito Processual Penal* 15 at 31.

[9] Mireille Hildebrandt, *Smart Technologies and the End(s) of Law: Novel Entanglements of Law and Technology* (Cheltenham, UK: Edward Elgar, 2015) at 159–185; Mathew Zaia, "Forecasting Crime? Algorithmic Prediction and the Doctrine of Police Entrapment" (2020) 18:2 *Canadian Journal of Law and Technology* 255 at 262; "Going Beyond", note 5 above, at section 2.1.

either do not identify "true positives," i.e., the people at risk of committing a crime, or which burden the public or a specific minority with unfair and expensive over-policing.[10] In any case, a risk assessment is a prognosis, and as such it always carries its own risks because it cannot be checked entirely; such risk assessments therefore raise ethical and legal issues when used as the basis for action.[11]

II.B Criminal Investigation and Fact-Finding in Criminal Proceedings

When a criminal case is opened regarding a particular matter, the suspicion that a crime actually occurred must be investigated. The authorities seek to substantiate this suspicion by collecting material to serve as evidence. The search for all relevant leads is an important feature of criminal proceedings, which are shaped by the ideal of finding the truth before a verdict is entered. Currently, the material collected as evidence increasingly includes digital evidence.[12]

Human–robot interactions in daily life can also lead to a targeted criminal investigation in a specific case. For example, a modern car programmed to monitor both driving and driver could record data that suggests a crime has been committed.[13] Furthermore, a driver's failure to react to take-over requests could factor into a prediction of the driving standards likely to be exhibited by an individual in the future.[14]

[10] For details, see Andrew G. Ferguson, "Policing Predictive Policing" (2016) 94:5 *Washington University Law Review* 1109; for possible remedies, see Sabine Gless, "Predictive Policing – In Defense of 'True Positives'" in Emre Bayamlıoğlu, Irina Baraliuc, Liisa Albertha Wilhelmina Janssens *et al.* (eds.), *Being Profiled: Cogitas Ergo Sum: 10 Years of Profiling the European Citizen* (Amsterdam, Netherlands: Amsterdam University Press, 2018) 76.

[11] Matthew Browning & Bruce A. Arrigo, "Stop and Risk: Policing, Data, and the Digital Age of Discrimination" (2021) 46:1 *American Journal of Criminal Justice* 298 at 310; Oskar J. Gstrein, Anno Bunnik, & Andrej Zwitter, "Ethical, Legal and Social Challenges of Predictive Policing" (2019) 3:3 *Católica Law Review, Direito Penal* 77 at 86–88.

[12] For a discussion on issues of using such material, see Alex Biedermann & Joëlle Vuille, "Digital Evidence, 'Absence' of Data and Ambiguous Patterns of Reasoning" (2016) 16 *Digital Investigation* S86.

[13] Andreas Winkelmann, "'Einzelraser' nach §315 d Abs. 1 Nr. 3 StGB und der Nachweis durch digitale Fahrzeugdate" ('Single Speeders' According to §315 d para. 1 no. 3 StGB and the Proof by Digital Vehicle File) (2023) 19:1 *Deutsches Autorecht* (German Car Law) 2 at 4–6.

[14] Empirical research using naturalistic driving data has been used to predict mild cognitive impairment and (oncoming) dementia in a longitudinal research on aging drivers: The scientists found that atypical changes in driving behaviors can be early signals of mental impairment using machine learning techniques on monthly driving data captured

For a while now, new technology has also played an important role in enhancing forensic techniques. DNA sample testing is one area that has benefited, but it has also faced new challenges.[15] Digitized DNA sample testing is less expensive, but it is based on an opaque data-generating process, which raises questions regarding its acceptability as criminal evidence.[16]

Beyond the forensic technological issues of fact-finding, new technology facilitates the remote testimony of witnesses who cannot come to trial as well as reconstructions of relevant situations through virtual reality.[17] When courts shut their doors during the COVID-19 pandemic, they underwent a seismic shift, adopting virtual hearings to replace physical courtrooms. It is unclear whether this transformation will permanently alter the justice landscape by offering new perspectives on court design, framing, and "ritual elements" of virtual trials in enhanced courtrooms.[18]

II.B.1 Taming the "Function Creeps"

Human–robot interaction prompts an even broader discussion regarding criminal investigation, as the field of inquiry includes not only AI tools designated as investigative tools, but also devices whose functions reach beyond their original intended purpose, termed "function creep."[19]

by in-vehicle recording devices; see Xuan Di, Rongye Shi, Carolyn DiGuiseppe *et al.*, "Using Naturalistic Driving Data to Predict Mild Cognitive Impairment and Dementia: Preliminary Findings from the Longitudinal Research on Aging Drivers (LongROAD) Study" (2021) 6:2 *Geriatrics* 45.

15 Steven P. Lund & Hariharan Iyer, "Likelihood Ratio as Weight of Forensic Evidence: A Closer Look" (2017) 122:27 *Journal of Research of National Institute of Standards Technology* 1 ["Likelihood Ratio"] at 1; Filipo Sharevski, "Rules of Professional Responsibility in Digital Forensics: A Comparative Analysis" (2015) 10:2 *Journal of Digital Forensics, Security and Law* 39 ["Digital Forensics"] at 39; Charles E.H. Berger & Klaas Slooten, "The LR Does Not Exist" (2016) 56:5 *Science and Justice* 388 ["The LR"]; Alex Biedermann & Joelle Vuille, "Understanding the Logic of Forensic Identification Decisions (Without Numbers)" (2018) *Sui Generis* 397.

16 Erin Murphy, "The New Forensics: Criminal Justice, False Certainty, and the Second Generation of Scientific Evidence" (2007) 95:3 *California Law Review* 721 ["New Forensics"] at 723–724.

17 Frederic I. Lederer, "Technology-Augmented and Virtual Courts and Courtrooms" in Michael McGuire & Thomas Holt (eds.), *The Routledge Handbook of Technology, Crime and Justice* (London, UK: Routledge, 2017) 518 at 525–526.

18 Meredith Rossner, David Tait, & Martha McCurdy, "Justice Reimagined: Challenges and Opportunities with Implementing Virtual Courts" (2021) 33:1 *Current Issues in Criminal Justice* 94 at 94, 97; Deniz Ariturk, William E. Crozier, & Brandon L. Garrett, "Virtual Criminal Courts" (2020) 2020 *University of Chicago Law Review Online* 57 at 67–68.

19 Paul W. Grimm, Maura R. Grossman, & Gordon V. Cormack, "Artificial Intelligence as Evidence" (2021) 19:1 *Northwestern Journal of Technology and Intellectual Property* 9 at 51–52.

An example would be drowsiness detection alerts, as the driving assistants generating such alerts were only designed to warn the driver about their performance during automated driving, not as evidence in a criminal court.

In her Chapter 9, Erin Murphy addresses the issue that while breathalyzers or DNA sample testing kits were designed as forensic tools, cars and smartphones were designed to meet consumer needs. When the data generated by consumer devices is used in criminal investigations, the technology is employed for a purpose which has not been fully evaluated. For example, the recording of a drowsiness alert, like other data stored by the vehicle,[20] could be a valuable source of evidence for fact-finding in criminal proceedings, in particular, a driver's non-response to alerts issued by a lane-keeping assistant or drowsiness detection system.[21] However, an unresolved issue is how a defendant would defend against such incriminating evidence. Murphy argues for a new empowerment of defendants facing "digital proof," by providing the defense with the procedural tools to attack incriminating evidence or introduce their own "digital proof."

A lively illustration of the need to take Murphy's plea seriously is the Danish data scandal.[22] Denmark uses historical call data records as circumstantial evidence to prove that someone has phoned a particular person or has been in a certain location. In 2019, it became clear that the data used was flawed because, among other things, the data processing method employed by certain telephone providers had changed without the police authorities' awareness. The judicial authorities eventually ordered a review of more than 10,000 cases, and consequently several individuals were released from prison. It has also been revealed that the majority of errors in the Danish data scandal were human error rather than machine error.

II.B.2 Need for a New Taxonomy

One lesson that can be learned from the Danish data scandal is that human–robot interaction might not always require new and complex

[20] See "Smart Vehicle", note 3 above, at 501.

[21] "Ca(r)veat Emptor", note 4 above, at 290; Sabine Gless, "AI in the Courtroom: A Comparative Analysis of Machine Evidence in Criminal Trials" (2020) 51:2 *Georgetown Journal of International Law* 195 ["AI in the Courtroom"] at 213.

[22] Lene Wacher Lentz & Nina Sunde, "The Use of Historical Call Data Records as Evidence in the Criminal Justice System – Lessons Learned from the Danish Telecom Scandal" (2021) 18 *Digital Evidence and Electronic Signature Law Review* 1 at 1–4.

models, but rather common sense, litigation experience, and forensic understanding. Telephone providers, though obliged to record data for criminal justice systems, have the primary task of providing a customer service, not preparing forensic evidence. However, when AI-generated data, produced as a result of a robot assessing human performance, are proffered as evidence, traditional know-how has its limits. If robot testimony is presented at a criminal trial for fact-finding, a new taxonomy and a common language shared by the trier of facts and experts are required. Rules have been established for proving that a driver was speeding or intoxicated, but not for explaining the process that leads an alert to indicate the drowsiness of a human driver. These issues highlight the challenges and possibilities accompanying digital evidence, which must now be dealt with in all legal proceedings, because most information is stored electronically, not in analog form.[23] It is welcome that supranational initiatives, such as the Council of Europe's Electronic Evidence Guide,[24] provide standards for digital evidence, although they do not take up the specific problems of evidence generated through human–robot interactions. To support the meaningful vetting of AI-generated evidence, Chapter 8 by Emily Silverman, Jörg Arnold, and Sabine Gless proposes a new taxonomy that distinguishes raw, processed, and evaluative data. This taxonomy can help courts find new ways to access and test robot testimony in a reliable and fair way.[25]

Part of the challenge in vetting such evidence[26] is to support the effective use of defense rights to challenge evidence.[27] It is very difficult for

[23] Paul W. Grimm, Daniel J. Capra, & Gregory P. Joseph, "Authenticating Digital Evidence" (2017) 69:1 *Baylor Law Review* 1.

[24] Council of Europe, "iPROCEEDS-2: Launching of the Electronic Evidence Guide v.3.0," www.coe.int/en/web/cybercrime/-/iproceeds-2-launching-of-the-electronic-evidence-guide-v-3-0#.

[25] One can bring a computer hard drive or a mobile phone to court, but the information stored is not accessible to the judges in the same way as printed information. Thus, jurisdictions must find a way to access email or mobile phone files or GPS data, and build expertise with computer forensics.

[26] For a similar discussion regarding DNA evidence, see: "Likelihood Ratio", note 15 above, at 1; "Digital Forensics", note 15 above, at 39; Nils Ommen, Markus Blut, Christof Backhaus *et al.*, "Toward a Better Understanding of Stakeholder Participation in the Service Innovation Process: More than One Path to Success" (2016) 69:7 *Journal of Business Research* 2409 at 2409; "The LR", note 15 above, at 388.

[27] "AI in the Courtroom", note 21 above, at 232–250; "New Forensics", note 16 above, at 723–724.

any fact-finder or defendant to pierce the veil of data, given that robots or other AI systems may not be able to explain their reasoning[28] and may be protected by trade secrets.[29]

II.C New Agenda on Institutional Safeguards and Defense Rights

The use of AI systems in law enforcement and criminal investigations, and the omnipresence of AI devices that monitor the daily life of humans, impact the criminal trial in significant ways.[30] One shift is from the traditional investigative-enforcement perspective of criminal investigations to a predictive-preventive approach. This shift could erode the theoretically strong individual rights of defendants in criminal investigations.[31] A scholarly debate has asked, what government action should qualify as the basis for a criminal proceeding as opposed to mere policing? What individual rights must be given to those singled out by AI systems? What new institutional safeguards are needed? And, given the ubiquity of smartphone cameras and the quality of their recordings, as well as the willingness of many to record what they see, what role can or should commercial technology play in criminal investigations?

In Chapter 7, Andrea Roth argues that the use of AI-generated evidence must be reconciled with the basic goals shared by both adversarial and inquisitorial criminal proceedings: accuracy, fairness, dignity, and public legitimacy. She develops a compilation of principles for every stage of investigation and fact-finding to ensure a reliable and fair process, one that meets the needs of human defendants without losing the benefits of new technology. Her chapter points to the notion that the use of AI devices in criminal proceedings jeopardizes the modern achievement of conceptualizing the defendant not as an object, but as a subject of the proceedings.

[28] Cynthia Rudin, "Stop Explaining Black Box Machine Learning Models for High Stakes Decisions and Use Interpretable Models Instead" (2019) 1:5 *Nature Machine Intelligence* 206 at 206.

[29] Eli Siems, Katherine J. Strandburg, & Nicholas Vincent, "Trade Secrecy and Innovation in Forensic Technology" (2022) 73:3 *UC Hastings Law Journal* 773 at 794–799.

[30] Mireille Hildebrandt & Bert-Jaap Koops, "The Challenges of Ambient Law and Legal Protection in the Profiling Era" (2010) 73:3 *Modern Law Review* 428 at 437–438.

[31] Brandon L. Garrett, "Big Data and Due Process" (2014) 99 *Cornell Law Review Online* 207 at 211–212.

It remains to be seen whether future courts and legal scholarship will be able to provide a new understanding of basic principles in criminal proceedings, such as the presumption of innocence. A new understanding is needed in view of the possibility that investigative powers will be exercised on individuals who are not the subjects of criminal investigations, but instead predictive policing,[32] as these individuals would not be offered traditional procedural protections. This is a complex issue doctrinally, because in Europe the presumption of innocence only applies after the charge. If there is no charge, there is, in principle, no protection. However, once a charge is leveled, the protection applies retroactively.

II.D Robo-Judges

After criminal investigation and fact-finding, a decision must be rendered. Could robots hand down a verdict without a human in the loop? Ideas relating to so-called robo-judges have been discussed for a while now.[33] In practice, "legal tech" and robot-assisted alternative dispute resolution have made progress,[34] as has robot-assisted human decision-making in domains where reaching a decision through the identification, sorting, and calibration of numerous variables is crucial. Instances of robots assisting in early release or the bail system in overburdened US systems, or in sentencing in China, have been criticized for various reasons.[35] However, some decision-making systems stand a good chance of being adopted in certain areas, because human–robot cooperation in making judicial decisions can facilitate faster and more affordable access to justice, which is a human right.[36] Countries increasingly provide online dispute resolutions that rely

[32] Lucia M. Sommerer, "The Presumption of Innocence's Janus Head in Data-Driven Government" in Emre Bayamlıoğlu, Irina Baraliuc, Liisa Albertha Wilhelmina Janssens *et al.* (eds.), *Being Profiled: Cogitas Ergo Sum: 10 Years of Profiling the European Citizen* (Amsterdam, Netherlands: Amsterdam University Press, 2018) ["Janus"] at 58–61; "Going Beyond", note 5 above.

[33] Daniel L. Chen, "Machine Learning and the Rule of Law" (2019) 1 *Revista Forumul Judecatorilor* (Judiciary Forum Review) 19.

[34] John Morison & Adam Harkins, "Re-engineering Justice? Robot Judges, Computerised Courts and (Semi) Automated Legal Decision Marking" (2019) 39:4 *Legal Studies* 618 ["Re-engineering Justice"].

[35] Ran Wang, "Legal Technology in Contemporary USA and China" (2020) 39 *Computer Law & Security Review* Article 105459, 11–14.

[36] Jasper Ulenaers, "The Impact of Artificial Intelligence on the Right to a Fair Trial: Towards a Robot Judge?" (2020) 11:2 *Asian Journal of Law and Economics* Article 20200008.

almost entirely on AI,[37] and some may take the use of new technologies beyond that.[38]

When legal punishment entails the curtailment of liberty and property, and in some countries even death, things are different.[39] The current rejection of robo-judges in criminal matters is, however, not set in stone. Research on the feasibility of developing algorithms to assist in handing down decisions exists in jurisdictions as different as the United States,[40] Australia,[41] China,[42] and Germany.[43] If human–robot cooperation brings about more efficient and fair sentencing in a petty crime area, this will have wide-ranging implications for other human–robot interactions in legal proceedings, as well as other types of computer-assisted decision-making.

Obviously, this path is not without risk. Defendants today often only invoke their defense rights when they go to trial.[44] And as has been argued above, their confrontation right, which is necessary for reliable and fair fact-finding, is particularly at risk in the context of some robot evidence. A robot-assisted trial would have to grant an effective set of defense rights. Even the use of a robo-judge in a preliminary judgment could push defendants into accepting a plea bargain without making proper use of their trial rights. Some fear the inversion of the burden of proof, based on risk profiles and possibly even exotic clues like brain research.[45]

[37] For consumer disputes, see Feliksas Petrauskas & Eglė Kybartienė, "Online Dispute Resolution in Consumer Disputes" (2011) 18:3 *Jurisprudencija* 921 at 930; for family law, see Mavis Maclean & Bregje Dijksterhuis (eds.), *Digital Family Justice: From Alternative Dispute Resolution to Online Dispute Resolution?* (London, UK: Bloomsbury Publishing, 2019); in general, see "Re-engineering Justice", note 34 above, at 620–624.

[38] Regarding China, see Ray W. Campbell, "Artificial Intelligence in the Courtroom: The Delivery of Justice in the Age of Machine Learning" (2020) 18:2 *Colorado Technology Law Journal* 323.

[39] "Re-engineering Justice", note 34 above, at 625.

[40] *Loomis* v. *Wisconsin*, 881 N.W.2d 749 (Wis. 2016), cert. denied, 137 S.Ct. 2290 (2017).

[41] Nigel Stobbs, Daniel Hunter, & Mirko Bagaric, "Can Sentencing Be Enhanced by the Use of Artificial Intelligence?" (2017) 41:5 *Criminal Law Journal* 261 at 261–277.

[42] Yadong Cui, *Artificial Intelligence and Judicial Modernization* (Shanghai, China: Shanghai People's Publishing House and Springer, 2020).

[43] Tamara Deichsel, *Digitalisierung der Streitbeilegung* (Digitization of Dispute Resolution) (Baden-Baden, Germany: Nomos, 2022).

[44] William Ortman, "Confrontation in the Age of Plea Bargaining" (2021) 121:2 *Columbia Law Review* 451 at 451.

[45] "Janus", note 32 above, at 58–61.

As things stand today, using robo-judges to entirely replace humans is a distant possibility.[46] However, the risks of semi-automated justice comprise a more urgent need.[47] When an AI-driven frame of reference is admitted into the judging process, humans have difficulty making a case against the robot's finding, and it is therefore likely that an AI system would set the tone. We may see a robot judge as "fairer" if bias is easier to address in a machine than in a person. Technological advancement could reduce and perhaps eliminate a feared "fairness gap" by enhancing the interpretability of AI-rendered decisions and strengthening beliefs regarding the thoroughness of consideration and the accuracy of the outcome.[48] But until then, straightforward communication and genuine human connection seem too precious to sacrifice for the possibility of a procedurally more just outcome. As of now, it seems that machine-adjudicated proceedings are considered less fair than those adjudicated by humans.[49]

II.E Robo-Defense

Criminal defendants have a right to counsel, but this right may be difficult to exercise when defense lawyers are too expensive or hard to secure for other reasons. If it is possible for robots to assist judges, so too could they assist defendants. In routine cases with recurring issues, a standard defense could help. This is the business model of the start-up "DoNotPay."[50] Self-styled as the "world's first robot lawyer,"[51] it aims to help fight traffic tickets in a cheap and efficient way.[52] When DoNotPay's creator announced that his AI system could advise defendants in the courtroom using smart glasses that record court proceedings and dictate responses into their ear via AI text generators, he was threatened with criminal prosecution for the unauthorized practice of law.[53] Yet, the fact that well-funded, seemingly

[46] "Re-engineering Justice", note 34 above, at 632.

[47] Ibid.

[48] Benjamin M. Chen, Alexander Stremitzer, & Kevin Tobia, "Having Your Day in Robot Court" (2022) 36:1 *Harvard Journal of Law & Technology* 128 at 160–164.

[49] Ibid.

[50] DoNotPay, https://donotpay.com/ [DoNotPay].

[51] See also Maura R. Grossman, Paul W. Grimm, Daniel G. Brown *et al.*, "The GPTJudge: Justice in a Generative AI World" (2023) 23:1 *Duke Law & Technology Review* 1 at 21.

[52] Success rate of DoNotPay, note 50 above.

[53] For a news coverage, see Bobby Allyn, "A Robot was Scheduled to Argue in Court, Then Came the Jail Threats," *NPR* (January 25, 2023), www.npr.org/2023/01/25/1151435033/a-robot-was-scheduled-to-argue-in-court-then-came-the-jail-threats.

unregulated providers demonstrated a willingness to enter the market for low-cost legal representation might foreshadow a change in criminal defense.

Human–robot interaction might not only lower representation costs, but potentially also assist defendants in carrying out laborious tasks more efficiently. For example, if a large number of texts need to be screened for defense leads, the use of an AI system could speed up the process considerably. Furthermore, if a defendant has been incriminated by AI-generated evidence, it only makes sense to employ technology in response.[54]

II.F Robots as Defendants

Dismissed as science fiction in the past, scholars in the last decade have begun to examine the case for punishing robots that cause harm.[55] As Tatjana Hörnle rightly points out in her introduction to Part I of the volume, theorizing about attributing guilt to robots and actually prosecuting them in court are two different things. But if the issue is considered, it appears that similar problems arise in substantive and procedural law. Prominent among the challenges is the fact that both imputing guilt and bringing charges requires the defendant to have a legal personality. It only makes sense to pursue robots in a legal proceeding if they can be the subject of a legal obligation.

In 2017, the EU Parliament took a functional approach to confer robots with partial legal capacity via its "Resolution on Civil Law Rules

[54] "Ca(r)veat Emptor", note 4 above, at 294–295.

[55] Gabriel Hallevy, "The Criminal Liability of Artificial Intelligence Entities – From Science Fiction to Legal Social Control" (2010) 4:2 *Akron Intellectual Property Journal* 171 at 179; Eric Hilgendorf, "Können Roboter schuldhaft handeln?" (Can Robots Act Culpably?) in Susanne Beck (ed.), *Jenseits von Mensch und Maschine* (Beyond Man and Machine) (Baden-Baden, Germany: Nomos, 2012) at 119; Susanne Beck, "Intelligent Agents and Criminal Law – Negligence, Diffusion of Liability and Electronic Personhood" (2016) 86:4 *Robotics and Autonomous Systems* 138 ["Intelligent Agents"] at 141–142; Sabine Gless, Emily Silverman, & Thomas Weigend, "If Robots Cause Harm, Who Is to Blame? Self-Driving Cars and Criminal Liability" (2016) 19:3 *New Criminal Law Review* 412 at 412–424; Monika Simmler & Nora Markwalder, "Guilty Robots? Rethinking the Nature of Culpability and Legal Personhood in an Age of Artificial Intelligence" (2019) 30:1 *Criminal Law Forum* 1 ["Guilty Robots"] at 4; Ying Hu, "Robot Criminals" (2019) 52:2 *University of Michigan Journal of Law* 487 at 497–498; Ryan Abbott & Alex Sarch, "Punishing Artificial Intelligence: Legal Fiction or Science Fiction" (2019) 53:1 *University of California, Davies Law Review* 323 at 351.

on Robotics," which proposed to create a specific legal status for robots.[56] Conferring a legal personality on robots is based on the notion of a "legal personality" of companies or corporations. "Electronic personality" would be applied to cases where robots make autonomous decisions or otherwise interact with third parties autonomously.[57]

In principle, the idea of granting robots personhood dates back a few decades. A prominent early proposal was submitted by Lawrence Solum in 1992.[58] He posited the idea of a legal personality, although the idea was more akin to a thought experiment.[59] He highlighted the crucial question of incentivizing "robots": "what is the point of making a thing – which can neither understand the law nor act on it – the subject of a legal duty?"[60] More recently, some legal scholars claim that "there is no compelling reason to restrict the attribution of action exclusively to humans and to social systems."[61] Yet the EU proposal remains controversial for torts, and the proposal for legal personhood has not been taken up in the debate regarding AI systems in criminal justice.

II.G Risk Assessment Recommendation Systems (Bail, Early Release, Probation)

New technology not only changes how we investigate crime and search for evidence. Human–robot cooperation in criminal matters also has the potential to transform risk assessment connected to individuals in

[56] European Union, The European Parliament, Resolution of 16 February 2017 with Recommendations to the Commission on Civil Law Rules on Robotics (2015/2103(INL)), OJ 2015 C 252 (EU: Official Journal of the European Union, 2017) at para. 59.

[57] "Guilty Robots", note 55 above, at 9; "Intelligent Agents", note 55 above, at 141 f.; Antonio Ianni & Michael W. Monterossi, "Artificial Autonomous Agents and the Question of Electronic Personhood: A Path between Subjectivity and Liability" (2017) 26:4 *Griffith Law Review* 563 at 570; see also Gunther Teubner, "Digital Personhood? The Status of Autonomous Software Agents in Private Law" (2018) *Ancilla Juris* 106 at 113.

[58] Lawrence B. Solum, "Legal Personhood for Artificial Intelligences" (1992) 70:4 *North Carolina Law Review* 1231 ["Legal Personhood"] at 1231.

[59] For a debate of his arguments, see Bert-Japp Koops, Mireille Hildebrandt, & David-Oliver Jaquet-Chiffelle, "Bridging the Accountability Gap: Rights for New Entities in the Information Society?" (2010) 11:2 *Minnesota Journal of Law, Science & Technology* 497 at 518–532.

[60] "Legal Personhood", note 58 above, at 1239.

[61] Gunther Teubner, "Rights of Non-Humans? Electronic Agents and Animals as New Actors in Politics and Law" (2006) 33:4 *Journal of Law and Society* 497 at 502.

the justice system and the assignment of adequate responsive measures. A robot's capacity to analyze vast data pools and make recommendations based on this assessment potentially promises better risk assessment than humans.[62] Robots assist in decision-making during criminal proceedings in particular cases, as when they make recommendations regarding bail, advise on an appropriate sentence, or make suggestions regarding early release. Such systems have been used in state criminal justice branches in the United States, but this has triggered controversial case law[63] and a vigorous debate around the world.[64] What some see as more transparent and rational, i.e., "evidence-based" decision-making,[65] others denounce as deeply flawed decision-making.[66] It is important to note that in these cases, the final decision is always taken by a judge. However, the question is whether the human judge will remain the actual decision-maker, or becomes more and more of a figurehead for a system that crunches pools of data.[67]

[62] Vanessa Franssen & Alyson Berrendorf, "The Use of AI Tools in Criminal Courts: Justice Done and Seen to Be Done?" (2021) 92:1 *Revue Internationale de Droit Pénal* 199 at 206.

[63] Katherine Freeman, "Algorithmic Injustice: How the Wisconsin Supreme Court Failed to Protect Due Process Rights in *State* v. *Loomis*" (2016) 18:5 *North Carolina Journal of Law & Technology* 75.

[64] Arthur Rizer & Caleb Watney, "Artificial Intelligence Can Make Our Jail System More Efficient, Equitable, and Just" (2018) 23:1 *Texas Review of Law & Politics* 181; Han-Wei Liu, Ching-Fu Lin, & Yu-Jie Chen, "Beyond *State* v *Loomis*: Artificial Intelligence, Government Algorithmization and Accountability" (2019) 27:2 *International Journal of Law and Information Technology* 122 at 133–141; Hans Steege, "Algorithmenbasierte Diskriminierung durch Einsatz von Künstlicher Intelligenz" (Algorithm-Based Discrimination through the Use of Artificial Intelligence) (2019) 11 *Multimedia und Recht* 715. For a European view on such systems, see Serena Quattrocolo, *Artificial Intelligence, Computational Modelling and Criminal Proceedings: A Framework for A European Legal Discussion, Legal Studies in International, European and Comparative Criminal Law*, vol. 4 (Cham, Switzerland: Springer Nature, 2020); for a Canadian point of view, see Sara M. Smyth, "Can We Trust Artificial Intelligence in Criminal Law Enforcement?" (2019) 17:1 *Canadian Journal of Law and Technology* 99; for a comparison, see Simon Chesterman, "Through a Glass, Darkly: Artificial Intelligence and the Problem of Opacity" (2021) 69:2 *American Journal of Comparative Law* 271 at 287–294.

[65] Robert Werth, "Risk and Punishment: The Recent History and Uncertain Future of Actuarial, Algorithmic, and 'Evidence-Based' Penal Techniques" (2019) 13:2 *Sociology Compass* 1 at 8–10.

[66] John Lightbourne, "Damned Lies & Criminal Sentencing Using Evidence-Based Tools" (2016) 15:1 *Duke Law and Technology Review* 327 at 334–342.

[67] Marie-Claire Aarts, "The Rise of Synthetic Judges: If We Dehumanize the Judiciary, Whose Hand Will Hold the Gavel?" (2021) 60:3 *Washburn Law Journal* 511.

III Privacy and Fairness Concerns

The use of human–robot interaction in criminal matters raises manifold privacy and fairness concerns, only some of which can be highlighted here.

III.A Enhancing Safety or Paving the Way to a "Surveillance State"?

In a future where human–robot interactions are commonplace, one major concern is the potential for a "surveillance state" in which governments and private entities share tasks, thereby allowing both sides to avoid the regulatory net. David Gray takes on this issue when he asks whether our legal systems have the right tools to preserve autonomy, intimacy, and democracy in a future of ubiquitous human–robot interaction. He argues that the US Constitution's Fourth Amendment could provide safeguards, but it falls short due to current judicial interpretations of individual standing and the state agency requirement. Gray argues that the language of the Fourth Amendment, as well as its historical and philosophical roots, support a new interpretation, one that could acknowledge collective interests and guard privacy as a public good against threats posed by both state and private agents.

In Europe, the fear of a surveillance state has prompted manifold domestic and European laws. The European Convention on Human Rights (ECHR), adopted in 1950 in the forum of the Council of Europe, grants the right to privacy as a fundamental human right. The EU Member States first agreed on a Data Protection Directive (95/46/EC) in 1995, then proclaimed a right to protection of personal data in the Charter of Fundamental Rights of the EU in 2000, and most recently put into effect the General Data Protection Regulation (GDPR) in 2018. The courts, in particular the Court of Justice of the European Union (CJEU), have also shaped data protection law through interpretations and rulings.

Data processing in criminal justice, however, has always been an exception. It is not covered by the GDPR as such, but by the Directive (EU) 2016/680, which addresses the protection of natural persons regarding the processing of personal data by competent authorities for the purposes of the prevention, investigation, detection, or prosecution of criminal offenses or the execution of criminal penalties.[68] New proposals,

[68] European Union, The European Parliament, Official Journal of the European Union L 119 of 4 May 2016, OJ 2015 L 119 (EU: Official Journal of the European Union, 2016) [L 119] at 1.

such as regulation laying down harmonized rules on artificial intelligence (AI Act),[69] have the potential to undo current understandings regarding the dividing line between general regulation of data collection and police matters.

One major issue, concerning policing as well as criminal justice, pertains to facial recognition, conducted by either a fully responsible human via photo matching or by a robot using real-time facial recognition. When scanning masses of visual material, robots outperform humans in detecting matches via superior pattern recognition. This strength, however, comes with drawbacks, among them the reinforcement of inherent bias through the use of biased training materials in the machine learning process.

The use of facial recognition in criminal matters raises a number of issues, including public–private partnerships. Facial recognition systems need huge data pools to function, which can be provided by the authorities in the form of mug shots. Creating such data pools can, however, lead to the reinforcement of bias already existent in policing. Visual material could also be provided by private companies, but this raises privacy concerns if the respective individuals have not consented to be in the data pool. Data quality may also be problematic if the material lacks adequate diversity, which could affect the robot's capability to correctly match two pictures. In the past, authorities bought pictures and services from companies that later came under scrutiny for their lack of transparency and other security flaws.[70] If such companies scrape photos from social media and other internet sources without consent from individuals, the material cannot be used for matching, but without an adequate volume of photographs, there may be serious consequences such as wrongful identification. Similar arguments are raised regarding the use of genealogy databases for DNA-sample testing by investigation authorities.[71] The use of facial recognition for criminal justice matters may have even more profound effects. People might feel safer overall if criminals are identified, but

[69] Artificial Intelligence Act, note 1 above.

[70] Cf. Isadora Neroni Rezende, "Facial Recognition in Police Hands: Assessing the 'Clearview Case' from a European Perspective" (2020) 11:3 *New Journal of European Criminal Law* 375 at 389; for civil society challenges against Clearview AI in Europe, see "Challenge against Clearview AI in Europe," *Privacy International*, https://privacyinternational.org/legal-action/challenge-against-clearview-ai-europe.

[71] See e.g., Shanni Davidowitz, "23andEveryone: Privacy Concerns with Law Enforcement's Use of Genealogy Databases to Implicate Relatives in Criminal Investigations" (2019) 85:1 *Brooklyn Law Review* 185.

also less inclined to exercise legal rights that put them under the gaze of the authorities, such as taking part in demonstrations.[72]

The worldwide awareness of the use of robots in facial recognition has given rise to an international discussion about the need for universal normative frameworks. These frameworks are based on existing international human rights norms for the use of facial recognition technology and related AI use. In June 2020, the UN High Commissioner for Human Rights published a report concerning the impact of new technologies,[73] including facial recognition technology, focusing on the effect on human rights.[74] The report highlighted the need to develop a standard for privacy and data protection, as well as address accuracy and discriminatory impacts. The following year, the Council of Europe published Guidelines on Facial Recognition, suggesting that states should adopt a robust legal framework applicable to the different cases of facial recognition technology and implement a set of safeguards.[75] At the beginning of 2024, the EU Member States approved a proposal on an AI Act[76] that aims to ban certain facial recognition techniques in public spaces, but permits its use if prior judicial authorization is provided for the purpose of specific law enforcement.[77]

III.B Fairness and Taking All Interests in Consideration

Notwithstanding the many risks attached to the deployment of certain surveillance technology, it is clear that AI systems and robots can be put to use to

72 Kristine Hamann & Rachel Smith, *Facial Recognition Technology: Where Will It Take Us?* (Prosecutors' Center for Excellence, 2019), Art. 3, at 11–13; Johnathan W. Penney, "Understanding Chilling Effects" (2022) 106:3 *Minnesota Law Review* 1451.

73 United Nations, Report of the United Nations High Commissioner for Human Rights, Impact of New Technologies on the Promotion and Protection of Human Rights in the Context of Assemblies, Including Peaceful Protests, UN Doc. A/HRC/44/24 (United Nations: Office of the High Commissioner for Human Rights, 2020).

74 Ibid.

75 Council of Europe, Guidelines on Facial Recognition, adopted by the Consultative Committee of the Convention for the protection of individuals with regard to automatic processing of personal data (Council of Europe: Consultative Committee of the Convention for the protection of individuals with regard to automatic processing of personal data 2021), https://edoc.coe.int/en/artificial-intelligence/9753-guidelines-on-facial-recognition.html.

76 Proposal for a Regulation laying down harmonized rules on Artificial Intelligence (AI Act) COM/2021/206 final.

77 Michael Veale & Frederik Zuiderveen Borgesius, "Demystifying the Draft EU Artificial Intelligence Act: Analysing the Good, the Bad, and the Unclear Elements of the Proposed Approach" (2021) 22.4 *Computer Law Review International* 97–112 at 98.

support criminal justice in overburdened systems in which individuals face criminal justice systems under strain. For example, advanced monitoring systems might allow for finely adjusted bail or probation measures in many more situations than it is possible with current levels of human oversight.[78] Crowdsourced evidence from private cameras might provide exonerating evidence needed by the defense.[79] However, such systems raise fairness questions in many ways and require the balancing of interests in manifold respects, both within and beyond the criminal trial. Problems arising within criminal proceedings include the possible infringement of defense rights, as well as the need to correct bias and prevent discrimination (see Sections II.A and II.B.2).

A different sort of balancing of interests is required when addressing risks regarding the invasion of privacy.[80] Chapter 10 by Bart Custers and Lonneke Stevens outlines the increasing discrepancy between legal frameworks of data protection and criminal procedure, and the actual practices of using data as evidence in criminal courts. The structural ambiguity they detect has many features. They find that the existing laws in the Netherlands do not obstruct data collection but that the analysis of such evidence is basically unregulated, and data rights cannot yet be meaningfully enforced in criminal courts.

As indicated above, this state of affairs could change. In Europe, new EU initiatives and legislation are being introduced.[81] If the right to transparency of AI systems[82] and the right to accountability[83] can be enforced in criminal proceedings and are not modified by a specialized criminal justice regulation,[84]

[78] Mirko Bagaric, Jennifer Svilar, Melissa Bull *et al.*, "The Solution to the Pervasive Bias and Discrimination in the Criminal Justice System: Transparent and Fair Artificial Intelligence" (2021) 59:1 *American Criminal Law Review* 95 at 116 and 124; Mike Nellis, "From Electronic Monitoring to Artificial Intelligence: Technopopulism and the Future of Probation Services" in Lol Burke, Nicola Carr, Emma Cluley *et al.* (eds.), *Reimagining Probation Practice*, 1st ed. (London, UK: Routledge, 2022) 207.

[79] "Ca(r)veat Emptor", note 4 above, at 300–301.

[80] See, for a detailed discussion, Kate Weisburd, "Sentenced to Surveillance: Fourth Amendment Limits on Electronic Monitoring" (2019) 98:4 *North Carolina Law Review* 717 at 753–757.

[81] See e.g. relevant provisions in the Artificial Intelligence Act, note 1 above; European Union, European Commission, Proposal for a directive of the European Parliament and of the Council on adapting non-contractual civil liability rules to artificial intelligence (AI liability directive), COM/2022/496 final (Brussels: European Commission, 2022).

[82] Heike Felzmann, Eduard Fosch-Villaronga, Christoph Lutz *et al.*, "Towards Transparency by Design for Artificial Intelligence" (2020) 26:6 *Science and Engineering Ethics* 3333 ["Towards Transparency"] at 3335–3336.

[83] Paul De Hert & Guillermo Lazcoz, "When GDPR-Principles Blind Each Other: Accountability, Not Transparency, at the Heart of Algorithmic Governance" (2022) 8:1 *European Data Protection Law Review* 31.

[84] See e.g., L 119, note 68 above, at 1.

courts that want to make use of data gained through such systems might find that data protection regulation actually promises to assist in safeguarding the reliability of fact-finding. As always, the question is whether we can meaningfully identify, understand, and address the possibilities and risks posed by human–robot interaction. If not, we cannot make use of the technology.

The controversial debate on how the criminal justice system can adequately address privacy concerns[85] and the development of data protection law potentially point the way to a different solution. This solution lies not in law, but in technology, via privacy by design.[86] This approach can be taken to an extreme, until we arrive at what has been called "impossibility structures," i.e., design structures that prohibit human use in certain circumstances.[87] Using the example of driving automation, we find that the intervention systems exist on a spectrum. On one end of the spectrum, there are low intervention systems known as nudging structures, such as intelligent speed assistance and drowsiness warning systems. At the high intervention end of the spectrum are impossibility structures; rather than simply monitor or enhance human driving performance, they prevent human driving entirely. For example, alcohol interlock devices immobilize the vehicle if a potential driver's breath alcohol concentration is in excess of a certain predetermined level. These structures prevent drunken humans from driving at all, creating "facts on the ground" that replace law enforcement and criminal trials. It is very difficult to say whether it would be good to bypass human agency with such structures, the risk being that such legality-by-design undermines not only the human entitlement to act out of necessity, but perhaps also the privacy that comprises one of the foundations of liberal society, which could undermine democracy as a whole.[88]

[85] For a discussion on the protection offered by US Constitutional law regarding a rapidly developing technology, see Katherine J. Strandburg, "Home, Home on the Web and Other Fourth Amendment Implications of Technosocial Change" (2011) 70:3 *Maryland Law Review* 614.

[86] "Towards Transparency", note 80 above, at 3343–3344.

[87] Sabine Gless & Emily Silverman, "Create Law or Facts? Smart Cars and Smart Compliance Systems," *Oxford Business Law Blog* (March 17, 2023), https://blogs.law.ox.ac.uk/oblb/blog-post/2023/03/create-law-or-facts-smart-cars-and-smart-compliance-systems.

[88] See Michael L. Rich, "Should We Make Crime Impossible?" (2013) 36:2 *Harvard Journal Law & Public Policy* 795 at 802–804 for definition of terms, and "Smart Vehicle", note 3 above, at 500, for a reference to Professor Edward K. Cheng as the originator of the term "impossibility structures." For other attempts to define the term, see Edward K. Cheng, "Structural Laws and the Puzzle of Regulating Behavior" (2006) 100:2 *Northwestern University of Law Review* 655 at 664 ("type II structural controls"); Christina M. Mulligan, "Perfect Enforcement of Law: When to Limit and When to Use Technology" (2008) 14:4

IV The Larger Perspective

It seems inevitable that human–robot interaction will impact criminal proceedings, just as it has other areas of the law. However, the exact nature of this impact is unclear. It may help to prevent crime before it happens or it might lead to a merciless application of the law.

Legal scholars primarily point to the risks of AI systems in criminal justice and the need to have adequate safeguards in place. However, many agree that certain robots have the potential to make criminal proceedings faster, and possibly even fairer. One big, not yet fully scrutinized issue will be whether we can and will trust systems that generate information where the decision-making process is opaque to humans, even when it comes to criminal verdicts.[89]

Future lawmakers drafting criminal procedure must keep in mind what Tatjana Hörnle pointed out in her introduction to Part I of the volume, that humans tend to blame other humans rather than machines.[90] The same is true for bringing charges against humans as opposed to machines, as explained by Jeanne Gaakeer.[91] Part of the explanation for this view lies in the inherent perspectives of substantive and procedural law.[92] Criminal justice is tailored to humans, and it is much easier, for reasons rooted in human understanding and ingrained in the legal framework, to prosecute a human.[93] This appears to be the case when a prosecution can be directed against either a human or a human–robot cooperation,[94] and it would most probably also be the case if one had

Richmond Journal of Law & Technology 1 at 3 ("perfect prevention"); Timo Rademacher, "Of New Technologies and Old Laws: Do We Need a Right to Violate the Law?" (2020) 5:1 *European Journal for Security Research* 39 at 45.

89 See Chapter 6 in this volume.

90 See also Madeleine Clare Elish & Tim Hwang, "Praise the Machine! Punish the Human! The Contradictory History of Accountability in Automated Aviation," Data and Society, Comparative Studies in Intelligent Systems – Working Paper 1 (2015) at 2–3.

91 See Chapter 15 in this volume.

92 In this volume, Frode Pederson's Chapter 13 discusses how even narrative reflects a human orientation, which creates issues when dealing with robots.

93 Cf. Madeleine Elish, "Moral Crumple Zones: Cautionary Tales in Human–Robot Interaction (Pre-Print)" (2019) 5 *Engaging Science, Technology, and Society* 40.

94 Laurel Wamsley, "Uber Not Criminally Liable in Death of Woman Hit by Self-Driving Car, Prosecutor Says," *NPR* (March 6, 2019), www.npr.org/2019/03/06/700801945/uber-not-criminally-liable-in-death-of-woman-hit-by-self-driving-car-says-prosec (in the death of Elaine Herzberg, unsolved evidentiary issues presumably hampered prosecution: "After a very thorough review of all the evidence presented, this Office has determined that there is no basis for criminal liability for the Uber corporation arising from this matter ...").

to choose between prosecuting a visible human driver or a robot that guided automated driving.

With human–robot interaction now becoming a reality of daily life and criminal justice, it is time for the legal community to reconcile themselves to these challenges, and engage in a new conversation with the computer scientists, behavioral scholars, forensic experts, and other disciplines that can provide relevant knowledge. The digital shift in criminal justice will be manifold and less than predictable. Human–robot interaction might direct more blame in the direction of humans, but it might also open up various new ways to reconstruct the past and possibly assist in exonerating falsely accused humans. A basic condition for benefiting from these developments is to understand the different aspects of human–robot interaction and their ramifications for legal proceedings.

MAMAK ©

6

Human Psychology and Robot Evidence in the Courtroom, Alternative Dispute Resolution, and Agency Proceedings

SARA SUN BEALE AND HAYLEY LAWRENCE*

I Introduction

In the courtroom, the phrases artificial intelligence (AI) and robot witnesses ("robo-witnesses") conjure up images of a Star Wars-like, futuristic world with autonomous robots like C3PO taking the witness stand. Although testimony from a robo-witness may be possible in the distant future, many other kinds of evidence produced by AI are already becoming more common.

Given the wide and rapidly expanding range of activities being undertaken by robots, it is inevitable that robot-generated evidence and evidence from human witnesses who interacted with or observed robots will be presented in legal forums. This chapter explores the effects of human psychology on human–robot interactions (HRIs) in legal proceedings. In Section II, we review the research on HRI in other contexts, such as market research and consumer interactions. In Section III, we consider the effect the psychological responses detailed in Section II may have in litigation.

We argue that human responses to robot-generated evidence will present unique challenges to the accuracy of litigation, as well as ancillary goals such as fairness and transparency, but HRI may also enhance accuracy in other respects. For our purposes, the most important feature of HRI is the human tendency to anthropomorphize robots. Anthropomorphization can generate misleading impressions, e.g., that robots have human-like emotions and motives, and this tendency toward anthropomorphization can be manipulated by designing robots to make them appear more

* Sara Sun Beale, Charles L. B. Lowndes Professor of Law, Duke Law School; Hayley N. Lawrence, JD, LLM, Duke Law School, 2021.

trustworthy and believable. The degree of distortion caused by anthropomorphization will vary, depending on the design of the robot and other situational factors, like how the interaction is framed. The effects of anthropomorphization may be amplified by the simulation heuristic, i.e., how people estimate the likelihood that something happened based on how easy it is for them to imagine it happening, and the psychological preference for direct evidence over circumstantial evidence.[1] Moreover, additional cognitive biases may distort fact-finding or attributions of liability when humans interact with or observe robots.

On the other hand, robot-generated evidence may offer unique advantages if it can be presented as direct evidence via a robo-witness, because of the nature of a robo-witness's memory compared to that of a human eyewitness. We have concerns, however, about the degree to which the traditional methods of testing the accuracy of evidence, particularly cross-examination, will be effective for robot-generated evidence. It is unclear whether lay fact-finders, who are prone to anthropomorphize robots, will be able to understand and evaluate the information generated by complex algorithms, particularly those using unsupervised learning models.

Although it has played a limited role in litigation, AI evidence has been used in other legal forums. Section IV compares the use of testimony from autonomous vehicles (AVs) in litigation with the use of similar evidence in alternative dispute resolution (ADR) and the National Transportation Safety Board (NTSB). These contrasting legal infrastructures present an opportunity to examine AI evidence through a different lens. After comparing and contrasting AI testimony in ADR and NTSB proceedings with traditional litigation, the chapter suggests that the presence of expert decision-makers might help mitigate some of the problems with HRI, although other aspects of the procedures in each forum still raise concerns.

II The Psychology of HRI in Litigation

Although there is no universally agreed-upon definition of "robot," for our purposes, a robot is "an engineered machine that senses, thinks, and acts."[2] Practically speaking, that means the robot must "have sensors, processing ability that emulates some aspect of cognition," and the capacity

[1] See Section III.D.4.

[2] Patrick Lin, Keith Abney, & George Bekey, "Robot Ethics: Mapping the Issues for a Mechanized World" (2011) 175:5–6 *Artificial Intelligence* 942 at 943.

to act on its decision-making.[3] A robot must be equipped with programming that allows it to independently make intelligent choices or perform tasks based on environmental stimuli, rather than merely following the directions of a human operator, like a remote controlled car.[4] Under our definition, robots need not be embodied, i.e., they need not occupy physical space or have a physical presence. Of course, the fictitious examples of R2D2 and C3P0 fit our definition, but so too do the self-driving, guided steering, or automatic braking features in modern cars.

II.A Anthropomorphism

The aspect of HRI with the greatest potential to affect litigation is the human tendency to anthropomorphize robots.[5] Despite knowing that robots do not share human consciousness, people nevertheless tend to view robots as inherently social actors. As a result, people often unconsciously apply social rules and expectations to robots, assigning to them human emotions and sentience.[6] People even apply stereotypes and social heuristics to robots[7] and use the same language to describe interactions with robots and humans.[8] This process is unconscious and instantaneous.[9]

Rather than operating like an on-off switch, there are degrees of anthropomorphization, and the extent to which people anthropomorphize depends on several factors, including framing, interactivity or animacy,

[3] Ibid.

[4] Ibid.

[5] Kate Darling, "'Who's Johnny?': Anthropomorphic Framing in Human–Robot Interaction, Integration, and Policy" in Patrick Lin, Keith Abney, & Ryan Jenkins (eds.), *Robot Ethics 2.0: From Autonomous Cars to Artificial Intelligence* (New York, NY: Oxford University Press, 2017) 173 ["Who's Johnny"] at 173; see Chapter 13 in this volume.

[6] Ibid.

[7] Aaron Powers & Sara Keisler, "The Advisor Robot: Tracing People's Mental Model from a Robot's Physical Attributes" (paper delivered at the International Conference on Human–Robot Interaction, March 2–3, 2006), HRI '06: Proceedings of the 1st ACM SIGCHI/SIGART Conference on Human–Robot Interaction (New York, NY: Association for Computing Machinery, 2006) 218, www.cs.cmu.edu/~kiesler/publications/2006pdfs/2006_advisor-robot.pdf ["Advisor Robot"].

[8] Susan Fussell, Sara Kiesler, Leslie D. Setlock *et al.*, "How People Anthropomorphize Robots" (paper delivered at the International Human–Robot Interaction Conference, March 12–15, 2008), HRI '08: Proceedings of the 3rd ACM/IEEE International Conference on Human–Robot Interaction (New York, NY: Association for Computing Machinery, 2008) 145 at 149, www.cs.cmu.edu/~./kiesler/publications/2008pdfs/2008_anthropomorphize-bots.pdf.

[9] "Advisor Robot", note 7 above, at 2.

physical embodiment and presence, and appearance. Furthermore, these factors interact with one another. The presence (or absence) of a given characteristic impacts the anthropomorphizing effect of the other present characteristics.

II.A.1 Framing

How an HRI is framed significantly impacts human responses and perceptions about the robot and the interaction itself. Framing therefore has the potential to interfere with the accuracy of the litigation process when robot-generated evidence is presented. Framing generally refers to the way a human observer is introduced to an interaction, and in the case of robot-generated evidence, to a robot before the interaction actually begins. For example, does the robot have a name? Is the name endearing or human-like, e.g., "Marty" versus "Model X"? Is the robot assigned a gender? Is the robot given a backstory? What job or role is the robot intended to fulfil? Framing immediately impacts the human's perception of a robot. Humans use that introductory information to form a mental model about a robot, much as they do for people, assigning to it stereotypes, personal experiences, and human emotions through anthropomorphization.[10]

Two experiments demonstrate the power of framing to establish trust and create emotional attachments to robots. The first experiment involved participants riding in AVs, which are robots by our definition, and it demonstrates how framing can impact people's trust in a robot and how much blame they assign to it.[11] Each test group was exposed to a simulated crash that was unavoidable and clearly caused by another simulated driver. Prior to the incident, participants who had received anthropomorphic framing information about the car, including a name, a gendered identity, and a voice through human audio files, trusted the car more than participants who had ridden in a car with identical driving capabilities but for which no similar framing information had been provided ("agentic condition") and more than those in the "normal" condition who operated the car themselves, i.e., no autonomous capabilities.[12] After the incident, participants reported that they trusted the

[10] "Who's Johnny", note 5 above, at 180.

[11] Adam Waytz, Joy Heafner, & Nicholas Epley, "The Mind in the Machine: Anthropomorphism Increases Trust in an Autonomous Vehicle" (2014) 52 *Journal of Experimental Social Psychology* 113 at 115.

[12] Ibid.

anthropomorphically framed car more even though the only difference between the two conditions was the car having humanized qualities. Subjects in the anthropomorphized group also blamed the vehicle for the incident significantly less than the agentic group, perhaps because they unconsciously perceived the car as more thoughtful. Conversely, subjects in the normal condition who operated the car themselves assigned very little blame to the car. This makes sense because "[a]n object with no agency cannot be held responsible for any actions."[13] It is important that the anthropomorphized condition group perceived the car as more thoughtful, which mitigated some of the responsibility imputed to the vehicle.

The second experiment demonstrates that the way a robot's relationship to humans is framed, even by something as simple as giving the robot a name, can seriously impact the level of emotional attachment humans feel toward it. Participants were asked to observe a bug-like robot and then to strike it with a mallet.[14] The robot was introduced to one group of study participants with a name and an appealing backstory. "This is Frank. Frank is really friendly, but he gets distracted easily. He's lived at the Lab for a few months now. His favorite color is red."[15] The participants who experienced this anthropomorphic framing demonstrated higher levels of empathy and concern for the robot, showing emotional distress and a reluctance to hit it.[16]

Additionally, framing may impact whether, and to what degree, humans assume a robot has agency or free will. Anthropomorphism drives humans to impute at least a basic level of human "free will" to robots.[17] In other words, people assume that a robot makes at least some of its choices independently rather than as a simple result of its internal programming. This understanding is, of course, flawed. Although AI "neural networks" are modeled after the human brain to identify patterns and make decisions,

13 Ibid.

14 "Who's Johnny", note 5 above, at 181.

15 Kate Darling, Palash Nandy, & Cynthia Breazeal, "Empathic Concern and the Effect of Stories in Human–Robot Interaction" (paper delivered at the IEEE International Workshop on Robot and Human Communication (RO-MAN), August 31–September 1, 2015), 2015 24th IEEE International Symposium on Robot and Human Interactive Communication (RO-MAN) (Kobe, Japan: IEEE, 2015) 770 at 3, https://papers.ssrn.com/sol3/papers.cfm?abstract_id=2639689.

16 Ibid. at 11–12.

17 Neil Richards & William Smart, "How Should the Law Think about Robots?" in Ryan Calo, A. Michael Froomkin, & Ian Kerr (eds.), *Robot Law* (Cheltenham, UK: Edward Elgar, 2016) [*Robot Law*] 3 at 18.

robots do not consciously think and make choices as we do.[18] As robots operate more autonomously and are equipped with more anthropomorphous characteristics, humans will likely perceive them as having more agency or free will.[19]

II.A.2 Interactivity or Animacy

The interactivity or animacy of a robot also has a significant effect on HRI. Anthropomorphization drives people to seek social connections with robots,[20] and our innate need for social connection also causes humans to infer from a robot's verbal and non-verbal "expressions" that it has "emotions, preferences, motivations, and personality."[21] Social robots can now simulate sound, movement, and social cues that people automatically and subconsciously associate with human intention and states of mind.[22] Robots can motivate people by mimicking human emotions like anger, happiness, or fear, and demonstrate a pseudo-empathy by acting supportively.[23] They can apply peer pressure or shame humans into doing or not doing something.[24]

Humans form opinions about others based on voice and speech patterns,[25] and the same responses, coupled with anthropomorphization, can be used to make judgments about robots' speech. Many robots

[18] Instead, neural networks are comprised of a series of complex decision trees that are programmed to react according to environmental stimuli. Larry Hardesty, "Explained: Neural Networks," *MIT News* (April 14, 2017), http://news.mit.edu/2017/explained-neural-networks-deep-learning-0414.

[19] Matthias Scheutz, "The Inherent Dangers of Unidirectional Emotional Bonds between Humans and Social Robots" in Patrick Lin, Keith Abney, & George Bekey (eds.), *Robot Ethics: The Ethical and Social Implications of Robotics* (London, UK: MIT Press, 2012) 205 at 211–214.

[20] Ibid. at 205–221.

[21] Serena Marchesi, Davide De Tommaso, Jairo Perez-Osorio *et al.*, "Belief in Sharing the Same Phenomenological Experience Increases the Likelihood of Adopting the Intentional Stance Toward a Humanoid Robot" (2022) 3:3 *Technology, Mind, and Behavior* 1 (finding subjects with exposure to a human-like robot were more likely to rate the robot's actions as intentional).

[22] "Who's Johnny", note 5 above, at 175–176.

[23] Brian Jeffrey Fogg, "Computers as Persuasive Social Actors" in Brian Jeffrey Fogg, *Persuasive Technology: Using Computers to Change What We Think and Do* (San Francisco, CA: Morgan Kaufmann Publishers, 2003) 89 ["Persuasive Social Actors"] at 100.

[24] Ibid.

[25] Phil McAleer, Alexander Todorov, & Pascal Belint, "How Do You Say 'Hello'? Personality Impressions from Brief Novel Voices" (2014) 9:3 *PLoS ONE* 1; see also "Advisor Robot", note 7 above, at 1.

now communicate verbally, using verbal communication to persuade humans, establish a "relationship," or convey moods or a personality.[26] Certain styles of speech, accents, and vernacular are perceived as more authoritative, trustworthy, persuasive, or intelligent.[27]

II.A.3 Physical Presence and Physical Embodiment

Physical presence and physical embodiment also impact the extent to which people anthropomorphize a robot. A physically present robot is one that shares the same physical space with you. A physically embodied robot is one that has some sort of physical manifestation. A robot may be physically embodied, but not physically present. A familiar example is the Roomba vacuum robot. A Roomba in your house is physically present and physically embodied. But if you interact with C3PO, the gold robot from Star Wars, via video conference, C3PO is physically embodied, but not physically present. Instead, he is telepresent. Lastly, Apple's Siri is an example of a robot that is neither physically present nor physically embodied. The Siri virtual assistant is a voice with neither a physical appearance nor an embodiment outside the iPhone.

In experimental settings, a physically present, embodied robot affected HRI more than its non-embodied or non-present counterparts.[28] The combination of the robot's presence and embodiment fostered favorable attitudes among study participants. These findings are consistent with the assumptions that people perceive robot agents as social actors and typically prefer face-to-face interactions.[29] A review of multiple studies found that participants had more favorable attitudes toward co-present, physically embodied robots than toward telepresent robots, and that physically embodied robots were more persuasive and more trustworthy than

[26] "Persuasive Social Actors", note 23 above, at 101.

[27] See generally, Andrea Morales, Maura Scott, & Eric Yorkston, "The Role of Accent Standardness in Message Preference and Recall" (2012) 41:1 *Journal of Advertising* 33 ["Accent Standardness"] at 34 (studying people's accent preferences, noting, e.g., that "[s]ociolinguistic research shows that speakers with standard English accents are seen as having high social status and as being competent, smart, educated, and formal").

[28] Jamy Li, "The Benefit of Being Physically Present: A Survey of Experimental Works Comparing Copresent Robots, Telepresent Robots, and Virtual Agents" (2015) 77 *International Journal of Human-Computer Studies* 23 ["The Benefit"] at 33.

[29] "Accent Standardness", note 27 above, at 34.

their telepresent counterparts.[30] There was, however, no statistically significant difference between human perception of telepresent robots and non-embodied virtual agents like Siri. Overall, participants favored the co-present robot to the virtual agent and found the co-present robot more persuasive, even when its behavior was identical to that of the virtual agent. People paid more attention to the co-present robot and were more engaged in the interaction.

II.A.4 Appearance

Because of the power of anthropomorphism, the appearance or features of an embodied robot can influence whether it is viewed as likeable, trustworthy, and persuasive.

II.A.4.a Robot Faces Whether a robot is given a face, and what that face looks like, will have a significant impact on HRI. Humans form impressions almost instantly, deciding whether a person is attractive and trustworthy within one-tenth of a second of seeing their face.[31] Because humans incorrectly assume that robots are inherently social creatures, we make judgments about robots based on their physical attributes using many of the same mental shortcuts that we use for humans. Within the first two minutes of a human–robot interaction or observation, "people create a coherent, plausible mental model of the robot," based primarily on its physical appearance and interactive features like voice.[32]

Because humans derive many social cues from facial expressions, a robot's head and face are the physical features that most significantly affect HRI.[33] People notice the same features in a robot face that they notice about a human one: eye color and shape, nose size, etc.,[34] and researchers already have a basic understanding of what esthetic features humans like

[30] Twenty-four out of twenty-nine studies surveyed confirmed this point: see "The Benefit", note 28 above, at 33.

[31] Chad Boutin, "Snap Judgments Decide a Face's Character, Psychologist Finds," *Princeton University* (August 22, 2006), www.princeton.edu/news/2006/08/22/snap-judgments-decide-faces-character-psychologist-finds.

[32] See "Advisor Robot", note 7 above, at 6.

[33] Julia Fink, "Anthropomorphism and Human Likeness in the Design of Robots and Human–Robot Interaction" (paper delivered at the 4th International Conference, ICSR 2012, October 29–31, 2012) in Shuzi Sam Ge, Oussama Khatib, John-John Cabibihan *et al.* (eds.), *Social Robotics* (Berlin, Germany: Springer, 2012) 199 at 203 (noting that "most non-verbal cues are mediated through the face").

[34] People notice the same features they would notice unconsciously about a human face when they view a robot's face. Carl DiSalvo, Francine Gemperle, Jodi Forlizzi *et al.*, "All Robots

or dislike in robots. For example, robots with big eyes and "baby faces" are perceived as naïve, honest, kind, unthreatening, and warm.[35] Researchers are also studying how features make robot heads and faces more or less likeable and persuasive.[36] Manipulating the relative size of the features on a robot's head had a significant effect on not only study participants' evaluation of a robot, but also on whether they trusted it and would be likely to follow its advice.[37] A robot with big eyes was perceived as warmer and more honest and participants were thus more likely to follow its health advice.

II.A.4.b Physical Embodiment and Interactive Style When interacting with physically embodied robots, human subjects report that interactions with responsive robots, those with animated facial expressions, social gaze, and/or mannerisms, feel more natural and enjoyable than interactions with unanimated robots.[38] Embodied robots with faces can be programed to directly mirror subjects' expressions, or to indirectly mirror these expressions based on the robot's evaluation of the subject's perceived security, arousal, and autonomy. Study participants rated indirect mirroring robots highest for empathy, trust, sociability, and enjoyment,[39] and rated indirect mirroring and mirroring robots higher than the non-mirroring robots in empathy, trust, sociability, enjoyment, anthropomorphism, likeability, and intelligence.[40]

Generally, lifelike physical movement of robots, including "social gaze," or when a robot's eyes follow the subject it's interacting with,[41]

Are Not Created Equal: The Design and Perception of Humanoid Robot Heads" (paper delivered at the Conference on Designing Interactive Systems, June 25–28, 2002), DIS '02: Proceedings of the 4th Conference on Designing Interactive Systems: Processes, Practices, Methods, and Techniques (New York, NY: Association for Computing Machinery, 2002) 321 at 322, citeseerx.ist.psu.edu/viewdoc/download?doi=10.1.1.93.7443&rep=rep1&type=pdf ["Not Created Equal"].

35 "Advisor Robot", note 7 above, at 6.

36 "Persuasive Social Actors", note 23 above, at 92–93.

37 "Advisor Robot", note 7 above, at 6.

38 For a study examining the correlation between a co-present robot's emotional nonverbal response and a human's anthropomorphic response, see Friederike Eyssel, Frank Hegel, Gernot Horstmann *et al.*, "Anthropomorphic Inferences from Emotional Nonverbal Cues: A Case Study" (paper delivered at the 19th International Conference, September 13–15, 2010), 19th International Symposium in Robot and Human Interactive Communication (Viareggio, Italy: IEEE, 2010) 646 at 646.

39 "Not Created Equal", note 34 above, at 353–354 and 356.

40 Ibid.

41 See Debora Zanatto, Massimiliano Patacchiola, Jeremy Goslin *et al.*, "Priming Anthropomorphism: Can the Credibility of Humanlike Robots Be Transferred to

gestures, and human-like facial expressions, are highly correlated with anthropomorphic projection.[42] When those movements closely match humans' non-verbal cues, humans perceive robots as more human-like. This matching behavior, exemplified through non-verbal cues, like facial expressions, gestures, e.g., nodding, and posture, is known as behavioral mimicry.[43] Behavioral mimicry is critical for establishing rapport and empathy in human interactions,[44] and this phenomenon extends to HRI as well.[45]

II.B Other Cognitive Biases

A variety of other cognitive errors may distort fact-finding or the imposition of liability for the conduct of robots. For example, in experimental settings, subjects tended to blame human actors more than robots for the same conduct.

One study tested the allocation of blame for a hypothetical automobile accident in which a pedestrian has been killed by an automated car, and both the human driver and the automated system, a robot for our purposes, have made errors.[46] The "central finding is that in cases where a human and a machine share control of the car in hypothetical situations, less blame is attributed to the machine when both drivers make errors."[47]

Non-Humanlike Robots?" (paper delivered at the 2016 11th ACM/IEEE Conference on HRI, March 7–10, 2016), 2016 11th ACM/IEEE International Conference on Human–Robot Interaction (Christchurch: IEEE, 2016) 543 at 543–544 (finding that people perceived an anthropomorphic robot as more credible than its non-anthropomorphic counterpart when it used social gaze, as measured by willingness to change their response to a question based on information provided by the robot).

42 "Who's Johnny", note 5 above, at 174, 175–176.

43 Elise Owens, Ferguson W. H. McPharlin, Nathan Brooks *et al.*, "The Effects of Empathy, Emotional Intelligence and Psychopathy on Interpersonal Interactions" (2018) 25:1 *Psychiatry, Psychology and Law* 1 at 1–2.

44 Ibid.

45 Barbara Gonsior, Stefan Sosnowski, Christoph Mayer *et al.*, "Improving Aspects of Empathy and Subjective Performance for HRI through Mirroring Facial Expressions" (paper delivered at IEEE RO-MAN Conference, July 31–August 3, 2011), 2011 RO-MAN (Atlanta, GA: IEEE, 2011) 350 at 351, www.researchgate.net/publication/224256284_Improving_aspects_of_empathy_and_subjective_performance_for_HRI_through_mirroring_facial_expressions.

46 Edmond Awad, Sydney Levine, Max Kleiman-Weiner *et al.*, "Drivers Are Blamed More than Their Automated Cars When Both Make Mistakes" (2020) 4:2 *Nature Human Behaviour* 134 ["Drivers Are Blamed"].

47 Ibid. at 138.

In all scenarios, subjects attributed less blame to the automatic system when there was a human involved.

Other studies found that in experimental conditions subjects valued algorithmic predictions differently from human input. Coining the term "algorithmic appreciation," the authors of one study found that lay subjects adhered more to advice when they believed it came from an algorithm rather than a person.[48] But this "appreciation" for the algorithm's conclusions decreased when people chose between an algorithm's estimate and their own.[49] Moreover, experienced professionals who made forecasts on a regular basis relied less on algorithmic advice than did lay people, decreasing the professionals' accuracy. But other studies found "algorithmic aversion," with subjects showing more quickly losing confidence in algorithmic than human forecasters, after seeing both make the same mistake.[50]

III The Impact of the Psychology of HRI in Litigation

In this section, we assume that the psychological phenomena described above will occur outside the laboratory setting and, more specifically, in the courtroom. This is a significant assumption because it is difficult to perfectly extrapolate real-world behavior from experimental studies.[51]

The cognitive errors associated with people's tendency to anthropomorphize robots could distort the accuracy and fairness of the litigation process in multiple ways. The current prevalence of these errors may lead to the conclusion that the distortions arising from robot-generated evidence are no greater than those arising from other forms of evidence. Indeed, in some respects, robot-generated evidence might contribute to accuracy because it would be less subject to certain cognitive errors. There remain, however, difficult questions about how well the tools traditionally used

[48] Jennifer Logg, Julia Minson, & Don Moore, "Algorithm Appreciation: People Prefer Algorithmic to Human Judgment" (2019) 151 *Organisational Behavior and Human Decision Processes* 90 ["Algorithm Appreciation"].

[49] Ibid.

[50] Berkeley Dietvorst, Joseph Simmons, & Cade Massey, "Algorithmic Aversion: People Erroneously Avoid Algorithms after Seeing Them Err" (2015) 144:1 *Journal of Experimental Psychology: General* 114.

[51] Cf. "Adversarial Collaboration: An EDGE Lecture by Daniel Kahneman," *EDGE* (February 24, 2022), www.edge.org/adversarial-collaboration-daniel-kahneman (noting difficulty of replicating results of priming experiments).

to test accuracy in litigation can be adapted to robot-generated evidence, as well as questions about the distributional consequences of developing more persuasive robots.

III.A The Impact of Framing and Interactivity

Anthropomorphic framing and tailoring robots to preferences for certain attributes such as speech and voice patterns could distort and impair the accuracy of fact-finding in litigation. Anthropomorphic framing and design can cause humans to develop a false sense of trust and emotional attachment to a robot and may cause fact-finders to incorrectly attribute free will to it. These psychological responses could distort liability determinations if, e.g., jurors who anthropomorphized a robot held it, rather than its designers, responsible for its actions.[52] Indeed, in the automated car study discussed above,[53] because participants perceived the anthropomorphic car as being more thoughtful, they blamed it less than another car with the same automated driving capabilities. Anthropomorphism could also lead fact-finders to attribute moral blame to a robot. For example, in a study in which a robot incorrectly withheld a $20 reward from participants, nearly two-thirds of those participants attributed moral culpability to the robot.[54] Finally, tailoring voice and speech patterns to jurors' preferences could improve a robo-witness's believability, though these features would have no bearing on the reliability of the information provided.

On the other hand, the issues raised by anthropomorphization can be analogized to those already present in litigation. Fact-finders now use heuristics, or mental shortcuts, to evaluate a human witness based on her features, e.g., name, appearance, race, gender, mannerisms. In turn, this information allows jurors to form rapid and often unconscious impressions about the witness's motivations, personality, intelligence, trustworthiness, and believability. Those snap judgments may be equally as unfounded as those a person would make about a robot based on its appearance and framing. And just as a robot's programmed speech patterns may impact the fact-finder's perception of its trustworthiness

52 See *Robot Law*, note 17 above, at 19.

53 See notes 46–47 above and accompanying text.

54 Peter Kahn Jr., Takayuki Kanda, Hiroshi Ishiguro *et al.*, "Do People Hold a Humanoid Robot Morally Accountable for the Harm It Causes?" (paper delivered at the 7th ACM/IEEE International Conference, March 5–8, 2012), HRI '12: Proceedings of the 7th Annual ACM/IEEE International Conference on Human–Robot Interaction (New York, NY: Association for Computing Machinery, 2012) 33.

and believability, lay or expert human witnesses may be selected or coached to do the same thing. So, although robot-generated evidence and robo-witnesses may differ from their human counterparts, the issues their design and framing present in the litigation context are not entirely novel.

III.B The Impact of Robot Embodiment, Interactivity, and Appearance

Whether a robot is embodied and the form in which it is embodied have a significant impact on human perception. Assuming that these psychological responses extend to the litigation context, it may seem obvious that this would introduce serious distortions into the fact-finding process. But again, this problem is not unique to robots. As noted, humans apply the same unconscious heuristics to human faces, reacting more favorably depending on physical criteria, such as facial proportions, that have no necessary relationship to a witness's truthfulness or reliability. Arguably, the same random distortions could occur for human or robot witnesses. Indeed, assuming equal access to this technology, perhaps the fact that all robot witnesses can be designed to generate positive reactions could eliminate factors that currently distort the fact-finding process in litigation. For example, jurors will not discount the evidence of certain robo-witnesses on grounds such as implicit racial bias, or biases against witnesses who are not physically attractive or well spoken.

III.C The Impact of Other Cognitive Biases

In litigation, other cognitive biases about robots or their algorithmic programming may affect either the attribution of fault or the assessment of the credibility of robot-generated evidence, particularly evidence that is generated by algorithms.

The study discussed earlier, which found a greater tendency to attribute fault to a human rather than an automated system, has clear implications for liability disputes involving automated vehicles. As the authors of the study noted, the convergence of their experimental results with "real world public reaction" to accidents involving automated vehicles suggests that their research findings would have external validity, and that "juries will be biased to absolve the car manufacturer of blame in dual error cases."[55]

[55] "Drivers Are Blamed", note 46 above, at 139–140 (discussing the incidents with Tesla and Uber automated cars).

One of the experiments finding "algorithmic appreciation," which we characterize as the potential for overweighting algorithmic analysis, likely has some direct correlation in litigation, where an algorithm may be seen as more reliable than a variety of human estimates.[56]

III.D Testing the Fidelity of Robot-Generated Evidence in Litigation

Robot-generated evidence already plays a role in litigation proceedings. But how will that dynamic change as robots' capabilities mature to the point of testifying for themselves? We explore the possibilities below.

III.D.1 Impediments to Cross-Examination

It is unclear how adaptable the techniques traditionally used to test a human witness's veracity and reliability are to robot-generated evidence. In particular, the current litigation system relies heavily on cross-examination, based on the assumption that it allows the fact-finder to assess a witness's motivations, behavior, and conclusions. Cross-examination assumes that a witness has motivations, morality, and free will. But robots possess none of those, though fact-finders may erroneously assume that they do. Thus, it may be impossible to employ cross-examination to evaluate the veracity and accuracy of a robo-witness's testimony. Additionally, robot-generated evidence presents two distinct issues: the data itself, and the systems that create the data. Both need to be interrogated, which will require new procedures adapted to the kind of machine or robot evidence in question.[57]

III.D.2 The Difficulty in Evaluating and Challenging Algorithms

Adversarial litigation may also be inadequate to assess defects in a robot's programming, including the accuracy or bias of the algorithm.[58] The quality and accuracy of an algorithm depends on the training instructions and quality of the training data. Designers may unintentionally introduce bias into the algorithm, creating skewed results. For example, algorithms

[56] See "Algorithm Appreciation", note 48 above, at 151.

[57] See generally, Andrea Roth, "Machine Testimony" (2017) 126:1 *Yale Law Journal* 1972; see Chapters 7 and 9 in this volume.

[58] Regarding programmer liability, see Chapter 2 in this volume.

can entrench existing gender biases,[59] and facial recognition software has been criticized for racial biases that severely reduce its accuracy.[60]

It can be extraordinarily difficult to fully understand how an algorithm works, particularly an unsupervised one, in order to verify its accuracy. Unlike supervised learning algorithms, an unsupervised learning algorithm trains on an unlabeled dataset and continuously updates its own training based on environmental stimuli, generally without any external alterations or verification.[61] Although its original code remains the same, the way an unsupervised learning algorithm treats input data may change based on this continuous training. Data goes in and results come out, but how the algorithm reached that result may remain a mystery. Sometimes even the people who originally programmed these algorithms do not fully understand how they operate.

Juries may struggle to understand other complex technology, even with the assistance of experts, and unsupervised learning methods introduce a novel problem into the litigation process because even their creators may not know exactly how they work. This critical gap can only compound the difficulties introduced by anthropomorphism. Experts, even an algorithm's creators, may not be able to understand, let alone explain, how it reached certain conclusions, making it nearly impossible to verify those conclusions in legal proceedings using existing methods.[62]

III.D.3 The Advantages of Robot Memory

Although anthropomorphism can cause distortions, robot-generated evidence is not subject to other cognitive biases that currently impair fact-finding.[63]

The most significant impediment to an accurate evaluation of testimony is pervasive misunderstandings of how memories are formed and recalled. As a foundational matter, many people erroneously assume that our memories operate like recording devices, capturing all the details of a given event, etched permanently in some internal hard drive,

[59] See e.g. Nicol Turner Lee, Paul Resnick, & Genie Barton, "Algorithmic Bias Detection and Mitigation: Best Practices and Policies to Reduce Consumer Harms," *Brookings Institution* (May 22, 2019), www.brookings.edu/research/algorithmic-bias-detection-and-mitigation-best-practices-and-policies-to-reduce-consumer-harms/.

[60] Ibid.

[61] An unsupervised algorithm "tries to make sense by extracting features and patterns on its own."

[62] See Chapter 8 in this volume.

[63] Ibid.

available for instant recall at any moment.[64] But human memory formation is far more complex and fallible. Initially, our memories capture only a very small percentage of the stimuli in our sensory environment.[65] Because there are gaps, we often consciously or subconsciously look for filler information to complete the memory of a given event. Unlike a recording device, which would create a static memory, human memory is dynamic and reconstructive, meaning that post-event interactions or information may alter one's recollection of an event.[66] This susceptibility to influence is called suggestibility.[67] Outside influences can disturb the stability and accuracy of eyewitness memory over time, causing witnesses to misremember details about events they witnessed.[68] Moreover, when people are engaged in memory recall, their recollections are highly suggestible, increasing the likelihood that outside influences will taint their memories.[69]

Although the reliability of human memory depends on whether the witness accurately perceived the event in the first place, and whether the witness's memory degraded over time or was polluted by post-event information, jurors typically do not understand the complexity, malleability, and selectivity of memories.[70] Jurors' assessments are also subject to another cognitive error: the confidence-accuracy fallacy. Although jurors typically use eyewitness confidence as a proxy for reliability,[71] the

[64] "Elizabeth Loftus: How Can Our Memories Be Manipulated?" *NPR* (October 13, 2017), www.npr.org/transcripts/557424726 ["Manipulated"].

[65] Richard Schmechel, T. P. O'Toole, C. Easterly *et al.*, "Beyond the Ken? Testing Jurors' Understanding of Eyewitness Reliability Evidence" (2006) 46:2 *Jurimetrics* 177 ["Beyond the Ken"] at 195.

[66] Ibid.

[67] Elizabeth Loftus & Hunter Hoffman, "Misinformation and Memory: The Creation of New Memories" (1989) 118:1 *Journal of Experimental Psychology: General* 100 at 100 (noting that "postevent information can impair memory of an original event").

[68] A witness who is exposed to leading questions by investigators, recollections by other witnesses, or news reports that differ from her own memory may begin to remember the event differently in a way that aligns more closely with the narratives heard from others. According to expert Elizabeth Loftus, "[i]t's not that hard to get people to believe and remember things that didn't happen." "Manipulated", note 64 above.

[69] Elizabeth Loftus, "How Reliable is Your Memory?" (presentation delivered at TEDGlobal 2013: Think Again, June 11, 2013), www.ted.com/talks/elizabeth_loftus_how_reliable_is_your_memory.

[70] "Beyond the Ken", note 65 above, at 195.

[71] This causes jurors to "dramatically overestimate the accuracy of eyewitness identifications." Kevin Jon Heller, "The Cognitive Psychology of Circumstantial Evidence" (2006) 105:2 *Michigan Law Review* 241 ["Cognitive Psychology"] at 285; see also "Beyond the Ken", note 65 above, at 199 (31 percent of potential jurors stated a witness who was "absolutely certain"

correlation between witness confidence and accuracy is quite weak.[72] And because people tend to overestimate the reliability of their own memories,[73] witnesses are likely to be overly confident of their recollections, leading jurors to overvalue their testimony.

Robot testimony[74] would not share these vulnerabilities and may therefore be more reliable than human testimony. The common but incorrect understanding of the nature of human memory is in fact a fairly accurate representation of the way robots create memories, in that their internal decision-making systems operate much like a recording device. As a result, the information they record is verifiable and provable without additional corroboration, unlike a person's memory. Presumably, robot memory is not dynamic or suggestible. And in certain instances, a robot may actually capture a video recording of a given incident or interaction. As a result, a robo-witness's recollection of a given memory is likely to be more accurate than that of a human witness. Robot decision-making also takes into account more data than human decision-making processes can, which means a robot is capable of presenting a more thorough and accurate representation of what happened. Robot algorithms presumably would store the code from the time of the incident, recording, e.g., the environmental stimuli it perceived before making a fateful decision. In summary, robots capture more information than their human counterparts and do so more accurately, in part because they are less susceptible to post hoc manipulation or suggestibility. These advantages should enhance the accuracy of fact-finding. The potential to interrogate or challenge robot-generated evidence would depend on the nature of the robot and its memory function. For example, if a robot captures an incident by video recording, no further interpretation by third parties would be necessary. On the other hand, if the robot's "memories" take the form of algorithm sequences,

was "much more reliable" than the witness who was not, and approximately 40 percent of potential jurors agreed with the statement "an eyewitness' level of confidence in his or her identification is an excellent indicator of that eyewitness' reliability"). When evaluating the testimony of a confident witness and an unconfident witness, jurors identified the confident eyewitness as more reliable. Elizabeth Tenney, Robert J. MacCoun, Barabara A. Spellman *et al.*, "Calibration Trumps Confidence as a Basis for Witness Credibility" (2007) 18:1 *Psychological Science* 46 at 48.

72 "Beyond the Ken", note 65 above, at 198.

73 When asked to evaluate the reliability of their own memories, people vastly overestimated. "Beyond the Ken", note 65 above, at 196.

74 See Chapter 8 in this volume.

then an expert would be needed to interpret that data for a lay jury, akin to interpreting DNA test results.

Furthermore, because memory formation in robots operates like a recording device, confidence may indeed be a strong indicator of accuracy in future robot testimony.[75] Because the way robots form and recall memories is more similar to the commonly held understanding of memory, people's existing heuristics are likely to help them to understand and evaluate robot testimony more accurately than human eyewitness testimony. As a result, robot witnesses ostensibly would be more reliable and improve the accuracy of litigation outcomes. A robot's internal operating algorithm may also be able to produce a confidence interval for what it saw or why it made the decision it did. Experts could then interpret and explain this confidence interval to the lay jury.

III.D.4 The Preference for Direct Evidence and Eyewitness Testimony

Despite the well-documented unreliability of eyewitness testimony, several cognitive biases cause jurors to give it greater weight than circumstantial evidence, e.g., DNA evidence or fingerprints. Because of their preference for univocal evidence requiring fewer sequential inferences, jurors typically prefer direct evidence to circumstantial evidence.[76] Combined with the misunderstanding of memory described above, these phenomena threaten the jury's fact-finding mission.

Several features that distinguish eyewitness and circumstantial evidence cause jurors to draw erroneous conclusions about their relative accuracy. First, direct testimony is told as a narrative, from a single perspective that allows jurors to imagine themselves in the witness's shoes and to determine whether the proffered explanation is plausible. As a result, jurors tend to give greater weight to direct evidence like eyewitness testimony than to highly probative circumstantial evidence, such as DNA evidence, because direct evidence requires them to make fewer sequential inferences.[77] Eyewitness testimony is, at bottom, a story: "a

[75] Cf. John Wixted & Gary Wells, "The Relationship between Eyewitness Confidence and Identification Accuracy: A New Synthesis" (2017) 18:1 *Psychological Science in the Public Interest* 10 at 55 (noting that in ideal conditions confidence level at initial identification is actually a good proxy for accuracy).

[76] "Cognitive Psychology", note 71 above, at 267–268.

[77] Ibid. at 265, 267.

moment-by-moment account that helps [jurors] imagine how the defendant actually committed it."[78] In contrast, although abstract circumstantial evidence like DNA may be statistically more reliable than eye witness testimony, it does not allow the juror to visualize an incident happening.[79] Direct evidence is also univocal; when an eyewitness recalls the crime, she speaks with one voice, frequently in a singular, coherent narrative. Circumstantial evidence, by contrast, allows for, and often requires, many inferences. In this way, it is polyvocal; multiple pieces of evidence provide different snippets of the crime.[80] Jurors must fit those pieces together into a narrative, which is more difficult than following a single witness's story. Finally, eyewitness testimony can be unconditional. An eyewitness can testify that she is absolutely certain that the defendant committed the crime, or the defendant admitted as much.[81] In contrast, circumstantial evidence is inherently probabilistic.[82]

Jurors' preference for direct evidence is driven by the simulation heuristic. The simulation heuristic postulates that people estimate how likely it is that something happened based on how easy it is for them to imagine it happening; the easier it is to imagine, the more likely it is to have happened.[83] Studies have shown that when jurors listen to witness testimony, they construct a mental image of an incident that none of them witnessed.[84] Relatedly, the ease of simulation hypothesis posits that the likelihood a juror will acquit the defendant in a criminal case depends on her ability to imagine that the defendant did not commit the crime.[85]

A variety of factors could influence how the human preference for direct eyewitness testimony would interact with robot-generated testimony. As noted above, in experimental settings participants preferred and were more readily persuaded by embodied robots that were framed in an anthropomorphic fashion, and participants preferred certain attributes like faces and a mirroring conversational style. If a robot with the preferred design gave "eyewitness" testimony, it could provide a single

[78] Ibid. at 265.
[79] Ibid.
[80] Ibid. at 267.
[81] Ibid. at 268.
[82] Ibid.
[83] Ibid. at 260.
[84] Elizabeth Loftus, "Psychological Aspects of Courtroom Testimony" (1980) 347 *Annals of the New York Academy of Sciences* 27 at 27–28.
[85] "Cognitive Psychology", note 71 above, at 262.

narrative and speak in a confident univocal voice. Assuming that the same cognitive processes that guide jurors' evaluations of direct and circumstantial evidence apply equally to such evidence, jurors would give it greater weight than circumstantial evidence. In the case of direct robot testimony, however, many of the inadequacies of human eyewitness testimony would be mitigated or eliminated altogether because robot memory is not subject to the many shortcomings of human memory. In such cases, the cognitive bias in favor of a single, confident, univocal narrative would not necessarily produce an inaccurate weighting of the evidence. However, as noted above, jurors would likely employ the same unconscious preferences for certain facial features, interaction, and speech that they apply to human witnesses.

On the other hand, robot-generated evidence not presented by a direct robo-witness might not receive the same cognitive priority, regardless of its reliability, as human eyewitness testimony. But framing and designing robots to enhance anthropomorphization, like a car with voice software and a name, might elevate evidence of this nature above other circumstantial or documentary evidence. Perhaps in this context, anthropomorphization could enhance accuracy by evening out the playing field for some circumstantial or documentary evidence that jurors might otherwise give short shrift.

III.D.5 Distributional Issues

Resource inequalities are already a serious problem in the US litigation system. Because litigation is so costly, particularly under the American Rule in which each party bears its own costs in civil litigation,[86] plaintiffs without substantial personal resources are often discouraged from bringing suit, and outcomes in cases that are litigated can be heavily impacted by the parties' resources. Parties with greater resources may be more likely to present robot-generated evidence, and more likely to have robots designed to be the most persuasive witnesses. Disparate access to the best robot technology may well mean disparate access to justice, and this problem could increase over time as robot design is manipulated to take advantage of the distortions arising from heuristics and cognitive errors. On the other hand, as robots become ubiquitous in society, access to their "testimony" may become more democratized because more

[86] John Leubsdorf, "Does the American Rule Promote Access to Justice? Was that Why It Was Adopted?" (2019) 67 *Duke Law Journal Online* 257 at 257.

people across the socioeconomic spectrum may have regular access to them in their daily lives.

IV AI Testimony in Other Legal Proceedings

In this section, we consider the impact of HRI in legal proceedings other than litigation, specifically on ADR, with a focus on arbitration, and the specialized procedures of the NTSB. We do so for two reasons. First, in the United States, litigation is relatively rare, and most cases are now resolved by some form of ADR. That is likely to be true of disputes involving robo-witnesses and evidence about the actions of robots as well. Second, these alternatives address what Sections II and III identify as the critical problem in using robot-generated evidence in litigation: the tendency of humans, especially laypersons, to anthropomorphize robots and to misunderstand how human memory functions. In contrast, the arbitration process and the NTSB's procedures assign fact-finding either to subject matter experts or to decision-makers chosen for their sophistication and their ability to understand the complex technology at issue. In this section, we describe the procedures employed by the NTSB and in arbitration and consider how these forums might address the potential distortions discussed in Sections II and III.

IV.A Alternative Dispute Resolution

One way to address the issues HRI would raise in litigation is to resolve these cases through ADR. ADR includes "any means of settling disputes outside of the courtroom," but most commonly refers to arbitration or more informal mediation.[87] Arbitration resembles a simplified litigation process, in which the parties make opening statements and present evidence to an arbiter or panel of arbiters empowered to make a final decision binding on the parties and enforceable by courts.[88] Arbitration allows the parties to mutually select decision-makers with relevant industry or technical expertise. For example, in disputes arising from an AV, the parties could select an arbitrator with experience

[87] Cornell Legal Information Institute, "Alternative Dispute Resolution," www.law.cornell.edu/wex/alternative_dispute_resolution. Mediation is an informal alternative to litigation, in which adverse parties, operating through mediators, attempt to reach a settlement.

[88] American Bar Association, "Arbitration," www.americanbar.org/groups/dispute_resolution/resources/disputeresolutionprocesses/arbitration/.

in the AV industry. We hypothesize that an expert's familiarity with the technology could reduce the effect of the cognitive errors noted above, facilitate a more efficient process, and ensure a more accurate outcome. There is evidence that lay jurors struggle to make sense of complex evidence like MRI images.[89] An expert may be able to parse highly technical robot evidence more effectively. Likewise, individuals who are familiar with robot technology may be less likely to be influenced by the anthropomorphization that may significantly distort a lay juror's fact-finding and attribution of liability.

There are reasons for concern, however, about substituting arbitration for litigation. Although arbitral proceedings are adversarial, they lack many of the procedural safeguards available in litigation, and opponents of arbitration contend that arbitrators may be biased against certain classes of litigants. They argue that "arbitrators who get repeat business from a corporation are more likely to rule against a consumer."[90] More generally, consumer advocates argue that mandatory arbitration is anti-consumer because it restricts or eliminates altogether class action suits and because the results of arbitration are often kept secret.[91]

IV.B Specialized Procedures: The NTSB

Another more specialized option would be to design agency procedures particularly suited to the resolution of issues involving robot-generated evidence. The procedures of the NTSB demonstrate how such specialized procedures could work.

The NTSB is an independent federal agency that investigates transportation incidents, ranging from the crashes of Boeing 737 MAX airplanes to run-of-the-mill highway collisions. The NTSB acts, first and foremost, as a fact-finder; its investigations are "fact-finding proceedings with no adverse parties."[92] The NTSB has the power to issue subpoenas

[89] Teneille Brown & Emily Murphy, "Through a Scanner Darkly: Functional Neuroimaging as Evidence of a Criminal Defendant's Past Mental States" (2010) 62:4 *Stanford Law Review* 1119 at 1199–1201.

[90] Stephanie Zimmermann, "Trouble with Tesla: Couple Were Sold a Damaged Car, then Told They Can't Sue," *Chicago Sun Times* (September 28, 2019), https://chicago.suntimes.com/2019/9/27/20887609/tesla-arbitration-car-damage-repair-consumer-legal-chicago-kansas.

[91] Ibid.

[92] US Code of Federal Regulations (as amended February 3, 2023), Title 49 [49 CFR], §831.4(c).

for testimony or other evidence, which are enforceable in federal court,[93] but it has no binding regulatory or law enforcement powers. It cannot conduct criminal investigations or impose civil sanctions, and its factual findings, including any determination about probable cause, cannot be entered as evidence in a court of law.[94]

The NTSB's leadership and its procedures reflect its specialized mission. The five board members all have substantial experience in the transportation industry.[95] Its investigative panels use a distinctive, cooperative "party system," in which the subjects of the investigation are invited to participate in the fact-finding process, and incidents are investigated by a panel, run by a lead investigator who designates the relevant corporations or other entities as "parties."[96] A representative from the party being investigated is often named as a member of the investigative panel to provide the investigative panel with specialized, technical expertise.[97] At the conclusion of an investigation, the panel produces a report of factual findings, including probable cause; it may also make safety recommendations.[98]

The NTSB has two primary institutional advantages over traditional litigation, institutional competency and an incentive structure that fosters cooperation. First, unlike generalist judges or lay jurors, fact-finders at the NTSB are industry experts. Second, because the NTSB is prohibited from assigning fault or liability and its factual determinations cannot be admitted as evidence into legal proceedings, parties may have a greater incentive to disclose all relevant information. This would, in turn, promote greater transparency, informing consumers and facilitating the work of Congress and other regulators.

How would NTSB respond to cases involving robot-generated evidence? Certain aspects of the NTSB as an institution may make it a more accurate fact-finding process than litigation. First, finders of fact are a panel of industry and technical experts. Using experts who have either the education or the background to fully understand the technology means that an NTSB panel may be a more accurate fact-finder. Technical competence may also be a good antidote to the lay fact-finder tendency

[93] Ibid., §831.9(a)(3).

[94] United States Code (2018), Title 49, §1154(b).

[95] Biographies for all board members can be accessed from NTSB, "Board Member Speeches," www.ntsb.gov/news/speeches/Pages/Default.aspx.

[96] 49 CFR, note 92 above, §831.8 (authority of investigator in charge), §831.11(a)(1) (designation of parties by investigator in charge).

[97] NTSB, "The Investigative Process," www.ntsb.gov/investigations/process/Pages/default.aspx.

[98] 49 CFR, note 92 above, §831.4(a)–(b).

to anthropomorphize. The NTSB panel would also benefit from having the technology's designers at its disposal, as both the designer and manufacturer of an AV could be named party participants to an investigation. Second, because the NTSB experts may have been previously exposed to the technology, they also may be less susceptible to the cognitive errors in HRI. They are more likely to understand, e.g., how the recording devices in an AV actually function, so they will have to rely less on heuristics to understand the issue and reach a sound conclusion.

On the other hand, the NTSB process has been criticized. First, critics worry that the party system may hamstring the NTSB, because party participants are often the only source of information for a given incident, although the NTSB can issue subpoenas enforceable by federal courts.[99] Second, because NTSB proceedings are cooperative, their investigations do not benefit from the vetting process inherent in adversarial proceedings like litigation. Because the NTSB cannot make rules or undertake enforcement actions, critics worry the agency cannot do enough to address evolving problems. Finally, the NTSB may not have adequate resources to carry out its duties. Although it has the responsibility to investigate incidents in all modern modes of transportation, it is a fairly small agency with an annual operating budget of approximately $110 million and about 400 employees.[100] Its limited staff and resources mean that the agency must focus on high-volume incidents, incidents involving widespread technology or transportation mechanisms.

Perhaps most important, the NTSB process is not designed to allocate liability or provide compensation to individual victims, and it is entirely unsuited to the criminal justice process in which the defendant has a constitutional right to trial by jury.

IV.C A Real-Life Example and a Thought Experiment

IV.C.1 The Fatal Uber Accident

A recent event provides a real-life example of robot-generated evidence involving the forums we have described. In March 2018, an AV designed by Uber and Volvo struck and killed a pedestrian pushing a bicycle in

99 Jack London, "Issues of Trustworthiness and Reliability of Evidence from NTSB Investigations in Third Party Liability Proceedings" (2003) 68:1 *Journal of Air Law and Commerce* 39 at 48.

100 NTSB, "Fiscal Year 2020 Budget Request" (Washington DC: NTSB, 2019) at 7, 28, www.ntsb.gov/about/reports/Documents/NTSB-FY20-Budget-Request.pdf.

Tempe, Arizona.[101] During that drive, a person sitting in the driver's seat, the safety driver, was supposed to be monitoring the car's speed and looking out for any hazards in the road. But at the time of the crash, the safety driver was streaming TV on their phone. The car, equipped with multi-view cameras, recorded the entire incident, including the car's interior.

The NTSB investigated the incident and concluded that both human error and an "inadequate safety culture" at Uber were the probable causes of the crash.[102] It found that the automated driving system (ADS) first detected the victim-pedestrian 5.6 seconds before the collision, initially classifying the pedestrian and her bike as a vehicle and then a bicycle, and finally as an unknown object.[103] As a result, the system failed to correctly predict her forward trajectory. The car's self-driving system and its environmental sensors had been working properly at the time of the crash, but its emergency braking system was not engaged, depending solely on human intervention.[104] Finally, Uber's automated driving technology had not been trained to identify jaywalking pedestrians; in other words, the algorithm was not programmed to register an object as a pedestrian unless it simultaneously detected a crosswalk.[105]

Local authorities in Arizona declined to criminally prosecute Uber,[106] but they did charge the safety driver with criminal negligence,[107] and at the time of writing these charges were still pending. The victim's family settled with Uber out of court;[108] there was no arbitration or mediation.

[101] Ethan Sacks, "Self-Driving Uber Car Involved in Fatal Accident in Arizona," *NBC News* (March 20, 2018), www.nbcnews.com/tech/innovation/self-driving-uber-car-involved-fatal-accident-arizona-n857941.

[102] NTSB, "Highway Accident Report: Collision between Vehicle Controlled by Developmental Automated Driving System and Pedestrian" (Washington DC: NTSB, 2018), www.ntsb.gov/investigations/AccidentReports/Reports/HAR1903.pdf at v–vi (Executive Summary).

[103] Ibid. at 39.

[104] Ibid. at v.

[105] Ibid. at 16.

[106] "Uber 'Not Criminally Liable' for Self-Driving Death," *BBC* (March 6, 2019), www.bbc.com/news/technology-47468391.

[107] Kate Conger, "Driver Charged in Uber's Fatal 2018 Autonomous Car Crash," *The New York Times* (September 15, 2020), www.nytimes.com/2020/09/15/technology/uber-autonomous-crash-driver-charged.html.

[108] Kiara Alfonseca, "Uber Reaches Settlement with Family of Woman Killed by Self-Driving Car," *NBC News* (March 29, 2018), www.nbcnews.com/news/us-news/uber-reaches-settlement-family-woman-killed-self-driving-car-n861131.

If the civil case against Uber had gone to trial, how would the issues we have discussed play out, and how would the resolution by litigation compare to the NTSB's investigation and findings? The vehicle's video of the incident would reduce or eliminate concerns about the accuracy of human memory. Consequently, the AV's "memory" would likely improve the accuracy of the proceeding. It is unclear whether anthropomorphization would play any role. As we understand it, the robot controlling the AV had no physical embodiment, and it was not designed to have verbal interactions with jurors or with the safety driver. There was no anthropomorphic framing such as an endearing name, assigned gender, or backstory. Thus, the jury's tendency to anthropomorphize robots would likely play no significant role in its fact-finding or attribution of liability in this specific case. In a trial, the jury's task would be to comprehend complex technical information about the programming and operation of the algorithm that controlled the car. And although jurors would have the assistance of expert witnesses, it is doubtful whether they could reach more accurate conclusions about the causes of the accident than the NTSB panel. The NTSB's panel would readily comprehend the technical information, such as why the AV mischaracterized the pedestrian and her bike as an unknown object. Moreover, the jurors, presumably more than experts familiar with the technology, might be influenced by common cognitive biases to blame the human driver more than the AV.

IV.C.2 A Thought Experiment: Litigation Involving Fully Autonomous Robotaxis

Companies like Waymo and Cruise have begun deploying fully driverless taxis in certain cities. In June 2022, Cruise, a subsidiary of General Motors and supported by Microsoft, received approval to operate and charge fares in its fully driverless, fully autonomous "robotaxis" in parts of San Francisco.[109] The conditions under which these robotaxis can operate are limited. Cruise AVs are permitted to charge for driverless rides only during night-time hours, and are limited to a maximum speed of 30 miles per hour.[110] They can, however, operate in light rain

[109] Joann Muller, "Cruise's Robotaxis Can Charge You for Rides Now," *Axios* (June 6, 2022), www.axios.com/2022/06/06/cruise-driverless-taxi-san-fransisco.

[110] As of April 2023, Cruise had applied for permission to begin testing its AVs throughout California at speeds of up to 55 miles per hour (25 mph higher). Michael Liedtke, "No Driver? No Problem. Robotaxis Eye San Francisco Expansion," *AP News* (April 5, 2023), https://apnews.com/article/driverless-cars-robotaxis-waymo-cruise-tesla-684556379bb57425c8fdf35268e8046d.

and fog, frequent occurrences in San Francisco. Waymo, an Alphabet subsidiary, began carrying passengers in its robotaxis in less crowded Phoenix in 2020, and as of April 2023 it was giving free rides in San Francisco and awaiting approval to charge fares.[111] The potential safety benefits of autonomous taxis are obvious. A computer program is never tired, drunk, or distracted. And cars like Waymo's are equipped with sophisticated technology like lidar (light detection and ranging), radar, and cameras that simultaneously surveil every angle of the car's surroundings.

How would the psychology of HRI affect fact-finding and the allocation of liability if these driverless taxis were involved in accidents? Companies designing these robotaxis have many design options that might trigger various responses, including anthropomorphic projections and responses to the performance of the algorithms controlling the cars. They could seat an embodied, co-present robo-driver in the car; its features could be designed to evoke a variety of positive responses. Alternatively, and more inexpensively, the designers could create a virtual, physically embodied driver who would appear virtually on a computer screen visible to the passengers. In either case, the robot driver could be given a name, a backstory, and an appealing voice to interact with the rider. The robotaxi driver would play the same social function as today's Uber or taxi driver, but unlike their human counterparts, the robot drivers might play no role in actually operating the vehicle.

Design choices could affect ultimate credibility and liability judgments. For example, as experimental studies indicate, giving the car more anthropomorphic qualities, a name, an appearance, a backstory, etc. would make it more likeable, and as a result, people may be more hesitant to attribute liability to it – particularly if there is a human safety driver in the car. And if both the automated car and a car with a human driver were in an accident, the experimental studies suggest that the human driver would be blamed more. The fact-finders' evaluation of algorithmic evidence might also be affected by cognitive biases, including the tendency to discount algorithmic predictions once they have been shown to be in error, even if humans have made the same error.

This example also highlights other factors that may affect the ability of various fact-finders to resolve disputes arising from the complex and rapidly evolving technology in AVs. Arbitrators vary by specialty, and some may eventually specialize in disputes involving AVs. Finally,

[111] Ibid.

the NTSB is the most knowledgeable body that could handle disputes involving AVs. However, given the structural limitations of the agency, its decisions of fault are not legally enforceable against the parties involved.

V Conclusion

Human responses to robot-generated evidence will present unique challenges to the accuracy of litigation, as well as the transparency of the legal system and the perceptions of its fairness.

Robot design and framing have the potential to distort fact-finding both intentionally and unintentionally. Robot-generated evidence may be undervalued, e.g., because it is not direct evidence. But such evidence may also be overvalued because of design choices intended to thwart or minimize a robot's liability or perceived responsibility, and thus the liability of its designers, manufacturers, and owners. Although there are human analogs involving witness selection and coaching, they are subject to natural limits, limits which largely do not apply to the ex ante design-a-witness problem we may see with robots. Additionally, cognitive biases may distort assessments of blame and liability when human and robot actors are both at fault, leading to the failure to impose liability on the designers and producers of robots.

Testing the accuracy of robot-generated evidence will also create new challenges. Traditional cross-examination is ill-suited to this evidence, which may lead to both inaccurate fact-finding and a lack of transparency in the process that could undermine public trust. Cognitive biases can also distort the evaluation of evidence concerning algorithms. The high cost of accessing the most sophisticated robots and mounting the means to challenge them can exacerbate concerns about the fairness and accuracy of the legal system, as well as accessibility to justice. Accordingly, traditional trial techniques need to be adapted and new approaches developed, such as new testimonial safeguards.[112]

But the news concerning litigation is not all bad. If it is possible to reduce the distorting effects arising from cognitive errors, robot-generated evidence could improve the accuracy of litigation, capturing more data

[112] See "Machine Testimony", note 57 above (describing the potential infirmities of machine sources, providing a taxonomy of machine evidence that explains which types implicate credibility and explores how courts have attempted to regulate them, and offering a new "vision" of testimonial safeguards for machine sources of information).

initially and preserving it without the many problems that distort and degrade human memory.[113]

Finally, alternative forums, such as arbitration and agency proceedings, can be designed to minimize the evaluation of evidence and the imposition of liability on the basis of fact-finding by individuals who lack familiarity with the technology in question.

[113] See generally Andrea Roth, "Trial by Machine" (2016) 104:5 *Georgetown Law Journal* 1245 (documenting the rise of mechanical proof and decision-making in criminal trials as a means of enhancing objectivity and accuracy, at least when the shift toward the mechanical has benefited certain interests).

MAMAK ©
BLACK BOX

7

Principles to Govern Regulation of Digital and Machine Evidence

ANDREA ROTH

I Introduction

Criminal prosecutions now routinely involve technologically sophisticated tools for both investigation and proof of guilt, from complex software used to interpret DNA mixtures, to digital forensics, to algorithmic risk assessment tools used in pre-trial detention, sentencing, and parole determinations. As Emily Silverman, Jörg Arnold, and Sabine Gless's Chapter 8 explains, these tools offer not merely routine measurements, but also "evaluative data" akin to expert opinions.[1] These new tools, in critical respects, are a welcome addition to less sophisticated or more openly subjective forms of evidence that have led to wrongful convictions in the past, most notably eyewitness identifications, confessions, and statements of source attribution using "first generation"[2] forensic disciplines of dubious reliability, such as bite marks.[3]

Nonetheless, this new generation of evidence brings new costs and challenges. Algorithmic tools offer uniformity and consistency, but potentially at the expense of equitable safety valves to correct the unjust results that would otherwise flow from mechanistic application of rules. Such tools also may appear more reliable or equitable than they are, as fact-finders fail to identify sources of error or bias because the tools appear objective and are shrouded in black box secrecy. Even with greater transparency, some results, such as the decisions of deep neural networks engaged in deep

[1] See generally Chapter 8 in this volume.

[2] See Erin Murphy, "The New Forensics: Criminal Justice, False Certainty, and the Second Generation of Scientific Evidence" (2007) 95:3 *California Law Review* 721 ["New Forensics"] (comparing "first-generation" techniques, such as tool-marks and handwriting, to "second-generation" techniques, such as DNA and digital evidence).

[3] See generally Innocence Project, "DNA Exonerations in the United States (1989–2020)," https://innocenceproject.org/dna-exonerations-in-the-united-states/ (noting numerous exonerations in cases involving mistaken eyewitnesses, false confessions, and embellished forensic evidence).

learning, will not be fully explainable without sacrificing the very complexity that is the ostensible comparative advantage of artificial intelligence (AI). The lack of explainability as to the method and results of sophisticated algorithmic tools has implications for accuracy, but also for public trust in legal proceedings and participants' sense of being treated with dignity. As Sara Sun Beale and Haley Lawrence note in their Chapter 6 of this volume, humans have strong reactions to certain uses of robot "testimony" in legal proceedings.[4] Absent proper regulation, such tools may jeopardize key systemic criminal justice values, including the accuracy expressed by convicting the guilty and exonerating the innocent, fairness, public legitimacy, and softer values such as mercy and dignity.

In furtherance of these systemic goals, this chapter argues for four overarching principles to guide the use of digital and machine evidence in criminal justice systems: a right to front-end safeguards to minimize error and bias; a right of access both to government evidence and to exculpatory technologies; a right of contestation; and a right to an epistemically competent fact-finding process that keeps a human in the loop. The chapter offers legal and policy proposals to operationalize each principle.

Three caveats are in order. First, this chapter draws heavily on examples from the United States, a decentralized and adversarial system in which the parties themselves investigate the case, find witnesses, choose which evidence to introduce, and root out truth through contestation. Sabine Gless has described the many differences between the US and German approaches to machine evidence, distinguishing their adversarial and inquisitorial approaches, respectively.[5] Nonetheless, the principles discussed here are relevant to any system valuing accuracy, fairness, and public legitimacy. For example, although many European nations have a centralized, inquisitorial system, proposed EU legislation evinces concern over the rights of criminal defendants vis-à-vis AI systems, specifically the potential threat AI poses to a "fair" trial, the "rights of the defense," and the right to be "presumed innocent," as guaranteed by the EU Charter of Fundamental Rights.[6] As noted in Chapter 10 of

[4] See Chapter 6 in this volume.

[5] Sabine Gless, "AI in the Courtroom: A Comparative Analysis of Machine Evidence in Criminal Trials" (2020) 51:2 *Georgetown Journal of International Law* 195 ["AI in the Courtroom"].

[6] EU Charter of Fundamental Rights, 2000 (came into force in 2009), Title VI, Arts. 47–48; see also Artificial Intelligence Act, European Union (proposed April 21, 2021), COM(2021) 206 final 2021/0106, Explanatory Memorandum s. 3.5, https://eur-lex.europa.eu/legal-content/EN/TXT/?uri=celex%3A52021PC0206.

this volume by Bart Custers and Lenneke Stevens, European nations are facing similar dilemmas when it comes to the regulation of digital evidence in criminal cases.[7]

The second caveat is that digital and machine evidence is a wide-ranging and definitionally vague concept. Erin Murphy's Chapter 9 in this volume offers a helpful taxonomy of such evidence that explains its various uses and characteristics, which in turn determine how such evidence implicates the principles in Section II.[8] Electronic communications and social media, e.g., implicate authentication and access concerns, but not so much the need for equitable safety valves in automated decision-making. Likewise, biometric identifiers may raise more privacy concerns than use of social media posts as evidence. The key characteristics of digital evidence as cataloged by Murphy also affect which principles are implicated. For example, data created by a private person, and possessed by Facebook, might implicate the right to exculpatory information and the Stored Communications Act,[9] while resiliency or lack of data such as body-worn camera footage might require the state to adopt more stringent preservation and storage measures, and to allow defendants access to e-discovery tools. So long as the principles are followed when they apply, the delivery of justice can be enhanced rather than jeopardized by digital and machine proof.

The third caveat is that this chapter does not write on a blank slate in setting forth principles to govern the use of technology in rendering justice. A host of disciplines and governing bodies have adopted principles for "ethical or responsible" use of AI, from the US Department of Defense to the Alan Turing Institute to the Council of Europe. Recent meta-studies of these various sets of principles have identified recurring values, such as beneficence, autonomy, justice, explainability, transparency, fairness, responsibility, privacy, expert oversight, stakeholder-driven legitimacy, and "values-driven determinism."[10] More specifically, many countries

7 See Chapter 10 in this volume (exploring the shift toward digital evidence in Dutch criminal courts).

8 See Chapter 9 in this volume. Erin Murphy divides "technological evidence" into location trackers, electronic communications and social media, historical search or cloud or vendor records, "Internet of Things" and smart tools, surveillance cameras and visual imagery, biometric identifiers, and analytical software tools.

9 18 United States Code [18 USC], §§2701–2712.

10 See e.g. Luciano Floridi & Josh Cowls, "A Unified Framework of Five Principles for AI in Society" (2019) 1:1 *Harvard Data Science Review* (examining forty-seven principles promulgated since 2016, which map onto beneficence, non-maleficence, autonomy, justice,

already have a detailed legal framework to govern criminal procedure. In the United States, e.g., criminal defendants already have a constitutional right to compulsory process, to present a defense, to be confronted with the witnesses against them, to a verdict by a human jury, and to access to experts where necessary to a defense. But these rights were established at a time when cases largely depended on human witnesses rather than machines. The challenge here is not so much to convince nations in the abstract to allow a right to contest automated decision-making, but to explain how existing rights, such as the right of confrontation or right to pre-trial disclosure of the bases of expert testimony, might apply to this new type of evidence.

II The Principles

Principle I: The digital and machine evidence used as proof in criminal proceedings should be subject to front-end development and testing safeguards designed to minimize error and bias.

Principle I(a): Jurisdictions should acknowledge the heightened need for front-end safeguards with respect to digital and machine evidence, which cannot easily be scrutinized through case-specific, in-trial procedures.

To understand why the use of digital and machine evidence merits special front-end development and testing safeguards that do not apply to all types of evidence, jurisdictions should acknowledge that the current real-time trial safeguards built for human witnesses, such as cross-examination, are not as helpful for machine-generated proof.

and explicability); Anna Jobin, Marcello Ienca, & Effy Vayena, "The Global Landscape of AI Ethics Guidelines" (2019) 1:9 *Nature Machine Intelligence* 389–399 (reviewing 84 documents, which centered around transparency, justice and fairness, non-maleficence, responsibility, and privacy); Daniel Greene, Anna Lauren Hoffmann, & Luke Stark, "Better, Nicer, Clearer, Fairer: A Critical Assessment of the Movement for Ethical Artificial Intelligence and Machine Learning" (paper delivered at the Proceedings of the 52nd Hawaii International Conference on System Sciences, January 8, 2019), cited in Samuele Lo Piano, "Ethical Principles in Machine Learning and Artificial Intelligence: Cases from the Field and Possible Ways Forward" (2020) 7:1 *Humanities and Social Sciences Communications*, Article 9 (collecting meta-studies). The Council of Europe's 2020 Resolution on AI also includes these values, specifically mentioning "transparency, including accessibility and explicability," "justice and fairness," and "human responsibility for decisions." See Council of Europe, "Council of Europe and Artificial Intelligence," www.coe.int/en/web/artificial-intelligence.

A critical goal of any criminal trial is to ensure verdict accuracy by minimizing the chance of the fact-finder drawing the wrong inferences from the evidence presented. There are several different levers a system could use to combat inferential error by a jury. First, the system could exclude unreliable evidence so that the jury never hears it. Second, the system could implement front-end design and production safeguards to ensure that evidence is as reliable as it can be when admitted, or that critical contextual information about its probative value is developed and disclosed when the fact-finder hears it. Third, the system could allow parties themselves to explore and impeach, or attack the credibility/reliability of the evidence. Fourth, the system could adopt proof standards that limit the fact-finder's ability to render a verdict absent a proof threshold such as beyond a reasonable doubt, or type or quantum of evidence.

For better or worse, the American system of evidence pursues accuracy almost entirely through trial and back-end safeguards, the third and fourth levers described above. Although the United States still clings to the rule excluding hearsay, understood as out-of-court statements offered for their truth, that rule has numerous exceptions. And while US jurisdictions used to have stringent competence requirements for witnesses, these have given way to the ability to impeach witnesses once they testify or once their hearsay is admitted.[11] The parties conduct such impeachment through cross-examination, physical confrontation, and admission of extrinsic evidence such as a witness's prior convictions or inconsistent statements. In addition, the United States has back-end proof standards to correct for unreliable testimony, such as corroboration requirements for accomplice testimony and confessions. The US system has a similarly lenient admission standard with regard to physical evidence, requiring only minimal proof that an item such as a document or object is what the proponent says it is.[12]

Nonetheless, there are particular types of witness testimony that do require more front-end safeguards, ones that could work well for digital and machine evidence too. One example is eyewitness identifications. If an identification is conducted under unnecessarily suggestive circumstances, a US trial court, as a matter of constitutional due process, must conduct

[11] See e.g. Federal Rules of Evidence, United States (as amended on December 1, 2020) [Federal Rules of Evidence], Rules 602 (liberal competence standard), 806 (allowing impeachment of hearsay declarants), 608–609 (allowing impeachment by character-for-dishonesty evidence), and 613 and 801(d) (impeachment by inconsistent statements).

[12] See e.g. Federal Rules of Evidence, note 11 above, Rules 901 and 902 (imposing minimal authentication requirements).

a hearing to determine whether the identification is sufficiently reliable to be admitted against the defendant at trial.[13] Moreover, some lower US courts subject identification testimony to limits or cautionary instructions at trial, unless certain procedures were used during the identification, to minimize the risk of suggestivity.[14] Likewise, expert testimony is subjected to enhanced reliability requirements that question whether the method has been tested, has a known error rate, has governing protocols, and has been subject to peer review.[15] To a lesser extent, *confession* evidence is also subject to more stringent front-end safeguards, such as the requirement in some jurisdictions that stationhouse confessions be videotaped.[16]

The focus on front-end safeguards in these specific realms is not a coincidence. Rather, it stems from the fact that the problems with such testimony are largely cognitive, subconscious, or recurring, rather than a matter of one-off insincerity, and therefore not meaningfully scrutinized solely through cross-examination and other real-time impeachment methods.[17] These categories of testimony bear some of the same process-like characteristics that make digital and machine evidence difficult to scrutinize through cross-examination alone.

Even more so than these particular types of human testimony, digital and machine evidence bear characteristics that call for robust front-end development and testing safeguards before it gets to the courtroom. First, the programming of the algorithms that drive the outputs of many of the categories of proof discussed by Erin Murphy, including location trackers, smart tools, and analytical software tools, does not necessarily change from case to case.[18] Repeatedly-used software can be subject to testing to

[13] *Manson* v. *Brathwaite*, 432 U.S. 98 (1977).

[14] See e.g. *State* v. *Henderson*, 27 A.3d 872, 878 (NJ 2011) (establishing protocols for eyewitness identification procedures).

[15] See *Daubert* v. *Merrell Dow Pharmaceuticals, Inc.*, 509 U.S. 579 (1993) (setting forth a non-exhaustive list of factors trial courts should use in determining the scientific validity of an expert method). A minority of US state jurisdictions continue to adhere to the alternative *Frye* test, that looks to whether novel scientific methods are "general[ly] accept[ed]" in the scientific community. See *Frye* v. *United States*, 293 F. 1013 (DC Cir. 1923).

[16] See e.g. G. Daniel Lassiter, Andrew L. Geers, Ian M. Handley *et al.*, "Videotaped Interrogations and Confessions: A Simple Change in Camera Perspective Alters Verdicts in Simulated Trials" (2002) 87:5 *Journal of Applied Psychology* 867 at 867.

[17] See Edward Cheng & Alexander Nunn, "Beyond the Witness: Bringing a Process Perspective to Modern Evidence Law" (2019) 97:6 *Texas Law Review* 1077 ["Beyond the Witness"]; see also Jules Epstein, "The Great Engine that Couldn't: Science, Mistaken Identifications, and the Limits of Cross-Examination" (2007) 36:3 *Stetson Law Review* 727.

[18] See e.g. "New Forensics", note 2 above (noting this aspect of "second-generation" forensic techniques like DNA).

determine its accuracy under various conditions. Second, unlike eyewitnesses and confessions, where the declarant in some cases might offer significant further context through testimony, little further context can be gleaned from in-court scrutiny of any of the categories of proof Murphy describes.[19] To be sure, a programmer or inputter could take the stand and explain some aspects of a machine's output in broad strokes. But the case-specific "raw data," "measurement data," or "evaluative data"[20] of the machine is ultimately the product of the operation of the machine and its algorithms, not the programmer's own mental processes, and it is the machine's and algorithm's operation that must also be scrutinized. In short, the accoutrements of courtroom adversarialism, such as live cross-examination, are hardly the "greatest legal engine ever invented for the discovery of truth"[21] of the conveyances of machines.

Principle I(b): Jurisdictions should implement and enforce, through admissibility requirements, certain minimal development and testing procedures for digital and machine evidence.

Several development and testing safeguards should be implemented for any software-driven system whose results are introduced in criminal proceedings. The first is robust, independent stress testing of the software. Such standards are available,[22] but are typically not applied, at least in the United States, to software created for litigation. For example, a software expert reviewing the code of the Alcotest 7110, a breath-alcohol machine used in several US states, found that it would not pass industry standards. He documented 19,500 errors, nine of which he believed "could ultimately [a]ffect the breath alcohol reading."[23] A reviewing court held that such errors did not merit excluding the

19 See ibid.; see also Chapter 9 in this volume.

20 See Chapter 8 in this volume. The chapter defines "raw data" as data produced by a machine without any processing, "measurement data" as data produced by a machine after rudimentary calculations, and "evaluative data" as data produced by a machine according to sophisticated algorithmic methods that cannot be reproduced manually.

21 Prominent American evidence scholar John Henry Wigmore famously described cross-examination in this way, see John Henry Wigmore, *Evidence in Trials at Common Law*, vol. 5 (Boston, MA: Little, Brown & Co., 1974) at 32, s. 1367.

22 See e.g. Declaration of Nathaniel Adams, *People* v. *Hillary*, No. 2015–15 (New York County Court of St Lawrence, May 27, 2016) at 1–2 (on file with author) (listing citations to several governing bodies that have come together to promulgate industry standards for software development and testing).

23 See Supplemental Findings and Conclusions of Remand Court at 11, *State* v. *Chun*, No. 58,879 (NJ November 14, 2007), www.nj-dmv-dwi.com/state-v-chun-alcotest-litigation/.

reading, in part because the expert could not say with "reasonable certainty" that the errors caused a false reading in the case at hand,[24] but the court did require modifications of the program for future use.[25] In addition, Nathaniel Adams, a computer scientist and expert in numerous criminal cases in the United States, has advocated for forensic algorithms to be subject to the industry-standard testing standards of the Institute of Electrical and Electronic Engineers (IEEE).[26] Adams notes that STRMix, one of the two primary probabilistic genotyping programs used in the United States, had not been tested by a financially independent entity,[27] and the program's creators have disclosed more than one episode of miscodes potentially affecting match statistics, thus far, in ways that would underestimate but not overestimate a match probability.[28] Professor Adams' work helped to inspire a recent bill in the US Congress, the Justice in Forensic Algorithms Act of 2021, which would subject machine-generated proof in criminal cases to more rigorous testing, along with pre-trial disclosure requirements, defense access, and the removal of trade secret privilege from proprietary code.[29] And exclusion aside, a rigorous software testing requirement reduces the chance of misleading or false machine conveyances presented at trial.

Jurisdictions should also enact mandatory testing and operation protocols for machine tools used to generate evidence of guilt or innocence, along the lines currently used for blood-alcohol breath-testing

[24] Ibid.

[25] See *State* v. *Chun*, 943 A.2d 114, 129–30 (NJ 2008); see also Robert Garcia, "'Garbage in, Gospel Out': Criminal Discovery, Computer Reliability, and the Constitution" (1991) 38:5 *UCLA Law Review* 1043 at 1088 (citing GAO report finding deficiencies in software used by Customs Office to record license plates, and investigations of failures of IRS's computer system).

[26] See e.g. Nathaniel Adams, "What Does Software Engineering Have to Do with DNA?" (2018) May Issue *NACDL The Champion* 58 ["Software Engineering"] (arguing that software should be subject to industry-standard IEEE-approved independent software testing); Andrea Roth, "Machine Testimony" (2017) 126:7 *Yale Law Journal* 1972 ["Machine Testimony"] at 2023 (arguing for independent software testing as admissibility requirement).

[27] "Software Engineering", note 26 above.

[28] See *Final Report – Variation in STRMix Regarding Calculation of Expected Heights of Dropped Out Peaks* (STRMix, July 4, 2016) at 1–2 (on file with author) (acknowledging coding errors, but noting that errors would only underestimate the likelihood of contribution). Of course, an error underestimating the likelihood of contribution might also be detrimental to a factually innocent defendant in certain cases, such as where the defense alleges a third-party perpetrator.

[29] See United States, Bill HR 2438, Justice in Forensic Algorithms Act of 2021, 117th Cong., 2021, www.govtrack.us/congress/bills/117/hr2438.

equipment.[30] Such requirements need not be a condition of admission; in the breath-alcohol context, the failure to adhere to protocols goes to weight, not admissibility.[31] Even so, the lack of validation studies showing an algorithm's accuracy under circumstances relevant to the case at hand should, in some cases, be a barrier to admissibility. Jurisdictions should subject the conclusions of machine experts to validity requirements at the admissibility stage, similar to those imposed on experts at trial. Currently, the *Daubert* and *Frye* reliability/general acceptance requirements apply only to human experts; if the prosecution introduces machine-generated proof without a human interlocutor, the proof is subject only to general authentication and relevance requirements.[32]

Requiring the proponent to show that the algorithm is fit for purpose through developmental and internal validation before offering its results is key not merely for algorithms created for law enforcement but for algorithms created for commercial purposes as well. For example, while Google Earth results have been admitted as evidence of guilt with no legal scrutiny of their reliability,[33] scientists have conducted studies to determine its error rate with regard to various uses.[34] While error is inevitable in any human or machine method, this type of study should be a condition of admitting algorithmic proof.[35]

Such testing need not necessarily require public disclosure of source code or other levels of transparency that could jeopardize intellectual property interests. Instead, testing algorithms for forensic use could be done in a manner similar to testing of potentially patentable pharmaceuticals by

30 See e.g. Conforming Products List of Evidential Breath Alcohol Measurement Devices, 2012, 77 Fed. Reg. 35,747, 35,748 (prohibiting states from using machines except those approved by the National Highway Transportation Safety Administration).

31 See e.g. *People* v. *Adams*, 131 Cal. Rptr. 190, 195 (Ct. App. 1976) (holding that a failure to calibrate breath-alcohol equipment went only to weight).

32 See e.g. *People* v. *Lopez*, 286 P.3d 469, 494 (Cal. 2012) (admitting results of gas chromatograph, without testimony of expert); "Machine Testimony", note 26 above, at 1989–1990 (explaining that the hearsay rule does not apply to machines, heightening the need for alternative forms of scrutiny).

33 See e.g. *United States* v. *Lizarraga-Tirado*, 789 F.3d 1107, 1109 (9th Cir. 2015) (admitting Google Earth "pin" associated with GPS coordinates as evidence that defendant had been arrested on the US side of the US–Mexico border for purposes of an illegal re-entry prosecution).

34 See e.g. Shawn Harrington, Joseph Teitelman, Erica Rummel *et al.*, "Validating Google Earth Pro as a Scientific Utility for Use in Accident Reconstruction" (2017) 5:2 *SAE International Journal of Transport Safety* 135.

35 Cf. "Beyond the Witness", note 17 above (arguing that process-based evidence should be subject to testing to determine error rate).

the US Food and Drug Administration.[36] Others have made the point that scrutiny by "entrusted intermediate parties," behind closed doors, would avoid any financial harm to developers.[37] Of course, for algorithms that are open source, such concerns would be lessened.

One limit on validation studies as a guarantor of algorithmic accuracy is that most studies do not speak to whether an algorithm's reported score or statistic, along a range, is accurate. Studies might show that a software program boasts a low false positive rate in terms of falsely labeling a non-contributor as a contributor to a DNA mixture, but not whether its reported likelihood ratio might be off by a factor of ten. As two DNA statistics experts explain, there is no "ground truth" against which to measure such statistics:

> Laboratory procedures to measure a physical quantity such as a concentration can be validated by showing that the measured concentration consistently lies with an acceptable range of error relative to the true concentration. Such validation is infeasible for software aimed at computing a [likelihood ratio] because it has no underlying true value (no equivalent to a true concentration exists). The [likelihood ratio] expresses our uncertainty about an unknown event and depends on modeling assumptions that cannot be precisely verified in the context of noisy [crime scene profile] data.[38]

But systems are not helpless in testing the accuracy of algorithm-generated credit scores or match statistics. Rather, such results must be scrutinized using other methodologies, such as more complex studies that go beyond simply determining false positive rates, stress testing of software, examination of source code by independent experts, and assessment of whether various inputs, such as assumptions about the values of key variables, are appropriate.

Principle I(c): Jurisdictions should explicitly define what is meant by algorithmic fairness for purposes of testing for, and guarding against, bias.

Algorithms should also be tested for bias. The importance of avoiding racial and other bias in algorithmic decision-making is perhaps obvious,

[36] See e.g. Andrew Tutt, "An FDA for Algorithms" (2017) 69:1 *Administrative Law Review* 83 (suggesting that such a body could prevent problematic algorithms from going to market).

[37] Paul B. de Laat, "Algorithmic Decision-Making Based on Machine Learning from Big Data: Can Transparency Restore Accountability?" (2018) 31:4 *Philosophy & Technology* 525.

[38] Christopher D. Steele & David J. Balding, "Statistical Evaluation of Forensic DNA Profile Evidence" (2014) 1:1 *Annual Review of Statistics and Its Application* 361 at 380.

given that fairness is an explicitly stated value in nearly all promulgated AI standards in the meta-studies referenced in the introduction to this chapter. In addition, racial, gender, and other kinds of bias might trigger legal violations as well as ethical or policy concerns. To be sure, the Equal Protection Clause of the Fourteenth Amendment to the US Constitution guards only against state action that intentionally treats people differently because of a protected status, but if an algorithm simply has a disparate impact on a group, it will likely not be viewed as an equal protection violation. However, biased algorithms used in jury selection could violate the requirement that petit juries be drawn from a fair cross section of the population, and biased algorithms used to prove dangerousness or guilt at trial could violate statutory anti-discrimination laws or reliability-based admissibility standards.

In one highly publicized example of algorithmic bias from the United States, Pro Publica studied Northpointe's post-trial risk assessment tool Correctional Offender Management Profiling for Alternative Sanctions (COMPAS) and determined that the false positive rates, i.e., rates of those labeled "dangerous," but who did not reoffend, for Black subjects was much higher than for White subjects.[39] At the same time, however, other studies, including by Northpointe itself, noted that the algorithm is, in fact, racially non-biased if the metric is whether race has any predictive value in the model in determining dangerousness.[40] As Northpointe notes, Black and White subjects with the same risk score present the same risk of reoffending under the model.[41] The upshot was not that Pro Publica was wrong in noting the differences in false positive rates; it was that Pro Publica judged the algorithm's racial bias by only one particular measure.

The COMPAS example highlights the problems of testing algorithms for fairness without defining terms. As others have explained, it is impossible to have both equal false positive rates and predictive

[39] See Jeff Larson, Surya Mattu, Lauren Kirchner *et al.*, "How We Analyzed the COMPAS Recidivism Algorithm," *ProPublica* (May 23, 2016), www.propublica.org/article/how-we-analyzed-the-compas-recidivism-algorithm.

[40] See "Response to ProPublica: Demonstrating Accuracy, Equity, and Predictive Parity," *Northpointe Research Department* (July 8, 2016), www.equivant.com/response-to-propublica-demonstrating-accuracy-equity-and-predictive-parity/ ["Response to ProPublica"]; Jon Kleinberg, Sendhil Mullainathan, & Manish Raghavan, "Inherent Trade-Offs in the Fair Determination of Risk Scores," *Cornell University* (November 17, 2016), arxiv.org/abs/1609.05807v2 (arguing that algorithms like COMPAS cannot simultaneously satisfy all three possible means of measuring algorithmic fairness, and that it has predictive parity even with different false positive rates).

[41] "Response to ProPublica", note 40 above.

parity where two groups have different base rates.[42] So, in determining whether the algorithm is biased, one needs to decide which measure is the more salient indicator of the type of bias the system should care about. Several commentators have noted possible differences in definitions of algorithmic fairness as well.[43] Deborah Hellman argues that predictive parity alone is an ill-suited measure of algorithmic fairness because it relates only to beliefs, not outcomes.[44] In Hellman's view, a disparate false positive rate between groups is highly relevant to proving, though not dispositive of, normatively troubling unfairness.[45] While not all jurisdictions will agree with Hellman's take, the point is that algorithm designers should be aware of different conceptions of fairness, be deliberate in choosing a metric, and ensure that algorithms in criminal proceedings are fair under that metric. Jurisdictions could require what Osagie Obasogie has termed "racial impact statements" in the administrative law context,[46] to determine the effect of a shift in decision-making on racial groups. The Council of Europe has made a similar recommendation, calling on states to conduct "human rights impact assessments of AI applications" to assess "risks of bias/discrimination … with particular attention to the situation of minorities and vulnerable and disadvantaged groups."[47]

Finally, in determining algorithmic fairness, decision-makers should judge algorithms not in a vacuum, but against existing human-driven decision-making processes. For example, court reporters have been known to mistakenly transcribe certain dialects, such as African American Vernacular English (AAVE), in ways that matter to fact-finding

[42] See e.g. Richard Berk, Hoda Heidari, Shahin Jabbari *et al.*, "Fairness in Criminal Justice Risk Assessments: The State of the Art" (2021) 50:1 *Sociological Methods & Research* 3 (explaining that these two types of fairness are incompatible).

[43] See e.g. Dana Pessach & Erez Schmueli, "Algorithmic Fairness," *Cornell University* (January 21, 2020), https://arxiv.org/abs/2001.09784 (noting that COMPAS offered certain types of predictive parity, but that the odds of being predicted dangerous were worse for African-Americans than White subjects).

[44] Deborah Hellman, "Measuring Algorithmic Fairness" (2020) 106:4 *Virginia Law Review* 811.

[45] Ibid. at 840–841.

[46] Osagie K. Obasogie, "The Return of Biological Race? Regulating Race and Genetics Through Administrative Agency Race Impact Assessments" (2012) 22:1 *Southern California Interdisciplinary Law Journal* 1.

[47] "Justice by Algorithm – The Role of Artificial Intelligence in Policing and Criminal Justice Systems," Doc. 15156, report of the Committee on Legal Affairs and Human Rights, Resolution 2342 (Council of Europe, Parliamentary Assembly, 2020), https://pace.coe.int/en/files/28805/html ["Justice by Algorithm"].

in criminal proceedings.[48] If an AI system were to offer a lower, even if non-zero, error rate with regard to mistranscriptions of AAVE, the shift toward such systems, at least a temporary one subject to continued testing and oversight, might reduce, rather than exacerbate, bias.[49]

Principle II: Before trial or other relevant proceeding, the parties should have meaningful and equitable access to digital and machine evidence material to the proceeding, including exculpatory technologies and data.

Principle II(a): Pretrial disclosure requirements related to expert testimony should apply to digital and machine conveyances that, if asserted by a human, would be subject to such requirements.

Because digital and machine evidence cannot be cross-examined, parties cannot use the in-court trial process itself to discover the infirmities of algorithms or possible flaws in their results or opinions. As Edward Cheng and Alex Nunn have noted, enhanced pre-trial discovery must in part take the place of in-court discovery with regard to process-based evidence like machine conveyances.[50] Such enhanced discovery already exists in the United States for human experts, precisely because in-court examination alone is not a meaningful way for parties to understand and prepare to rebut expert testimony. Specifically, parties in criminal cases are entitled by statute to certain information with regard to expert witnesses, including notice of the basis and content of the expert's testimony and the expert's qualifications.[51] Disclosure requirements in civil trials are even more onerous, requiring experts to prepare written reports that include the facts or data relied on.[52] Moreover, proponents of expert testimony must not discourage experts from speaking with the opposing party,[53] and in criminal trials, proponents must also disclose certain prior statements, or Jencks material, of witnesses after they testify.[54] These requirements

48 See e.g. Taylor Jones, Jessica Rose Kalbfeld, Ryan Hancock *et al.*, "Testifying While Black: An Experimental Study of Court Reporter Accuracy in Transcription of African American English" (2019) 95:2 *Language: Linguistic Society of America* 216.

49 Whether AI voice-recognition-driven court reporting systems are more accurate than human stenographers remains to be seen.

50 "Beyond the Witness", note 17 above.

51 See e.g. Federal Rules of Criminal Procedure, United States (as amended December 1, 2022) [Federal Rules of Criminal Procedure], Rule 16(a)(1)(G).

52 See Federal Rules of Criminal Procedure, note 51 above, Rule 26(a)(2)(B)(ii).

53 See e.g. *Gregory* v. *United States*, 369 F.2d 185, 188 (DC Cir. 1966) ("Both sides have an equal right, and should have an equal opportunity, to interview [state witnesses]").

54 See e.g. 18 USC, note 9 above, Jencks Act, 18 USC §3500(b).

also facilitate parties' ability to consult with their own experts to review the opposing party's evidence or proffered expert testimony.

Using existing rules for human experts as a guide, jurisdictions should require that parties be given access to the following:

(1) The evidence and algorithms themselves, sufficient to allow meaningful testing of their assumptions and running the program with different inputs. One probabilistic genotyping software company, TrueAllele, offers defendants access to its program, with certain restrictions, albeit only for a limited time and without the source code.[55] This sort of "black box tinkering" not only allows users to "confront" the code "with different scenarios," thus "reveal[ing] the blueprints of its decision-making process,"[56] but also approximates the posing of a hypothetical to a human expert. Indeed, the ability to tinker might be just as important as access to source code; data science scholars have written about the limits of transparency and the superior promise of reverse engineering in understanding how inputs relate to outputs.[57] Along these lines, Jennifer Mnookin has argued that a condition for admissibility of computer simulations should be that "their key evidence-based inputs are modifiable," allowing the opposing party to "test the robustness of the simulation by altering the factual assumptions on which it was built and seeing how changing these inputs affects the outputs."[58]

(2) The training or software necessary to use or test the program. In the United States, criminal defendants have reported that certain trainings are off limits to non-law-enforcement; e.g., for using the Cellebrite program to extract digital evidence from a cell phone, or for using DNA genotyping software. Moreover, only certain defense experts are able to buy the software for their own use, and some academic researchers have been effectively denied research licenses to study proprietary forensic software. Instead, the defense and academic communities should presumptively be given a license to access

[55] See State's Response to Defense Motion to Compel, *State* v. *Fair*, No. 10-1-09274-5 (Wash. Sup. Ct. April 1, 2016) at 21 (representations made by TrueAllele as to defense access to its program).

[56] Maayan Perel & Niva Elkin-Koren, "Black Box Tinkering: Beyond Transparency in Algorithmic Enforcement" (2017) 69:5 *Florida Law Review* 181.

[57] Nick Diakopoulos, "Algorithmic Accountability Reporting: On the Investigation of Black Boxes" (2013) *Tow Center for Digital Journalism* 30, https://academiccommons.columbia.edu/doi/10.7916/D8ZK5TW2.

[58] Jennifer Mnookin, "Repeat Play Evidence: Jack Weinstein, 'Pedagogical Devices,' Technology, and Evidence" (2015) 64:2 *DePaul Law Review* 571 at 573.

to all software used by the government in generating evidence of guilt, to facilitate independent validity testing.

(3) A meaningful account of the assumptions underlying the machine's results or opinion, as well as the source code and prior output of software, where necessary to a meaningful understanding of those assumptions. Human experts can be extensively questioned both before and during trial, offering a way for parties to understand and refute their methods and conclusions. Digital and machine evidence cannot be questioned in the same way, but proponents should be required to disclose the same type of information about methods and conclusions that a machine expert witness would offer, if it could talk. Likewise, Article 15(1)(h) of General Data Protection Regulation (GDPR)[59] gives a data subject the right to know of any automated decision-making to which he is subject, and if so, the right to "meaningful information about the logic involved." While the GDPR may apply only to private parties rather than criminal prosecutions, the subject's dignitary interest in understanding the machine's logic would presumably be even greater in the criminal realm.

In particular, where disclosure of source code is necessary to meaningful scrutiny of the accuracy of machine results,[60] the proponent must allow access. As discussed in Principle I, source code might be important in particular to scrutinize scores or match statistics, where existing studies reveal only false positive rates. A jurisdiction should also require disclosure of prior output of the machine, covering the same subject matter as the machine results being admitted.[61] For human witnesses, such prior statements must be disclosed in many US jurisdictions to facilitate scrutiny of witness claims and impeachment by inconsistency. For machines, parties should have to disclose, e.g., the results of all prior runs of DNA

59 General Data Protection Regulation, EU 2016, Regulation (EU) 2016/679 (with effect from May 25, 2018).

60 See e.g. Andrew Morin, Jennifer Urban, Paul D. Adams *et al.*, "Shining Light into Black Boxes" (2012) 336:6078 *Science* 159 at 159 ["Shining Light"] ("Common implementation errors in programs … can be difficult to detect without access to source code"); Erin E. Kenneally, "Gatekeeping Out of the Box: Open Source Software as a Mechanism to Assess Reliability for Digital Evidence" (2001) 6:13 *Virginia Journal of Law and Technology* 13 (arguing that access to source code is necessary to prevent or unearth many structural programming errors).

61 See e.g. *United States* v. *Liebert*, 519 F.2d 542, 543, 550–51 (3d Cir. 1975) (entertaining the possibility that the defense was entitled to view the IRS program's prior reports of non-filers to determine their accuracy, but determining that access was not necessary to impeach the program).

software on a sample, all potentially matching reference fingerprints reported by a database using a latent print from a crime scene,[62] or calibration data from breath-alcohol machines.[63]

(4) Access to training data. Defendants and their experts should have access to underlying data used by the machine or algorithm in producing its results. In countries with inquisitorial as compared to adversarial systems, defendants should have access to "any data that is at the disposal of the court-appointed expert."[64] For example, for a machine-learning model labeling a defendant a "sexual psychopath" for purposes of a civil detention statute, the defendant should have access to the training dataset. Issues of privacy, i.e., the privacy of those in the dataset, have arisen, but are not insurmountable.[65]

To be sure, access alone does not guarantee that defendants will understand what they are given. But access is a necessary condition to allowing defendants to consult with experts who can meaningfully study the algorithms' performance and limits.

Principle II(b): Jurisdictions should not allow claims of trade secret privilege or statutory privacy interests to interfere with a criminal defendant's meaningful access to digital and machine evidence, including exculpatory technologies and data.

While creators of proprietary algorithms routinely argue that source code is a trade secret,[66] this argument should not shield code from discovery in a criminal case, where the code is material to the proceedings.[67] Of course, if proprietors can claim substantive intellectual property rights in their algorithms, those rights are still enforceable through licensing fees and civil lawsuits.

[62] State officials generally refuse defense requests for access to the other reported near matches, notwithstanding arguments that these matches might prove exculpatory. See generally Simon A. Cole, "More than Zero: Accounting for Error in Latent Fingerprint Identification" (2005) 95:3 *Journal of Criminal Law and Criminology* 985.

[63] Kathleen E. Watson, "COBRA Data and the Right to Confront Technology against You" (2015) 42:2 *North Kentucky Law Review* 375 at 381–382. But see *Turcotte* v. *Dir. of Revenue*, 829 S.W.2d 494, 496 (Mo. Ct. App. 1992) (holding that the state's failure to file timely maintenance reports on a breath-alcohol machine did not "impeach the machine's accuracy").

[64] "AI in the Courtroom", note 5 above, at 248.

[65] See e.g. Emiliano De Cristofaro, "An Overview of Privacy in Machine Learning," *Cornell University* (May 18, 2020), https://arxiv.org/abs/2005.08679.

[66] See generally Rebecca Wexler, "Life, Liberty, and Trade Secrets: Intellectual Property in the Criminal Justice System" (2018) 70:5 *Stanford Law Review* 1343.

[67] Ibid. (arguing that trade secrets doctrine should not apply in criminal cases).

Likewise, criminal defendants should have meaningful access to exculpatory digital and machine evidence, including the ability to subpoena witnesses who can produce such evidence in criminal proceedings where such evidence is material. Rebecca Wexler has explored the asymmetries inherent in US statutes such as the Stored Communications Act, which shields electronically stored communications from disclosure and has an exception for "law enforcement," but not for criminal defendants, however material the communications might be to establishing innocence. Such asymmetries are inconsistent not only with basic adversarial fairness, but arguably also with the Sixth Amendment compulsory process.[68]

Principle II(c): Jurisdictions should apply a presumption in favor of open-source technologies in criminal justice.

In the United States, the public has a constitutional right of access to criminal proceedings.[69] With regard to human witnesses, the public can hear the witnesses testify and determine the strength and legitimacy of the state's case. The public should likewise be recognized as a stakeholder in the development and use of digital and machine evidence in criminal proceedings. The Council of Europe's guidelines for use of AI in criminal justice embrace this concept, requiring Member States to "meaningfully consult the public, including civil society organizations and community representatives, before introducing AI applications."[70]

The most direct way to ensure public scrutiny of such evidence would be through open-source software. Scholars have discussed the benefits of open-source software in terms of facilitating "crowdsourcing"[71] and "ruthless public scrutiny"[72] as means of testing models and algorithms for hidden biases and errors. Others have gone further, arguing that software should

[68] See generally Rebecca Wexler, "Privacy Asymmetries: Access to Data in Criminal Defense Investigations" (2021) 68:1 *UCLA Law Review* 212.

[69] See *In re. Oliver*, 333 U.S. 257 (1948); Sixth Amendment to the US Constitution (right to a "public trial").

[70] "Justice by Algorithm", note 47 above, at 9.3.

[71] Cathy O'Neil, *Weapons of Math Destruction* (New York, NY: Crown Books, 2016) [*Weapons of Math Destruction*] at 211 (calling for "crowdsourcing campaigns" to offer feedback on errors and biases in datasets and models); see also Frank Pasquale, *The Black Box Society: The Secret Algorithms that Control Money and Information* (Cambridge, MA: Harvard University Press, 2015) at 208 (arguing for open source software in determining credit scores).

[72] Holly Doremus, "Listing Decisions under the Endangered Species Act: Why Better Science Isn't Always Better Policy" (1997) 75:3 *Washington University Law Quarterly* 1029 at 1138.

be open source whenever used in public law.[73] Public models would have the benefit of being "transparent" and "continuously updated, with both the assumptions and the conclusions clear for all to see."[74] States could encourage adoption of open-source software through drastic means, excluding output from adjudication, or more modest means, such as offering monetary incentives or prizes for development of open source replacements.

Principle II(d): Jurisdictions should make investigative technologies equally available to criminal defendants for potential exculpatory purposes, regardless of whether the state used the technology in a given case.

As Erin Murphy notes in Chapter 9 of this volume, defendants have two compelling needs with regard to digital and machine evidence: a meaningful chance to attack the government's proof, and a meaningful chance to discover and present "supportive defense evidence."[75] Just as both defendants and prosecutors have the ability to interview and subpoena witnesses, defendants should have an equal ability to wield new technologies that are paid for by the state when prosecutors seek to use them. If a defendant is accused of a crime based on what he believes to be a human analyst's erroneous interpretation of a complex DNA mixture, the defendant should be given the ability to use a probabilistic genotyping program, like TrueAllele, to attack these results. Of course, this access would be costly, and might reasonably be denied in cases where it bears no relevance to the defense, as determined *ex parte* by a judge. But if defendants have a due process right to access to defense experts where critical to their defense,[76] they should have such a right of access to exculpatory algorithms as well.

Principle III: Criminal defendants should have a meaningful right of contestation with respect to digital and machine evidence including, at a minimum, a right to be heard on development and testing procedures and meaningful access to experts.

Much has been written about a right of contestation by data subjects with regard to results of automated decision-making processes.[77] In the

[73] "Shining Light", note 60 above (arguing for open-source software for public law uses).

[74] *Weapons of Math Destruction*, note 71 above.

[75] See Chapter 9 in this volume.

[76] See *Ake* v. *Oklahoma*, 470 U.S. 68 (1986).

[77] See e.g. *Recommendation CM/Rec(2020)1 on the Human Rights Impacts of Algorithmic Systems* (Council of Europe, Committee of Ministers, 2020) at 9, 13 ("[a]ffected individuals and groups should be afforded effective means to contest relevant determinations and decisions … [which] should include an opportunity to be heard, a thorough review of the decision and the possibility to obtain a non-automated decision");

US criminal context, defendants already enjoy, at least in theory, a right to present a defense, encompassing a cluster of rights, including the right to be confronted by the witnesses against them, to testify in their own defense, and to subpoena and present witnesses in their favor. In the United States, a criminal defendant's right of contestation essentially encompasses everything already discussed with regard to access to the state's evidence, as well as to some exculpatory electronic communications. In addition, the US Supreme Court has held that the right to present a defense exists even where the government presents scientific evidence of guilt that a trial judge might deem definitive. The fact that an algorithm offers compelling evidence of guilt cannot preclude a defendant from offering a defense case.[78]

In addition to pre-trial access to the evidence itself, and information about its assumptions and processes, other rights that are key to a meaningful ability to contest the results of digital and machine evidence include the ability to consult experts where necessary. David Sklansky has argued that a right to such expert testimony, and not merely in-court cross-examination, should be deemed a central part of the Sixth Amendment right of confrontation.[79]

The importance of a right of contestation in the algorithmic design process might be less obvious. But in a changing world in which machine evidence is not easily scrutinized at the trial itself, the adversarialism upon which common law systems are built might need to partially shift from the trial stage to the design and development stage. Carl DiSalvo has coined the term "adversarial design"[80] to refer to design processes that incorporate political contestation among different stakeholders. While adversarial design would not be a case-specific process, it could still involve representatives from the defense community. Others have suggested appointing a "defender general" in each jurisdiction[81] who could inject adversarial scrutiny into various recurring criminal justice issues at the front end. Perhaps such a representative could oversee defense involvement in the design, testing, and validation of algorithms. This process would supplement, not supplant, case-specific machine access and discovery.

OECD, Council on Artificial Intelligence, *Recommendation of the Council on Artificial Intelligence*, 2020, OECD/LEGAL/0449, at s. 1.3.iv, https://legalinstruments.oecd.org/en/instruments/OECD-LEGAL-0449.

78 See *Holmes* v. *South Carolina*, 547 U.S. 319 (2006).

79 See David A. Sklansky, "Hearsay's Last Hurrah" (2009) 2009:1 *Supreme Court Review* 1.

80 Carl DiSalvo, *Adversarial Design* (Cambridge, MA: The MIT Press, 2012).

81 See Daniel Epps & William Ortman, "The Defender General" (2020) 168:6 *University of Pennsylvania Law Review* 1469.

The right of contestation with regard to sophisticated AI systems, the methods of which may well never be meaningfully understood by the parties, might also need to incorporate a right to delegated contestation, in the form of the right to another machine's scrutiny of the results. Other scholars have noted the possibility of "reversible" algorithms that would audit themselves or each other,[82] or have suggested that one machine opinion alone should be deemed legally insufficient for a conviction, in the absence of corroboration from a second expert system.[83]

At the trial itself, the right of contestation should first include the right to argue for exclusion of the evidence on reliability (*Frye*/*Daubert*) and/or authenticity grounds. In the US federal system, proponents of digital and machine evidence must present sufficient evidence to persuade the factfinder that the evidence is what the proponent says it is, e.g., that an email is from a particular sender.[84] In China, courts have used blockchain technology to facilitate authentication of electronically stored information.[85] Jurisdictions' authenticity method might reasonably change as the ability for malfeasors to falsify evidence changes in the future. Likewise, litigants should have the right to insist on exclusion of machine evidence if inputs are not proven accurate. For example, in the United Kingdom, a "representation" that is made "other than by a person" but that "depends for its accuracy on information supplied (directly or indirectly) by a person" is not admissible in criminal cases without proof that the "information was accurate."[86] In some cases, this showing will require testimony from the inputter.[87]

82 See Matthias Möller & Cornelis Vuik, "On the Impact of Quantum Computing Technology on Future Developments in High-Performance Scientific Computing" (2017) 19:4 *Ethics and Information Technology* 253.

83 See "Machine Testimony", note 26 above, at 2038.

84 See Federal Rules of Evidence, note 11 above, Rule 901(9) (allowing admission of a live witness to prove that a "process or system" produces an accurate result), and Rule 902(13), (14) (allowing admission of electronically stored and generated information upon presentation of a certification from a qualified witness who can attest to how the process works).

85 See e.g. Zhuhao Wang, "China's E-Justice Revolution" (2021) 105:1 *Judicature* 37 (noting how blockchain is used for authentication of electronic evidence); Ran Wang, "Legal Technology in Contemporary USA & China" (2020) 39:10549 *Computer Law & Security Review* 1 at 4.

86 Criminal Justice Act 2003, United Kingdom, c. 44, s. 129(1). If the inputter's "purpose" is "to cause … a machine to operate on the basis that the matter is as stated," it is treated as hearsay (see s. 115(3)), requiring the live testimony of the inputter (see s. 114(1)). The provision "does not affect the operation of the presumption that a mechanical device has been properly set or calibrated" (see s. 129(2)).

87 See e.g. ibid. (requiring inputter testimony); Gert Petrus van Tonder, "The Admissibility and Evidential Weight of Electronic Evidence in South African Legal Proceedings:

Principle IV: Criminal defendants should have a right to a factfinding process that is epistemically competent but that retains a human in the loop, so that significant decisions affecting their liberty are not entirely automated.

Principle IV(a): While parts of the criminal process can be automated, human safety valves must be incorporated into the process to ensure a role for equity, mercy, and human moral judgment.

Both substantive criminal law and criminal procedure in the United States have become more mechanical over the past few decades, from mandatory arrest laws, to sentencing guidelines, to laws criminalizing certain quantities of alcohol in drivers' blood.[88] The more mechanical that the system becomes on the front end via, e.g., mandatory arrest, prosecution, liability rules, and sentencing, the more that safety valves such as prosecutorial, fact-finder, and sentencing discretion become critical to avoid inequities, i.e., results that are legal but unjust.[89] Moreover, mechanical regimes reduce the possibility of mercy, understood to mean leniency or grace, beyond what a defendant justly deserves. While mercy may be irrational, it is a pedigreed and "important moral virtue" that shows compassion and a shared humanity.[90]

As digital and machine evidence accelerate the mechanization of justice, jurisdictions should ensure that human actors are still able to exercise equity and mercy at the charging, guilt, and/or punishment stages of criminal justice. Not only are humans needed to ensure that laws are not applied mechanically. They are needed because they are literally human – they bring a human component to moral judgment that is necessary, if not for dignity, then at least for public legitimacy[91] and, in turn, for

A Comparative Perspective" (LLM thesis, University of Western Cape, May 2013), etd.uwc.ac.za/xmlui/bitstream/handle/11394/4833/VanTonder_gp_llm_law_2013.pdf (requiring live testimony of signer of documents).

88 See generally Andrea Roth, "Trial by Machine" (2016) 104:5 *Georgetown Law Journal* 1245 ["Trial by Machine"] (noting how various aspects of American criminal justice have become more mechanical).

89 See e.g. Martha C. Nussbaum, "Equity and Mercy" (1993) 22:2 *Philosophy & Public Affairs* 83 at 93 and n. 19 (explaining that equity "may be regarded as a 'correcting' and 'completing' of legal justice").

90 Jeffrie G. Murphy, "Mercy and Legal Justice" in Jeffrie G. Murphy & Jean Hampton, *Forgiveness and Mercy* (Cambridge, UK: Cambridge University Press, 1998) 162 at 176.

91 Meg Leta Jones, "Right to a Human in the Loop: Political Constructions of Computer Automation and Personhood from Data Banks to Algorithms" (2017) 47:2 *Social Studies of Science* 216 at 231.

enforcement of criminal law.[92] In the United States, scholars have written since the 1970s of the illegitimacy of verdicts based solely on "naked statistical evidence," based on personhood concerns.[93] Moreover, humans add to the fact-finding process as well, rendering AI systems fairer without having to make such systems less accurate through simplification.[94] Corroborating these observations, recent AI guidelines and data privacy laws reflect the public's desire to keep humans in the loop with regard to automated decision-making, from the Council of Europe's call to "ensure that the introduction, operation and use of AI applications can be subject to effective judicial review,"[95] to the EU Directive prohibiting processes that produce an "adverse legal effect" on a subject "based solely on automated processing," without appropriate "safeguards for the rights and freedoms of the data subject, at least the right to obtain human intervention on the part of the controller."[96]

More concretely, criminal liability should not be based solely on an automated decision. Red light cameras are the closest the United States has come to fully automated liability, but thus far, such violations end only in a mailed traffic ticket rather than a criminal record. Moreover, in jurisdictions with juries, the power of jury nullification should continue undisturbed. It may well be that jurors' ability to decide historical fact, e.g., "was the light red?", could be curtailed, so long as their ability to decide evaluative data, e.g., "did the defendant drive 'recklessly'?", is preserved.[97] Indeed, some historical fact-finding might be removed from lay jurors, if they lack the "epistemic competence" to assess the evidence's probative value.[98]

[92] See generally Tom Tyler, "Procedural Justice, Legitimacy, and the Effective Rule of Law" (2003) 30:1 *Crime & Justice* 283 (explaining the role of procedural justice in inspiring compliance with law).

[93] See e.g. Laurence Tribe, "Trial by Mathematics: Precision and Ritual in the Legal Process" (1971) 84:6 *Harvard Law Review* 1329.

[94] See e.g. Katharine Miller, "When Algorithmic Fairness Fixes Fail: The Case for Keeping Humans in the Loop," *Stanford University: Institute for Human-Centered AI* (November 2, 2020), https://hai.stanford.edu/blog/when-algorithmic-fairness-fixes-fail-case-keeping-humans-loop.

[95] "Justice by Algorithm", note 47 above, at 9.13.

[96] See European Commission, Directive (EU) 2016/680 of April 27, 2016 (OJ 4.5.2018, L 119, 89), Art. 11.

[97] Others have called for this; see e.g. Josh Bowers, "Legal Guilt, Normative Innocence, and the Equitable Decision Not to Prosecute" (2010) 110:7 *Columbia Law Review* 1655 at 1723; Anna Roberts, "Dismissals as Justice" (2017) 69:2 *Alabama Law Review* 327 (discussing Model Penal Code §2.12).

[98] See e.g. Scott Brewer, "Scientific Expert Testimony and Intellectual Due Process" (1998) 107:6 *Yale Law Journal* 1535 at 1551 (arguing for a due process right to an "epistemically competent" fact-finder).

Jurisdictions could still ensure that humans remain in the loop by disallowing machine experts from giving dispositive testimony on ultimate questions of fact,[99] prohibiting detention decisions based solely on a risk assessment tool's score, and requiring a human expert potentially liable for injustices caused by inaccuracies to vouch for the results of any machine expert, before introducing results in a criminal proceeding.

Principle IV(b): Jurisdictions should ensure against automation complacency by developing effective human–machine interaction tools.

Keeping a human in the loop would be useless if that human deferred blindly to a machine. For example, if sentencing judges merely rubber-stamped scores of risk assessment tools, there would be little reason to ensure that judges remain in the loop.[100] Likewise, if left to their own devices, juries might irrationally defer to the apparent objectivity of machines.[101] A human in the loop requirement should entail the development of tools to guard against automation complacency. One underused tool in this regard is jury instructions. For example, where photographs are admitted as silent witnesses, the jury hears little about lens, angle, speed, placement, cameraperson bias, or other variables that might lead it to draw a false inference from the evidence. The jury should be educated about the effect of these variables on the image they are assessing.[102] Ultimately, jurisdictions should draw from the fields of human factors engineering, and human–computer interaction and collaboration, in designing ways to ensure a systems approach that keeps humans in the loop while leveraging the advantages of AI.

Principle IV(c): Jurisdictions should establish a formal means for stakeholders to challenge uses of digital and machine evidence that are fundamentally inconsistent with principles of human-delivered justice.

[99] Cf. Federal Rules of Evidence, note 11 above, Rule 704 (prohibiting expert witnesses from giving opinions as to whether criminal defendants have the mental state required).

[100] See Sonja B. Starr, "Evidence-Based Sentencing and the Scientific Rationalization of Discrimination" (2014) 66:4 *Stanford Law Review* 803 at 866–868 (suggesting that actuarial instruments drive judicial sentencing decisions).

[101] R. A. Bain, "Comment, Guidelines for the Admissibility of Evidence Generated by Computer for Purposes of Litigation" (1982) 15:4 *UC Davis Law Review* 951 at 961 (noting that fact-finders might be unduly "awed by computer technology").

[102] See Benjamin V. Madison III, "Seeing Can Be Deceiving: Photographic Evidence in a Visual Age – How Much Weight Does It Deserve?" (1984) 25:4 *William & Mary Law Review* 705 at 740 (arguing for jury instructions along these lines for photographs); see generally Jessica M. Silbey, "Judges as Film Critics: New Approaches to Filmic Evidence" (2004) 37:2 *University of Michigan Journal of Law Reform* 493 (suggesting trial safeguards for explaining testimonial infirmities of images to fact-finders).

Keeping a human in the loop also necessarily means taking steps to ensure against inappropriate uses of AI that threaten softer systemic values like dignity. For example, certain machines might be condemned as inherently dehumanizing, such as the penile plethysmograph[103] or deception detection.[104] Just as some modes of obtaining evidence are rejected as violating substantive due process, such as forcibly pumping a suspect's stomach to find evidence of drug use,[105] modes of determining guilt should be rejected if the public views them as inhumane. Other jurisdictions might decide that the "right to explanation" is so critical to public legitimacy that overly complex AI systems must be abandoned in criminal adjudication, even if such systems promise more accuracy.[106] Whatever approach jurisdictions adopt regarding these issues, they should resolve such issues first, and only then look for available technological enhancements of proof, rather than vice versa. Numerous scholars have written about the seduction of quantification and measurement,[107] and the Council of Europe expressly included in its guidelines for the use of AI in criminal justice that Member States should "ensure that AI serves overall policy goals, and that policy goals are not limited to areas where AI can be applied."[108]

III Conclusion

The principles for governing digital and machine evidence articulated in this chapter attempt to move beyond the adversarial/inquisitorial divide, and incorporate the thoughtful recent work of so many scholars, policymakers, and stakeholders worldwide in promulgating guidelines for the ethical and benevolent use of AI in decision-making affecting peoples'

[103] "Trial by Machine", note 88 above (describing the penile plethysmograph and arguing that its use violates dignitary interests of subjects).

[104] See ibid. (discussing personhood objections to various forms of lie detection evidence).

[105] See *Rochin* v. *California*, 342 U.S. 165 (1952).

[106] See e.g. "Justice by Algorithm", note 47 above, at 9.9 (Member States should "ensure that the essential decision-making processes of AI applications are explicable to their users and those affected by their operation").

[107] See e.g. Andrea Saltelli, "Ethics of Quantification or Quantification of Ethics?" (2020) 116:102509 *Futures* 1 (discussing "metric fixation"); "Trial by Machine", note 88 above, at 1281 (quoting Sally Engle Merry, *The Seductions of Quantification: Measuring Human Rights, Gender Violence and Sex Trafficking* (Chicago, IL: University of Chicago Press, 2016) (exploring the distorting effects of the quest for measurable indicators in the context of human rights)).

[108] "Justice by Algorithm", note 47 above, at 9.3.

lives. Applied to a common law adversarial criminal system such as that in the United States, these principles may manifest in existing statutory and constitutional rights, albeit in new ways. Applied to other nations' systems, these principles will manifest differently, perhaps because such systems already recognize the need for "out of court evidence gathering"[109] to ensure meaningful evaluation of complex evidence. On the other hand, as Sabine Gless has suggested, continental systems might find that party-driven examinations have an underappreciated role to play in ensuring reliability of machine evidence.[110]

As AI becomes more sophisticated, one key goal for all justice systems will be to ensure that AI is not merely given an objective to accomplish, such as "determine whether this witness is lying" or "determine if this person contributed to this DNA mixture," but is programmed to continually look to humans to express and update their preferences. If the former occurs, AI will preserve itself at all costs, and may engage in behavior antithetical to human values, to get there.[111] Only if machines are taught to continually seek feedback can AI remain benevolent. We cannot simply program machines to achieve the goals of criminal justice – public safety, social cohesion, equity, the punishment of the morally deserving, and the vindication of victims. We will have to ensure that humans have the last word on what justice means and how to achieve it.

109 "AI in the Courtroom", note 5 above, at 251.

110 "AI in the Courtroom", note 5 above, at 249.

111 See generally Stuart Russell, *Human Compatible: Artificial Intelligence and the Problem of Control* (New York, NY: Penguin Books, 2019).

MAMA K ©
1101
10110!
...

8

Robot Testimony?

A Taxonomy and Standardized Approach to the Use of Evaluative Data in Criminal Proceedings

EMILY SILVERMAN, JÖRG ARNOLD, AND SABINE GLESS*

I Drowsy at the Wheel?

In 2016, the Swiss media reported a collision involving a sports car and a motor scooter that resulted in serious injuries to the rider of the scooter.[1] Charges were brought against the car driver on the grounds that he was unfit to operate his vehicle. Driving a motor vehicle while unfit to do so is a crime pursuant to the Swiss Traffic Code[2] and one for which negligence suffices to establish culpability.[3] Although the accused denied consciously noticing that he was too tired to drive, prosecuting authorities claimed that he should have been aware of his unfitness, as the car's driving assistants had activated alerts several times during the journey.[4] Media coverage of the event did not report whether or how the accused defended himself against these alerts.

We refer to these alerts as "evaluative data" because they combine data with some form of robot evaluation. We argue that acknowledging this novel category of evidence is necessary because driving assistants

* We wish to express our gratitude to the Swiss National Science Foundation for ongoing support as well as to NYU's Jean Monnet Program for providing a forum in which to discuss our results.

1 See e.g. "Swiss Politician Fined Over Crash That Injured 17-Year-Old," *The Local* (October 31, 2016), www.thelocal.ch/20161031/swiss-politician-fined-over-crash-that-injured-17-year-old.

2 *Straßenverkehrsgesetz* (StVG), SR 741.01 (as of January 1, 2020), Art. 91, para. 2, www.admin.ch/opc/de/classified-compilation/19580266/index.html.

3 Ibid. Art. 100, para. 1.

4 Some weeks after the accident, the car driver accepted a summary penalty order. With such an order, the public prosecutor's office fixes a penalty for a criminal offense that will be enforced if the accused does not ask for the matter to be dealt with under the normal procedure by a court, Swiss Criminal Procedure Code, SR 312.0 (with effect from January 1, 2011) [Swiss CrimPC], Arts. 352–356, www.fedlex.admin.ch/eli/cc/2010/267/en.

and other complex information technology (IT) systems outfitted with artificial intelligence (AI) do more than simply employ sensors that engage in relatively straightforward tasks such as measuring the distance between the vehicle and lane markings. Driving assistants also evaluate data associated with indicators that they deem potential signs of fatigue, such as erratic steering movements or a human driver's drooping eyelids. They interpret this data and decide autonomously whether to alert the driver to drowsiness. When introduced into a criminal proceeding, this evaluative data can be referred to as a kind of robot testimony because it conveys an assessment made by a robot based on its autonomous observation.

This chapter aims to alleviate deficits in current understandings of the contributions such testimony can make to truth-finding in criminal proceedings. It explains the need to vet robot testimony and offers a taxonomy to assist in this process. In addition to a taxonomy of robot testimony, the chapter proposes a standardized approach to the presentation and evaluation of robot testimony in the fact-finding portion of criminal trials. Analysis focuses on a currently hypothetical criminal case, in which a drowsiness alert is proffered as evidence in a civil law jurisdiction such as Switzerland or Germany.

The chapter first introduces robot testimony and outlines the difficulties it poses when offered as evidence in criminal proceedings (Section II). Second, we propose a taxonomy for and a methodical way of using the results of a robot's assessment of human conduct (Section III). Based on traditional forensic science, robot testimony must first be grounded in the analog world, using a standardized approach to accessibility, traceability, and reproducibility. Then, with the help of forensic experts and the established concepts of source level and activity level, the evidence can be assessed on the offense level by courtroom actors, who are often digital laypersons (Section IV). As robot witnesses cannot be called to the stand and have their assessments subjected to cross-examination, the vetting of robot testimony in the courtroom poses a number of significant challenges. We suggest some ways to meet these challenges in Section V. In our conclusion, we call for legislatures to address the lacunae regarding the use of robot testimony in criminal proceedings, and we consider how criminal forensics might catch up with the overall debate on the trustworthiness of robots, an issue at the core of the current European debate regarding AI systems in general (Section VI). An outline of questions that stakeholders might want to ask when vetting robot testimony via an expert is presented in the Appendix.

II Introducing Robot Testimony

A core problem raised when defending oneself against a robot's evaluation of one's conduct, not to mention one's condition, is the overwhelming complexity of such an assessment. A car driver, as a rule, does not have the tools necessary to challenge the mosaic of components upon which the robot's evaluation is based, including the requisite knowledge of raw data, insights into source code, or the capacity for reverse engineering; this is certainly the case in a driving assistant's assessment that the human driver is drowsy.[5]

II.A A New Generation of Forensic Evidence Generated by Robots

Today, various makes of cars are equipped with robots, understood as artificially intelligent IT systems capable of sensing information in their environment, processing it, and ultimately deciding autonomously whether and how to respond.[6] Unlike rule-based IT systems, these robots decide themselves whether to act and when to intervene. Due in part to trade secrets, little is known about the detailed functioning of the various types of driving assistants in different car brands, but the general approach taken by drowsiness detection systems involves monitoring the human driver for behavior potentially indicative of fatigue. The systems collect data on the driver's steering movements, sitting posture, respiratory rate, and/or eyelid movements, etc.; they evaluate these indicators for signs of drowsiness or no signs of drowsiness; and, finally, on the basis of complex algorithms and elements of machine learning, choose whether to issue an alert to the driver.[7]

Robots that issue such alerts do so on the basis of the definition of drowsiness on which they were trained. They compare the data collected from the human driver they are monitoring with their training data, and then decide by means of the comparison whether or not the driver is drowsy. This use of training data creates several problems. If the robot

[5] For a more detailed discussion as to what information should be accessible, see Edward Imwinkelried, "Computer Source Code: A Source of the Growing Controversy over the Reliability of Automated Forensic Techniques" (2016) 66:1 *DePaul Law Review* 97.

[6] For the definition of robot, see Chapter 6 in this volume ("an engineered machine that senses, thinks, and acts," citing Patrick Lin, Keith Abney, & George Bekey, "Robot Ethics: Mapping the Issues for a Mechanized World" (2011) 175:5–6 *Artificial Intelligence* 942 at 943.

[7] Muhammad Ramzan, Hikmat U. Khan, Shahid Mahmood Awan *et al.*, "A Survey on State-of-the-Art Drowsiness Detection Techniques" (2019) 7 *Institute of Electrical and Electronics Engineers Access* 61904 ["Drowsiness Detection"] at 61908; for a legal assessment of such evidence, see Sabine Gless, Fred Lederer, & Thomas Weigend, "AI-Based Evidence in Criminal Trials?" (2024) 59:1 *Tulsa Law Review* 1.

is trained on data from drivers who have round eyes when they are wide awake and droopy eyes when they are sleepy, the robot will issue a drowsiness alert if the driver they are monitoring is droopy-eyed, even if that particular driver's eyes are droopy when he or she is rested.[8] Another difficulty that humans face when attempting to challenge an alert is that, on the one hand, it is not possible for all training data fed into the system to be recorded, and on the other hand, there is a lack of standards governing the data recorded from the driver. A provision requiring the implementation of a uniform data storage system in all automated vehicles, such as the Data Storage System for Automated Driving (DSSAD),[9] could resolve some of these issues and contribute to the advancement of a standardized, methodological approach to vehicle forensics.

Robots became mandatory for safety reasons in cars sold in the European Union beginning in 2022,[10] thus laying the groundwork for an influx of robot testimony in criminal proceedings. The hallmark of this data is the digital layer of intelligence added when robots evaluate human conduct and record their assessments. Up until now, there has been no taxonomy that facilitates a robust and common understanding of what sets evaluative data apart from raw data (Section III.A.1) or measurement data (Section III.A.2). The following sections first detail the difficulties raised by robot data, and then propose a taxonomy of raw data, measurement data, and evaluative data.

II.B Evidentiary Issues Raised by Robot Testimony

Basic questions arise as to the conditions under which the prosecution, the defense counsel, and the courts should be able to tap into the vast emerging pool of evaluative data and how robot testimony might be of assistance in the criminal process. Under what circumstances can evaluations

8 For different ways to train systems to detect drowsiness, see Elena Magán López, M. Paz Sesmero Lorente, Juan Manuel Alonso-Weber *et al.*, "Driver Drowsiness Detection by Applying Deep Learning Techniques to Sequences of Images" (2022) 12:3 *Applied Sciences* 1145; Samy Bakheet & Ayoub Al-Hamadi, "A Framework for Instantaneous Driver Drowsiness Detection Based on Improved HOG Features and Naïve Bayesian Classification" (2021) 11:2 *Brain Sciences* 240.

9 For details, see European Union, The European Parliament, & The Council of the European Union, Regulation (EU) 2019/2144 of 27 November 2019 on Type-Approval Requirements for Motor Vehicles, OJ 2019 L 325, ECE/TRANS/WP.29/2020/81 (EU: Official Journal of the European Union, 2019) [Regulation 2019/2144].

10 See ibid., as well as *Straßenverkehrsgesetz (SVG) (Entwurf)* (Swiss Reform Proposal), BBl 2021 3027 (December 29, 2021), www.fedlex.admin.ch/eli/fga/2021/3027/de.

generated by robots involved in robot–human interactions serve as evidence in criminal trials? And in the context of the hypothetical example used in this chapter, can alerts issued by a drowsiness detection system serve as meaningful evidence that a specific human driver was on notice of his or her unfitness?

Answers to these questions depend on many factors and require a more comprehensive analysis than can be given here.[11] This chapter therefore focuses on one fundamental challenge facing fact-finders:[12] their capacity as digital laypersons, with the help of forensic experts, to understand robot testimony.

One of the problems encountered when assisting digital laypersons to understand robot testimony is the fact that robot testimony is not generated by a dedicated set of forensic tools. While radar guns, breathalyzers, and DNA test kits are designed expressly for the purpose of producing evidence,[13] driving assistance systems are consumer gadgets swept into an evidentiary mission creep.[14] They monitor lane keeping, sitting posture, and respiratory rate, etc. from the perspective of safety. Car manufacturers are currently free to configure them as they see fit, so long as they satisfy the standards set by the applicable type approval regulations,[15] which are the minimum set of regulatory, technical, and safety requirements required before a product can be sold in a particular country. The lack of commonly accepted forensic standards causes manifold problems, as it is unclear how a drowsiness detection system distinguishes between a driver sitting awkwardly in the driver's seat due to fatigue and a driver sitting awkwardly due to, say, a vigorous physical workout. To the best of our knowledge, these systems do not include baseline data for a specific driver, but are trained on available data chosen by the manufacturer. To address questions as to whether their results should be admissible as evidence in a court of law, and if so, what

11 For issues raised when using new technology for evidentiary purposes, see Edward Imwinkelried, "The Admissibility of Scientific Evidence: Exploring the Significance of the Distinction between Foundational Validity and Validity as Applied" (2020) 70:3 *Syracuse Law Review* 817 ["Scientific Evidence"] at 818–820.

12 In this chapter, the term "fact-finder" is used to refer to the legal actor responsible for determining the facts in a criminal case, i.e., judge or bench in a case that goes to trial, or prosecutor in a case disposed of by summary penalty order.

13 See Erin Murphy, "The New Forensics: Criminal Justice, False Certainty, and the Second Generation of Scientific Evidence" (2007) 95:3 *California Law Review* 721 at 723–724.

14 See Paul Grimm, Maura Grossmann, & Gordon Cormack, "Artificial Intelligence as Evidence" (2021) 19:1 *Northwest Journal of Technology and Intellectual Property* 9 (using the term "function creep").

15 For details, see e.g. the Appendixes to Regulation 2019/2144, note 9 above.

the information content of such data really is, a taxonomy to ground expert evidence is needed. Before drowsiness alerts and other evaluative data generated by non-forensic robots that serve primarily consumer demands can be used in court, a special vetting process may also be necessary, and possibly even a new evidentiary framework (see Section VI). One solution could be to require manufacturers to provide source code, training data, and data on validation testing, and to require manufacturers to share information regarding potential programming errors. The need for such information is clear but access is not yet possible, as confidentiality issues associated with proprietary data and the protection of trade secrets will first have to be addressed by legislatures or the courts.

As the use of robots to monitor human conduct becomes more common, robots' assessments may seem reminiscent of eyewitness testimony. As things stand today,[16] however, robots – unlike human witnesses – cannot be brought into the courtroom and confronted directly. They cannot be called to the stand and asked to explain their assessments under cross-examination. Instead, digital forensic experts serve as intermediaries to bridge this gap. These experts aim to translate a robot's message into a form that is comprehensible to lawyers. But in order to do so, experts must have access to the data recorded by the robot as well as the tools to secure and the competence to interpret this data. Experts must also clearly define their role in the fact-finding process. On what subjects should they be permitted to opine, e.g., that a drowsiness alert indicates that an average person, according to the training material used, was likely drowsy when the alert was issued? And could such testimony be rebutted with evidence regarding, e.g., the accused's naturally drooping eyelids, due perhaps to advanced age, or habitually relaxed sitting posture?

II.C Searching for the Truth with the Help of Robots

In most criminal justice systems, statutory provisions and case law aim to render the evidentiary process rational and transparent while upholding the principle of permitting the fact-finder to engage in the unfettered assessment of evidence. The parties have a vital interest in participating in this crucial step of the trial. In our hypothetical example of drowsiness

[16] For a visionary account of future courtrooms, see Frederic Lederer, "Technology-Augmented and Virtual Courts and Courtrooms" in M. R. McGuire & Thomas Holt (eds.), *The Routledge Handbook of Technology, Crime and Justice* (London, UK: Routledge, 2017) 518 at 525–526.

alerts, the prosecution will claim that alerts issued by the driving assistants were triggered by the accused's drowsy driving, and the defense will counter that the driving assistants issued false alarms, perhaps by wrongly interpreting certain steering movements or naturally drooping eyelids as signs of drowsiness. The law provides little guidance on how to address such conflicting claims. The law also offers little guidance as to how the parties, the defense in particular, can participate in the vetting of robot testimony or question the admissibility or reliability of such evidence.[17] One difficulty is that forensic experts and lawyers have not yet developed sufficiently differentiated terminology; often all data stored in a computer system or exchanged between systems is simply labeled digital evidence.[18] Yet such a distinction is crucial, as failing to make distinctions runs the risk of lumping together very different kinds of information. If these kinds of data are to be of service in the fact-finding process, they must always be interpreted in the context of the circumstances in which they originated.[19]

Inquisitorial-type criminal procedures, in particular, seem vulnerable to the risks posed by robot testimony, thanks to their broad, truth-seeking missions. For example, Article 139 of the Swiss Criminal Procedure Code (Swiss CrimPC) states that "in order to establish the truth, the criminal justice authorities shall use all the legally admissible evidence that is relevant in accordance with the latest scientific findings and experience."[20] The Swiss CrimPC is silent, however, as to what "legally admissible evidence that is relevant in accordance with the latest scientific findings and experience" actually is. While case law and scholarship have provided an abundance of views on the admissibility in court of a small number of recognized categories of evidence, until now, they have provided little guidance on how to proceed when technological advances create new kinds of evidence that do not fall within these categories. There is consensus that

[17] For a discussion on issues concerning scientific evidence, cf. Edward Imwinkelried, "Improving the Presentation of Expert Testimony to the Trier of Fact: An Epistemological Insight in Search of an Evidentiary Theory" (2020) 52:1 *Arizona State Law Journal* 49 at 57–59.

[18] Eoghan Casey, *Digital Evidence and Computer Crime*, 3rd ed. (London, UK: Academic Press, 2011) at 7.

[19] For further analysis, see Alex Biedermann & Joëlle Vuille, "Digital Evidence, 'Absence' of Data and Ambiguous Patterns of Reasoning" (2016) 16:S86–S96 *Digital Investigation* S86 at S90; Joëlle Vuille & Franco Taroni, "Measuring Uncertainty in Forensic Science" (2021) 24:1 *Institute of Electrical and Electronics Engineers Instrumentation & Measurement Magazine* 5 at 8.

[20] Swiss CrimPC, note 4 above, Art. 139, www.fedlex.admin.ch/eli/cc/2010/267/en#a165.

these new types of evidence must comply with existing rules of presentation and accepted *modi operandi*.[21] In cases in which specialist knowledge and skills are necessary, Article 182 of the Swiss CrimPC, e.g., requires the court to ask an expert "to determine or assess the facts of the case."[22] In a rather surprising parallel to an approach broadly seen as adversarial in nature, if a party wishes to challenge an expert's determination or assessment, it can target the source and the reliability of the data, the expert's methodology, or specific aspects of the expert's interpretation, such as statistical reasoning.[23]

The strengthening of fair trial principles and defense rights in vetting evidence can be seen in recent decisions taken by the German Constitutional Court (*Bundesverfassungsgericht*) that recognize access to raw data, i.e., the initial representation of physical information in digital form, as a prerequisite for an effective defense.[24] In November 2020, e.g., the Constitutional Court held that defendants in speeding cases have the right, in principle,[25] to inspect all data generated for fact-finding purposes, including raw data.[26]

[21] For the *Daubert/Frye* test in the United States, see Andrea Roth, "Machine Testimony" (2017) 126:1 *Yale Law Journal* 1972 ["Machine Testimony"] at 1981–1983; for the more principled-driven "systematic approach" in Germany, see Sabine Gless, "AI in the Courtroom: A Comparative Analysis of Machine Evidence in Criminal Trials" (2020) 51:2 *Georgetown Journal of International Law* 195 ["AI in the Courtroom"] at 234–237.

[22] Joelle Vuille & Franco Taroni, "Measuring Uncertainty in Forensic Science" (2021) 24:1 *IEEE Instrumentation & Measurement Magazine* 5 at 5–9; Steven Lund & Hari Iyer, "Likelihood Ratio as Weight of Forensic Evidence: A Closer Look" (2017) 122:27 *Journal of Research of National Institute of Standards and Technology* 1; Filipo Sharevski, "Rules of Professional Responsibility in Digital Forensics: A Comparative Analysis" (2015) 10:2 *Journal of Digital Forensics, Security and Law* 39; Nils O. Ommen, Markus Blut, Christof Backhaus *et al.*, "Toward a Better Understanding of Stakeholder Participation in the Service Innovation Process: More than One Path to Success" (2016) 69:7 *Journal of Business Research* 2409.

[23] Edward Imwinkelried, "The Importance of Forensic Metrology in Preventing Miscarriages of Justice: Intellectual Honesty About the Uncertainty of Measurement in Scientific Analysis" (2014) 7:2 *John Marshall Law Journal* 333 ["Forensic Metrology"] at 353–362.

[24] Raw data is comparable to DNA taken from blood samples on a murder weapon in the analog world.

[25] The court conceded, however, a practical need for procedural flexibility in small-scale crimes *en masse*, i.e., certain traffic violation cases: see *BVerfG Beschluss* (Order of German Federal Constitutional Court) of November 12, 2020, 2 BvR 1616/18.

[26] Ibid. nos. 32–34 and 50–55. The Constitutional Court based its decision on two articles of the *Grundgesetz* (German Basic Law) (with effect from May 23, 1949), Art. 2, para. 1 (which grants a general right of liberty and autonomy) and Art. 20, para. 3 (which captures a specific aspect of the rule of law – *Rechtsstaatlichkeitsprinzip*).

III A Taxonomy for the Use of Robot Testimony

Robot testimony is a potentially useful addition to the evidentiary process, but only if its meaning for a case can be communicated to the fact-finder in a comprehensible way. In order to facilitate this communication, we propose a taxonomy of robot testimony. The taxonomy distinguishes between three types of machine-readable data, beginning with the least complex form and ending with the most complex form. We also suggest how the taxonomy can be used in practice, by differentiating circumstantial information, which refers to the context in which the data is found (Section III.B), from information content, the forensically relevant information that the expert can deduce from the properly identified data (Section III.C).

III.A Categories of Machine-Readable Data

The term "data" is widely used, both in everyday language and in the legal context, but while the term was used as a synonym for any kind of information in the past, digitalization has led to changes in its usage. Today, the term is often used to mean any kind of machine-readable information.[27] This meaning is still very broad. When coupled with the lack of a legal definition in the law of criminal procedure, a broad definition can cause problems in situations where a finer distinction is required, e.g., when machine-readable information is introduced as evidence in a criminal case and a forensic expert is needed to explain the exact nature of the information being proffered. This chapter suggests that there are three categories of data: raw data, measurement data, and evaluative data.

III.A.1 Raw Data

Digital forensic experts define raw data as the initial representation of physical information in digital form. Raw data generated by sensors, e.g., captures measurements of physical indicators such as time or frequency, mass, angles, distances, speed, acceleration, or temperature. Raw data can also convey the status information of a technical system, i.e., on/off, operation status, errors, failure alarms, etc., or the rotational speed measured by sensors placed at the four wheels of a vehicle. It is necessary to keep in mind that raw data, the basic currency of information for digital forensics,

[27] "Data is the representation of information in a form that can be processed by a machine": Dino Buzzetti, "Digital Editions and Text Processing" in Marilyn Deegan & Kathryn Sutherland (eds.), *Text Editing, Print and the Digital Word* (Farnham, UK: Ashgate, 2009) 46.

may contain errors, and that tolerances[28] must be considered. In order for this kind of information to be understood, it must be processed by algorithms, but at least in theory, its validity could always be checked by a human, e.g., by using a stopwatch, physically measuring the distance traveled, or checking whether a system was turned on or off.

Where a system operates as intended, the raw data produced by the system is deemed objective, although verification and interpretation[29] as well as an assessment supplied by a forensic expert may be necessary. Once the raw data has been collected, it is available for processing by algorithms into one of the other data categories, i.e., measurement data or, with the participation of AI-based robots, evaluative data.

III.A.2 Measurement Data

At present, the most important category of data is probably measurement data. This category is produced when raw data is processed with the help of algorithms. Given sufficient time and resources, if the algorithms involved are accessible, measurement data can theoretically be traced back to the original raw data. For example, the measurement data generated by the tachometer is vehicular speed. With the help of an algorithm, a tachometer calculates vehicular speed by taking the average of the raw data noted by rotational sensors located at each of the four wheels of a vehicle, known as wheel speed values. Wheel slip, another example of measurement data, is produced by calculating the difference between the four separate wheel speed values. In the event of an accident, this kind of processed data enables a forensic expert to testify about wheel slip and/or skidding, and state whether the vehicle was still under the control of the driver by the time of the incident or whether the driver had already lost control of it. While the raw data in this example would not mean very much to fact-finders, they could understand the meaning of the speed or wheel slip of a vehicle at a particular moment.

The distinction between raw data and measurement data is a clear one, in theory, but it can become blurred. For example, raw data must be made

[28] In terms of measurement, the difference between the maximum and minimum dimensions of permissible errors is called the "tolerance." The allowable range of errors prescribed by law, such as with industrial standards, can also be referred to as tolerance; see Measurement Fundamentals, "What Is Tolerance?" www.keyence.co.in/ss/products/measure-sys/measurement-selection/basic/tolerance.jsp.

[29] Sandra Wachter & Brent Mittelstadt, "A Right to Reasonable Inferences: Re-Thinking Data Protection Law in the Age of Big Data and AI" (2019) 2019:2 *Columbia Business Law Review* 494 at 510–511.

readable, and therefore processed, before it can be interpreted. This difficulty does not, however, call the taxonomy offered by the chapter into doubt as a matter of principle, but rather shows the importance of having categories that support differentiation, similar to the way in which the distinction between a fact and an opinion in evidence law distinguishes between two kinds of evidence.[30]

III.A.3 Evaluative Data

The third category of data in our taxonomy is new, and we call it evaluative data. This kind of data is the product of a robot's autonomous assessment of its environment. In contrast to measurement data, the genesis of evaluative data cannot, by definition, be completely verified by humans because the digital layer inherent to robot testimony cannot be completely reconstructed.

Evaluative data causes problems for fact-finding on several different levels. Using the drowsiness alert hypothethical,[31] a human cannot reconstruct the exact reckoning of a drowsiness detection system that monitors a human for behavior indicative of fatigue, because while this robot does continuously measure and evaluate the driver's steering movements and tracks factors such as sitting posture and eyelid movements, the robot does not record all its measurements. It evaluates these indicators for signs of drowsiness or no signs of drowsiness, and when it determines that the threshold set by the programmer or by the system itself has been reached, it issues an alert to the driver and records the issuance of the alert.

This system cannot explain its evaluation of human conduct regarding a particular episode.[32] In fact, the operation by which a driving assistant reaches its conclusion in a particular case is almost always an impenetrable process, thanks to the simultaneous processing of a plethora of data in a given situation, the notorious black box problem of machine learning, and walls of trade secrets.[33] In the field of digital forensics, evaluative data is therefore a novel category of evidence that requires careful scrutiny.

[30] Richard O. Lempert, Samuel R. Gross, James S. Liebman *et al.*, *A Modern Approach to Evidence*, 5th ed. (St. Paul, MN: West Academic Publishing, 2014) [*Modern Approach*] at 5.

[31] For more details, see "Drowsiness Detection", note 7 above, at 61904–61919.

[32] Cynthia Rudin, "Stop Explaining Black Box Machine Learning Models for High Stakes Decisions and Use Interpretable Models Instead" (2019) 1:5 *Nature Machine Intelligence* 206.

[33] "Machine Testimony", note 21 above; Rebecca Wexler, "Life, Liberty, and Trade Secrets: Intellectual Property in the Criminal Justice System" (2018) 70:5 *Stanford Law Review* 1343; "AI in the Courtroom", note 21 above.

It may be possible to vet the reliability of this category of data by focusing on the configuration of the system's threshold settings for issuing an alert and then searching for empirical methods by which to test the robustness of its results. Before that point can be reached, however, fact-finders need a functional taxonomy and a standardized methodological approach so they can understand whether, or rather under what conditions, they can challenge a system's issuance of drowsiness alerts.

Using evaluative data for evidentiary purposes raises questions on a number of levels, some of which are linked to the factual level of circumstantial information (Section III.B) and to information content (Section III.C). For example, the question arises as to whether the issuance of a drowsiness alert can be used to prove that the accused driver was drowsy or whether it can only be used to prove that an average person could be deemed drowsy given the data recorded by the robot while the accused was driving. Other questions pertain to the evidentiary level, such as whether the issuance of an alert can be used to prove that the driver was on notice of unfitness, or whether the issuance of an alert could even be used to prove that the driver was in fact unfit to operate the vehicle.

III.B Circumstantial Information

Raw data, measurement data, and evaluative data require a context, referred to in the field of forensics as circumstantial information,[34] to enable fact-finders to draw meaningful inferences that can be used to establish facts in a legal proceeding. In our drowsiness alert hypothetical, when a driver is charged with operating a vehicle while unfit to do so, the data read out of the car is useful only if it can be established what the data means for that particular car, what the normal operating conditions of the car are, who was driving the car at the time of the accident, etc. It is important to explain what kinds of data were recorded in the run-up to the drowsiness alert and to determine whether the manufacturer submitted the relevant validation data for that specific system. Otherwise, the machine learning mechanisms cannot be vetted. It might turn out, e.g., that the training data and machine learning methods used to teach robots to distinguish between drowsy and not drowsy differ significantly between the systems used by different manufacturers.

[34] Robert Cook *et al.*, "A Hierarchy of Propositions: Deciding Which Level to Address in Casework" (1998) 38:4 *Science & Justice* 231 ["Hierarchy of Propositions"]; for the notion of "circumstantial evidence" in law, see *Modern Approach*, note 30 above, at 217–219.

The furnishing of circumstantial information is an important and delicate step in the communication between forensic experts and lawyers. While courts in continental Europe, and judges and/or juries in other jurisdictions, are mandated to determine the truth, the role of a forensic expert is a different one. The forensic expert's task is to keep an open mind and to focus solely on evaluating the forensic findings in light of propositions offered by court or parties (see Section IV.D).[35] In our drowsiness alert hypothetical, the expert will be asked to assess the data read out of the car in light of the proposition of the prosecution, namely that the accused was in fact the driver of the car and alerts were issued because the driver was driving while drowsy, as well as pursuant to the proposition of the defense, namely that the issuance of alerts was due to circumstances completely unrelated to the driver's fitness to operate the vehicle. In order truly to assist the court, experts must avoid stepping outside the boundaries of scientific expertise. They must not step into the role of the fact-finder.

III.C Information Content

Once experts have explained the details of the relevant data and provided the requisite circumstantial information, the court and the parties should be in a position to formulate their propositions about its information content. In this context, information content is understood as the forensically relevant information deduced from raw, measurement, and evaluative data. In our hypothetical, the fact-finders ought to be able to decide whether, in their view, the alerts issued by the drowsiness detection system are evidence that the human driver was in fact unfit to operate a vehicle or whether the alerts are better interpreted as false alarms.

In a Swiss or German courtroom, the expert will be asked not only to present and verify the information content of a particular piece of evidence, but to provide a sort of likelihood ratio regarding the degree to which the various propositions are supported.[36] While this approach is not universal,[37] such an obligation is important in cases where evaluative

[35] For more detail on the expectation that experts provide a meaningful quantitative measure of uncertainties, see "Forensic Metrology", note 23 above, at 353–362.

[36] Joelle Vuille & Joerg Arnold, "L'appréciation des preuves techniques en matière de circulation routière – les traces numériques" (Assessment of Forensic Traffic Data – Digital Evidence) (2019) 3 *Circulation Routière* 60; on the expectation in the United States that experts provide a meaningful quantitative measure of uncertainties, see "Forensic Metrology", note 23 above, at 353–362.

[37] For case law in the United States discussing the role of likelihood in the context of DNA evidence, see "Forensic Metrology", note 23 above, at 370, n. 77.

data is proffered as evidence. Evaluative data in the form of drowsiness alerts cannot simply be taken at face value, and experts must therefore have the right conceptual tools with which to assess it.

IV A Standardized Approach to Interpreting Robot Testimony

Having established a tri-part taxonomy for the use of robot testimony, we now suggest a standardized approach regarding its interpretation in a court of law. Legal actors can draw on existing concepts[38] in concert with the new taxonomy proposed here, but the traditional approach will have to be modified so as to accommodate the special needs of assessing evaluative data for fact-finding in a criminal case. A sort of tool kit is needed to test whether a robot generates trustworthy evidence. In our hypothetical, the question can be framed as whether a drowsiness detection system reliably detects reasonable parameters related to a human driver's fitness to operate a vehicle.

In principle, the general rules for obtaining and presenting evidence in a criminal case apply to robot testimony. In our hypothetical, the vehicle involved in the accident will be seized. Subsequently, the search for analog evidence will follow existing provisions of the applicable code of criminal procedure regarding the admissibility and reliability of potential evidence. As far as digital evidence is concerned, various modifications stemming from the particularities of using bits and bytes for fact-finding will apply,[39] and specific risks of error will have to be addressed. For known problems, such as the loss of information during the transmission of data, solutions may already be at hand.[40] But new problems arise, including, e.g., the sheer volume of data that may be relevant if it becomes necessary to validate a specific alert issued by a vehicle's drowsiness detection system. In such cases, it is essential for stakeholders to understand what is meant by accessibility (Section IV.A) and traceability (Section IV.B) of relevant data, as well as the reproducibility (Section IV.C) and interpretation (Section IV.D) of results provided by the expert.

38 See "Hierarchy of Propositions", note 34 above.

39 For details on the technology, see "SWGDE Best Practices for Archiving Digital and Multimedia Evidence" (Scientific Working Group on Digital Evidence, 2020), www.swgde.org/documents/published-complete-listing; for a discussion on the need to update procedural codes, see Orin Kerr, "Digital Evidence and the New Criminal Procedure" (2005) 105:1 *Columbia Law Review* 279 ["New Criminal Procedure"] at 285–287.

40 Take, e.g., the verification of raw data by means of checksums (or hash values). Paul Grimm, Daniel Capra, & Gregory Joseph, "Authenticating Digital Evidence" (2017) 69:1 *Baylor Law Review* 1 ["Authenticating Digital Evidence"] at 17 and 41.

IV.A Accessibility

An expert should first establish what data is available, i.e., raw, measurement, or evaluative, and how it was accessed. Digitalization poses a challenge to procedural codes tailored to the analog world because data and its information content are not physically available and cannot be seized. This characteristic of data may lead to problems with regard to location and accessibility. For example, even if the data recorded by a driving assistant is stored locally in a car's data storage device, simply handing over the device to the authorities or granting them access to it will probably not suffice. Decrypting tools[41] will have to be made available to the forensic expert, and the difficulties associated with decryption explained to the fact-finder.

Some regulations pertaining to accessibility are being pursued, e.g., the movement in Europe toward a DSSAD. As early as 2006, uniform data requirements were introduced in the United States to limit the effects of accessibility problems with regard to car data; these requirements govern the accuracy, collection, storage, survivability, and retrievability of crash event data, e.g., for vehicles equipped with Event Data Recorders (EDRs) in the 5 seconds before a collision.[42] In 2019, working groups were established at the domestic and international levels to prepare domestic legislation on EDRs for automated driving.[43] And in 2020, the UN Economic Commission for Europe (UNECE) began working toward the adoption of standardized technical regulations relevant for type approval.[44] The UNECE aims to define the availability and accessibility of data and to establish read-out standards.[45] It would also require cars to have a

[41] For issues involving compelled decryption, see Orin Kerr & Bruce Schneier, "Encryption Workarounds" (2018) 106:4 *Georgetown Law Journal* 989; Laurent Sacharoff, "Unlocking the Fifth Amendment: Passwords and Encrypted Devices" (2018) 87:1 *Fordham Law Review* 203.

[42] National Highway Traffic Safety Administration (NHTSA) Event Data Recorders Rules, 49 CFR Pt. 563, www.law.cornell.edu/cfr/text/49/part-563 [Data Recorders Rules].

[43] For Germany, see *Bundestagsdrucksache* (Bundestag Document) BT-Drs 19/16250 of December 30, 2019 (Ger.); for a publication prepared under the auspices of the UNECE's WP 29, see also United Nations, UN Economic and Social Council, Revised Framework Document on Automated/Autonomous Vehicles, ECE/TRANS/WP.29/2019/34 (Geneva: UN, 2019).

[44] OEDR is discussed at United Nations, UN Economic and Social Council, Proposal for a New UN Regulation on Uniform Provisions Concerning the Approval of Vehicles with Regards to Automated Lane Keeping System, ECE/TRANS/WP.29/2020/81 (Geneva: UN, 2020) ["Uniform Provisions"] at Chapter 7, DSSAD at Chapter 8.

[45] Cf. United Nations, Agreement Concerning the Adoption of Harmonized Technical United Nations Regulations for Wheeled Vehicles, Equipment and Parts, E/ECE/TRANS/505/Rev.3/Add.156 of March 4, 2021, no. 8 'Data Storage System for Automated Systems'; reading out the data will be possible by using On-Board Diagnostics Port, 2nd generation (OBD II port), launched in 1996, for further information, see UNECE, "Automated Driving," https://unece.org/automated-driving.

standardized data storage system.[46] However, these efforts will not lead to the recording of all data that might possibly be relevant for the establishment of facts in a criminal court.

IV.B Traceability: Chain of Custody

The second step toward the use of machine-readable data is a chain of custody that ensures traceability. A chain of custody should be built from the moment data is retrieved to the moment it is introduced in the courtroom. Data retrieval, also called read-outs of data, is the process by which raw data, and if relevant decrypted data, is translated into readable and comprehensible information. The results are typically documented in a protected report that is accessible to defined and identified users by means of a pre-set access code.[47] To ensure traceability, every action taken by the forensic expert must be documented, including when and where the expert connected to the system, what kind of equipment and what software was used, what was downloaded, e.g., file name, file size, and checksum,[48] and where the downloaded material was stored.[49]

Traceability can be supported when a standard forensic software is used, e.g., the Crash Data Retrieval tool designed to access and retrieve data stored in the EDRs standard in cars manufactured in the United States.[50] In each country, the legislature could ensure the traceability of data generated by driving assistance systems by establishing a requirement to integrate a data storage system as a condition of type approval. Such a step could eliminate the difficulties currently associated with the traceability of data.

46 Uniform Provisions, note 44 above, at Chapter 7.

47 E.g. the forensic expert will use the vehicle identification number (VIN) when accessing an EDR.

48 A checksum is a value that represents the number of bits in a transmission message and is used by IT professionals to detect high-level errors within data transmissions; see "Checksum," *TechTarget*, www.techtarget.com/searchsecurity/definition/checksum.

49 See ISO/IEC 27043:2015 Information Technology, Security Techniques, Incident Investigation Principles and Processes (International Organization for Standardization, 2015), www.iso.org/standard/44407.html; ISO/IEC 27037:2012 Guidelines for Identification, Collection, Acquisition and Preservation of Digital Evidence (International Organization for Standardization, 2012); ISO/IEC 27040 Storage Security (International Organization for Standardization, 2015).

50 See Data Recorders Rules, note 42 above; Jeremy Daily, Nathan Singleton, Elizabeth Downing *et al.*, "The Forensics Aspects of Event Data Recorders" (2008) 3:3 *Journal of Digital Forensics, Security and Law* 29; Nhien-An Le-Khac, Daniel Jacobs, John Nijhoff *et al.*, "Smart Vehicle Forensics: Challenges and Case Study" (2020) 109 *Future Generation Computer Systems* 500 at 503.

IV.C *Reproducibility*

The third basic requirement for establishing trustworthy robot testimony is reproducibility.[51] Simply stated, the condition of reproducibility is met if a second expert can retrieve the data, run an independent analysis, and produce the same results as the original expert. Whether this condition can be achieved in the foreseeable future probably depends less on having comprehensive access to all theoretically relevant data and more on the development of smart software that can evaluate the reliability of a specific robot's testimony. This software could work by analyzing the probability of error on the basis of simulations using the raw and measurement data recorded by the robot, looking for bias, and testing the system's overall trustworthiness.

Reproducibility in the context of evaluative data generated by a consumer product is particularly challenging. Driving assistants issue alerts on the basis of a plethora of data processed in a particular driving situation, and as noted above, only a subset of the data is stored. This subset is the only data available for forensic analysis. Reproducibility therefore currently depends on ex ante specifications of what data must be stored, and what minimum quality standards the stored data must meet in order to ensure that an incident can be reconstructed with the reliability necessary to answer both factual and legal questions.

In our drowsiness alert hypothetical, a key requirement for reproducibility would be the unambiguous identification of the vehicle at issue and of the data storage device if there is one. In addition, the report generated during the retrieval process must contain all necessary information about the conditions under which that process took place, e.g., VIN, operator, software version, time, and date. This discussion regarding reproducibility demonstrates the crucial importance of establishing minimum specifications for data storage devices, specifications that could probably be implemented most efficiently at the car's type-approval stage. As these specifications are responsible for ensuring reproducibility, they ought to be defined in detail by law and standardized internationally.

IV.D *Interpretation Using the Three-Level Approach*

The fourth step of a sound standardized approach to the use of machine-readable data in court requires the data to be interpreted systematically

[51] Craig Cooley, "Forensic Science and Capital Punishment Reform: An 'Intellectually Honest' Assessment" (2007) 17:2 *George Mason University Civil Rights Law Journal* 299 at 353.

in light of the propositions of the courtroom actors.[52] When courts lack the specialist knowledge necessary to determine or assess the facts of the case, they look to forensic experts.[53] In order to bridge the knowledge gap, lawyers and forensic experts need a common taxonomy, a common understanding of the scientific reasoning that applies to the evaluation of data,[54] and a common understanding of the kinds of information that forensic science can deliver.

Following an established approach in forensic science, three levels of questions and answers should be recognized: source level, activity level, and offense level.[55] These levels help, first, to distinguish pure expert knowledge (source level) from proposition-based evaluation of forensic findings by the expert in a particular case (activity level), and second, to distinguish these two levels from the court's competences and duties in fact-finding (offense level).

In our drowsiness alert hypothetical, before deciding whether to convict or acquit the accused, the court will want to know whether there is any data to be found in the driving assistance system's data storage system (source level), whether alerts have been issued (activity level), and whether there is any other evidence that might shed light on the driver's fitness or lack thereof to operate a vehicle (offense level).

IV.D.1 Source Level

In forensic methodology, the source level is associated with the source of evidence. The first question is whether any forensic traces in analog or digital form are available, and if so what kind of traces, e.g., blood, drugs, fibers, or raw data. Source-level answers are normally simple results with defined tolerances;[56] the answer may simply be yes, no, or undefined.

In the context of digital evidence such as our drowsiness alert hypothetical, the source-level question would be whether there is any relevant

[52] "Hierarchy of Propositions", note 34 above.

[53] See Swiss CrimPC, note 4 above, Art. 182 and German Code of Criminal Procedure (as amended March 25, 2022), Art. 75.

[54] Colin Howson & Peter Urbach, *Scientific Reasoning: The Bayesian Approach*, 3rd ed. (Chicago, IL: Open Court, 2006).

[55] "Hierarchy of Propositions", note 34 above.

[56] The definition of tolerance limits and the accuracy of results in forensic science are subjects of intense and ongoing discussions. See "ENFSI Guideline for Evaluative Reporting in Forensic Science" (European Network of Forensic Science Institutes, 2015), https://enfsi.eu/wp-content/uploads/2016/09/m1_guideline.pdf.

data stored in a data storage device. Such data, if any, would enable the forensic expert to answer source-level questions regarding, e.g., the values of physical parameters such as speed, wheel slip, heart rate, or recently detected status information. In the context of airbags, the evaluation of the values recorded or the temporal development of these physical parameters leads to the decision to deploy the airbag, with storage of the respective data in the EDR, or not to deploy the airbag, normally without data storage. In the context of a drowsiness alert, the system produces either an alert and storage of the respective data in the DSSAD or a non-alert, normally without data storage.

IV.D.2 Activity Level

On the activity level, forensic experts evaluate a combination of source-level results and circumstantial information on the basis of propositions related to the event under examination. Complex communication between experts and fact-finders that covers the different categories of data as well as circumstantial information is required. In our drowsiness alert hypothetical, the question would be whether the drowsiness detection system issued an alert and whether and how the human driver reacted.

By addressing the activity level, experts provide fact-finders with the knowledge they need to evaluate the validity of propositions regarding a past event, e.g., when there are competing narratives concerning a past event. Regarding a drowsiness alert, the expert might present findings that support the prosecution's proposition, namely, that the drowsiness detection system's alerts were the consequence of the driver's posture in the driver's seat or other drowsiness indicators. Or, in contrast, the findings might support the defense's proposition, namely that the alerts were not a consequence of the human driver's conduct, but rather were a reaction of the driving assistant to external disturbances.

IV.D.3 Offense Level

In the context of a criminal case, the offense level addresses questions related to establishing an element of the offense charged. In this ultimate step of fact-finding, the task of the expert has ended, and the role of the court as adjudicator begins. In our drowsiness alert hypothetical, the legal question the fact-finder must answer is whether or not the driver was unfit to operate a motor vehicle. This task may be a difficult one if the expert is able to provide information on a robot's functioning or its general capacity to monitor a human's conduct, but is unable to provide information relevant to the question of whether the actual driver was unfit in the run-up to the accident.

V Unique Challenges Associated with Vetting Robot Testimony

The proposed standardized approach to proffering evaluative data as evidence in criminal proceedings illustrates the need for a sound methodology. It also simultaneously highlights the limits of the traditional approach with robot testimony. One of the parties may want to use an alert issued by a drowsiness detection system as evidence of a human driver's unfitness to operate a vehicle, but forensic experts may not be able to offer sufficient insights to verify or refute the system's evaluation. Crucial questions of admissibility or weight of the evidence are left unanswered when experts can attest only that the drowsiness detection system issued an alert before the accident occurred. If experts cannot retrieve sufficient data or sufficient circumstantial information, they may not be able to provide the fact-finder with the information necessary to assess the evidentiary value of the alert. The fact-finder cannot simply adopt the driving assistant's evaluation, as doing so would fail to satisfy the judicial task of conclusively assessing evidence. The question as to the grounds upon which judges can disregard such evidence remains an open one.[57]

The problems raised in vetting robot testimony become even clearer when the defense's ability to challenge the trustworthiness of observations and evaluations generated by a robot are compared to the alternatives available to check and question measurement data generated by traditional forensic tools. If, e.g., the defense wants to question the results of a radar gun in a speeding case, the relevant measurement data, i.e., the whole dataset of frequency values, calculated speed values, and the additional measurements performed by the radar gun, can be accessed. This information can reveal whether or not a series of measurements appears to be robust.[58] Furthermore, if the defense wishes to cast doubt on an expert's findings and develop another proposition to explain the results of the radar gun, the court could require law enforcement authorities to offer a second dataset based on an independent measurement method, e.g., a videotaping of the radar gun's

[57] For an analysis of this fundamental problem when facing machine evidence, see "Machine Testimony", note 21 above, at 1982–1983.

[58] For a proposal to use error rates when testing facial recognition, see "Scientific Evidence", note 11 above, at 838.

measurement and its environment. This would allow for independent verification and would make it possible to check for factors that may have distorted the measurements, such as truck trailers parked on the street or the surface reflections of buildings.[59]

In contrast, if the defense wishes to challenge robot testimony such as a drowsiness detection system's alert, new and unresolved issues with regard to both facts and law may arise.[60] As mentioned above, driving assistants are consumer gadgets designed to enhance road safety. They are neither approved nor certified forensic tools designed to generate evidence for criminal proceedings. It is currently left to the programmer of the driving assistance system or the manufacturer of the car to develop a robust machine learning process for the system that leads to the establishment of a threshold for issuing an alert and to determine what information to store for potential evaluation, ex ante, of the robot's assessment. The decision-making power of the programmer or producer regarding the shaping of a smart product's capacity to observe and record is limited only if there are regulations that require the storage of particular data in a particular form.

Parties challenging drowsiness alerts can try their luck by challenging different kinds of data. Measurement data, which generally describes physical facts in a transparent way, appears to be the most objective information, and the corresponding information content seems relatively safe from legal attack. In contrast, evaluative data, including records of decisions taken or interventions launched by a robot, appears to be much closer to the contested legal questions and thus a more appropriate target for legal challenge. Counsel could argue that the dataset containing information about the incident does not allow for robust testing of alternative scenarios, or that no validation exists for the thresholds for issuing an alert set by machine learning, thereby rendering an expert's probability ratios worthless, or that someone might have tampered with the data. These arguments show that in order to do their jobs properly, lawyers must be capable of understanding not only how data is generated, retrieved, and accessed, but also how evidence can be evaluated, interpreted, verified, and vetted with regard to its information content and to the integrity of the data.

[59] See *Entscheid Obergericht Kanton Zürich* (Decision of the Upper Court of Zurich, Switzerland) of November 10, 2016, SB160168-O/U/cwo (Ger.).

[60] A promising approach could be to crowdsource data; see Sabine Gless, Xuan Di, & Emily Silverman, "Ca(r)veat Emptor: Crowdsourcing Data to Challenge the Testimony of In-Car Technology" (2022) 62:3 *Jurimetrics* 285.

VI A Look to the Future

VI.A Criminal Procedure Reform

A robot's capacity to assess its environment autonomously, and possibly self-modify its algorithms, is a development that holds promise for numerous fields of endeavor, and a sophisticated driving assistant that handles an enormous amount of data when monitoring an individual driver for specific signs of drowsiness holds great promise for fact-finding. The challenge will be to update procedural codes in a way that empowers courts to decipher this new form of evidence methodically, with the help of forensic experts who should be able fully to explain the specific operations undertaken by the robot in question.

Currently, doubts about the trustworthiness of a robot's evaluation of a human driver's fitness seem well-founded, given the fact that car manufacturers are free to shape a drowsiness detection system's alert as a feature of their brand and may even construct its capacity to observe in such a way as to favor their own interests.[61] Our chapter argues that the use of robot testimony must be supported with a clear taxonomy, a standardized methodological approach, and a statutory regime.[62]

Up until now, most procedural codes have opted for a blanket approach to evidence and for "technological neutrality," even in the context of complex scientific evidence.[63] Yet there are many arguments that support the enactment of specific regulations for courts to rely on when using data as evidence, and that speak for the rejection of a case-by-case approach. Differences between data and other exhibits proffered as evidence in criminal cases, such as documents or photographs of car wrecks, seem obvious.[64] Raw, measurement, and evaluative data cannot be comprehended by the naked eye. Experts are needed not only to access the data and to ensure traceability, but also to interpret it. Fact-finders are dependent on experts when faced with the task of retracing the steps by means of which data is seized from computers,[65] from databases storing traffic data, and

61 "AI in the Courtroom", note 21 above, at 213–214.

62 For a detailed discussion on the need to update procedural codes, see "New Criminal Procedure", note 39 above, at 289–306.

63 Codes of criminal procedure provide few specific rules, e.g., with regard to DNA sampling, Swiss CrimPC, note 4 above, Art. 255, and the Law on DNA Profiles, Switzerland, SR 363 (with effect from June 20, 2003).

64 This chapter will not address limitations on the gathering of evidence due to privacy rights.

65 For a perspective from the United States, see "New Criminal Procedure", note 39 above, at 309–310.

from other data carriers. They must also rely on experts to explain how data is retrieved from cloud computing services. As yet, fact-finders have no legal guidance on how to ensure that the chain of custody is valid and the data traceable and reproducible.

Fact-finders also face serious challenges when they have to fit digital evidence into a human-centered evidentiary regime designed with the analog world in mind. In German criminal proceedings, all evidence, including digital evidence, must be presented pursuant to four categories defined by law (*Strengbeweisverfahren*[66]), namely expert evidence, documentary evidence, evidence by personal inspection, and testimony; digital evidence is not defined by law as a separate category.[67] If a courtroom actor wants to use a driving assistant's alert as evidence, the alert must be introduced in accordance with the rules of procedure governing one of these categories. Most probably, the court will call an expert to access relevant data, to explain the data-generating process, and to clarify how the data was obtained and how it was stored, but there is no guidance in the law as to how to account for the fact that drowsiness detection assistants issue alerts based on their own evaluation of the driver and that experts cannot retrace this evaluation completely when reading out the system.

VI.B Trustworthy Robot Testimony

Situations in which robots assess human behavior represent a potentially vast pool of evidence in our digital future, and legal actors must find a way to exploit the data. With a taxonomy for the use of robot testimony in legal proceedings and clearly defined roles for lawyers and forensic experts in the fact-finding process, particularly if a standardized approach is used to vet this new evidence, the law can do its bit to establish the trustworthiness of robot testimony.

Time is of the essence. With driving assistants already aboard cars, courts will soon be presented with new forms of robot testimony, including that provided by drowsiness detection systems. If evaluative data, which is set to be a common by-product of automated driving thanks

[66] For further details on the German *Strengbeweis*, see Michael Bohlander, *Principles of German Criminal Procedure*, 2nd ed. (Oxford, UK: Hart, 2021) at 145–146.

[67] Sabine Gless & Thomas Wahl, "The Handling of Digital Evidence in Germany" in Michele Caianiello & Alberto Camon (eds.), *Digital Forensic Evidence. Towards Common European Standards in Antifraud Administrative and Criminal Investigations* (Alphen aan den Rijn, Netherlands: Wolters Kluwer, 2021) 52.

to the requirement that new cars in some countries be equipped with integrated driving assistants, is to be proffered as evidence in criminal trials, legislatures must ensure that the robots' powers of recollection are as robust as possible.[68] And not only the law must take action. New and innovative safety nets can be provided by different disciplines to ensure the trustworthiness of robot testimony. One option would be for these safety nets to take the form of an official certification process for consumer robot products likely to be used as witnesses, similar to the process that ensures the accuracy of forensic tools such as radar guns.[69] Ex ante certification might not solve all the problems, because in practice, drowsiness detection systems depend on many different factors, any one of which could easily distort the results, such as a driver not sitting upright due to a back injury, a driver wearing sunglasses, etc. Technical testing ex post, perhaps with the help of AI, might be a better solution; it could, at least, supplement the certification process.[70]

Evaluative data generated by robots monitoring human conduct cannot be duly admitted as evidence in a criminal case until technology and regulation ensure its accessibility, traceability, and to the greatest extent possible reproducibility, as well as provide a sufficient amount of circumstantial information. Only when this has been achieved can the real debate about trustworthy robot testimony begin, a debate that will encompass the whole gamut of current deliberations concerning the risks posed by AI and its impact on human life.

APPENDIX

Vetting Robot Testimony Via an Expert

If robot testimony is proffered as evidence in a criminal proceeding, this chapter has suggested that because direct communication with a robot is impossible, a forensic expert could serve as a sort of mouthpiece for this witness. The following list, inspired by routine questions regarding

[68] A minimum prerequisite is the adoption of legal regulations for DSSADs; see Uniform Provisions, note 44 above, at Chapter 9.

[69] For details on new certification approaches, see "Machine Testimony", note 21 above, at 2023–2027; for certification of authenticity of digital evidence in general, see "Authenticating Digital Evidence", note 40 above, at 46–54.

[70] Sabine Gless & Thomas Weigend, "Intelligente Agenten als Zeugen im Strafverfahren?" (Intelligent Agents as Witnesses in Criminal Proceedings) (2021) 76:12 *Juristenzeitung* 612 at 618–620.

digital evidence, offers a brief insight into what stakeholders might want to ask when vetting a robot via an expert. This list works together with our proposed taxonomy for robot testimony in Section III above, and the standardized approach to using robot testimony for fact-finding in Section IV.

First, the expert must address questions surrounding issues of accessibility:

- How is the relevant raw data defined when the robot is initially certified for use?
- Where is the relevant raw data originally stored, who can access it, and how?
- Who is authorized to access this data?

Second, the expert must address the issue of traceability:

- How is the raw data processed?
- Where are the relevant algorithms implemented, how are they documented, and who has access to them?
- How can processed data be verified by forensic experts? Does verification require knowledge of the source code, or can other techniques be used?

Third, the expert must address the issue of reproducibility (this is probably where robot testimony differs most from other forms of digital evidence):

- How is an assessment, e.g., of human behavior, generated when complex algorithms and machine learning elements are involved?
- What raw and measurement data recorded in that process is accessible for use in forensic testing?
- If a self-modifying system is involved, how are algorithms modified "en route," and how are subsequent decisions generated?

The overall goal of this set of questions is to build what we refer to in our taxonomy as information content, i.e., what can actually be learned from the robot testimony.

GUILTY
NOT GUILTY
NOT GUILTY
NOT GUILTY

9

Digital Evidence Generated by Consumer Products

The Defense Perspective

ERIN E. MURPHY*

I Introduction

In courtrooms across the world, criminal cases are no longer proved only through traditional means such as eyewitnesses, confessions, or rudimentary physical evidence like the proverbial smoking gun. Instead, prosecutors increasingly harness technologies, including those developed and used for purposes other than law enforcement, to generate criminal evidence.[1]

This kind of digital data may take different forms, including raw data, data that is produced by a machine without any processing; measurement data, data that is produced by a machine after rudimentary calculations; and evaluative data, data that is produced by a machine according to sophisticated algorithmic methods that cannot be reproduced manually.[2] These distinctions are likewise evident in the array of consumer products that can now be tapped to produce evidence in a criminal case. A mobile phone can be used to track the user's location via raw data in the form of a readout of which tower the cell phone "pinged," via measurement data reflecting the triangulation of data towers accessed along a person's route, or with evaluative data generated by a machine-learning algorithm to predict the precise location of a person, such as a specific shop in a shopping mall.[3] In all three forms, the use of such data presents new evidentiary challenges, although it is the evaluative data that raises the most issues as a result of both its precision and impenetrability.

* I am deeply grateful to Safeena Mecklai for her outstanding research assistance.

1 See e.g. Ian N. Friedman & Eric C. Nemecek, "#Trending: Traditional Crimes Meet Nontraditional Evidence" (2018) *The Champion* 20; Erin Murphy, "The New Forensics: Criminal Justice, False Certainty, and the Second Generation of Scientific Evidence" (2007) 95:3 *California Law Review* 721 at 729–730.

2 See Chapter 8 in this volume.

3 See e.g. Haiyang Jiang, Mingshu He, Yuanyuan Xi *et al.*, "Machine-Learning-Based User Position Prediction and Behavior Analysis for Location Services" (2021) 12:5 *Information* 180.

As scholars begin to tackle the list of questions raised by these new forms of evidence, one critical perspective is often omitted: the view of the criminal defendant. Yet, just as digital evidence serves to prove the guilt of an accused, so too can it serve the equally important role of exculpating the innocent. As it stands now, law fails to adequately safeguard the rights of a criminal defendant to conduct digital investigations and present digital evidence. In a world increasingly reliant on technological forms of proof, the failure to afford full pre-trial rights of discovery and investigation to the defense fatally undermines the presumption of innocence and the basic precepts of due process.

Persons accused of crimes have two compelling needs with regard to digital evidence. First, criminal defendants must be granted the power to meaningfully attack the government's digital proof, whether offered by the government to prove its affirmative case or to counter evidence tendered by the defense.[4] For example, the defense might challenge cell site location records that purport to show the defendant's location at the scene of the crime. Or they might contest cell site records offered by the government to undermine a defense witness's claim to have witnessed the incident. The defendant is attacking the government's proffered digital evidence in both cases, but in the first variation, the attack responds to the government's evidence in its case-in-chief, whereas the second variation responds to evidence proffered by the government to counter a defense claim or witness.

The defense's use of digital evidence in this way differs from the second category, which might be called supportive defense evidence. A defendant must be able to access and introduce the defendant's own digital proof, in order to support a defense theory or to attack the government's non-digital evidence. For example, the defendant might use digital data to show that the defendant is innocent, to reinforce testimony offered by a defense witness, or to support a claim that another person in fact committed the offense. Classic examples of such use would be DNA evidence that proves there was another perpetrator, or surveillance footage that reveals the perpetrator had a distinguishing mark not shared by the defendant. A defendant might also use such evidence to bolster a legal claim. In the United States, e.g., the defendant might use digital proof to argue that evidence must be suppressed because it was obtained in violation of the Constitution.[5] Or a defendant might use digital evidence to

[4] See Chapter 7 in this volume (recognizing five key rights of the accused).

[5] *United States* v. *Scott*, No. 2:17-CR-20489-TGB, 2018 WL 2197911, at *5 (ED Mich. May 14, 2018).

attack the non-digital evidence in the government's case, like a defendant who introduces the cell-site records that show that the government's witness was not at the scene, or offers the victim's social media posts to prove that the victim still possessed the property the defendant allegedly stole. What links these examples of supportive defense evidence is that the defense introduces digital proof of its own; it does not just attack the digital proof offered by the government.

In both cases – when the defense aims to attack government digital proof, or when it aims to introduce its own digital proof – the defendant cannot effectively mount a defense without access to and the ability to challenge complex forms of digital proof. Yet, in all too many jurisdictions, the legal system has embraced the government's use of technological tools to inculpate a defendant[6] without reckoning with the equivalent needs of the accused.[7] Baseline principles such as those enshrined in the Fifth and Sixth Amendments to the US Constitution and Article 6 of the European Convention on Human Rights sketch broad rights, but how those rights are actually implemented, and the governing rules and statutes that embody those values, may vary dramatically.[8] In the United States, criminal defendants have few positive investigatory powers,[9] and are largely dependent on rules that mandate government disclosure of limited forms of evidence or the backstop of the constitutional rights of due process, confrontation, and compulsory process.[10]

6 The Electronic Frontier Foundation and the Reynolds School of Journalism created a database of police surveillance technologies, which is a helpful compilation of some police surveillance practices. See Atlas of Surveillance, https://atlasofsurveillance.org/.

7 See e.g. Rebecca Wexler, "Privacy Asymmetries: Access to Data in Criminal Defense Investigations" (2021) 68:1 *UCLA Law Review* 212 ["Privacy Asymmetries"]; Sabine Gless, "AI in the Courtroom: A Comparative Analysis of Machine Evidence in Criminal Trials" (2020) 51:2 *Georgetown Journal of International Law* 195; Rebecca Wexler, "Life, Liberty and Trade Secrets: Intellectual Property in the Criminal Justice System" (2018) 70:5 *Stanford Law Review* 1343 ["Life, Liberty"]; Andrea Roth, "Trial by Machine" (2016) 104:5 *Georgetown Law Journal* 1245 ["Trial by Machine"]; Andrea Roth, "Machine Testimony" (2017) 126:1 *Yale Law Journal* 1972; Erin Murphy, "The Mismatch between Twenty-First-Century Forensic Evidence and Our Antiquated Criminal Justice System" (2014) 87:3 *South California Law Review* 633; Joshua A. T. Fairfield & Erik Luna, "Digital Innocence" (2014) 99:5 *Cornell Law Review* 981 ["Digital Innocence"] at 1056; Brandon L. Garrett, "Big Data and Due Process" (2014) 99 *Cornell Law Review Online* 207; Erin Murphy, "Databases, Doctrine and Constitutional Criminal Procedure" (2010) 37:3 *Fordham Urban Law Journal* 803.

8 See generally Wayne R. LaFave, Jerold H. Israel, Nancy J. King *et al.*, *Criminal Procedure*, 4th ed. (St. Paul, MN: Thomson Reuters, 2015) [*Criminal Procedure*] at ss. 20.2(c) and 20.3.

9 Ion Meyn, "Discovery and Darkness: The Information Deficits in Criminal Disputes" (2014) 79:3 *Brooklyn Law Review* 1091 at 1095–1096 and 1108–1114.

10 Ibid. at 1113–1114.

Even when the defense is entitled to certain information, existing legal tools may be inadequate to effectively obtain and utilize it. Criminal defendants must typically rely on either a court order or subpoena to obtain information from third parties, but both of those mechanisms are typically understood as intended for the purpose of presenting evidence at trial, not conducting pre-trial investigation.[11] And even sympathetic courts struggle to determine whether and how much to grant requests. As one high court observed when addressing a defendant's request for access to a Facebook post, "there is surprisingly little guidance in the case law and secondary literature with regard to the appropriate inquiry."[12]

Finally, generally applicable substantive laws may also thwart defense efforts to use technological evidence. For example, privacy statutes in the United States typically include law enforcement exceptions,[13] but as Rebecca Wexler has observed, those same statutes effectively "bar defense counsel from subpoenaing private entities for entire categories of sensitive information," and in fact "[c]ourts have repeatedly interpreted [statutory] silence to categorically prohibit defense subpoenas."[14]

Without robust reconsideration of the rights necessary to empower defendants in each of these endeavors, the digitalization of evidence threatens to bring with it the demise of due process and accurate fact-finding. The first step in articulating these critical defensive rights, however, is to identify and classify the scope of such evidence and its pertinent features. Such analysis serves two purposes. First, it crystallizes the need for robust defense pre-trial rights, including rights to discovery, compelled process, and expert assistance, as well as substantive and procedural entitlements to confront such evidence and mount an effective defense at trial. Second, cataloging these technologies helps point the way toward a comprehensive framework for defense access and disclosure, one that can account for the many subtle variations and features involved in each technology – one that is wholly lacking now.

To facilitate deeper inquiry into the proper scope and extent of the criminal defendant's interest in digital proof, this chapter presents a

[11] *Criminal Procedure*, note 8 above, at s. 20.2(d).

[12] *Facebook, Inc.* v. *Superior Court*, 471 P.3d 383, 387 (Cal. 2020) [*Facebook* v. *Superior Court*].

[13] See e.g. Erin Murphy, "The Politics of Privacy in the Criminal Justice System: Information Disclosure, the Fourth Amendment, and Statutory Law Enforcement Exemptions" (2013) 111:4 *Michigan Law Review* 485 ["Politics of Privacy"].

[14] See e.g. "Privacy Asymmetries", note 7 above, at 215.

taxonomy of defensive use of technological evidence. Section II identifies and provides examples for seven categories of such data: location trackers, electronic communications and social media, historical search or cloud or vendor records, the "Internet of Things" and smart tools, surveillance cameras, biometric identifiers, and analytical software tools. Although the examples in this chapter are drawn primarily from legal cases in the United States, these technologies are currently in broad use around the world. Section III then considers ten separate characteristics that attend these technologies, and how each may affect the analysis of the proper scope of defense access. Section IV concludes.

II A Taxonomy of Digital Proof

The first step in articulating the issues that confound defense access to digital proof is to outline the general categories into which such technologies fall. Of course, digital information is used throughout the criminal justice process, e.g., in pre-trial bail and detention risk assessments and post-conviction at the time of sentencing. This chapter, however, focuses only on the use of such digital evidence to investigate and prove or disprove a defendant's guilt.

In addition, although it might at first glimpse be appealing to attempt to draw sharp distinctions between consumer products and forensic law enforcement technologies, those categories prove illusory in this context.[15] The line between consumer and law enforcement either collapses, or is simply arbitrarily drawn, when it comes to defense investigation. For example, what difference does it make if law enforcement uses surveillance video from a police camera versus security footage from a *Ring* doorbell-camera or private bank? What does it matter if the facial recognition software is used on a repository of high school yearbooks versus police mugshots? Are questions of access so different when DNA testing was done via a public lab versus by a private lab, or whether the search was in a commercial versus law enforcement database?

Even if such a line were drawn, it may be difficult to defend in principle. Suppose law enforcement obtains data from an X (formerly Twitter) account, and then uses a proprietary law-enforcement software to do

[15] See Chapter 8 in this volume, and regarding the limited reach of the Fourth Amendment of the US Constitution to state agents and not private actors, see Chapter 11.

language analysis of the account. Is that a consumer product or law enforcement tool? Or if law enforcement secretly signs an agreement with a consumer DNA database to enable testing and searches for police purposes, is that a consumer tool or law enforcement tool? All too often, the lines between the two will break down as increasingly public–private cooperation generates evidence pertinent for a criminal case.

Of course, concerns about the reliability of evidence may differ when the evidence derives from a consumer product used by the general public as opposed to a forensic tool used only by law enforcement. Regulatory regimes and market incentives exercise an oversight function for commercial applications, and the financial incentives that ensure reliability for commercial products may be lacking in the law enforcement context. But those safeguards are not a substitute for a defendant's opportunity to access and challenge technological evidence, because reliability of the government's proof is not the only value at stake. The defense must have a meaningful right to access or challenge technological evidence, as a means of testing the non-digital aspects of the government's proof as well as bolster its own case. Thus, in taxonomizing digital evidence, this chapter acknowledges but does not differentiate between technology created and used by general consumers versus those created primarily or exclusively by police.

II.A Location Data

The general label "location data" covers a wide array of technological tools that help establish the presence or absence of a person in a particular place and, often, time. Location evidence may derive from mobile phone carriers that either directly track GPS location or indirectly provide cell-site location services, license plate scanning technology, electronic toll payment systems, or even "smart" cars or utility meters that can indicate the presence or absence of persons or the number of persons in a particular space at a particular time.

The use of such technologies to implicate a defendant is obvious. Evidence that a defendant was in a particular location at a particular time may prove that a defendant had access to a particular place, support an inference that the defendant committed an act, or reinforce a witness's assertions. For example, evidence that shows that the defendant's cell phone was at that location where a dead body was found can strengthen the prosecution's identification of the defendant as the perpetrator. But just as such evidence inculpates, so too might it exculpate. A criminal defendant might seek to introduce such evidence to contest a government victim or witness's account, or prove bias or collusion by witnesses.[16]

Location data also has supportive defense power, in that it could establish an alibi, prove the presence of an alternative perpetrator, or contradict a line of government cross-examination. A law enforcement officer or witness may be shown to have arrived at the scene after a pivotal moment, or left prior to a critical development. An alleged third-party perpetrator may be proved to have accessed a controlled site, or to have interacted with culpable associates.

The inability of defendants to access such information directly often leaves them reliant upon either the thoroughness of government investigators or the willingness of a court to authorize subpoenas for such information. For example, one police report described cases in which police used license-plate-reading cameras to support each defendant's claim of innocence, and thus to exonerate individuals from false accusations.[17] But such open-minded and thorough investigation is not always the norm. In some cases, the government may have little incentive to seek information that contradicts the government's theory or calls into question the government's proof.

In *Quinones* v. *United States*,[18] the defendant alleged that his counsel was ineffective for failing to seek location data including both GPS and license plate readings that the defendant argued would support his claim that he had not been residing for months in the location where firearms were found, but rather had only recently visited. The court rejected the claim, stating that the defendant "fails to provide any indication that such evidence even exists, and if so, what that evidence would have revealed," and that "[a] license plate reader would merely indicate that a certain vehicle was at a certain location at a specific time, but such would not conclusively prove the location of an individual."[19] Another court

[16] Kathleen McWilliams, "New Haven Man Jailed for 17 Years Freed after Judge Vacates Murder, Robbery Convictions," *Hartford Courant* (April 25, 2018), www.courant.com/breaking-news/hc-br-vernon-horn-released-wrongful-conviction-20180425-story.html.

[17] Press Release, "Grosse Ile Police Department Exonerates Two Individuals Using Fixed License Plate Reader Cameras," *Vigilant Solutions* (February 4, 2016), www.police1.com/police-products/traffic-enforcement/license-plate-readers/press-releases/grosse-ile-police-department-exonerates-two-individuals-using-fixed-license-plate-reader-cameras-SyndPZ00572XK92v/.

[18] 2020 WL 1509386 (SD W. Va. Jan. 9, 2020) (slip copy) [*Quinones* v. *United States*].

[19] *Quinones* v. *United States*, note 18 above, at *9. See also *Harrison* v. *Baker*, No. 3:18CV85-HEH, 2019 WL 404974, at *4 (ED Va. Jan. 31, 2019); *Blackman* v. *United States*, No. CIV.A. 2:12-02509, 2014 WL 1155444, at *4 (DNJ Mar. 21, 2014); *United States* v. *Medina*, 918 F.3d 774, 786 (10th Cir.), cert. denied, 139 S.Ct. 2706 (2019).

likewise rejected a defendant's claim that the defense attorney's failure to seek such information constituted ineffective assistance, reasoning that the defendant had offered "no reason, beyond his own speculation, to believe that the GPS records would have bolstered his defense ...."[20] The dismissive tone regarding the potential evidence in *Quinones* is also evident in other cases, such as *People* v. *Wells*. In that case, the court dismissed the significance of automatic toll records, noting that "[t]here was no individual camera for the FasTrak lane. These inherent limitations in the underlying videotape evidence made it possible for defendant's car to pass through undetected ...."[21]

But of course, the very point of investigation is to find information that is not already known, including information that impeaches or contradicts critical witnesses, and to present such evidence, even though it may be equivocal. As one law firm wrote in a post that underscored the importance of location records, obtaining the complainant's location data aided the firm in convincing the government that the complaint was unfounded.[22]

The point of these cases is not so much that such evidence is always decisive. Rather, they highlight the discrepancy between the ease, even if not unfettered,[23] with which courts recognize that access to and introduction of such evidence is critical to building a government case, while dismissing its importance in mounting a defense. One press report from Denmark noted, in connection with the revelation that up to 1,000 cases may have been tainted by erroneous mobile geolocation data which precipitated the release of 30 persons from pre-trial detention, the fact that such errors went unchecked is "obviously very concerning for the

[20] *Cooper* v. *Griffin*, 16-CV-0629 (VEC) (BCM), 2019 WL 1026303, at 11 (SDNY Feb. 11, 2019), report and recommendation adopted, 16-CV-0629 (VEC), 2019 WL 1014937 (SDNY Mar. 4, 2019).

[21] *People* v. *Wells*, No. A112173, 2007 WL 466963, at 6 (Cal. Ct. App. Feb. 14, 2007), as modified on denial of reh'g (Mar. 13, 2007); *Jackson* v. *Lee*, 10-CIV-3062 (LAK) (AJP), 2010 WL 4628013 at 13 (SDNY Nov. 16, 2010), report and recommendation adopted, 10-CIV-3062 (LAK), 2010 WL 5094415 (SDNY Dec. 10, 2010).

[22] "The Importance of Subpoenaing Cell Phone GPS-Data Records in California Criminal Cases," *HG.org*, www.hg.org/legal-articles/the-importance-of-subpoenaing-cell-phone-gps-data-records-in-california-criminal-cases-51299.

[23] See e.g. *Carpenter* v. *United States*, 138 S.Ct. 2206 (2018); Case C-623/17, *Privacy International* v. *Secretary of State for Foreign and Commonwealth Affairs and others*; Joint Cases C-511/18, *La Quadrature du Net and others*, C-512/18, *French Data Network and others*, and C-520/18, *Ordre des barreaux francophones et germanophone and others*.

functioning of the criminal justice system and the right to a fair trial."[24] Yet the preceding discussion suggests that a court could well reject a defense request for such information out-of-hand.

II.B *Electronic Communications and Social Media*

The advent of mobile devices has changed the manner in which people communicate, and exponentially increased the amount of that communication. As one leading treatise puts it: "E-mail is inordinately susceptible to revealing 'smoking gun' evidence."[25] Email and text messages comprise a significant fraction of digital records of communication, but social media accounts on platforms such as Facebook, Snapchat, Instagram, and X (formerly known as Twitter) also provide fertile ground for data.[26] Although criminal defendants typically have access to their own records, historical information including deleted material or material generated by other persons may not be as readily obtainable.

In one high-profile case in England, a man spent three years in prison in connection with a rape allegation. He contended the encounter was innocent, but it was only when his family was able to locate an original thread of Facebook messages by the complainant that it was revealed that she had altered the thread to make the incident appear non-consensual.[27] In a similar case in the United States, the court dismissed as critical to an effective defense the effort to obtain Facebook evidence.[28]

[24] "Danish Data Retention: Back to Normal after Major Crisis," *EDRi* (November 6, 2019), https://edri.org/our-work/danish-data-retention-back-to-normal-after-major-crisis/; see also Lene Wacher Lentz & Nina Sunde, "The Use of Historical Call Data Records as Evidence in the Criminal Justice System – Lessons Learned from the Danish Telecom Scandal" (2021) 18 *Digital Evidence and Electronic Signature Law Review* 1 ("To support the ability of the defence to challenge the evidence, the prosecution must provide a transparent presentation of the data and the processes as a whole, with all the inherent risk of errors and uncertainties").

[25] Monique C. M. Leahy, "Recovery and Reconstruction of Electronic Mail as Evidence" in *American Jurisprudence Proof of Facts*, 3d at section 1, vol. 41 (Rochester, NY: Lawyers Cooperative Publishing, 2020).

[26] Emily R. West, "Nolensville Homicide Suspect Wants Snapchat in Trial," *Tennessean* (August 22, 2019), www.tennessean.com/story/news/local/williamson/2019/08/22/nolensville-murder-robert-ward-jonathon-elliott-snapchat/2083867001/ ["Nolensville"].

[27] Matthew Diebel, "Man Convicted of Rape Is Freed after Sister-in-Law Finds Deleted Facebook Messages that Prove His Innocence," *USA Today* (January 3, 2018), www.usatoday.com/story/news/world/2018/01/02/man-convicted-rape-freed-after-sister-law-finds-deleted-facebook-messages-prove-his-innocence/995197001/.

[28] *Williams* v. *Davis*, No. 3:15-CV-331-M (BH), 2017 WL 1155855, at *7 (ND Tex. Feb. 13, 2017), report and recommendation adopted, No. 3:15-CV-331-M, 2017 WL 1155845 (ND Tex. Mar.

Such discovery difficulties can occur even for high-profile defendants; the actor Kevin Spacey had trouble obtaining an unaltered copy of the complainant's cell phone records.[29]

Not every court has disregarded defense requests. In another case, the defendant sought the complainant's emails in part to dispute the prosecution's characterization of him as a predatory sadist, but the trial court denied the request, asserting that the defendant could simply "obtain the information contained in the e-mails from other sources, i.e., speaking directly with the persons who communicated with the complainant in these e-mails."[30] In reversing, the appellate court observed that the evidence had particular power not only to undermine the prosecution's depiction of the defendant, but also the complainant's portrayal as a "naïve, overly trusting, overly polite and ill-informed" person.[31]

Despite the critical role that written communications and correspondence can play as evidence, defendants often have trouble convincing courts of their value, and overcoming significant legal hurdles. Ironically, "[t]he greatest challenge may be ascertaining and obtaining electronic evidence in the possession of the prosecution."[32] That is because, like location data, defendants often "must successfully convince the court that without 'full and appropriate' pretrial disclosure and exchange of ESI, the defendant lacks the ability to mount a full and fair defense."[33]

In the United States, access to electronic communications is one of the few areas expressly covered by statutory law, but that law also restricts the defense. Only governmental entities are expressly permitted to subpoena electronic communications from the service provider; other persons are dependent on access to the records from the person who created

27, 2017). See also "Nolensville", note 26 above; *In the Interest of R.A.P., a Minor Appeal of R.A.P.*, No. 930 WDA 2019, 2020 WL 1910515, at *10 (Pa. Super. Ct. Apr. 20, 2020).

29 "Spacey's Defense Claims Deleted Text Messages Will 'Exonerate' Him," *NBC Boston* (June 2, 2019), www.nbcboston.com/news/local/spaceys-defense-claims-deleted-text-messages-will-exonerate-him/108067/.

30 *People* v. *Jovanovic*, 176 Misc.2d 729, 730 (NY Sup. Ct. 1997), rev'd 263 A.D.2d 182 (NY App. Div. 1999).

31 Ibid., 263 A.D.2d 182, 200, 700 N.Y.S.2d 156, 170 (1999). See also "Nolensville", note 26 above.

32 Daniel B. Garrie, Esq., The Honorable Maureen Duffy-Lewis, & Daniel K. Gelb, Esq., "'Criminal Cases Gone Paperless': Hanging with the Wrong Crowd" (2010) 47:2 *San Diego Law Review* 521 at 523.

33 Ibid. "ESI" refers to electronically stored information.

or received the communication, who may not have the records or be reluctant to share them.[34] There is also a demonstrated reluctance on the part of social media and other provider companies to support defense cases.[35] One public defender described Facebook and Google as "terrible to work with," noting that "[t]he state's attorney and police get great information, but we get turned down all the time. They tell us we need to get a warrant. We can't get warrants. We have subpoenas, and often they ignore them."[36] And in one high-profile case, Facebook accepted a $1,000 fine for contempt rather than comply with the court's order to disclose information for the defense, citing its belief that the order contradicted the federal law on stored communications.[37]

Eventually, the California Supreme Court directly confronted the problem of defense access in its decision in *Facebook, Inc.* v. *Superior Court of San Diego County*.[38] In that case, the defendant subpoenaed Facebook to obtain non-public posts and messages made by a user who was also a victim and witness in an attempted homicide case. Articulating a seven-part test for determining when to quash third-party subpoenas, the court also laid out a series of best practices for such requests that included a presumption against granting them *ex parte* and under seal.[39] Although the court's opinion offers a roadmap for similar cases in the future, it is remarkable that the availability of such a critical and important form of evidence remains relatively uncertain in many jurisdictions.

[34] Jenia I. Turner, "Managing Digital Discovery in Criminal Cases" (2019) 109:2 *Journal of Criminal Law and Criminology* 237 at 262; "Digital Innocence", note 7 above, at 1055.

[35] Andrew Cohen, "How Social Media Giants Side with Prosecutors in Criminal Cases," *The Marshall Project* (January 15, 2018), www.themarshallproject.org/2018/01/15/how-social-media-giants-side-with-prosecutors-in-criminal-cases; "Digital Innocence", note 7 above, at 1056.

[36] Kashmir Hill, "Imagine Being on Trial. With Exonerating Evidence Trapped on Your Phone," *The New York Times* (22 November 2019), www.nytimes.com/2019/11/22/business/law-enforcement-public-defender-technology-gap.html ["Being on Trial"]. See also Jeffrey D. Stein, "Why Evidence Exonerating the Wrongly Accused Can Stay Locked Up on Instagram," *The Washington Post* (September 10, 2019), www.washingtonpost.com/opinions/2019/09/10/why-evidence-exonerating-wrongly-accused-can-stay-locked-up-instagram/.

[37] See generally Maura Dolan, "After that $5 Billion Fine, Facebook Gets Dinged Again: $1000 by Judge Overseeing Murder Trial," *Los Angeles Times* (July 26, 2019), www.latimes.com/california/story/2019-07-26/facebook-twitter-fined-private-postings-gang-trial ["$5 Billion Fine"].

[38] *Facebook* v. *Superior Court*, note 12 above.

[39] *In re. Facebook (Hunter)*, 417 P.3d 725 (Cal. 2018). An *ex parte* proceeding or ruling is made without notice to or response from the opposing side.

II.C Historical Search, Cloud, Crowdsourced, and Vendor Records

It is not only social media and electronic messaging services that retain records of individuals. A vast network of automated and digital records has arisen documenting nearly every aspect of daily life, including Google search histories, vendor records from companies like Amazon, find my iPhone searches, meta-data stored when files are created, uploaded, or changed, or cloud-stored or backed-up records.

These records are commonly used tools to establish a defendant's guilt.[40] But they might be equally powerful means of exculpating or partially exculpating an accused by identifying another perpetrator, undermining or disputing testimony by a government witness, or bolstering and reinforcing a defense witness, as in the case of a record showing that a phone's flashlight feature was on, or history of purchases or searches, or crowdsourced data from a traffic app that proves the accident was the fault of a hazard along a roadway.[41]

In one exceptional case, the defendant successfully defeated the charges only after his attorney – at New York's Legal Aid Society, which unlike most defenders has its own forensic laboratory – was able to retrieve stored data that proved the defendant's innocence.[42] The defendant was charged with threatening his ex-wife, but insisted he had in fact been on his way to work at the time. Fortunately, the Legal Aid Society had invested in its own digital forensics lab at the cost of roughly $100,000 for equipment alone. Using the defendant's cell phone, the defense analyst produced a detailed map of his morning, which established that he was 5 miles from the site of the alleged assault. Software applications like "Oxygen Forensic Detective" provide a suite of data extraction, analysis, and organization tools, for mobile devices, computers, cloud services, and more,[43] but it is safe to say that there are few if any defenders that could have performed that kind of analysis in-house, and only a handful that could have apportioned expert funds to outsource it.

[40] See e.g. *Walters* v. *State*, 206 So. 3d 524 (Miss. 2016) (admitting Google Earth images); "Ellington Husband Accused of Killing Wife Searched 'Poison' Online: Court Documents," *NBC Connecticut* (January 3, 2020), www.nbcconnecticut.com/news/local/ellington-husband-accused-of-killing-wife-searched-poison-online-court-documents/2205136/ ["Ellington Husband"].

[41] See e.g. Sabine Gless, Xuan Di, & Emily Silverman, "Ca(r)veat Emptor: Crowdsourcing Data to Challenge the Testimony of In-Car Technology" (2022) 62:3 *Jurimetrics* 285.

[42] "Being on Trial", note 36 above. Cf. *State* v. *Bray*, 383 P.3d 883 (Ct. Ap. Oreg. 2016).

[43] See e.g. Oxygen Forensics, www.oxygen-forensic.com/en/products/oxygen-forensic-detective.

II.D "Internet of Things" and "Smart Tools"

An emerging category of digital records that could be lumped under the prior heading of historical search records arises from the Internet of Things (IoT) and smart tools. This general heading encompasses a broad array of technologies. Some simply record and generate data from commonplace household items and tools, without any real evaluative function, including the following: basic "wearables" that measure one's pulse or temperature; medical monitoring devices like pacemakers; personal home aids like Siri, Echo, or Alexa; basic automotive data such as speed or mileage indicators; or even "smart" toys, lightbulbs, vacuums, toothbrushes, or mattresses.[44] These devices record everything from ambient sounds to specific requests, including passive and active biomedical information like weight, respiratory rate, sleep cycles, or heartbeat; and time in use or mode of use.

This category also includes tools that may have true evaluative function, including real-time analysis and feedback. For example, this category includes fully or semi-autonomous vehicles or medical instruments that do not just detect information and record it, but also process and respond to those inputs in real time.

Such information has a range of both inculpatory and exculpatory uses. The government readily accesses such information, and may do so even more in the future. For example, residents in Texas awoke one morning to find that their "smart" meters had raised the temperature overnight to avoid a burnout during a heat wave.[45] Used selectively, this technology could aid law enforcement. As one report summarized:[46]

[44] "With My Fridge as My Witness?!" *Privacy International* (June 28, 2019), https://privacyinternational.org/long-read/3026/my-fridge-my-witness ["Fridge as My Witness"]; "Ellington Husband", note 40 above; *United States* v. *Smith*, 2017 WL 11461003 (D. NH 2017); Lauren Pack, "Defense Wants Middletown Man's Pacemaker Evidence Tossed in Arson Case," *Journal News* (June 6, 2017), www.springfieldnewssun.com/news/crime--law/defense-wants-middletown-man-pacemaker-evidence-tossed-arson-case/jZeYV7KjWdncLIZqNbYW2I/; Stephen Jordan, "Apple Health App Data Being Used as Evidence in Murder Trial in Germany," *Digital Trends* (January 14, 2018), www.digitaltrends.com/mobile/apple-health-app-murder-germany/.

[45] Tyler Sonnemaker, "Texas Power Companies Automatically Raised the Temperature of Customers' Smart Thermostats in the Middle of a Heat Wave," *Business Insider* (June 21, 2021), www.businessinsider.com/texas-energy-companies-remotely-raised-smart-thermostats-temperatures-2021-6.

[46] "Fridge as My Witness", note 44 above.

> Everyday objects and devices that can connect to the Internet – known as the Internet of Things (IoT) or connected devices – play an increasing role in crime scenes and are a target for law enforcement. … We believe that a discussion on the exploitation of IoT by law enforcement would benefit from the views of a wide spectrum of voices and opinions, from technologists to criminal lawyers, forensic experts to civil society.

In one especially prominent case, James Bates was charged with strangling and drowning a man, based in part on evidence from Amazon Echo and a smart water meter. The water evidence presumably showed a five-fold uptake in usage that police said corresponding to spraying down the crime scene.[47] But after reviewing the Amazon Echo evidence, prosecutors dropped the case, noting that they could not definitively prove that the accused had committed the murder.[48] In Bates' case, it was not clear that either the government *or* the defense could easily access the evidence, as Amazon initially refused its release to either party, but relented when Bates agreed to allow government access. In another case, investigators again sought Amazon Echo data in connection with a homicide; tellingly, the defense asked "to hear these recordings as well," as they believed them exculpatory.[49]

Some data within this category may exclusively be held in the defense's hand. For example, fitness or health data is often preserved on the user's own devices, and thus could be shared with defense counsel without seeking the permission of either the government or the vendor. In one case, police used data from a complainant's Fitbit to determine

[47] Sara Jerome, "Smart Water Meter Data Considered Evidence in Murder Case," *Water Online* (January 3, 2017), www.wateronline.com/doc/smart-water-meter-considered-evidence-murder-case-0001; Dillon Thomas, "Bentonville PD Says Man Strangled, Drowned Former Georgia Officer," *5 News* (February 23, 2016), www.5newsonline.com/article/news/local/outreach/back-to-school/bentonville-pd-says-man-strangled-drowned-former-georgia-officer/527-0e573fa0-4ff9-457d-8ed1-b4c27762e189; Kathryn Gilker, "Bentonville Police Use Smart Water Meters as Evidence in Murder Investigation," *5 News* (December 28, 2016), www.5newsonline.com/article/news/local/outreach/back-to-school/bentonville-police-use-smart-water-meters-as-evidence-in-murder-investigation/527-e74e0aa5-0e2a-4850-a524-d45d2f3fd048.

[48] Colin Dwyer, "Arkansas Prosecutors Drop Murder Case that Hinged on Evidence from Amazon Echo," *NPR: The Two-Way* (November 29, 2017), www.npr.org/sections/thetwo-way/2017/11/29/567305812/arkansas-prosecutors-drop-murder-case-that-hinged-on-evidence-from-amazon-echo.

[49] Minyvonne Burke, "Amazon's Alexa May Have Witnessed Alleged Florida Murder, Authorities Say," *NBC News* (November 2, 2019), www.nbcnews.com/news/us-news/amazon-s-alexa-may-have-witnessed-alleged-florida-murder-authorities-n1075621.

that the allegations were false,[50] and in another, the government relied on the readings from a suspect's health app to document activity consistent with dragging the victim's body down a hill.[51] But it is just as easy to imagine that the accused might seek to introduce such evidence to show that they had a heart rate consistent with sleep at the time of a violent murder, or that sounds or images from the time of an incident contradict the government's claim.

But of course, in other cases, the data will not be the defendant's data. The accused may seek data from devices owned or operated by a witness, decedent, victim, or even an alleged third-party perpetrator. In the Bates case described above, Bates claimed to have gone to sleep, leaving the decedent and another friend downstairs in the hot tub. The friend claimed to have left just after midnight, and his wife corroborated that claim, thus ruling him out as a suspect. But suppose evidence from a device contradicted those claims? Perhaps the friend's fitness tracker showed that in fact his heart had been racing and he had been moving around vigorously exactly around the time of the murder? Or maybe his "smart" door lock or lighting system would show he arrived home much later than he had claimed. Obtaining such evidence may be difficult for law enforcement, but it is all but impossible for the defense. Again, to quote one report, "[i]n criminal investigations, it is likely that the police will have access to more information and better tools than the witness, victim or suspect."[52]

II.E Surveillance Cameras and Visual Imagery

The overwhelming presence of surveillance tools in contemporary society make visual imagery another critical source of digital defense evidence. In some cities, cameras record nearly every square inch of public space, and are particularly trained on critical areas such as transportation hubs or commercial shopping areas. There have even been reports of the use of drones to conduct domestic policing surveillance in the

50 Criminal Complaint: Affidavit of Probable Cause Continuation, and Order from *Pennsylvania* v. *Risley*, http://online.wsj.com/public/resources/documents/2016_0421_PAvRisley.pdf (Fitbit data contesting victim's account).

51 Philip Kuhn, "Die Version vom Handeln im Affekt ist mit dem heutigen Tag obsolet" (The Option of Acting in Effect Is Obsolete Today), *Welt* (August 1, 2018), www.welt.de/vermischtes/article172287105/Mordprozess-Hussein-K-Die-Version-vom-Handeln-im-Affekt-ist-mit-dem-heutigen-Tag-obsolet.html.

52 "Fridge as My Witness", note 44 above.

United States, and a federal appeals court recently ruled a municipality's "spy plane" surveillance unconstitutional.[53] Private cameras also increasingly record or capture pertinent information, as homeowners use tools like Nest or Ring and businesses install security systems. Individuals may also advertently or inadvertently generate visual records, such as the tourist snapping photos who accidentally captures a robbery, the film crew that unknowingly records a linchpin piece of evidence, or the citizen-journalist who records a police killing.[54]

In perhaps one of the most dramatic examples – so dramatic it inspired a documentary[55] – a man charged with capital murder was able to exonerate himself using media footage that established his alibi.[56] Juan Catalan was charged with murdering a witness who planned to testify against his brother in a separate case, based on the testimony of an eyewitness to the killing. But Catalan explained that he had attended a baseball game at Dodger Stadium on the night of the killing. The prosecutor didn't believe him, but his defense attorney did, and with permission of the stadium he examined all the internal camera footage from the game that night. Although none of that footage turned up evidence of Catalan's presence, Catalan recalled that a film crew had been present that night, gathering footage for a popular television show. The show producers allowed the attorney to review their material, which revealed images of Catalan that corroborated his account. Based on that evidence, and cell phone records placing him at the stadium, the case was dismissed.

In Catalan's case, the defense was able to secure voluntary compliance with private entities, the stadium, the television producers, and the cell phone company. But what if material is held by an entity that does not

[53] See *Leaders of a Beautiful Struggle and others* v. *Baltimore Police Department*, 2 F.4th 330 (4th Cir. 2021) (en banc), https://law.justia.com/cases/federal/appellate-courts/ca4/20-1495/20-1495-2021-06-24.html; Cade Metz, "Police Drones Are Starting to Think for Themselves," *The New York Times* (December 5, 2020), www.nytimes.com/2020/12/05/technology/police-drones.html?action=click&module=News&pgtype=Homepage. But see Timothy M. Ravich, "Courts in the Drone Age" (2015) 42:2 *Northern Kentucky Law Review* 161 at 164, n. 5.

[54] See e.g. "Darnella Frazier," *The Pulitzer Prizes: The 2021 Pulitzer Prize Winner in Special Citations and Awards*, www.pulitzer.org/winners/darnella-frazier.

[55] Christopher Campbell, "New Netflix True-Crime Doc Shows How 'Curb Your Enthusiasm' Saved a Man from Death Row," *Thrillist* (September 29, 2017), www.thrillist.com/entertainment/nation/netflix-documentary-long-shot-curb-your-enthusiasm-death-row.

[56] Kirsten Fleming, "How 'Curb Your Enthusiasm' Saved This Man from Prison," *New York Post* (September 23, 2017), https://nypost.com/2017/09/23/how-curb-your-enthusiasm-saved-this-man-from-prison/.

willingly share its data? For example, in many localities, law enforcement operates the public surveillance cameras, i.e., the very persons who are accusing the defendant of the offense. For good or bad reasons, law enforcement may act as gatekeepers of the data, but when they deny defense requests in order to protect privacy interests, they privilege their own assessment of the relevance of such data or simply act in self-interest to safeguard their case from attack.

In an example from New York, a defense attorney subpoenaed surveillance footage held by the New York Police Department to corroborate the accused's exculpatory account. The prosecutor reluctantly disclosed a portion of the video, claiming that it was only required to disclose video as required by its statutory discovery obligations and the Brady rule,[57] but the defendant asserted an "independent right to subpoena video that will exonerate her."[58] The court, reviewing the arguments, stated:[59]

> [S]ince the inception of this case, the defense forcefully and persistently attempted to obtain surveillance footage that had the potential to "undercut" the complainant's claims and to corroborate his client's claim that she was not present at nor involved in any criminal activity … The defense, however, in contrast to Cruz, could not simply subpoena this potentially exculpating evidence because the footage was held by the NYPD …. Here, the defense compellingly argued that if immediate action was not taken, the recordings, which are maintained by the NYPD's VIPER Unit for a period of no more than 30 days, would be destroyed.

Ultimately ruling on various motions in the case, the court held that the US Constitution and state laws supported the court's preservation order, even if the state's discovery rules did not.[60] But the closeness of the fight demonstrates the extent to which the defense must overcome significant hurdles to access basic information.

[57] *Brady* v. *Maryland*, 373 U.S. 83 (1963) (requiring the prosecutor to disclose of exculpatory information to the defense). But see Angela J. Davis, *Arbitrary Justice: The Power of the American Prosecutor* (New York, NY: Oxford University Press, 2007) at 130–131.

[58] *People* v. *Swygert*, 57 Misc. 3d 913 (NY Crim. Ct. 2017) [*People* v. *Swygert*] at 921–922. See also J. W. August, "Attorney: Security Video Exonerates Dina Shacknai in Death of Rebecca Zahau," *NBC San Diego* (April 20, 2017), www.nbcsandiego.com/news/local/security-video-dina-shacknai-in-death-of-rebecca-zahau/12795/; *People* v. *Butler*, 61 Misc.3d 1009 (NY Sup. Ct. 2018).

[59] *People* v. *Swygert*, note 58 above, at 922. See also Beth Schwartzapfel, "Defendants Kept in the Dark about Evidence, Until It's Too Late," *The New York Times* (August 7, 2017), www.nytimes.com/2017/08/07/nyregion/defendants-kept-in-the-dark-about-evidence-until-its-too-late.html.

[60] *People* v. *Swygert*, note 58 above, at 923–924.

II.F Biometric Identifiers

Biometric identifiers are increasingly used for inculpatory proof, but they also can exculpate or exonerate defendants. Biometrics include familiar techniques such as fingerprinting and blood typing, but also more sophisticated or emerging methods like probabilistic DNA analysis that relies on algorithms to make "matches," iris scanning, facial recognition technologies, or gait or speech analysis.

This category of digital proof may be the most familiar in terms of its exonerative use and thus perhaps requires the least illustration. The Innocence Project sparked a global movement to use DNA testing to free wrongfully convicted persons.[61] But biometric identifiers might also be used by the defense more generally, such as to identify eyewitnesses or alternate suspects, or to bolster the defense. In a disputed incident, biometric evidence might support the defense version, e.g., DNA on the couch but not the bed, over that of the prosecution.

Because of the particular power of DNA, there have been extensive legal analysis of the myriad legal hurdles for the defense in preserving, obtaining, and testing physical evidence,[62] including the fact that physical evidence is typically in the hands of the government, and the tools and expertise required to analyze it may exceed the reach of even well-resourced defense counsel.

II.G Analytical Software Tools

The final category of digital proof overlaps in many ways with the preceding groups, and focuses primarily on the evaluative data generated by machines. The label "analytical software tools" generally describes computer software that is used to reach conclusions or conduct analyses that mimic or exceed the scope of human cognition.

By way of example, prosecutors often rely on artificial intelligence (AI) and machine learning to identify complex patterns or process incomplete data. Perhaps the most common form of such evidence is found in the "probabilistic genotyping systems" used by the government to untangle difficult or degraded DNA samples. An accused could likewise marshal

[61] Innocence Project, www.innocenceproject.org/.

[62] See generally Brandon L. Garrett, "Towards an International Right to Claim Innocence" (2017) 105:4 *California Law Review* 1173; Brandon L. Garrett, "Claiming Innocence" (2008) 92:6 *Minnesota Law Review* 1629. See generally Erin E. Murphy, *Inside the Cell: The Dark Side of Forensic DNA* (New York, NY: Nation Books, 2015).

those tools defensively, either to challenge the system's interpretation of evidence or to uncover supportive defense evidence.

Defense teams have often sought access to the algorithms underlying probabilistic genotyping software that returns inculpatory results used by the prosecution. But companies typically refuse full access, raising trade secret claims that are accepted uncritically by courts.[63] Such software might also be sought by the defense for directly exculpatory reasons, not just to call into question the accuracy of the government's approach,[64] but also to demonstrate that a different party perpetrated the offense or that another interpretation of the evidence is possible.[65]

DNA profiles are not the only targets for analytical software. Evidence from facial recognition software can cast new light on grainy surveillance video,[66] or a speech pattern analysis. As one commentator explains:[67]

> … in a blurry surveillance video or an unclear audio recording, the naked eye and ear may be insufficient to prove guilt beyond a reasonable doubt, but certain recognition algorithms could do so easily. Lip-reading algorithms might tell jurors what was said on video where there is no audio available. A machine might construct an estimation of a perpetrator's face from only a DNA sample, or in other DNA analysis of corrupted samples.

Of course, the same could be true for the defense. Software could corroborate a defense claim or undermine the credibility of a government witness. It could also aid the defense in identifying other witnesses to the event or alternative perpetrators. In a case where inculpatory evidence was seized from a computer, the defense successfully argued for suppression of the evidence by obtaining information about how the software used to search the computer worked, thereby showing the search exceeded its permissible scope.[68]

[63] See e.g. "Life, Liberty" and "Trial by Machine", both note 7 above.

[64] See e.g. *United States* v. *Gissantaner*, 417 F. Supp.3d 857 (WD Mich. 2019) (holding the government's probabilistic DNA results evidence inadmissible because they lacked reliability).

[65] See e.g. Katherine Kwong, "The Algorithm Says You Did It: The Use of Black Box Algorithms to Analyze Complex DNA Evidence" (2017) 31:1 *Harvard Journal of Law & Technology* 275 at 287–288 (citing defense uses of TrueAllele).

[66] See e.g. Ben Fox Rubin, "Facial Recognition Overkill: How Deputies Cracked a $12 Shoplifting Case," *CNET* (March 19, 2019), www.cnet.com/news/facial-recognition-overkill-how-deputies-solved-a-12-shoplifting-case/.

[67] Patrick W. Nutter, "Machine Learning Evidence: Admissibility and Weight" (2019) 21:3 *University of Pennsylvania Journal of Constitutional Law* 919 at 921.

[68] Jack Gillum, "Prosecutors Dropping Child Porn Charges after Software Tools Are Questioned," *ProPublica* (April 3, 2019), www.propublica.org/article/prosecutors-dropping-child-porn-charges-after-software-tools-are-questioned.

III Characteristics of Digital Proof

The preceding section provides a general overview of the digital shift in evidence in criminal prosecutions, and identifies the ways in which such evidence might likewise be critical to the defense. And as the preceding section demonstrates, it is not the case that the data's reliability is a defendant's only concern. The defense also requires access to digital proof for the same reasons that the government does – because digital evidence can help find or bolster witnesses, establish a critical fact, or impeach a claim. But the preceding part also reveals just how little guidance exists, either as a matter of rules-based guidance or judicial opinion, for those attempting to craft a meaningful defense right to access and use this material. This part identifies the critical questions that must be answered, and values that must be weighed, in devising a regime of comprehensive access to such information for defensive or exculpatory purposes.

1. Who "owns" and who "possesses" the data. Perhaps the most important question with regard to technological forms of evidence is who owns and who possesses the data. Ownership is critical because, as with physical items, the right to share or disclose data often rests in the hands of the owner. Possession is also critical because, as with physical items, a possessor may disclose information surreptitiously without permission or knowledge of the owner.

The most straightforward cases involve physical items owned and possessed by the accused or a person sympathetic to the accused's interest, in which the data is stored locally in the instrument. Such might be the case for a security camera owned by the defendant, or an electronic device with stored files. In these cases, the owner can make the evidence available to the defense.

But many technological forms of evidence will not be accessed so simply. As a general matter, ownership might be in public, governmental hands, such as police or public housing surveillance footage, or private hands, such as a private security camera. Even the category of private ownership is complex – ownership may be as simple as belonging to a private individual, or as complex as ownership held by a publicly traded large corporate entity. In some cases, ownership may even cross categories. Digital information in particular may have multiple "owners," e.g., a user who uploads a picture to a social media site may technically own the intellectual property, but the terms of service for the site may grant the site-owner a broad license to use or publicize the material.[69]

[69] See e.g. Instagram, "Terms of Use," https://help.instagram.com/.

When possession is divorced from ownership, a new suite of problems arises. Even when an owner is sympathetic or willing to share information with the defense, access may nonetheless be thwarted by an entity or person in possession of the data. Possession may also make access questions difficult because the reach of legal process may not extend to a physical site where information is kept. Possessors may also undermine the right of owners to exclude, e.g., if a security company grants visual access to the interior of a home against the wishes of the owner.

In both cases, obtaining data from third-party owners or possessors runs the further risk of disclosing defense strategies or theories. The government may have the capacity to hide its use of technology behind contracts with non-disclosure clauses or vague references to "confidential informants." Human Rights Watch has labeled this practice "parallel construction" and documented its use.[70] But a criminal defendant may not be able to operate stealthily, relying instead on the goodwill of a third party not to disclose the effort or a court's willingness to issue an *ex parte* order.

2. Who created the data. In many cases, answering questions of ownership and possession will in turn answer the question of creation. But not always. An email may be drafted by one person, sent to a recipient who becomes its legal "owner," and then possessed or stored by a third party. Or an entity may "create" information or data by collecting or analyzing material owned or possessed by another, e.g., a DNA sample sent for processing through analytical software; the data is created by the processing company, and the physical sample tested may be "owned" or possessed by the government.

Data created by the defendant perhaps poses only ancillary obstacles when it comes to a defendant's access to information. If anything, a defendant's claim to having created data may bolster their claim to access, even if they neither own nor possess it.[71] Some jurisdictions even specifically bestow upon an individual the right to access, correct, and delete data.[72] But it may also be the case that the diffusion

[70] "Dark Side: Secret Origins of Evidence in US Criminal Cases," *Human Rights Watch* (January 9, 2018), www.hrw.org/report/2018/01/09/dark-side/secret-origins-evidence-us-criminal-cases#.

[71] Cf. *O'Grady* v. *Superior Court*, 44 Cal.Rptr.3d 72 (2006).

[72] Pollyanna Sanderson, Katelyn Ringrose, & Stacey Gray, "It's Raining Privacy Bills: An Overview of the Washington State Privacy Act and Other Introduced Bills," *Future of Privacy Forum* (January 13, 2020), https://fpf.org/2020/01/13/its-raining-privacy-bills-an-overview-of-the-washington-state-privacy-act-and-other-introduced-bills/ ["Privacy Bills"].

of claims in data may complicate rules for access and use by the defense. Imagine a piece of technology or evidence possessed by one party, owned by another person, and created by still another person – with disputes between the parties about whether or not to release the information.

3. For what purpose was the data created. Another factor that must be considered in contemplating defense access is the source of the data and the purpose for which it was created. Much of the information that the defense may seek to access for exculpatory purposes will have likely been created for reasons unrelated to the criminal matter. For example, an automated vacuum may record the placement of the furniture in the room so that it can efficiently clean, but such data might be useful to show the layout at the time of the robbery. Or a search engine may store entered searches to optimize results and targeted advertising, but the record may suggest that a third party was the true killer. Such purpose need not be singular, either. The person searching the internet has one goal, but the internet search engine company has a different objective. The critical point is that the reason the information is there may help shed light on the propriety of defense access.

By way of example, the most compelling case for unconstrained access to the defense might be for data that was created specifically for a law enforcement purpose. In the national security context in the United States, a statutory frame exists to resolve some of these claims.[73] Conversely, the most difficult case for access might be for information privately created for personal purposes unrelated to the criminal case. Although no single factor should determine the capacity and scope of access, the extent to which data or information is created expressly with a criminal justice purpose in mind may shed light on the extent to which such information should also be made accessible to an accused.

4. With what permissions was the data created. A related point arises with regard to how much of the general public is swept into a data disclosure, and the extent to which participants implicated by its disclosure are aware of the risks posed by broader dissemination. Open access to surveillance footage is troubling because it has the potential to implicate the privacy rights of persons other than the accused, who have no relation to the crime and who may not even know that they appear in the footage. Although we might tolerate those rights

[73] Cf. "Digital Innocence", note 7 above, at 1045–1048.

being compromised when it is only law enforcement who will access the information, or when used by a private operator with little incentive to exploit it, giving access to defense attorneys may create cause for concern. Persons in heavily policed neighborhoods may fear that, after viewing an image in surveillance, attorneys will be incentivized to accuse a third party of the crime simply out of expedience rather than in good faith. But such concerns may be minimized when creators or owners voluntarily provide data to law enforcement for law enforcement purposes.

5. How enduring or resilient is the data and who has the authority to destroy it. A central concern about defense access to data is that, without prompt and thorough access, such data will be destroyed before the defendant has a chance to request its preservation, if not disclosure. Some forms of evidence may be incredibly resilient. For example, cloud computing services or biometric identifiers of known persons may be highly resilient to destruction or elimination.

But other forms of data may be transient in nature, or subject to deliberate interference by an unwilling owner or holder of the data. Surveillance cameras notoriously run on short time loops, automatically erasing and retaping data in limited increments. Social media or other sites may promise total erasure of deleted material, not just superficial elimination from a single device.

Meaningful defense access to technological tools for exculpatory purposes requires attentiveness to timing, such that a defendant is able to access the material before its destruction. Even if the entitlement extends no farther than preservation, with actual access and use to be decided later, that would significantly impact a defendant's capacity to make use of this information.

6. The form, expertise, and instrumentation required to understand or present the data. Generally speaking, evidentiary form is likely to be a less pertinent consideration in any framework for defense access than are questions related to ownership or possession. What import is it if the data is on a hard drive or flash drive? What matters is who owns it and who has it.

Nevertheless, any comprehensive scheme for meaningful defense access must consider form inasmuch as certain forms at the extreme may entail greater or lesser burdens on the party disclosing the information. Data diffused over a large and unsearchable system may provide important information to a defense team, but even turning over that data may present a significant challenge to its holder. In the Catalan case above, the surveillance video that exonerated him was physically held by the stadium officials and the production company. Fortunately, it was rather confined, as it covered one day and one game. It was the defense attorney who pored through the footage, isolating the exculpatory images.

But what if the records go beyond a single episode, or require special instrumentation to interpret. Information that requires that a holder devote significant time or resources to make the data available, or that is not readily shareable or accessible without expertise or instrumentation, may pose much more significant hurdles to open defense access. Some defense claims may actually be requests for access to services, rather than disclosure of information. For example, a defense request to run a DNA profile in the national database or to query a probabilistic genotyping system with a different set of parameters is less about traditional disclosure than about commandeering the government's resources to investigate a defense theory. The same could be true for location data from a witness's phone or search records from a particular IP address. The sought information is less an item than a process, a process to be conducted by a third party, not the defense.

7. What are the associated costs or expenses, and are there even available experts for the defense. A critical logistical, if not legal, hurdle to defense access to digital and technological evidence is the cost associated with seeking, interpreting, and introducing such evidence. Most of the forms of evidence described require some degree of expertise to extract, interpret, and understand, much less to explain to a judge, attorney, or juror. To the extent that the information also seeks an operational process or other search measure, the owner or possessor of the information may justly charge a fee for such services. Even more troubling, some vendors may restrict access to the government, or there may not be an available defense expert to hire given the lack of a robust market.

In this way, cost alone can preclude equitable access. For example, even assuming the defendant could get access to the probabilistic software used to interpret a complicated DNA crime sample, and assuming the vendor who contracted with the government would agree to run a defense query, the vendor may nonetheless charge for the service. Routine costs like copying fees or hourly rates can quickly put even routine investigative efforts beyond the capacity of a criminal defense lawyer, as the vast majority of defendants are indigent and there may be insufficient public funds available or such funds may be jealously guarded by judicial officials.[74]

The introduction of this evidence also may require payment of expert fees so that the attorney is able to understand and clearly present the findings. Such costs can make defense lawyers reluctant even to pursue exculpatory evidence, because actually obtaining and using it appears insurmountable.

One still more troubling possibility is that some subpoenaed parties will actively choose to defy orders rather than comply. As discussed above, social media companies Facebook and Twitter (now X) both refused to turn over posts requested by the defense in a criminal case, leading the judge to hold them in contempt and fine each $1,000 – the maximum allowed under the law.[75] With fines capped statutorily, a company wealthy enough or unlikely to be a repeat player might simply choose non-compliance.

8. What are the privacy implications of divulging the data. Perhaps the most apparent and central concern raised by defense access to digital data relates to privacy. The nature of the material sought and the scope of what it reveals, along with the number of persons implicated by defense disclosure, is perhaps equal only to concerns about unnecessary "fishing expeditions" or wasted resources as a basis for the reluctance to provide generous access to the defense. Whereas the government is bound to act in the interest of the public, and thus in theory should minimize harm to innocent third parties in the course of its investigations, the defense is entitled to act only in furtherance of the interest of the accused.

At one end of the spectrum, some technological evidence will reveal deeply private or personal data belonging to a person wholly unrelated to the criminal offense. The DNA sequence or entire email history of a witness, or extensive public surveillance of a small community, obviously implicate profound interests. But at the other end of the spectrum, discrete bits of information created by the defendant him- or herself pose little concern when sought by the same defendant.

And of course, non-digital forms of evidence can raise the same concerns. As such, there are already mechanisms available to limit the privacy impact of revealing information to the defense. In prosecution

[74] See e.g. Stephen A. Saltzburg, "The Duty to Investigate and the Availability of Expert Witnesses" (2018) 86:4 *Fordham Law Review* 1709 at 1720 ("[R]eluctance to appoint defense experts is rooted in cost to the government and inertia; i.e., a history of not routinely providing defense experts at the request of defense counsel").

[75] "$5 Billion Fine", note 37 above.

investigations, it is not unusual to have a "taint team" that reviews sensitive information and passes along only the incriminating material to the prosecutor in the case. Or a judge can take on the responsibility to review material *in camera*, i.e., outside of the view of the parties and their attorneys, and disclose only evidence that is relevant to the defense.

In short, privacy is understandably a central and driving concern, but it should not be a definitive reason to close the door on broad defense access to exculpatory or defensive material.

9. What legal restrictions, whether substantive, procedural, or jurisdictional, limit access or use. The final critical inquiry incorporates some aspects of the privacy concerns just discussed, but goes beyond them. Namely, any comprehensive effort to provide defense access to digital and technological evidence must square with existing legal regimes surrounding disclosure and use of such evidence, whether as a matter of comprehensive or targeted privacy laws, intellectual or physical property, trade secret, or evidence. At a basic level, the data may straddle jurisdictions – created in one place, processed in another, and then used somewhere else. Legal restrictions may also be loosely lumped into substantive and procedural limitations, differentiating between substantive constraints such as privacy laws and procedural impediments such as jurisdictional rules.

Background statutory regimes that may conflict with defense access are imperative to consider, because jurisdictions increasingly have adopted such restrictions in response to complaints about privacy.[76] Although law enforcement is routinely afforded exceptions to privacy statutes,[77] there is rarely any mention of any equivalent route of access for a criminal defendant.[78] Moreover, even outside the realm of privacy law, there may be other statutory limitations on disclosure or access, such as legal non-disclosure agreements. Or jurisdictions may point to regulatory regimes aimed at reliability as sufficient to safeguard all of the defendant's interests.[79]

[76] See e.g. Paul M. Schwartz, "Global Data Privacy: The EU Way" (2019) 94:4 *New York University Law Review* 771; Electronic Privacy Information Center, "Face Surveillance and Biometrics," https://epic.org/issues/surveillance-oversight/face-surveillance/; "Privacy Bills", note 72 above.

[77] See generally "Politics of Privacy", note 13 above.

[78] See generally "Privacy Asymmetries", note 7 above.

[79] See e.g. Federal Institute of Metrology METAS, "Legal Metrology – Regulating Measurement and Ensuring Its Binding Implementation," *Swiss Confederation*, www.metas.ch/metas/en/home/gesmw/gesetzliches-messwesen---messen-regeln---.html.

IV Conclusion

Digital proof is here, and it is here to stay. Such proof has already assumed a prominent place in the prosecution of criminal suspects. But all too often, the ability of the defense to access and utilize such evidence depends on happenstance rather than formal right. By cataloging and characterizing this critical form of proof, the chapter hopes to support efforts to formalize and standardize a defendant's ability to marshal defense evidence for exculpatory and adversarial purposes as readily as the government does to inculpate.

MAMAK ©

10

Data as Evidence in Criminal Courts

Comparing Legal Frameworks and Actual Practices

BART CUSTERS AND LONNEKE STEVENS

I. Introduction*

Technology has rapidly changed our society over the past decades. As a result of the ubiquitous digitalization of our society, people continuously leave digital traces behind. Some have already referred to this as "digital exhaust."[1] People are often monitored without being aware of it, not only by camera surveillance systems, but also by their own smartphones and by other devices they use to access the internet.

Information about the whereabouts, behavior, networks, intentions, and interests of people can be very useful in a criminal law context. It is used mainly for guiding criminal investigations, as it may provide clues on potential suspects, witnesses, etc., but it can also constitute evidence in courts, as the data may confirm specific actions and behavior of actors. In other words, digital data can be used to find out exactly what happened, understood in the legal context as finding the truth, and try to prove what happened, understood in the legal context as providing evidence. This chapter focuses on the use of digital data as evidence in criminal courts. The large amounts of potentially useful data now available may cause a shift in the types of evidence presented in courts, in that there may be more digital data as evidence, in addition to or at the cost of other types of evidence, such as statements from suspects, victims, and witnesses.[2]

* A preliminary version of this chapter was published as Bart Custers & Lonneke Stevens, "The Use of Data as Evidence in Dutch Criminal Courts" (2021) 29:1 *European Journal of Crime, Criminal Law and Criminal Justice* 25.

[1] Bruce Schneier, "The Battle for Power on the Internet," *The Atlantic* (October 24, 2013), www.theatlantic.com/technology/archive/2013/10/the-battle-for-power-on-the-internet/280824/.

[2] Data within a criminal procedural context means information that needs to be found and/or understood by means of certain techniques and expertise; thus, a witness statement is not data, but a DNA profile is.

However, in many jurisdictions, the legal provisions setting the rules for the use of evidence in criminal courts were formulated long before these digital technologies existed. As a result of ongoing technological developments, there seems to be an increasing discrepancy between legal frameworks and actual practices. The chapter investigates this disconnect by analyzing the relevant legal frameworks in the European Union for processing data in criminal courts and then comparing and contrasting these with actual court practices.

The relevant legal frameworks are criminal law and data protection law. Data protection law is mostly harmonized throughout the European Union, via the General Data Protection Regulation (GDPR)[3] and by regulation more specifically tailored to the criminal law context, via Directive 2016/680, also known as the Law Enforcement Directive (LED).[4] Criminal law, however, is mostly national law, with limited harmonization throughout the European Union. For this reason, criminal law is considered from a national perspective in this chapter. Criminal law in the Netherlands is taken as an example to illustrate the issues that may arise from using data as evidence in criminal courts.

Although Dutch criminal law may not be representative for all EU Member States, the discrepancies between EU data protection law and Dutch criminal law may be similar to other EU Member States. As such, the Netherlands may serve as a helpful example of how legal provisions dealing with the use of evidence in criminal courts is not aligned with developments in data as evidence.

We also think that reviewing the use of data as evidence in courts in the Netherlands may be interesting for other jurisdictions, because it can provide some best practices as well as identify caveats and pitfalls that can perhaps be avoided in other countries. We see two major arguments supporting such a claim. First, the issues of using data as evidence in courts are likely to be the same across Europe, as the technologies available are not confined to one or particular jurisdictions. This point also applies to the forensic standards that are applied, as these also have an international scope and nature, either because they are established by international standardization organizations such as ISO,[5]

[3] General Data Protection Regulation, EU 2016, Regulation (EU) 2016/679 (with effect from May 25, 2018) [GDPR].

[4] The Data Protection Law Enforcement Directive, EU 2016, Directive (EU) 2016/680 (with effect from May 5, 2016) [LED].

[5] International Organization for Standardization, www.iso.org/home.html.

CEN-CENELEC,[6] and ETSI[7], or, if created on a national level, are at least aligned among forensics experts from different countries. Second, the legal frameworks for using data as evidence in courts are highly comparable. This is particularly the case for data protection law, which is highly harmonized across the European Union. Criminal law may not be harmonized that much across the European Union, but the norms and standards for evidence and fair trial are fleshed out in large part by the European Convention on Human Rights (ECHR) and Court of Justice of the European Union (CJEU) case law. All this means that the basic situation regarding technology and forensic practices and the relevant legal boundaries are more or less the same across the European Union, although national interpretations and practices within these confines may vary.

There are two other reasons to use the Netherlands as an example in this chapter, both related to the fact that the Netherlands is in the forefront of relevant regulation. First, international legal comparisons show that the Netherlands is a front runner in privacy and data protection law in several aspects.[8] The Netherlands implemented national legislation with higher levels of data protection than strictly necessary for compliance with EU data protection laws. Typical examples are data breach notification laws and mandatory privacy impact assessments that already existed in the Netherlands before the GDPR came into force in 2018.[9] Also, when looking at the criminal law context, the Netherlands was among the first countries to have specific acts for the police and the judiciary dealing with the processing of personal data in criminal law, long before EU Directive 2016/680 (the LED, see section III.C) came into force.[10] If there exists a

[6] CEN stands for European Committee for Standardization (*Comité Européen de Normalisation*) and CENELEC stands for European Committee for Electrotechnical Standardization (*Comité Europeén de Normalisation Électrotechnique*), www.cencenelec.eu/.

[7] European Telecommunications Standards Institute, www.etsi.org/.

[8] Bart Custers, Alan M. Sears, Francien Dechesne *et al.*, *EU Personal Data Protection in Policy and Practice* (Heidelberg, Germany: Asser/Springer, 2019) [*EU Personal Data*].

[9] Christopher Kuner, "The European Commission's Proposed Data Protection Regulation: A Copernican Revolution in European Data Protection Law" (2012) *Bloomberg BNA Privacy and Security Law Report* 1.

[10] The introduction of EU Directive 2016/680 required few changes in the Dutch legal framework for processing personal data in criminal law. In comparison, in Italy, there were no specific laws or regulations for the protection of personal data in criminal law, apart from the general legislation for criminal investigation and the GDPR. As such, Italy needed to draft entirely new legislation. In other countries, such as Germany, Sweden, and Romania, this topic was dealt with in their Police Acts, which often needed further elaboration to comply with this EU Directive. *EU Personal Data*, note 8 above.

disconnect between legal frameworks and actual practices with regard to data as evidence in criminal courts in a country that seems to be a regulatory front runner, in this case the Netherlands, similar problems may also exist in other EU Member States.

Second, the Netherlands is among the front runners in digital forensics and cybercrime legislation.[11] The Netherlands was among the initiators of the Convention on Cybercrime, adopted by the Council of Europe in 2001, which includes provisions that relate to the processing of police data.[12] This Convention regulates, among other things, the protection of personal data and international cooperation, including the exchange of personal data in criminal law cases between authorities of different countries. Also, the Netherlands ratified a series of legal instruments that aim to advance the cooperation and sharing of information between Member States, such as the Prüm Treaty[13] (for exchanging DNA data, fingerprints, and traffic data), the Schengen Information System[14] (for international criminal investigation information), the Visa Information System[15] (for visa data, including biometrical data), and the Customs Information System[16] and Eurodac[17] (for fingerprints

[11] Susan Brenner & Bert-Jaap Koops, "Approaches to Cybercrime Jurisdiction" (2004) 4:1 *Journal of High Technology Law* 1; Bert-Jaap Koops, "Cybercrime Legislation in the Netherlands" (2005) 2005:4 *Cybercrime and Security* 1.

[12] European, Council of Europe, Convention on Cybercrime, ETS No. 185 (Budapest: Council of Europe, 2001) Arts. 19–21.

[13] European Union, The Council of the European Union, Council Decision 2008/615/JHA on the Stepping Up of Cross-border Cooperation, Particularly in Combating Terrorism and Cross-border Crime, OJ 2008 L 210 (EU: Official Journal of the European Union, 2008).

[14] European Union, The Council of the European Union, Council Decision 2007/533/JHA on the Establishment, Operation and Use of the Second Generation Schengen Information System (SIS II), OJ 2007 L 205 (EU: Official Journal of the European Union, 2007).

[15] European Union, The European Parliament, & The Council of the European Union, Regulation (EC) No. 767/2008 of The European Parliament and of The Council Concerning the Visa Information System (VIS) and the Exchange of Data Between Member States on Short-Stay Visas (VIS Regulation), OJ 2008 L 218 (EU: Official Journal of the European Union, 2008).

[16] European Union, The Council of the European Union, Council Decision 2009/917/JHA on the Use of Information Technology for Customs Purposes, OJ 2009 L 323 (EU: Official Journal of the European Union, 2009).

[17] European Union, The Council of the European Union, Council Regulation (EC) 2725/2000 Concerning the Establishment of 'Eurodac' for the Comparison of Fingerprints for the Effective Application of the Dublin Convention, OJ 2000 L 316 (EU: Official Journal of the European Union, 2000); European Union, The Council of the European Union, Council Regulation (EC) 407/2002 Laying Down Certain Rules to Implement Regulation

of asylum seekers and stateless people). The institutional regulations for Europol, Eurosur, and Eurojust contain provisions for the exchange of criminal law information between Member States.

In short, the Netherlands appears to be among the first countries in the European Union to develop both privacy and data protection, and digital forensics and cybercrime legislation. This characteristic is relevant because if there is a disconnect between legal frameworks and actual practices with regard to data as evidence in criminal courts in a country that seems to be in the forefront of regulation, in this case the Netherlands, it may be expected that similar problems also exist in other EU Member States.

In the Netherlands, a founding member of the European Union and its predecessors, there has been an extensive debate in society and in politics on how to balance using data in a criminal law context and protecting the right to privacy.[18] This debate has influenced the legal frameworks that regulate the use of data in criminal law. There are competing legal frameworks regulating this area: on the one hand, criminal law, including both substantive and procedural criminal law, and, on the other hand, privacy law, more specifically data protection law. It is important to note that both legal frameworks provide rules for allowing and restricting the use of personal data in criminal law, as sometimes there is a misunderstanding that criminal law would only or mainly allow the collection and processing of data, whereas data protection law would only or mainly restrict such data collection and processing.

The focus of this chapter is the discrepancy between legal frameworks and actual practices. First, the relevant legal frameworks for processing data in Dutch criminal courts are analyzed, i.e., Dutch criminal procedure law and EU data protection law). After this legal analysis, current court practices are examined, mainly by looking at typical case law and current developments in society and technology.

2725/2000 Concerning the Establishment of 'Eurodac' for the Comparison of Fingerprints for the Effective Application of the Dublin Convention, OJ 2002 L 62 (EU: Official Journal of the European Union, 2002).

[18] Together with France and Italy, the Netherlands had a debate focused on privacy versus security. This culminated in a referendum on the proposed Intelligence Agencies Act that extended powers for intelligence agencies, which voters turned down. Since this referendum was not binding, the Dutch government accepted the act anyway and abolished this type of referendum; see Charlotte Wagenaar, "Beyond For or Against? Multi-Option Alternatives to a Corrective Referendum" (2019) 62:1 *Electoral Studies* Article 102091. This case shows a clear tension between the general public's commitment to privacy issues versus the government's priority of national security, and perhaps also of criminal law enforcement.

This chapter is structured as follows. Section II provides a brief general introduction to Dutch criminal procedure law. Section III provides a brief general introduction to EU data protection law and to some extent its implementation in Dutch data protection law, focusing on the GDPR and the LED respectively. Section IV investigates the actual use of evidence in Dutch criminal courts by focusing first on current court practices as reflected in case law, and second on current developments in society and technology. Section V compares current court practices with the developments in society and technology, in order to see whether there is a need to change court practices or the underlying legal frameworks.

II Criminal Procedure Law: The Example of the Netherlands

As the Netherlands is used as an example of national law in this chapter, some background information is provided regarding Dutch criminal law. The Dutch Code of Criminal Procedure (Dutch CCP)[19] dates back to 1926. Back then, the Code was characterized as "moderately accusatorial" since it introduced more rights for the defense than before that time.[20] Today, however, the suspect remains to a large extent the object of investigation, rather than, e.g., the victim, which has become increasingly important in Dutch criminal law in recent decades.[21] This is especially the case in the stages of police investigation, before the start of the trial. Although over the years more possibilities for the defense to influence the earlier investigation were introduced, such as the right to contra-expertise during police investigation in Article 150b of the Dutch CCP, the defense and the prosecutor are far from equal parties. Basically, the room for maneuver for the defense largely depends on the prosecutor's goodwill, as it is the prosecutor who leads the criminal investigation.[22]

19 *Wetboek van Strafrecht* (Dutch Code of Criminal Procedure), Netherlands (1926) [Dutch CCP].

20 See Lonneke Stevens, *Het nemo-teneturbeginsel in strafzaken: van zwijgrecht naar containerbegrip* (The Nemo Tenetur Principle in Criminal Cases: From the Right to Remain Silent to an All-Purpose Concept, PhD thesis, Tilburg University) (Nijmegen, Netherlands: Wolf Legal Publishers, 2005) at ch. 3.

21 Cf. Jo-Anne Wemmers, Rien van der Leeden, & Herman Steensma, "What Is Procedural Justice: Criteria Used by Dutch Victims to Assess the Fairness of Criminal Justice Procedures" (1995) 8:4 *Social Justice Research* 329.

22 For more details, see Jeroen Chorus, Ewoud Hondius, & Wim Voermans (eds.), *Introduction to Dutch Law*, 5th ed. (Alphen aan den Rijn, Netherlands: Kluwer Law International, 2016).

A more accurate description of Dutch criminal procedure would therefore be "moderately inquisitorial."[23]

Fundamental to the position of the defense is the right to silence in Article 29 of the Dutch CCP. Rights and principles such as the privilege against self-incrimination, the equality of arms, and the presumption of innocence are not explicitly laid down in the Dutch CCP. They apply, however, directly to Dutch criminal procedure through Article 6 of the ECHR.

The Dutch CCP has been amended and supplemented many times since its creation in 1926. As a result, the Dutch CCP now looks more like a patchwork instead of structured and clear-cut Code. This is also one of the reasons that the legislator started the major, still-running project "Modernisation Criminal Procedure" (*Modernisering Strafvordering*) in 2014. This revision of legislation was not finished as of 2023, and it will take several more years before it is finished. The idea is to revise the Dutch CCP in order to make criminal procedure, among other things, more accessible and efficient.[24] Another aim of the revision is to tackle one of the greater challenges criminal procedures face nowadays, those of keeping up with technological developments in criminal investigation practice and developing an overall framework for regulating criminal investigation in the digital era. The Dutch CCP is still very much an analog-style Code that regulates the searching of homes, the seizure of letters, wiretapping, the questioning of witnesses, etc. Various digital investigation methods can be conducted on the basis of existing powers, e.g., a computer that was seized in a home can be searched just like a diary or a pistol that was seized in a home,[25] and several new digital investigation methods have been laid down in the Dutch CCP, e.g., the network search of Article 125j of the Dutch CCP or the hacking powers in Article 126nba of the Dutch CCP,[26] but many digital methods

[23] Geert Corstens, Matthias Borgers, & Tijs Kooijmans, *Het Nederlands strafprocesrecht* (Dutch Criminal Procedure Law) (Deventer, Netherlands: Kluwer, 2018) [*Het Nederlands*] at 10.

[24] See Documenten Modernisering Wetboek van Strafvordering, www.rijksoverheid.nl/documenten/publicaties/2017/11/13/documenten-modernisering-wetboek-van-strafvordering; Platform Modernisering Strafvordering, www.moderniseringstrafvordering.nl/.

[25] See Bert-Jaap Koops & Jan-Jaap Oerlemans, "Formeel strafrecht en ICT" (Substantive Criminal Law and ICT) in Bert-Jaap Koops & Jan-Jaap Oerlemans (eds.), *Strafrecht en ICT* (The Hague, Netherlands: Sdu Uitgevers, 2018) 117 at 125–127.

[26] Introduced with the Computer Crime Law III, Netherlands (in force since March 2019). See also Ronald Pool & Bart Custers, "The Police Hack Back: Legitimacy, Necessity and Privacy Implications of the Next Step in Fighting Cybercrime" (2017) 25:2 *European Journal of Crime, Criminal Law and Criminal Justice* 123.

are still unregulated. Awaiting legislation, some gaps have been filled provisionally by the Supreme Court, in cases where the defense questioned the legitimacy of certain methods. One important discussion concerns the legitimacy of searching a smartphone that was seized from a suspect after arrest. In 2017, the Supreme Court ruled that the general power of a policeman to "seize and search objects the suspect carries with him when arrested" in Articles 94 and 95 of the Dutch CCP can be the basis of a smartphone search under the condition that the infringement on the right to privacy remains limited.[27] In cases where the infringement exceeds a limited search, such a search should be conducted or authorized by the public prosecutor. When it is foreseeable that the privacy-infringement will be "serious" (*zeer ingrijpend*), the investigatory judge needs to be involved.

The smartphone ruling of the Supreme Court needs to be understood from the perspective of the procedural legality principle that is laid down in Article 1 of the Dutch CCP. This article states that criminal procedure can only take place as foreseen by law,[28] which means that the police cannot use investigation methods that infringe fundamental rights which are not explicitly grounded in a sufficiently detailed and explicit statutory investigation power. However, investigation methods that are not explicitly regulated in the Dutch CCP, like the seize and search powers in Articles 94 and 95 of the Dutch CCP mentioned above, and that only cause minor infringements, can be based on Article 3 of the Police Act.[29] This Article contains the general description of the task carried out by the police: "it is the task of the police to maintain the legal order in accordance with the rules and under the subordination of the competent authority."[30] In case law, several digital investigation methods have been found to constitute only a minor infringement and therefore did not need to be explicitly regulated.[31] For example, sending stealth text

[27] Dutch Supreme Court (via www.rechtspraak.nl), HR 4 April 2017, *NJ* 2017, 229, ECLI:NL:HR:2017:584; see also the case note of Lonneke Stevens, "Onderzoek in een smartphone: Zoeken naar een redelijke verhouding tussen privacybescherming en werkbare opsporing" (Smartphone Searches: Balancing Privacy Protection and Criminal Investigation Practices) (2017) *Ars Aequi* 730 at 730–735. For an explanation in English, see Bryce Clayton Newell & Bert-Jaap Koops, "From Horseback to the Moon and Back: Comparative Limits on Police Searches of Smartphones upon Arrest" (2020) 72:1 *Hastings Law Journal* 229 ["From Horseback"].

[28] "Law" meaning formal acts of Parliament.

[29] *Het Nederlands*, note 23 above, at 29–30.

[30] Police Act 1993, Netherlands (with effect from December 9, 1993), Art. 3.

[31] This approach is also taken in some proposals in the United States, such as the American Bar Association (ABA) Model Standards for Criminal Justice: Law Enforcement Access

messages[32] to someone's cell phone can in principle be based on the general police task description, except when this is done for such a period or with such frequency and intensity that a complete image is revealed of certain aspects of someone's private life.[33] The smartphone case, in which a very general power to seize was found to be a sufficient statutory basis for a limited smartphone search, builds on this settled case law.[34] In its legislative draft on digital investigation, the "Modernisation" legislator has incorporated the so-called "pyramid-structure" of the smartphone case, i.e., within the categories of limited, more than limited, and serious intrusions. A larger privacy infringement demands a higher approval authority, so instead of the police, a prosecutor or investigatory judge is required. Also, limited intrusions do not have to be explicitly regulated, while more than limited and serious intrusions are in need of more detailed and stringent legislation. To distinguish between the different levels of privacy intrusion, the legislator uses the concept of "systematicness" (*stelselmatigheid*).[35] This means that, e.g., a "forseeably systematic" computer or network search can be ordered by the public prosecutor, while a "foreseeably serious systematic" computer or network search also needs a warrant from the investigating judge.[36] The same regime applies to research in open sources.[37] The post-smartphone case law already demonstrates that the category of seriously systematic is almost non-existent in practice.[38] Although the introduction of the pyramid structure is also based on the practical premise that the investigating judge should not be overburdened within the context of digital investigations, this does raise serious concerns about the level of legal protection.

to Third Party Records (2013), www.americanbar.org/groups/criminal_justice/standards/law_enforcement_access/. US courts have so far largely rejected this approach.

32 Stealth text messaging refers to sending a text message to a cell phone without the phone acknowledging receipt, in order to generate traffic data with the phone's location that can be ordered from a telecoms provider.

33 Dutch Supreme Court, HR 1 July 2014, *NJ* 2015, 114, ECLI:NL:HR:2014:1563.

34 See Dutch Supreme Court, HR 4 April 2017, *NJ* 2017, 229, ECLI:NL:HR:2017:584.

35 It was initially the Commission "Modernisation of criminal investigation in the digital era" (Koops-Commission) that suggested the use of *systematicness* as a structuring concept; see the advice in: Netherlands, Commissie modernisering opsporingsonderzoek in het digitale tijdperk, *Regulering van opsporingsbevoegdheden in een digitale omgeving* (Regulating Criminal Investigation Powers in Digital Environments), s. l. (Netherlands: Commissie modernisering opsporingsonderzoek in het digitale tijdperk, 2018) ["Koops-Commission"].

36 See the proposal for the *Nieuw Wetboek van Strafvordering* (Proposed Code of Criminal Procedure), Netherlands (as amended July 2020) [Proposed CCP], Arts. 2.7.39 and 2.7.41.

37 Ibid., Art. 2.8.8.

38 "From Horseback", note 27 above, at 264–268.

III Dutch and EU Data Protection Law

III.A GDPR and LED

In 2016, the European Union issued the final text for the GDPR, revising the EU legal framework for personal data protection. This legislative instrument, well known throughout the European Union, is directly binding for all EU Member States and their citizens.[39] To a large extent, the GDPR carried over the contents of the EU Data Protection Directive from the 1995 version it replaced, most notably the so-called principles for the fair processing of personal data, although the GDPR, which came into force in May 2018, received a lot of attention, probably due to the significant fines that were introduced for non-compliance. The European Union also issued with comparatively little fanfare Directive 2016/680, on protecting personal data processed for the purposes of law enforcement.[40] This much less well-known directive, referred to as the LED, which can be considered a *lex specialis* for the processing of personal data in the context of criminal law, had to be implemented into national legislation of each EU Member State by May 2018, coinciding with the date the GDPR came into force.

III.B The GDPR

Since the GDPR is directly binding for all Member States and their citizens, strictly speaking no further implementation is required. Nevertheless, some countries, including the Netherlands,[41] implemented national legislation to further implement the GDPR. The GDPR allows EU Member States to further elaborate on provisions in the GDPR that leave room for additional provisions at a national level.

The scope of the GDPR is restricted to personal data, which is defined in Article 4(1) as any information relating to an identified or identifiable natural person (the data subject). This excludes anonymous data and data

[39] GDPR, note 3 above, on the protection of natural persons with regard to the processing of personal data and on the free movement of such data, and repealing Directive 95/46/EC (General Data Protection Regulation) [2016] OJ L 119.

[40] LED, note 4 above, on the protection of natural persons with regard to the processing of personal data by competent authorities for the purposes of the prevention, investigation, detection, or prosecution of criminal offenses or the execution of criminal penalties, and on the free movement of such data, and repealing Council Framework Decision 2008/977/JHA [2016] OJ L 119/89.

[41] In the Netherlands, the GDPR was implemented via the *Uitvoeringswet AVG* (GDPR Execution Act), Netherlands (with effect from May 25, 2018).

relating to legal persons. Data on deceased people is not personal data and therefore beyond the scope of the GDPR.[42] For collecting and processing personal data, there are several provisions that data controllers have to take into account. First of all, all processing has to be lawful, fair, and transparent under Article 5(1). Furthermore, the purposes for which the data are collected and processed have to be stated in advance (purpose specification), the data may not be used for other purposes (purpose or use limitation), and data may only be collected and processed when necessary for these purposes (collection limitation or data minimization). Data has to be accurate and up to date (data quality). When data is no longer necessary, it has to be removed (storage limitation). The data needs to be processed in a way that ensures appropriate security and has to be protected against unlawful processing, accidental loss, destruction, and damage (data integrity, confidentiality). Furthermore, the data controller is responsible for compliance under Article 5(2) (accountability).

Data subjects have several so-called data subject rights regarding their personal data under the GDPR, including a right to transparent information on the data collected and the purposes for which it is processed (Articles 12–14), a right to access to their data (Article 15), a right to rectification (Article 16), a right to erasure (Article 17), a right to data portability (Article 20), and a right not to be subject to automated decision-making (Article 22).

The GDPR is relevant in a criminal law context for all data controllers that are not within the scope of the LED. For example, private investigators and government agencies in the migration domain are subjected to the GDPR. Also, when companies apply camera surveillance or other technologies that collect personal data, the data collected and processed are subject to the GDPR. As soon as the police or the public prosecution service request such data for criminal investigation, the data comes within the scope of the LED rather than the GDPR.[43] Law enforcement agencies can request data from individuals and companies at any time during a criminal investigation, but handing over such data is on a voluntary basis. It is only when law enforcement agencies have obtained a court warrant that handing over the data is mandatory. If relevant, any such information may be used as evidence in court cases.

[42] Edina Harbinja, "Does the EU Data Protection Regime Protect Post-Mortem Privacy and What Could Be the Potential Alternatives?" (2013) 10:1 *SCRIPTed* 19.

[43] Although the GDPR is less relevant than the LED in a criminal law context, we use the GDPR as a starting point in this section, because we expect Europeans readers of this chapter to be more familiar with the GDPR.

III.C *The Law Enforcement Directive (LED)*

In 2012, the European Commission presented the first draft of a Directive that would harmonize the processing of personal data in criminal law matters.[44] The debate regarding the Directive between the European Parliament, the Commission, and the Council continued for four years. After amendments, the legislative proposal was adopted in 2016, in its current version as EU Directive 2016/680 (the LED). The deadline for implementation in national legislation was two years, with a final deadline in May 2018. Directive 2016/680 repealed the Framework Decision 2008/977/JHA as of that date.

The aim of the LED is twofold. It ensures the protection of personal data processed for the prevention, investigation, detection and prosecution of crimes, and the execution of criminal penalties. It also facilitates and simplifies police and judicial cooperation between Member States and, in general, more effectively addresses crime. This two-pronged approach is similar to that of the GDPR and the Framework Decision.

The LED is a data protection regime alongside the GDPR. The LED specifically focuses on data processing by "competent authorities," as defined in Article 3(7). Competent authorities include:

> (a) any public authority competent for the prevention, investigation, detection or prosecution of criminal offences or the execution of criminal penalties, including the safeguarding against and the prevention of threats to public security, or
>
> (b) any other body or entity entrusted by Member State law to exercise public authority and public powers for the purposes of the prevention, investigation, detection or prosecution of criminal offences or the execution of criminal penalties, including the safeguarding against and the prevention of threats to public security.

Perhaps the most obvious competent authorities are police forces and public prosecution services, but there may be a variety of competent

[44] This section of the chapter is partially based on Mark Leiser & Bart Custers, "The Law Enforcement Directive: Conceptual Issues of EU Directive 2016/680" (2022) 5:3 *European Data Protection Law Review* 367 ["Conceptual Issues"].

European Union, European Commission, Proposal for a Directive of the European Parliament and of the Council on the Protection of Individuals with Regard to the Processing of Personal Data by Competent Authorities for the Purposes of Prevention, Investigation, Detection or Prosecution of Criminal Offences or the Execution of Criminal Penalties, and the Free Movement of Such Data, COM (2012) 10 final (EU: European Commission, 2012).

authorities in the national criminal law of EU Member States. For example, in the domain of execution of criminal penalties, competent authorities may include the "regular" prison system, juvenile correction centers, forensic psychiatric centers, probation authorities, etc.

The scope of the LED is limited to the processing of personal data by the competent authorities for the specific purposes of the prevention, investigation, detection, or prosecution of criminal offenses or the execution of criminal penalties (Articles 1 and 2). This includes the safeguarding against and the prevention of threats to public security (Recital 11). As such, it should be noted that not all personal data processed by law enforcement agencies and the judiciary is within the scope of the LED. For example, when law enforcement agencies or the judiciary are processing personnel data regarding their staff, for paying wages or assessing employee performance, the GDPR applies rather than the LED. The GDPR is also applicable to personal data processing regarding borders, migration, and asylum.

With regard to the protection of personal data, the LED includes, similar to the GDPR, a set of principles for the fair processing of information, such as lawful and fair processing, purpose limitation, accuracy of data, adequate security safeguards, and responsibility of the data controller in Article 4 of the LED. Transparency is strived for as much as possible, but it is obvious that there are clear limitations to transparency in the interest of ongoing criminal investigations. This can lead to interference with the principle of equality of arms (Article 6 of the ECHR), as the defense may not be entitled to review some relevant data, and in practice, the defense may only get what the prosecutor decides to give. Essentially, the rights granted to data subjects can be difficult to invoke, at least in a meaningful way. National data protection authorities are eligible to handle any complaints regarding actors in the criminal justice system that do not comply with the LED provisions, and such cases can also be brought to courts. However, for data subjects, it can be hard to get access to data on themselves if they do not know which data actually exists. Contrary to the GDPR regime of high fines, the LED regime leaves setting maximum fines to national legislation. No EU Member State has implemented significant fines for LED non-compliance, something that obviously does not contribute to strict enforcement.

Personal data should be collected for specified, explicit, and legitimate purposes within the LED's scope, and should not be processed for purposes incompatible with the purposes of the prevention, investigation, detection, or prosecution of criminal offenses or the execution of criminal penalties, including the safeguarding against and the prevention of threats to public security. Some of these principles are problematic, particularly when data is transferred from a GDPR regime into the context of law enforcement.[45] Also, the protection provided under the GDPR may decrease, from a data subject's perspective, when law enforcement agencies get access to data collected by private parties.[46] While the GDPR is not very specific about time limits for data storage and review,[47] the LED requires clear establishment of time limits for storage and review.[48] The LED states that Member States should provide for appropriate time limits to be established for the erasure of personal data or for a periodic review of the need for the storage of personal data. Article 5(1)(e) of the GDPR states that personal data should be kept no longer than necessary, but does not mention a number of days, months, or years. The Article 29 Working Party issued an opinion that argues that time limits should be differentiated.[49] Storage time limits vary across Member States and for different situations, including different types of data subjects and different crimes. For example, in Germany, data storage duration is limited depending on the types of persons: ten years for adults, five years for adolescents, and two years for children.[50] Data on whistleblowers and informants can only be stored for one year, but can be extended to three years. In the Netherlands, the storage of personal data by the police is limited to one year, which can be extended to five years if the data is necessary for the police tasks.[51] In the United

[45] Catherine Jasserand, "Subsequent Use of GDPR Data for a Law Enforcement Purpose: The Forgotten Principle of Purpose Limitation?" (2018) 4:2 *European Data Protection Law Review* 152.

[46] Catherine Jasserand, "Law Enforcement Access to Personal Data Originally Collected by Private Parties: Missing Data Subjects' Safeguards in Directive 2016/680?" (2018) 34:1 *Computer Law & Security Report* 154.

[47] GDPR, note 3 above, Art. 5(1)(e) states that personal data should be kept no longer than necessary, but does not mention a number of days, months, or years. Note that Arts. 13 and 14 of the GDPR require data controllers to inform the data subject on storage times if they inquire about this.

[48] LED, note 4 above, Art. 5; see also Teresa Quintel, "European Union – Article 29 Data Protection Working Party Opinion on the Law Enforcement Directive" (2018) 4:1 *European Data Protection Law Review* 104.

[49] European Union, European Commission, Opinion on Some Key Issues of the Law Enforcement Directive (EU 2016/680) – wp258, WP 2017/258 (EU: European Commission, 2017).

[50] *Bundesgrenzschutzgesetz 1994* (Federal Border Protection Act 1994), Germany (with effect from/as amended 1994), § 35.

[51] *Wet Politiegegevens* (Police Data Act), Netherlands (with effect from/as amended 1 October 2022) [Police Data Act], Art. 8.

Kingdom, section 39(2) of the Data Protection Act 2018[52] requires that appropriate time limits must be established for the periodic review of the need for the continued storage of personal data for any of the law enforcement purposes.[53]

The LED offers explicit protection for special, i.e., sensitive, categories of data, such as data relating to race, ethnicity, political opinions, religion, trade union membership, sexual orientation, genetic data, biometric data, health data, and sex life data. The use of perpetrator profiles and risk profiles is explicitly allowed.

The LED also provides a list of data subject rights, such as the right to information, the right to access, the right to rectification, the right to erasure, and the right to restriction of the processing. Since these data subject rights can only be invoked if this does not interfere with ongoing investigations, these rights can be somewhat misleading. Some data subject rights mentioned in the GDPR, such as the right to data portability and the right to object to automated individual decision-making, are not included in the LED. The absence of the right to object to automated decision-making offers more leeway for law enforcement to use profiling practices, such as perpetrator profiling and risk profiling.

In the Netherlands, there already existed specific legislation for the processing of personal data in criminal law before the LED came into force. The Police Data Act (*Wet politiegegevens*) ("Wpg")[54] regulated the use of personal data for police agencies, and the Justice and Prosecution Data Act (*Wet justitiële en strafvorderlijke gegevens*) ("Wjsg")[55] regulates the use of personal data by the public prosecution services and the judiciary. Contrary to other EU Member States, where sometimes entirely new legislation had to be drafted, the Netherlands merely had to adjust existing legislation when implementing Directive 2016/680.

Both the Wpg and the Wjsg already strongly resembled the LED in terms of structure, scope, and contents, which meant that only a few changes were required. Also, the rights of data subjects, international cooperation, and supervision by data protection authorities were already regulated. Elements that were missing included concepts like Privacy

[52] Data Protection Act 2018, UK, c. 12 (with effect from May 25, 2018).

[53] In comparison, this feature is largely missing in US regulatory frames.

[54] Police Data Act, note 51 above.

[55] *Wet justitiële en strafvorderlijke gegevens* (Justice and Prosecution Data Act), Netherlands (with effect from/as amended July 1, 2022).

by Design, Privacy by Default, and Privacy Impact Assessments.[56] The Netherlands already introduced data breach notification laws in 2016, prior to the GDPR, but these laws did not apply to the police, prosecution services, and the judiciary – a change brought about by the LED.

Across the European Union, implementation of the LED in national legislation proceeded slowly. In February 2018, a few months before the implementation deadline of May 2018, only a few countries, such as Germany, Denmark, Ireland, and Austria, had implemented the directive. The Netherlands had implemented the directive with some delay: the revised Wpg and Wjsg came into force in January 2019, more than half a year after the May 2018 deadline. Other countries, such as Belgium, Finland, and Sweden, were later, but they implemented the directive by 2019. However, there was also a group of countries, including Spain, France, Latvia, Portugal, and Slovenia, that had not yet accomplished implementation by 2019. In January 2019, the European Commission sent reasoned opinions to Bulgaria, Cyprus, Greece, Latvia, the Netherlands, Slovenia, and Spain for failing to implement the LED, and urged the Czech Republic and Portugal to finalize the LED's implementation.[57] In July 2019, the European Commission lodged an infringement action against Greece and Spain before the CJEU for failing to transpose the LED into national legislation.[58] Since then, Greece passed Law 4624/2019 of August 29, 2019, implementing the LED. Latvia and Portugal transposed the LED in August 2019, while Spain had not yet adopted such an act. Also as of August 2019, six out of the 16 federal states (*Länder*) of Germany had not yet passed laws transposing the LED, which led the European Commission to send a formal notice, the first step of infringement proceedings.[59] As of May

[56] Privacy by design and privacy by default are based on the idea that technology usually can be designed in different ways within provided requirements, resulting in the same functionality. However, some designs can be more privacy-friendly and other less privacy-friendly. Privacy by design aims to include privacy as a value into the design. Privacy by default aims to set defaults in technology in a privacy-friendly mode, e.g., opt-in instead of opt-out. Privacy impact assessments are risk assessments of new technologies, business models, policies, or other plans in which personal data are being processed. The risk assessments focus on privacy risks of the data subjects.

[57] European Commission, "January Infringements Package: Key Decisions" (January 24, 2019), https://ec.europa.eu/commission/presscorner/detail/en/MEMO_19_462.

[58] European Commission, "Data Protection: Commission Decides to Refer Greece and Spain to the Court for Not Transposing EU Law" (July 25, 2019), https://ec.europa.eu/commission/presscorner/detail/EN/IP_19_4261.

[59] European Commission, "Infringement Proceedings: Commission Takes Legal Action against Germany in 17 Cases" (July 25, 2019), https://ec.europa.eu/commission/presscorner/detail/en/inf_23_142.

2020, Germany had not yet fully transposed the LED, and the European Commission has sent a reasoned opinion. The same action was taken against Slovenia, which also failed to transpose the LED.[60] On February 25, 2021, the CJEU sanctioned Spain with a €15 million fine and a daily penalty of €89,000 for its ongoing failure to transpose the LED into national legislation.[61] In April 2022, the European Union launched an infringement procedure against Germany after detecting a gap in the transposition of the LED in relation to activities of Germany's federal police.[62]

IV Evidence in Dutch Criminal Law

IV.A Basic Principles

As in many countries, the evidentiary system in criminal cases in Dutch criminal law is based on the principle of establishing the substantive truth. This goal is expressed in the Dutch CCP by the requirement that a judge may assume that the offense charged is proven only if the judge "is convinced."[63] This means that a high degree of certainty must exist that the suspect has committed the offense. The judge must be convinced by the contents of legal evidence. The latter is the evidence that the Dutch CCP considers admissible in criminal proceedings. It includes the judge's own perception, statements by the suspect, statements by a witness, statements by an expert, and written documents per Article 339 of the Dutch CCP. This summary is so broad that hardly any evidence can be indicated that the law does not consider admissible.[64] Digital data as evidence will usually be submitted in the form of written police statements that report the results of an investigation.[65]

There are only few rules in the Dutch CCP that govern the reliability of evidence. Relevant to any kind of evidence is the obligation for the judge

[60] European Commission, "May Infringements Package: Key Decisions" (May 14, 2020) at "Data Protection: Commission Urges GERMANY and SLOVENIA to Complete the Transposition of the Data Protection Law Enforcement Directive," https://ec.europa.eu/commission/presscorner/detail/en/inf_20_859.

[61] C-658/19, Court of Justice of the European Union, February 25, 2021, ECLI:EU:C:2021:138.

[62] European Union, European Commission, First Report on Application and Functioning of the Data Protection Law Enforcement Directive (EU) 2016/680 ("LED"), COM/2022/364 final (Brussels: European Commission, 2022), https://eur-lex.europa.eu/legal-content/EN/TXT/HTML/?uri=CELEX:52022DC0364&from=EN.

[63] There is no constitutional provision with the same content.

[64] An example of such an exception is what the lawyer puts forward during the hearing.

[65] The data itself is often stored in police databases or at the Netherlands Forensic Institute (NFI).

to justify his rejection of a "plea against the use of unreliable evidence" in Article 359, paragraph 2 of the Dutch CCP, i.e., a defense objection to evidence. This means that if the judge decides *not* to exclude the contested evidence, he or she must give reasons why. The better the defense substantiates the plea of unreliability, the more an explanation is required from the court. Furthermore, there are the so-called minimum evidence rules in relation to statements. For example, the judge may not convict[66] on the basis of a statement by only one witness or by the suspect only. Because there is always a chance that the witness or the suspect will not tell the truth, the law requires a second piece of evidence for conviction. However, case law demonstrates that this requirement is very easily met.[67] A final and increasingly important example concerns criteria for assessing expert evidence. These criteria, developed by the Supreme Court, hold that if the reliability of expert evidence is disputed, the judge should examine whether the expert has the required expertise and, if so, which method(s) the expert used, why the expert considers that the method(s) is (are) reliable, and the extent to which the expert has the ability to apply that method in a professional manner.[68]

Apart from reliability, the legitimacy of evidence may also be challenged in court. Article 359a of the Dutch CCP provides for attaching consequences to the unlawful gathering of evidence. Depending on the circumstances, the judge can decide to decrease the severity of the punishment, to exclude the evidence, or declare the case inadmissible for prosecution.[69] In practice, cases are almost never affected by unlawfully obtained evidence. Courts rarely impose consequences for unlawfully obtained evidence, and if they do, cases may not be affected by this, because the requirements the Supreme Court laid down in its case law regarding the scope of Article 359a of the Dutch CCP are rather restricted.[70]

66 An important exception is that evidence that the suspect has committed the offense charged *can* – not *must* – be assumed by the judge on the basis of an official report by an investigating officer. See Dutch CCP, note 19 above, § 344(2).

67 For an overview and interpretation of the case law, see the case note M. J. Borgers in Dutch Supreme Court, July 7, 2015, *NJ* 2015, 488, ECLI:NL:HR:2015:1817.

68 HR 27 January 1998, *NJ* 1984, 404. Assessing the reliability of the ways in which data is secured may depend on the methods and technologies used; see e.g. Eric Van Buskirk & Vincent Liu, "Digital Evidence: Challenging the Presumption of Reliability" (2006) 1:1 *Journal of Digital Forensic Practice* 19.

69 If the case is declared inadmissible for prosecution, the court will not allow litigation to start because the eligibility criteria of procedural criminal law are not met.

70 See e.g. HR 19 February 2013, *NJ* 2013, 308; see also *Het Nederlands*, note 23 above, at 884–886.

IV.B Current Court Practices: Increasing Use of Digital Evidence

Traditionally, statements of witnesses and suspects are important evidence in criminal cases. The general feeling is, however, that things are changing. Criminal investigations into organized crime in particular do not rely on witnesses, and investigations increasingly build a case by combining location data via phone locations or automatic number plate recognition, user data of phones and computers, the internet, etc.[71] The Dutch police increasingly and with success invest in "data-driven investigation," and high-tech detectives have gained access to various encrypted communication providers that were used by organized crime groups such as Ennetcom, EncroChat, and Sky ECC.[72] An international coalition of investigators even built their own communication app "Anom," which was gladly used by ignorant criminals. The downside of these celebrated successes, however, is that there is no capacity to read the millions of intercepted messages.[73]

Moreover, the absence of adequate rules discussed in Section II, and the legitimacy of digital investigation methods, are serious issues. But due to the restricted interpretation of Article 359a of the Dutch CCP (discussed above), the courts almost never attach a serious consequence to the fact that evidence was gathered illegally. Next, there is the problem of territorial jurisdiction.[74] The data in the Ennetcom-seizure, e.g., was owned by a Dutch company, but stored on a Canadian server. As a result of this, the Dutch police could not investigate the data without permission of the Canadian authorities. In order to comply with the Canadian judicial requirements for access to the data, the Dutch investigatory judge and the prosecutor interpreted the Dutch

[71] Desiree de Jonge, "Verdediging in tijden van digitale bewijsvoering" (Legal Defense in the Age of Digital Evidence) in Patrick Petrus Jacobus van der Meij (ed.), *Aan de slag. Liber amicorum Gerard Hamer* (The Hague, Netherlands: Sdu Uitgevers, 2018) 125 ["Verdediging"].

[72] See "Dutch Police 'Read' Blackberry Emails," *BBC News* (January 12, 2016), www.bbc.com/news/technology-35291933; Robert Wright, "Hundreds Arrested across Europe as French Police Crack Encrypted Network," *The Financial Times* (June 8, 2021).

[73] "Judicial System Overwhelmed after Gaining Access to Encrypted Chats," *NL Times* (June 14, 2021), https://nltimes.nl/2021/06/14/judicial-system-overwhelmed-gaining-access-encrypted-chats.

[74] In relation to investigation in the cloud, see also Jan-Willem van den Hurk & Sander de Vries, "Cybercrime. Waar worden gegevens in de 'cloud' opgeslagen en welke juridische consequentie heeft het antwoord op die vraag? Een speurtocht langs het traditionele juridisch kader en actuele wetgeving en jurisprudentie leidt tot een opmerkelijke conclusie" (2019) *Strafblad* 34.

procedural rules very broadly. The defense objected, but in the end the trial judge authorized the course of action.[75]

Next to issues of legitimacy, digital evidence raises questions of reliability as well as on defense rights. We illustrate this with the case of the "Webcam blackmailer," in which the reliability of a keylogger and the right to equality of arms were both discussed.[76] In this case, the suspect was tried, among other things, for threatening and spreading sexual images of underage girls via the internet, as well as for extorting various males with information on them having "webcam sex." The discussion regarding the keylogger,[77] elaborately described in the verdict, clearly demonstrates the effort non-expert litigants have to make to understand how these kinds of technical devices work. To a large extent, they need to rely on expert witnesses for determining reliability. Even more interesting in this case are the attempts of the defense to get access to all the data that was found and produced by the police, including the complete copies that were made of the computers, all the results of the keylogger, all the Skype conversations with the victims, WE-logs, VPN-logs, etc. The defense brought forward an alternative scenario, and argued that in order to properly assess the selection and interpretation of the incriminating evidence, it is necessary to have access to all the data. Indeed, this request seems reasonable from the perspective of the right to equality of arms. All information that can be relevant for the case must be seen and checked by the defense. However, by Dutch law, the prosecution determines what is relevant and made available. This rule has always been the object of discussion between defense attorneys and prosecution, but this debate is given a new dimension in the context of big sets of technical data.[78] The police have their own software to search and select data, and they may not always be willing to provide insight into their investigative methods. Furthermore, the amount of data can be enormous, as in the Ennetcom, EncroChat, and Sky ECC examples above, and for that reason the effort to make it accessible for the defense will be too. There now seems to be a court policy developing in early cases in which decrypted data is used, allowing the defense to search the secondary dataset at the Netherlands Forensic Institute (NFI) with the

[75] See e.g. para. 6 of the verdict of the Court of Amsterdam, April 19, 2018, ECLI:NL:RBAMS:2018:2504.

[76] Court of Appeal Amsterdam, December 14, 2018, ECLI:NL:GHAMS:2018:4620.

[77] A keylogger is a device or software that registers, typically in a covert manner, all keystrokes on a keyboard.

[78] See also "Verdediging", note 71 above.

search engine "Hansken."[79] Hansken was developed by the NFI to investigate large amounts of seized data. In the Webcam blackmailer case, the Court of Appeal dismissed the request of the defense with the argument that they were on a phishing expedition and had had plenty of opportunity to challenge the evidence. Nonetheless, this case illustrates that the Dutch CCP needs provisions to ensure insight into issues generated by automated data analysis, for the defense, but also for the judge.[80]

IV.C Developments in Society and Technology: New Issues of Quality and Assessment of Evidence

As observed in the beginning of the chapter, people are increasingly leaving digital traces everywhere all the time. People are often monitored without being aware of it, by camera surveillance systems, by their own smartphones, and on other devices they use to access the internet. This generates data that can be useful for law enforcement to collect evidence and to find out what happened in specific cases. In the Netherlands, many surveillance systems are in place for law enforcement to rely on. These are mostly private systems from which data is requested if needed.

The data we are referring to here is digital data, usually large amounts of data, in different formats such as statistics, as well as audio, video, etc., that can only be accessed via technological devices. In the past, forensic experts also provided technical data, such as fingerprints or ballistics, to criminal investigations and provided clarifications when testifying in courts, but the current use of data as evidence is significantly different. In the past, forensic data was collected in a very specific, controlled, and targeted way, mostly at the crime scene. Currently, it is possible to collect very large amounts of data, not necessarily specifically targeted to one individual or connected to a specific crime scene. For some of these relatively new data collection methods, no protocols even exist yet. In this subsection, we discuss three issues regarding the quality of evidence that arise as a result of the characteristics of digital data.

[79] See e.g. the rulings of the Court of Amsterdam, April 19, 2018 ECLI:NL:RBAMS:2018:2504 and April 1, 2021, ECLI:NL:RBAMS:2021:1507.

[80] See Koops-Commission, note 35 above, at 27; see also Maša Galič, "De rechten van de verdediging in de context van omvangrijke datasets en geavanceerde zoekmachines in strafzaken: een suggestie voor uitbreiding" (Rights of the Defendant in the Context of Large Datasets and Advanced Search Engines in Criminal Cases) (2021) 2:2 *Boom Strafblad* 41 ["De rechten"].

The first issue concerns the reliability of data. Digital data can be volatile and manipulated, which means that the litigating parties and the judge would need an instrument to assess the originality of the data. This instrument can be found in procedures on how to seize digital data in a controlled and reproducible way. For example, when a copy of a hard disc of a computer is made, it is very important to have a fixed procedure or protocol, including timestamps, so that it is clear to all litigating parties that the data was not tampered with or accidentally altered. Even with such procedures and protocols in place, creating a copy of the data on a seized computer can be complicated. For example, Bitcoin and other cryptocurrencies cannot be copied, even though they are essentially data on a computer. Seizure of cryptocurrencies therefore requires specific protocols. Another technological issue is that of streaming data and data in the cloud. Such data can also be hard to record or securely copy, and if so, much depends on the timing. Forensic experts in the Netherlands and other countries are working on new methods and protocols for securing digital data. A detailed discussion is beyond the scope of this chapter.[81]

The second issue concerns the large amounts of data that can arise during criminal investigations in relation to the principle that the litigating parties need to have access to all relevant data, incriminating and exonerating. For example, in the Netherlands, law enforcement uses a significant amount of wiretapping to find clues for further investigation in criminal cases. This yields large amounts of data that can be hard to process by humans, as it would require listening to all audio files collected. Voice recognition technologies may be helpful to process such data in automated ways. Also, camera surveillance, including license plate recognition systems, may yield large amounts of data. Again, such data can be hard to process by humans going through all images. Analytics software may be useful to speed up such processes.

The large amounts of data routinely collected in criminal cases therefore calls for automated search and analysis. When using software tools to go through large amounts of data to find specific data or to disclose specific patterns, one problem may be that humans may find it hard to follow how the software works, particularly when such tools are very advanced. However, if it is not transparent how particular conclusions

[81] For more details, see e.g. Jan-Jaap Oerlemans, *Investigating Cybercrime*, PhD thesis, Leiden University (Leiden, Netherlands: Meijers Research Institute and Graduate School of the Leiden Law School of Leiden University, 2017).

were drawn from the data, this could be an issue when such conclusions are used in courts as evidence.[82] According to the principle of equality of arms, it should be possible to contest all evidence brought up by any of the process parties. However, search and analysis tools may be programmed in such a way that they aim to find incriminating evidence in datasets, and there may be exonerating pieces of evidence in the databases that the tools may not show.[83]

A detailed legal framework may be lacking, but courts still seem increasingly reliant on experts and computer systems. A typical example here are risk assessment models, usually based on algorithms, that provide risk scores for recidivism rates. In several of the United States, the system Correctional Offender Management Profiling for Alternative Sanctions (COMPAS) is used to assess recidivism risks.[84] In their decisions, courts place considerable weight on these models, or rather the results they spit out. In the Netherlands, the probation services use a system called RISC (*Recidive inschattings schalen*). Part of that system is the Oxford Risk of Recidivism Tool, an actuarial risk assessment tool that can be used to predict statistical risks.[85] These models increasingly play a role in the work of probation services and the decisions of courts.

The use of such models offers several benefits, such as fair assessments done in more structured and objective ways. Subjective assessors can be prone to human failure or can be influenced by bias and prejudice. If the models are self-learning, they can also recognize and

[82] The increasing use of AI in a criminal law context can raise such issues; see Bart Custers, "Artificiële intelligentie in het Strafrecht: een overzicht van actuele ontwikkelingen" (Artificial Intelligence in Criminal Law: An Overview of Current Developments) (2021) 4 *Computerrecht* 330; for a more general discussion, see Daniel Solove, *The Digital Person; Technology and Privacy in the Information Age* (New York, NY: New York University Press, 2004). Regarding the interpretation of equality of arms in relation to large datasets, see "De rechten", note 80 above. See also *Sigurður Einarsson and others* v. *Iceland*, App. No. 39757/15, ECtHR (June 4, 2019); and see Sabine Gless, "AI in the Courtroom: A Comparative Analysis of Machine Evidence in Criminal Trials" (2020) 51:2 *Georgetown Journal of International Law* 195; Sabine Gless, Xuan Di, & Emily Silverman, "Ca(r)veat Emptor: Crowdsourcing Data to Challenge the Testimony of In-Car Technology" (2022) 62:3 *Jurimetrics* 285.

[83] Toon Calders & Bart Custers, "What Is Data Mining and How Does It Work?" in Bart Custers, Toon Calders, Bart Schermer *et al.* (eds.), *Discrimination and Privacy in the Information Society*, no. 3 (Heidelberg, Germany: Springer, 2013) 27. For more on the responsibility of programmers, see Chapter 2 in this volume.

[84] "Practitioner's Guide to COMPAS Core" (Northpointe, 2015), https://assets.documentcloud.org/documents/2840784/Practitioner-s-Guide-to-COMPAS-Core.pdf.

[85] OXRISK, "OXREC: Oxford Risk of Recidivism Tool," https://oxrisk.com/oxrec-nl-2-backup/.

incorporate new trends and developments. This ability obviously can also increase efficiency and reduce costs. However, there is also criticism of these instruments, because they do not seem to outperform assessments by human experts, and there are risks similar to human assessments, such as bias that can lead to discrimination.[86] In the United States, COMPAS seemed to systematically assign higher recidivism risks to Afro-Americans.[87] It is often argued that these models do not process any ethnicity data and, therefore, cannot be discriminating.[88] However, characteristics like ethnicity can easily be predicted and are therefore often reconstructed by self-learning technologies, without being visible to users.[89] Furthermore, it should be noted that the false positive rate for African-Americans is higher in COMPAS, but race has no predictive value. In other words, suspects from different ethnic backgrounds with the same risk score have the same risk of reoffense.

The third issue is related to difficulties in estimating the strength of the evidence. All datasets contain inaccurate data or gaps to some extent. Incorrect or incomplete data is not always problematic from a data analytics perspective, but it may reduce some of the accuracy and reliability of analysis results and thus affect the conclusions that can be drawn from it.[90] When based on large amounts of data, some minor errors and gaps in the data will hardly affect the final results. However, in cases of limited data, errors might have crucial impacts on the evidence. For example, cell phone data can be used in a court case to prove

[86] Gijs Van Dijck, "Algoritmische risicotaxatie van recidive: Over de Oxford Risk of Recidivism tool (OXREC), ongelijke behandeling en discriminatie in strafzaken" (Algorithmic Risk Assessment of Recidivism) (2020) 95:25 *Nederlands Juristenblad* 1784.

[87] Julia Angwin, Jeff Larson, Surya Mattu *et al.*, "Machine Bias," *ProPublica* (May 23, 2016), www.propublica.org/article/machine-bias-risk-assessments-in-criminal-sentencing.

[88] Marjolein Maas, Ellen Legters, & Seena Fazel, "Professional en risicotaxatie-instrument hand in hand: hoe de reclassering risico's inschat" (Professional and Risk Assessment Work Together: How Probation Organisations Assess Risks) (2020) 1814 *Nederlands Juristenblad* 2055.

[89] Cf. Faisal Kamiran, Toon Calders, & Mykola Pechenizkiy, "Techniques for Discrimination-Free Predictive Models" in Bart Custers, Toon Calders, Bart Schermer *et al.* (eds.), *Discrimination and Privacy in the Information Society*, no. 3 (Heidelberg, Germany: Springer, 2013) 223.

[90] Bart Custers, "Effects of Unreliable Group Profiling by Means of Data Mining" in Gunter Grieser, Yuzuru Tanaka, & Akihiro Yamamoto (eds.), *Lecture Notes in Artificial Intelligence*, vol. 2843 (Berlin, Germany; New York, NY: Springer-Verlag, 2003) 290; for more on malfunctioning technology, which is also related to reliability, see Chapter 13 in this volume.

that a suspect was at the crime scene at a particular time. If this conclusion is based on data from three cell phone masts, but one of them is unreliable, then the result may not be entirely accurate. The conclusion could be, e.g., that the probability that the suspect can be pinpointed to the location is 75 percent. This problem with accuracy also brings in all the assessment problems that humans, including judges, may have when dealing with probabilities and risks, including the so-called prosecutor's fallacy and the defense attorney's fallacy.[91]

Despite all these issues, the changing technological landscape does provide many opportunities for the use of data as evidence in courts. When used properly, the use of data could be more objective than the use of statements from suspects, victims, and witnesses.[92] People may easily forget specific details of a past situation and their memories may even distort after some time. Many psychological mechanisms might be at play. In very stressful situations, when people are the victim of a crime or witnessing serious crime, they may experience time in different ways, often thinking it takes longer than in reality, or they may invoke coping mechanisms that block particular information in their brains. Witnesses who are not directly involved in a crime they are witnessing may be paying less attention to details, and the evidence they can produce in their statements may therefore be limited. Research has shown that memories also fade over time for all actors.[93]

Objective digital data, e.g., from cell phones, may easily fill in the blanks in people's memories and rectify any distortions that have occurred. Such data can readily confirm where people were at a particular moment and can disclose connections between people. The data can help prove that some statements are wrong or confirm that some statements are indeed correct. Data can also help to avoid tunnel vision and other biases that law enforcement officers conducting criminal investigations may have.

[91] Both fallacies are errors in statistical reasoning involving a test for an occurrence, such as a match in fingerprints or DNA; the prosecutor's fallacy exaggerates the probability of a criminal defendant's guilt, whereas the defense attorney's fallacy typically underestimates it. See William Thompson & Edward Schumann, "Interpretation of Statistical Evidence in Criminal Trials: The Prosecutor's Fallacy and the Defense Attorney's Fallacy" (1987) 11 *Law and Human Behavior* 167.

[92] The same applies to statements and testimonies by robots; see Chapters 6 and 8 in this volume.

[93] Geralda Odinot, Amina Memon, David La Rooy *et al.*, "Are Two Interviews Better than One? Eyewitness Memory across Repeated Cognitive Interviews" (2013) 8:10 *PLoS ONE* e76305.

Altogether, the use of data as evidence in courts can be a valuable asset. It can be more accurate, detailed, unprejudiced, and objective than statements. But this is only the case if some of the pitfalls and issues mentioned above are properly avoided. Data can be manipulated, the tools for analysis can be biased and discriminating, and the probabilities resulting from any analysis can be subject to interpretation fallacies.

Regarding categories of evidence, in general we see an increase in the use of data as evidence in courts, but not necessarily a decrease in the use of statements from suspects, victims, and witnesses. This decrease is not to be expected any time soon, as statements remain important, for more than evidentiary reasons, such as the procedural justice experienced by all parties in court. As such, the use of data as evidence is a valuable addition to statements, but not a replacement.

The European Union seems to expect that data as evidence will become increasingly important. A relevant development on the EU level that needs to be discussed here is the draft Regulation on e-evidence.[94] To make it easier and faster for law enforcement and judicial authorities to obtain electronic evidence needed to investigate and eventually prosecute criminals and terrorists, the European Commission proposed new rules in April 2018 in the form of a Regulation and a Directive. Both proposals focus on swift and efficient cross-border access to e-evidence, in order to effectively fight terrorism and other serious and organized crime.[95] The proposal for the directive focuses on harmonized rules for appointing legal representatives when gathering evidence in criminal proceedings.[96] The proposal for the regulation focuses on European production and preservation orders for electronic evidence in criminal matters.[97] The production order will allow judicial authorities to obtain electronic evidence

[94] European Union, European Commission, Proposal for a Regulation of the European Parliament and of The Council on European Production and Preservation Orders for Electronic Evidence in Criminal Matters, COM/2018/225 final – 2018/0108 (COD) (Strasbourg: European Commission, 2018), https://eur-lex.europa.eu/legal-content/EN/TXT/?uri=COM%3A2018%3A225%3AFIN [Production and Preservation].

[95] European Council, "European Council Conclusions, 18 October 2018" (October 18, 2018), www.consilium.europa.eu/en/press/press-releases/2018/10/18/20181018-european-council-conslusions/.

[96] European Union, European Commission, Proposal for a Directive of the European Parliament and of the Council Laying Down Harmonised Rules on the Appointment of Legal Representatives for the Purpose of Gathering Evidence in Criminal Proceedings, COM/2018/226 final – 2018/0107 (COD) (Strasbourg: European Commission, 2018).

[97] Production and Preservation, note 94 above.

directly from services in other Member States. These legal instruments have not yet been adopted by the European Union, as strong privacy, data protection, and privacy safeguards are still under scrutiny. However, it may be expected that, once adopted, this regulation will further increase the use of electronic evidence in court cases in the European Union over the next few years.

V Conclusion

In this chapter, we focused on the increasing discrepancy between legal frameworks and actual practices regarding the use of data as evidence in criminal courts. The two legal frameworks under consideration are criminal law and data protection law. Since the EU harmonization of criminal law is very limited, we used the example of the Netherlands to further examine the use of data as evidence in criminal courts. Even though the Netherlands is a front runner in the areas of privacy and data protection law, as well as digital forensics and cybercrime, large parts of its criminal law were developed before digital evidence existed. Data protection law, which is more recent, is highly harmonized throughout the European Union via the GDPR and the LED.

The two major legal frameworks of criminal law and data protection law are not fully integrated and adjusted to each other. There seems to be a structural ambiguity here. When it comes to regulating data as evidence, these frameworks together need to cover three separate but intertwined activities: (1) collection of data; (2) processing and analysis of data, including storage, selecting, combining; and (3) evaluation of data.[98] In the Netherlands, the Dutch CCP covers the collection and evaluation, while the processing is mainly the domain of the Wpg and Wjsg in accordance with the LED.

Based on the analysis of the existing legal frameworks, the actual use of data as evidence in criminal courts, and developments in society and technology, we have four major observations, regarding the final aspect of our research question: i.e., what is needed next. A first observation regarding regulation is that the existing legal frameworks in the Netherlands barely or not at all obstruct the collection of data for evidence. Hence, the legal

[98] Obviously, this is a simplification. A more detailed analysis would need to include more steps, such as access to data, access to evaluations of data, destruction of data, etc.; cf. David Gray, *The Fourth Amendment in an Age of Surveillance* (Cambridge, UK: Cambridge University Press, 2017).

frameworks essentially allow law enforcement agencies and public prosecutors to make use of the opportunities that data can offer as evidence in criminal courts. Although many digital investigation methods are not provided for in the Dutch CCP, and as a result, fundamental issues on privacy are debated, this seems to have few consequences for the legitimacy of data as evidence in specific cases. This is partly due to the fact that, in the Netherlands, illegally gathered evidence rarely leads to serious consequences. The Supreme Court case law thus reflects the importance given to crime fighting. Another explanation is that the debate on how to define and protect the right to digital privacy within criminal procedure is still in its infancy.

Our second observation is that regulation regarding collection via the Dutch CCP and regulation on processing and analysis via the Wpg and Wjsg is not integrated. As with other written law, these legal frameworks use different language and definitions, have different structures, and lack any cross-reference to one another. The Dutch CCP is not specifically aimed at what can be done with data once collected, but what can be done with data is also relevant for the evaluation of the extent of the privacy intrusion, and hence the design of the investigation powers. An integrated approach is also necessary for other reasons. Under data protection law, data subjects have a series of data subject rights they can invoke, such as the right to information, transparency, and access. These rights can be somewhat of a farce, as people may not know about them and how to invoke them and, if they do, they may be blocked in cases where a criminal investigation is still ongoing.[99]

Our third observation concerns the absence of regulation of automated data analysis during all stages in the criminal justice system, including the prevention, investigation, detection, or prosecution of criminal offenses, the use of data as evidence in criminal courts, and the execution of criminal penalties. Automated data analysis raises fundamental questions regarding the equality of arms, and because all parties should have access to all relevant data and be able to assess data selection, we would like to argue that introducing some additional provisions for regulating data analytics, subsequent to data collection, would be appropriate. We have not seen any similar provisions in the legislation of other EU Member States,[100] but we did encounter an example of such

[99] "Conceptual Issues", note 44 above.

[100] Bart Custers, Francien Dechesne, Alan M. Sears *et al.*, "A Comparison of Data Protection Legislation and Policies across the EU" (2017) 34:2 *Computer Law & Security Review* 234.

a provision in the Dutch Intelligence Agencies Act (*Wet Inlichtingen- en Veiligheidsdiensten*).[101] Article 60 of this Act states that the Dutch intelligence agencies are empowered to perform automated data analytics on their own datasets and open sources. The data can be compared and used for profiling and pattern recognition. Since no similar provision exists in criminal law, it is unclear whether law enforcement agencies are allowed to do the same. We are not arguing that they should or should not be allowed to do this, but we would like to argue that there should be more clarity regarding this issue.

The absence of regulation of data analysis raises issues regarding privacy and data protection of the data subjects whose data is being processed, but it can also raise issues regarding equality of arms during litigation in courts. Normally, suspects have access to all evidence brought forward in their case, including any data underlying the evidence. In practice, defendants may only get what prosecutors grant them, and they may not be aware of what is missing. Furthermore, if data analysis is based on large amounts of data, and that data includes the data of others,[102] a suspect may not be granted access to it; the GDPR prevents this in order to protect privacy and personal data. As a result, a suspect may not have full transparency regarding the data on which the analysis was based and may be unable to reproduce the analysis.[103] If the data analytics involve very sophisticated self-learning technology such as AI, the prosecutor may not even know how the data analysis took place.

Finally, as a fourth observation, what may also need further attention is the level of court expertise in dealing with digital data as evidence. Given

[101] *Wet Inlichtingen- en Veiligheidsdiensten* (Intelligence Agencies Act), 2017, Netherlands (as amended 1 January 2022).

[102] E.g. risk assessments of individuals can only be made in comparison with data of others; typically, a suspect has a high risk *in comparison with* other suspects or the general population.

[103] In the United States, a joint working group of the Department of Justice and the Administrative Office of the US Courts drafted guidelines for electronically stored information discovery production in federal criminal cases and how to inform defendants at an early stage about this; see US Department of Justice and Administrative Office of the US Courts Joint Working Group on Electronic Technology in the Criminal Justice System, "Recommendations for Electronically Stored Information (ESI) Discovery Production in Federal Criminal Cases" (Washington, DC: Department of Justice, 2012), www.uscourts.gov/sites/default/files/finalesiprotocolbookmarked.pdf. Because technology changes rapidly, there are no specific requirements for the manner or timing of the disclosure of the information. Instead, organizations in the criminal law system are required to develop best practices.

the increasing importance of data as evidence in criminal courts, it is imperative that judges understand some of the basics of how data is collected and processed before it results in the evidence that is presented to them. In order to evaluate the reliability and strength of the data-evidence, they have to be very aware of any of the pitfalls and issues mentioned in the previous section. Judges should be able to contest different types of data brought forward as evidence, even if the data is not contested by any of the litigating parties. For this reason, further training in this area may be important, as well as procedural rules identifying the basis for judicial assessment of how data was seized.

In view of these observations, we conclude that, on the one hand, there are perhaps no major obstructions in the existing legal frameworks for the use of data as evidence in criminal courts, but that, on the other hand, much of this area is in practice still a work in progress. In order to find the right balance between the interests of law enforcement and the rights of subjects in criminal cases, further work is needed. Further work would include research, but obviously also the development of case law, as the balancing of interests approach is at the heart of what courts do, most notably supreme courts, and particularly in search and seizure jurisprudence. Since criminal law and data protection law are more or less separate legal frameworks, they need to be further aligned, not necessarily by adjusting the legislation, but at least in detailing the actual practices and policies of law enforcement agencies further. The absence of any regulation regarding automated data analysis is a major concern and may have considerable consequences for data subjects and their rights in criminal cases. We suggest that, after further research, regulation be considered. Regulation can be done via legislation, but perhaps also via policies. And, finally, further training of actors in courts may be required to make all of this work.

When looking at the developments in society and technology, we expect that the use of data as evidence in courts will significantly increase in the coming decades. This means that the issues identified in this chapter, such as limited effectiveness of data subject rights provided in the LED and issues regarding the principle of equality of arms during litigation, may become more pressing in the near future. It is therefore important to further prepare both courts and law enforcement agencies for these challenges, as suggested above.

However, having said this, we do not expect that the use of other types of evidence in criminal courts, such as statements from suspects, victims, or witnesses, will fall out of use. We think it is important to consider the use of digital evidence in criminal courts as an addition to the use of statements and other types of evidence, not as a replacement. Humans seek to understand evidence by means of stories, which means that regardless of its digital nature, data will always need to fit into a story – the stories of suspects, victims, and witnesses.[104]

[104] Kiel Brennan-Marquez, "Plausible Cause: Explanatory Standards in the Age of Powerful Machines" (2017) 70:4 *Vanderbilt Law Review* 1249.

MAMA K ©

11

Reconsidering Two US Constitutional Doctrines

Fourth Amendment Standing and the State Agency Requirement in a World of Robots

DAVID GRAY

I Introduction

A wide array of robot technologies now inhabit our life worlds – and their population grows every day. The extent, degree, and diversity of our interactions with these technologies serve daily notice that we now live in an unprecedented age of surveillance. Many of us carry with us personal tracking devices in the shape of cellular phones allowing service providers and "apps" to monitor our locations and movements. The GPS chips embedded in smart devices provide detailed location data to a host of third parties, including apps, social media companies, and public health agencies. Wearable devices monitor streams of biological data. The IoT is populated by a dizzying array of connected devices such as doorbells, smart speakers, household appliances, thermostats, and even hairbrushes, which have access to the most intimate, if often quotidian, details of our daily lives. And then there is the dense network of surveillance technologies such as networked cameras, license plate readers, and radio frequency identification (RFID) sensors deployed on terrestrial and airborne platforms, including autonomous drones, that document our comings and goings, engagements and activities, any time we venture into public. Increasingly, these systems are backed by AI technologies that monitor, analyze, and evaluate the streams of data produced as we move through physical and online worlds, many of which also have the capacity and authority to take action. What once was the stuff of dystopian fiction is now a lived reality.

Privacy scholars have quite reasonably raised concerns about threats to fundamental rights posed by robots. For example, Frank Pasquale has advanced a trenchant critique of black-box algorithms, which have displaced human agents in a variety of contexts.[1] On the other hand,

[1] Frank Pasquale, *The Black Box Society: The Secret Algorithms that Control Money and Information* (Cambridge, MA: Harvard University Press, 2015).

we readily invite robots into our lives to advance personal and social goals. Some play seemingly minor roles, such as autonomous vacuums and refrigerators capable of tracking their contents, determining when supplies are low, and submitting online orders. Others less so, such as fitness monitors that summon emergency medical personnel when they determine their human partners are in crisis, or mental wellness apps that utilize biometric data to recommend, guide, and monitor therapy.

Because they entail constant and intimate contact, these human–robot interactions challenge our conceptions of self, privacy, and society, stretching the capacities of our legal regimes to preserve autonomy, intimacy, and democratic governance. Prominent among these challenges are efforts to understand the role of constitutions as guarantors of rights and constraints on the exercise of power. In the United States, this is evident in conversations about the Fourth Amendment and technology.

The Fourth Amendment provides that: "The right of the people to be secure in their persons, houses, papers, and effects, against unreasonable searches and seizures, shall not be violated, and no warrants shall issue, but upon probable cause, supported by oath or affirmation, and particularly describing the place to be searched, and the persons or things to be seized." Since the Supreme Court's pivotal 1967 decision in *Katz* v. *United States*,[2] the Fourth Amendment has been cast as a guarantor of privacy, which suggests that it might have a role to play in normalizing, protecting, and regulating the relationships among us, our technologies, corporations, and government agencies. Specifically, we might imagine the Fourth Amendment protecting us from threats to privacy posed by robots or securing our relationships with robots against threats of interference or exploitation. Unfortunately, doctrinal rules developed by the US Supreme Court have dramatically reduced the capacity of the Fourth Amendment to serve either role. Some of these rules have earned considerable attention, including the public observation doctrine[3] and the third party doctrine.[4] Others have so far avoided close scrutiny.

[2] 389 U.S. 347 (1967) [*Katz* v. *United States*].

[3] Under the public observation doctrine, police may make observations from any place where they lawfully have a right to be without triggering Fourth Amendment regulations. See David Gray, *The Fourth Amendment in an Age of Surveillance* (Cambridge, UK: Cambridge University Press, 2017) [*Age of Surveillance*] at 78–84.

[4] Under the third party doctrine, government agents may acquire from third parties through lawful means information voluntarily shared with those parties without triggering Fourth Amendment protections. See ibid. at 84–89.

This chapter examines two doctrinal rules in this more obscure category that are particularly salient to robot–human interactions. The first is that privacy is a personal good, limiting standing to bring Fourth Amendment challenges to those who have suffered violations of their personal expectations of privacy. The second is that the Fourth Amendment can only reach the actions of state agents. This chapter will show that neither is required by the text or history of the Fourth Amendment. To the contrary, the text, history, and philosophical lineage of the Fourth Amendment favor a broader understanding of privacy as a public good that "shall be" secure against threats of intrusive surveillance and arbitrary power by both government and private actors, whether human or robotic. This reading should lead us to alter our understanding of a variety of Fourth Amendment doctrines,[5] including rules governing standing and the state agency requirement, thereby enhancing the potential of the Fourth Amendment to play a salutary role in efforts to understand, regulate, and even protect human–robot interactions.

Before turning to that work, it is worth pausing for a moment to wonder whether we would be better off abandoning the Fourth Amendment to these doctrinal rules and focusing instead on legislation or administrative regulation as a means to govern robot–human interactions. There are good reasons to doubt that we would be better off. Legislatures generally, and the US Congress in particular, have failed to take proactive, comprehensive action as new technologies emerge.[6] Instead, this is an area where Congress has tended to follow the courts' lead. A good example is the Wire Tap Act,[7] passed in 1968 right after the Court's landmark decision in *Katz*. Most important, however, is that accepting the degradation of any constitutional right out of deference to the political branches turns constitutional democracy on its head. The whole point of constitutional rights is to guarantee basic protections regardless of legislative sanction or inaction. At any rate, defending constitutional rights does not exclude legislative action. For all of these reasons, we should question the doctrinal rules that seem to limit the scope of constitutional rights rather than accepting them in the hope that legislatures or executive agencies will ride to the rescue.

[5] *Age of Surveillance*, note 3 above, at 190–299.

[6] *United States* v. *Jones*, 565 U.S. 400 (2012) at 429–430 (Alito, J., concurring).

[7] 18 USC §§2510 et seq.

II Fourth Amendment Standing

Established Fourth Amendment doctrine imagines that privacy is a personal good.[8] This received truth traces back to the Supreme Court's 1967 opinion in *Katz*.[9] Confronted with the unregulated deployment and use of emerging surveillance technologies, including wiretaps and electronic eavesdropping devices, the *Katz* Court adopted a novel definition of "search" as a violation of a subjectively manifested "expectation of privacy … that society is prepared to recognize as 'reasonable.'"[10] Applying this definition, the *Katz* Court held that eavesdropping on telephone conversations is a "search," and therefore subject to Fourth Amendment regulation.

Once hailed as progressive, *Katz*'s revolutionary potential has been dramatically limited by its assumption that privacy is a personal good.[11] This point is manifested most clearly in the Court's decisions governing Fourth Amendment "standing." "Standing" is a constitutional rule limiting the jurisdiction of US courts. To avail themselves of a court's jurisdiction, Article III, section 2, of the US Constitution requires litigants to show that they have suffered a legally cognizable injury caused by the opposing party, and that the court can provide relief. Fourth Amendment standing shares a conceptual kinship with Article III standing, but is neither jurisdictional nor compelled by the text. It is, instead, derivative of the assumption in *Katz* that privacy is a personal good. Thus, a litigant must establish that his "own Fourth Amendment rights [were] infringed by the search and seizure which he seeks to challenge."[12]

Fourth Amendment standing doctrine hamstrings efforts to challenge overreaching and even illegal conduct. Consider *United States* v. *Payner*.[13] There, Internal Revenue Service (IRS) agents suspected that taxpayers were using a Bahamian bank to hide income and avoid paying federal taxes. Unable to confirm those suspicions, agents decided to steal records from Michael Wolstencroft, a bank employee. To facilitate their plan, agents hired private investigators Norman Casper and

[8] *Alderman* v. *United States*, 394 U.S. 165 (1969) at 174 ("Fourth Amendment rights are personal rights").

[9] Ibid. (citing *Katz* v. *United States*).

[10] *Katz* v. *United States*, note 2 above, at 361 (Harlan, J., concurring).

[11] *Katz* v. *United States*, note 2 above, at 350 ("[The Fourth] Amendment protects individual privacy against certain kinds of governmental intrusion.…"). This assumption underwrites both the third-party and public observation doctrines.

[12] *Rakas* v. *Illinois*, 439 U.S. 128 (1978) at 133.

[13] 447 U.S. 727 (1980) [*United States* v. *Payner* (1980)].

Sybol Kennedy. Kennedy established a relationship with Wolstencroft and arranged to go to dinner with him.[14] During their dinner date, Wolstencroft left his briefcase in Kennedy's apartment. Casper retrieved the briefcase and delivered it to IRS agent Richard Jaffe. Caspar and Jaffe broke into the briefcase and copied its contents, including hundreds of pages of bank documents. They then replaced the documents, relocked the briefcase, and returned it to Kennedy's apartment. This fantastic criminal conspiracy was carried out with the full knowledge and approval of supervisory agents at the IRS.

Among the stolen documents were records showing that Payner used Wolstencroft's bank to hide income. Based on this evidence, Payner was charged with filing a false tax return. At trial, he objected to the introduction of the stolen documents on the grounds that they were the fruits of a conspiracy to violate the Fourth Amendment. District Judge John Manos granted Payner's motion and condemned the government's actions as "outrageous."[15] In an effort to deter similar misconduct in the future, Judge Manos suppressed the stolen documents, concluding that "[i]t is imperative to signal all likeminded individuals that purposeful criminal acts on behalf of the Government will not be tolerated in this country and that such acts shall never be allowed to bear fruit."[16] The government appealed to the Supreme Court.

Writing for the Court in *Payner*, Justice Lewis Powell acknowledged that the government intentionally engaged in illegal activity and did so on the assumption that it would not be held accountable. He also agreed that: "No court should condone the unconstitutional and possibly criminal behavior of those who planned and executed this 'briefcase caper.'"[17] Nevertheless, Justice Powell held that Payner could not challenge the government's illegal conduct because Payner's personal "expectation of privacy" was not violated. The briefcase belonged to Wolstencroft. The documents belonged to the bank. Payner had no personal privacy interest in either. He therefore did not have "standing" to challenge the government's illegal actions.

Payner shows how treating privacy as a personal good prevents many criminal litigants from challenging illegal searches and seizures. That may seem defensible in the context of a criminal case, where demonstrably

14 *United States* v. *Payner*, 434 F. Supp. 113 (1977) at 119–121.

15 Ibid., at 130–131.

16 Ibid.

17 *United States* v. *Payner* (1980), note 13 above, at 733.

guilty defendants seek to avoid responsibility by suppressing reliable evidence. But what about public-minded civil actions? Consistent with its English heritage, US law allows for civil actions seeking equitable relief in the form of declaratory judgments and injunctions. Given the different interests at stake in this context, and the decidedly public orientation of these actions, one might expect to see a more expansive approach to questions of standing when litigants bring Fourth Amendment suits designed to benefit "the people" by challenging the constitutionality of search and seizure practices and demanding reform. Unfortunately, doctrinal rules governing Fourth Amendment standing make it nearly impossible to pursue declaratory or injunctive relief in most circumstances.[18] The culprit, again, is the assumption that privacy is a personal good. *Los Angeles* v. *Lyons*[19] offers a vivid example.

Adolph Lyons sued the Los Angeles Police Department (LAPD) and the City of Los Angeles after officers put him in a chokehold during a traffic stop. The chokehold was applied with such intensity that Lyons lost consciousness and suffered damage to his larynx. Given that he was the person assaulted, Lyons clearly had standing to bring a civil action alleging violations of his Fourth Amendment rights. To his credit, however, Lyons was interested in more than personal compensation. He wanted to use his suit to compel the LAPD to modify its practices, policies, and training on the use of force. Those remedies would have benefited not just Lyons, but also the people of Los Angeles and the United States generally, enhancing the people's collective security against unreasonable seizures. Unfortunately, the Court dismissed these equitable claims on the grounds that Lyons did not have standing.

In order to demonstrate standing to pursue injunctive relief, the Court held, Lyons would need to "establish a real and immediate threat that he would again be stopped for [a] traffic violation, or for any other offense, by an officer or officers who would illegally choke him into unconsciousness without any provocation or resistance on his part."[20] That is a virtually insurmountable burden, but it is entirely consistent with the Court's assumption that privacy and Fourth Amendment rights are personal goods. No matter how public-minded he might be, or how important the legal questions presented, Lyons could not

[18] See Jennifer E. Laurin, "Trawling for Herring: Lessons in Doctrinal Borrowing and Convergence" (2011) 111:3 *Columbia Law Review* 670.

[19] 461 U.S. 95 (1983).

[20] Ibid. at 105.

pursue judicial review of LAPD chokehold practices because he could not establish that his personal Fourth Amendment rights were in certain and immediate danger. It did not matter that the LAPD was still engaging in a pattern and practice of using dangerous, unjustified chokeholds, jeopardizing the Fourth Amendment rights of the people of Los Angeles as a whole. Those practices, and the threats they posed, did not violate Lyons' personal interests, so he was powerless to demand change.

Both the assumption that privacy is a personal good and the derivative rules governing Fourth Amendment standing have consequences for robot–human interactions. For example, they can be deployed to insulate from judicial review the kinds of electronic data-gathering that are essential for robotic actors and easily conducted by robots. A ready example is *Clapper* v. *Amnesty International*.[21] There, a group of attorneys, journalists, and activists challenged the constitutionality of a provision of the FISA Amendments Act, 50 USC §1881a, granting broad authority for government agents to surveil the communications of non-US persons located abroad. The plaintiffs argued that this authority imperiled their abilities to maintain the confidence of their sources and clients, compromising their important work. While admitting that plaintiffs' concerns were theoretically valid, the Supreme Court held that they did not have standing to challenge the law precisely because their fears were theoretical. In order to establish standing, the plaintiffs needed to demonstrate that their communications had actually been intercepted or were certain to be intercepted pursuant to authority granted by §1881a. As a result, the authority granted by §1881a remained in place, condemning "the people," individually and collectively, to a state of persistent insecurity in their electronic communications against both human and robot actors.

Courts have also wielded rules governing Fourth Amendment standing to limit the ability of service providers to protect their customers' privacy interests. For example, in *California Bankers Association* v. *Shultz*, the Supreme Court concluded that banks do not have standing to raise Fourth Amendment claims on their customers' behalf when contesting a subpoena for financial records.[22] In *Ellwest Stereo Theaters, Inc.* v. *Wenner*, the Ninth Circuit Court of Appeals held that an adult entertainment operator had "no standing to assert the fourth amendment

[21] 568 U.S. 398 (2013).
[22] 416 U.S. 21 (1974).

rights of his customers."[23] In a 2012 case where investigators subpoenaed Twitter for messages posted by political protestors along with location data, a New York trial court decided that Twitter did not have standing to object on Fourth Amendment grounds.[24] In 2017, a federal court in Seattle found that Microsoft Corporation did not have Fourth Amendment standing to challenge the gag order provisions of 18 USC §2705(b), which the government routinely invoked when compelling providers of data, internet, and communication services to disclose information relating to their customers.[25]

We are likely to see more of these kinds of decisions in coming years as courts continue to wrestle with new and emerging technologies. Consider, as an example, Amazon's Ring.

Ring is an internet-connected doorbell equipped with cameras, microphones, and speakers that allows owners to monitor activity around their front doors through a smartphone, tablet, or computer, whether they are inside their homes or in another time zone. Ring is capable of coordinating with other smart devices to provide users with access and control over many aspects of their home environments. There is also a Ring device for automobiles. Although Ring does not make independent intelligent choices or perform tasks based on environmental stimuli, it represents the kinds of technologies that inhabit the IoT, which includes a rapidly rising population of robots. Some of these robots gather stimuli directly through their onboard sensors. Others draw on sensorial inputs from other devices, such as Ring. Either way, devices like Ring represent a critical point of engagement for robots and humans as we grant intimate access to our lives and the world outside our front doors in order to obtain the convenience and benefits of robotic collaborators. As recent experiences with Ring show, that access is ripe for exploitation.

In August 2019, journalists revealed that Amazon had coordinated with hundreds of law enforcement agencies to allow them access to

[23] 681 F.3d 1243 (1982) at 1248.

[24] *People* v. *Harris*, 945 N.Y.S.2d 505 (NY Crim. Ct. 2012); Megan Guess, "Twitter Hands over Sealed Occupy Wall Street Protestor's Tweets," *Ars Technica* (September 14, 2012), https://arstechnica.com/tech-policy/2012/09/twitter-hands-over-occupy-wall-street-protesters-tweets/.

[25] *Microsoft Corp.* v. *United States Dep't of Justice*, No. C16-0538JLR (W. Dist. Wash., Feb. 8, 2017), slip opinion at 39–45. Microsoft ultimately settled with the Department of Justice; US, Office of the Deputy Attorney General, Policy Regarding Applications for Protective Orders Pursuant to 18 USC §2705(b) (Washington, DC: US Department of Justice, October 19, 2017), www.documentcloud.org/documents/4116081-Policy-Regarding-Applications-for-Protective.html.

video images and other information gathered by Ring without seeking or securing a court order or the explicit permission of owners.[26] It is hard to imagine a starker threat to the security of the people guaranteed by the Fourth Amendment than a program granting law enforcement access to our home environments. But who has standing to challenge this program? Criminals prosecuted using evidence from a Ring doorbell do not. That is the lesson from *Payner*. Owners of Ring doorbells do not, unless they can show that their personal devices have been exploited. That is the lesson from *Clapper*. But even a Ring owner who can show that her device was exploited cannot challenge the program writ large or demand programmatic reform. That is the lesson from *Lyons*. As a result, the Fourth Amendment appears to be functionally powerless, both to protect these sites of human–robot interaction,[27] and to protect the public from robotic exploitation via these kinds of devices and the data they generate. As an example of technologies in this latter category, consider facial recognition, which is capable of conducting the kinds of independent analysis once the sole province of carbon-based agents.[28]

Rules governing Fourth Amendment standing are not the only culprits in the apparent inability of the Fourth Amendment to regulate robot–human interactions. As the next section shows, the state agency requirement also limits the role of the Fourth Amendment in protecting and regulating many robot–human interactions.

III The State Agency Requirement

Conventional doctrine holds that the Fourth Amendment binds state agents, not private actors.[29] This state agency requirement limits the capacity of the Fourth Amendment to regulate and protect many human–robot interactions. Justice Samuel Alito recently explained why:

[26] Kim Lyons, "Amazon's Ring Now Reportedly Partners with More than 2,000 US Police and Fire Departments," *The Verge* (January 31, 2021), www.theverge.com/2021/1/31/22258856/amazon-ring-partners-police-fire-security-privacy-cameras.

[27] For an in-depth discussion of government access to information shared with robots, see Chapter 8 in this volume.

[28] See David Gray, "Bertillonage in an Age of Surveillance: Fourth Amendment Regulation of Facial Recognition Technologies" (2021) 24:1 *SMU Science and Technology Law Review* 3; for a considered discussion of evidentiary issues relating to robot-generated evidence, see Chapters 7, 9, and 10 in this volume.

[29] *Burdeau* v. *McDowell*, 256 U.S. 465 (1921) at 475.

> The Fourth Amendment restricts the conduct of the Federal Government and the States; it does not apply to private actors. But today, some of the greatest threats to individual privacy may come from powerful private companies that collect and sometimes misuse vast quantities of data about the lives of ordinary Americans.[30]

Many, if not most, of the robot–human interactions that challenge our conceptions of privacy, fracture social norms, destabilize our institutions, and that will most likely play central roles in our lives, are produced, deployed, and controlled by private companies. Smart speakers and other IoT devices, wearable technologies, and the myriad software applications that animate phones, tablets, and televisions are all operated by private enterprises. Some of these corporations have more immediate effects on our lives than government entities, and pose greater threats to our privacy, autonomy, and democratic institutions than government entities, but they stand immune from constitutional constraint because they are not state agents. As a consequence, the Fourth Amendment appears unable "to protect [the public] from this looming threat to their privacy."[31]

Here again, Ring provides a good example. Ring is part of a larger ecosystem of connected devices designed, sold, and supported by Amazon. In addition to Ring, many folks have other Amazon products in their homes, including Alexa-enabled devices, which are equipped with microphones and voice recognition technologies. These devices allow users to play music, operate televisions, order goods and services, make phone calls, and even adjust the lighting using voice commands. This ecosystem is increasingly open to devices capable of making independent choices. These are all wonderful human–robot interactions, but they come with the cost of allowing Amazon and its affiliates access to our homes and lives. By virtue of the state agency requirement, that relationship stands outside of Fourth Amendment regulation. Amazon, directly or through its robot intermediaries, is at liberty to threaten the security of the people in their persons and homes without fear of constitutional constraint so long as they do not directly coordinate with government agencies.

Must it be this way? Or does the Fourth Amendment have more to say about robot–human interactions than is suggested by rules governing standing and the state agency requirement? As the next sections argue, the text and history of the Fourth Amendment suggest that it does.

[30] *Carpenter* v. *United States*, 138 S.Ct. 2206 (2018) [*Carpenter* v. *United States*] at 2261 (Alito, J., dissenting).

[31] Ibid. at 2261.

IV Challenging Fourth Amendment Standing

The Fourth Amendment undeniably protects collective interests and recognizes that privacy is a public rather than an exclusively private good. That is evident in the text, which uses the phrase "the people" instead of "persons."[32] This choice was deliberate.[33] Those who drafted the Fourth Amendment had competing models to choose from, as represented in various state constitutions, some of which employed "persons"[34] and others "the people."[35] The drafters demonstrated awareness of these alternatives by guaranteeing Fifth Amendment protections to "persons"[36] and Sixth Amendment rights to "the accused."[37] By choosing "the people," the First Congress aligned the Fourth Amendment with political rights protected elsewhere in the Constitution,[38] such as the First Amendment right to assemble and petition the government[39] and the Article I right of the people to elect their representatives.[40] That makes sense in light of contemporaneous experiences with general warrants and writs of assistance, which showed how search and seizure powers could be weaponized to silence political speech. As we shall see, those cases contributed to founding-era concerns that general warrants and writs of assistance threatened the collective security of the people, not just those who were actually the subject of searches and seizures, because the very existence of broad, indiscriminate licenses to search and seize threatened the security of the people as a whole.[41]

32 See David Gray, "Dangerous Dicta" (2015) 72 *Washington & Lee Law Review* 1181 (explaining why dicta in *District of Columbia* v. *Heller*, 554 U.S. 570 (2008) at 580, n. 6, suggesting that Fourth Amendment rights are individual rather than collective finds no support in the text or history of the Fourth Amendment).

33 *Age of Surveillance*, note 3 above, at 149.

34 Massachusetts Constitution, US, Declaration of Rights (1780), Art. XIV.

35 Pennsylvania Constitution, US, Declaration of Rights (1776), Art. X.

36 US Constitution, Fifth Amendment.

37 US Constitution, Sixth Amendment.

38 *Age of Surveillance*, note 3 above, at 150–154.

39 US Constitution, First Amendment.

40 US Constitution, Art. I.

41 *Wilkes* v. *Wood*, 8 Eng. Rep. 489 (CP 1763) [*Wilkes* v. *Wood*] at 498 ("discretionary power … to search wherever their suspicions may chance to fall … certainly may affect the person and property of every man in this kingdom, and is totally subversive of the liberty of the subject"); *Entick* v. *Carrington*, 95 Eng. Rep. 807 (KB 1765) [*Entick* v. *Carrington*] at 817 ("[W]e can safely say there is no law in this country to justify the defendants in what they have done; if there was, it would destroy all the comforts of society …"). For an extended defense of this reading of the Fourth Amendment, see *Age of Surveillance*, note 3 above, at 134–172.

The text of the Fourth Amendment reflects founding-era understandings that security against arbitrary searches and seizures was an essential feature of democratic society. The founders understood how searches and seizures could be used to oppress thought and speech. But they also understood the idea, well-established since the time of the ancients, that security in our persons, houses, papers, and effects is essential to processes of ethical, moral, and intellectual development, which in turn are essential to the formation and sustenance of citizens capable of performing the duties of democratic government.[42] This is privacy as a public good. The Fourth Amendment guarantees that public good by securing space for liberty, autonomy, civil society, and democracy against threats of oppressive scrutiny.

The Supreme Court is not completely blind to the collective interests at stake in the Fourth Amendment. Consider, as an example, its exclusionary rule jurisprudence. Most Fourth Amendment claims arise in the context of criminal trials where the remedy sought is exclusion of illegally seized evidence.[43] The idea that illegally seized evidence should be excluded at trial is not derived from the text or history of the Fourth Amendment.[44] In fact, nineteenth-century jurists rejected the idea.[45] The exclusionary rule is, instead, a prudential doctrine justified solely by its capacity to prevent Fourth Amendment violations[46] by deterring police officers from violating the Fourth Amendment in the future.[47] Although illegal evidence is excluded in the cases of particular defendants, there is no individual right to exclude evidence seized in violation of the Fourth Amendment.[48] To the contrary, the Court has made clear that admitting

[42] Elvin T. Lim, "The Federalist Provenance of the Principle of Privacy" (2015) 75:1 *Maryland Law Review* 415 at 419, 425–428.

[43] Richard Myers, "Fourth Amendment Small Claims Court" (2013) 10 *Ohio State Journal of Criminal Law* 567 at 584.

[44] *United States* v. *Leon*, 468 U.S. 897 (1984) [*United States* v. *Leon*] at 906.

[45] See e.g. *United States* v. *La Jeune Eugenie*, 26 F. Cas. 832 (CCD Mass. 1822) at 843–844 ("In the ordinary administration of municipal law the right of using evidence does not depend, nor, as far as I have any recollection, has ever been supposed to depend upon the lawfulness or unlawfulness of the mode, by which it is obtained"); *Commonwealth* v. *Dana*, 43 Mass. (2 Met.) 329 (1841) at 337 ("If the search warrant were illegal, or if the officer serving the warrant exceeded his authority … this is no good reason for excluding the papers seized as evidence …").

[46] *Elkins* v. *United States*, 364 U.S. 206 (1960) at 217; *Age of Surveillance*, note 3 above, at 219–221.

[47] *United States* v. *Calandra*, 414 U.S. 338 (1974) at 348.

[48] *Davis* v. *United States*, 564 U.S. 229 (2011) at 236–237; *Stone* v. *Powell*, 428 U.S. 465 (1976) at 486; *United States* v. *Janis*, 428 U.S. 433 (1976) at 454.

evidence seized in violation of the Fourth Amendment "works no new Fourth Amendment wrong."[49] In making this prudential case for the exclusionary rule on general deterrence grounds, the Court recognizes that there is more at stake in a particular search or seizure than the personal privacy of a specific person.

The Court's awareness of the collective interests at stake in Fourth Amendment cases is not limited to its exclusionary rule jurisprudence. For example, in *Johnson* v. *United States*, decided in 1948, the Court noted that "[t]he right of officers to thrust themselves into a home is also a grave concern, not only to the individual, but to a society which chooses to dwell in reasonable security and freedom from surveillance."[50] Similarly, in *United States* v. *Di Re*, the Court concluded that "the forefathers, after consulting the lessons of history, designed our Constitution to place obstacles in the way of a too permeating police surveillance, which they seemed to think was a greater danger to a free people than the escape of some criminals from punishment."[51] Of course, these sentiments were issued before *Katz*, which shifted the focus to individual interests.

Importantly, however, *Katz* did not close the door, and there is some evidence that the Supreme Court may be ready to rethink rules governing Fourth Amendment standing in light of new challenges posed by emerging technologies. The strongest evidence comes from the Court's decision in *Carpenter* v. *United States*.[52] There, the Court was asked whether the Fourth Amendment regulates governmental access to cell site location information (CSLI). CSLI has been a boon to law enforcement. It can be used to track suspects' past movements and to establish their proximity to crimes. That is precisely what investigators did in *Carpenter*. Based on information from a co-conspirator, they knew that Carpenter was involved in a string of armed robberies. In order to corroborate that information, they obtained several months of CSLI for Carpenter's phone, establishing his proximity to several robberies. At trial, Carpenter objected to the admission of this evidence on Fourth Amendment grounds.

In light of the Court's views on standing and the state agency requirement, there was good reason to think that the government would prevail. After all, it was Carpenter's cell phone company who, of its own

[49] *United States* v. *Leon*, note 44 above, at 906.

[50] 33 U.S. 10 (1948) [*Johnson* v. *United States*] at 14.

[51] 332 U.S. 581 (1948) at 595.

[52] *Carpenter* v. *United States*, note 30 above.

accord, tracked his phone and stored his location information. It certainly did not appear to be acting as a state agent. Moreover, the information was recorded in the company's business records. If Payner did not have standing to challenge the search of banking records, then why would Carpenter have standing to challenge the search of cellular service records? Despite these challenges, the Supreme Court held that the "location information obtained from Carpenter's wireless carriers was the product of a search."[53] In doing so, the Court seemed to return to the pre-*Katz* era:

> The "basic purpose of this Amendment," our cases have recognized, "is to safeguard the privacy and security of individuals against arbitrary invasions by governmental officials." The Founding generation crafted the Fourth Amendment as a "response to the reviled 'general warrants' and 'writs of assistance' of the colonial era, which allowed British officers to rummage through homes in an unrestrained search for evidence of criminal activity." In fact, as John Adams recalled, the patriot James Otis's 1761 speech condemning writs of assistance was "the first act of opposition to the arbitrary claims of Great Britain" and helped spark the Revolution itself .... [our] analysis is informed by historical understandings "of what was deemed an unreasonable search and seizure when [the Fourth Amendment] was adopted." On this score our cases have recognized some basic guideposts. First, that the Amendment seeks to secure "the privacies of life" against "arbitrary power." Second, and relatedly, that a central aim of the Framers was "to place obstacles in the way of a too permeating police surveillance."[54]

This reasoning marks a potential broadening of the Court's approach to Fourth Amendment questions. Along the way, the Court seemed to recognize the important collective dimensions of the Fourth Amendment.[55]

The majority opinion in *Carpenter* does not directly address the question of Fourth Amendment standing. Nevertheless, Justices Anthony Kennedy and Clarence Thomas make clear that something potentially revolutionary is afoot in their dissenting opinions. For his part, Justice Kennedy reminds us that the Court's precedents "placed necessary limits on the ability of individuals to assert Fourth Amendment interests in property to which they lack a requisite connection."[56] "Fourth Amendment

[53] Ibid. at 2217.

[54] Ibid. at 2213–2214, citations omitted.

[55] David Gray, "Collective Rights and the Fourth Amendment after *Carpenter*" (2019) 79:1 *Maryland Law Review* 66 at 67–85.

[56] *Carpenter* v. *United States*, note 30 above, at 2227 (Kennedy, J., dissenting), citations omitted.

rights, after all, are personal," he continues, "[t]he Amendment protects '[t]he right of the people to be secure in their … persons, houses, papers, and effects' – not the persons, houses, papers, and effects of others." In the case of the business records at issue in *Carpenter*, Justice Kennedy concluded that they belonged to the cellular service provider "plain and simple." Consequently, Carpenter, like Payner, "could not assert a reasonable expectation of privacy in the records." Justice Thomas was even more pointed in his criticism, lambasting the majority for endorsing the idea that individuals can "have Fourth Amendment rights in someone else's property."[57]

The *Carpenter* majority offers no direct response to these charges, but there are hints consistent with the arguments sounding in the collective rights reading of the Fourth Amendment advanced in this chapter. For example, the Court recognizes that allowing government agents unfettered access to CSLI implicates general, collective interests rather than the specific interests of an individual. As Chief Justice John Roberts, writing for the majority, points out, cellular phones are ubiquitous, to the point that there are more cellular service accounts with US carriers than there are people. Furthermore, most people "compulsively carry cell phones with them all the time … beyond public thoroughfares and into private residences, doctor's offices, political headquarters, and other potentially revealing locales."[58] From these facts, the majority concludes that granting unfettered governmental access to CSLI would facilitate programs of "near perfect surveillance, as if [the Government] had attached an ankle monitor to the phone's user."[59] "Only the few without cell phones could escape this tireless and absolute surveillance."[60] This exhibits a keen awareness that the real party of interest in the case was "the people" as a whole. At stake was "the tracking of not only Carpenter's location but also everyone else's, not for a short period, but for years and years."[61] Denying customers' standing to challenge government access to those records would leave the people insecure against threats of broad and indiscriminate surveillance – exactly the kind of "permeating police surveillance" the Fourth Amendment was designed to prevent.[62]

[57] Ibid. at 2241–2242 (Thomas, J., dissenting).
[58] Ibid. at 2218, citations omitted.
[59] Ibid.
[60] Ibid.
[61] Ibid. at 2219.
[62] Ibid. at 2214.

Recognizing the collective dimensions of the Fourth Amendment provides good grounds for reconsidering rules governing Fourth Amendment standing. As the founders saw it, any instance of unreasonable search and seizure in essence proposed a rule, and the Fourth Amendment prohibits endorsement of any rule that threatens the security of the people as a whole.[63] It follows that anyone competent to do so ought to be able to challenge a proposed rule and the practice or policy it recommends. To be sure, a citizen challenging search and seizure practices should be limited in terms of the remedy she can seek. Actions at law seeking compensation should be limited to individuals who have suffered a direct, compensable harm. On the other hand, anyone competent to do so should have standing to bring actions seeking equitable relief in the form of declaratory judgments condemning search and seizure practices or injunctions regulating future conduct. Neither should we require the kind of surety of future personal impact reflected in the Court's decisions in *Lyons* and *Clapper*. The founding generation recognized that the very existence of licenses granting unfettered discretion to search and seize threaten the security of the people as a whole. Why, then, would we not permit a competent representative of "the people" to challenge a statute, policy, or practice that, by its very existence, leaves each of us and all of us to live in fear of unreasonable searches and seizures?

Expanding the scope of Fourth Amendment standing would enhance human–robot interactions by allowing competent persons and groups to challenge efforts to exploit those interactions. It would likewise enhance our security against robotic surveillants. It would allow the activist groups like those who brought suit in *Clapper* to challenge legislation granting broad access to electronic communications and other data sources likely to play a role on robot–human interactions. It would allow technology companies to challenge government demands for the fruits and artifacts of our engagements with technologies. It would also license competent individuals and organizations to seek declaratory and injunctive relief when companies and government agencies exploit our relationships with robots and other technologies or seek to deploy robotic monitors. There is no doubt that this expanded access to the courts would enhance the security, integrity, and value of our interactions with a wide range of technologies that inhabit our daily lives, both directly and indirectly, by increasing pressure on the political branches to act.

[63] David Gray, "The Fourth Amendment Categorical Imperative" (2017) 116 *Michigan Law Review Online* 14 at 31–34.

V Reconsidering the State Agency Requirement

Contemporary doctrine holds that the Fourth Amendment applies only to state agents, and primarily the police. A closer look at the text and history of the Fourth Amendment suggests that it is not, and was not conceived to be, so narrow in scope.

To start, there is the simple fact that the police as we know them today did not exist in eighteenth-century America. That was not for lack of models or imagination. By the late eighteenth century, uniformed, paramilitary law enforcement agencies with general authority to investigate crimes were familiar in continental Europe. But England had rejected efforts to adopt that model, at least in part because members of the nobility feared privacy intrusions by civil servants. When Sir Robert Peel was able to pass the Metropolitan Police Act in 1829, establishing the Metropolitan Police Force, the "Peelers" (later "Bobbies") were limited to maintaining the peace and did not have authority to investigate crimes. America was a decade behind England, with police forces making their first appearances in Boston (1838) and New York (1845). It was not until the late nineteenth century that professionalized, paramilitary police forces with full authority to investigate crime became a familiar feature of American society. By then, the Fourth Amendment was a venerable centenarian.

By dint of this historical fact, we know that the Fourth Amendment was not drafted or adopted with police officers as its sole or even primary antagonists. The text reflects this, making no mention of government agents of any stripe. Who then, was its target? The historical record suggests that it was overstepping civil functionaries, including constables, administrative officials, tax collectors, and their agents, as well as private persons. This is evidenced by the complicated role of warrants in eighteenth-century common law.

Contemporary Fourth Amendment wisdom holds that the warrant requirement plays a critical prospective remedial role, guarding the security of citizens against threats of unreasonable search and seizure by interposing detached and neutral magistrates between citizens and law enforcement.[64] Among others, Laura Donohue has made a persuasive case that the "unreasonable searches" targeted by the Fourth Amendment were searches conducted in the absence of a warrant conforming to the probable cause, particularity, oath, and return

[64] *Johnson* v. *United States*, note 50, at 13–14.

requirements described in the warrant clause.[65] But, as Akhil Amar has pointed out, the eighteenth-century history of warrants is somewhat more complicated.[66] Some of those complications highlight the role of private persons in conducting searches and seizures.

In a world before professional, paramilitary police forces, private individuals bore significant law enforcement responsibilities. In his commentaries, Blackstone recognized the right of private persons to effect arrests on their own initiative or in response to a hue and cry.[67] Searches and seizures in support of criminal investigations often were initiated by civilians who might go to a justice of the peace to swear-out a complaint against a suspected thief or assailant.[68] So, too, a plaintiff in a civil action could swear-out a warrant to detain a potential defendant.[69] A justice of the peace would, in turn, exercise his authority through functionaries, such as constables, who, as William Stuntz has noted, were "more like private citizens than like a modern-day police officer,"[70] or even civilian complainants themselves, by issuing a warrant authorizing those persons to conduct a search or seizure.[71] These private actors could conduct

[65] Laura K. Donohue, "Original Fourth Amendment" (2016) 83:3 *University of Chicago Law Review* 1181; Laura K. Donohue, "The Fourth Amendment in a Digital World" (2017) 71:4 *NYU Annual Survey of American Law* 553.

[66] Akhil Reed Amar, *The Constitution and Criminal Procedure: First Principles* (London, UK: Yale University Press, 1998) [*Constitution and Criminal Procedure*] at 3–20.

[67] William Blackstone, *Commentaries on the Laws of England: A Facsimile of the First Edition of 1765–1769*, vol. 4 (Chicago, IL: University of Chicago Press, 1979) at 286–290.

[68] *Constitution and Criminal Procedure*, note 66 above, at 12; William Stuntz, "The Substantive Origins of the Fourth Amendment" (1995) 105:2 *Yale Law Journal* 393 ["Substantive Origins"] at 401. See also James Otis, "In Opposition to Writs of Assistance" in William Jennings Bryan (ed.), *The World's Famous Orations* (New York, NY: Funk & Wagnalls, 1906) 27 ["In Opposition"] at 29 (describing common law cases "in which the complainant has before sworn that he suspects his goods are concealed" providing grounds for "warrants to search such and such houses, specially named").

[69] *Bell* v. *Clapp*, 10 Johns R. 263 (NY 1813) at 269; *Grumon* v. *Raymond*, 1 Conn. 40 (1814) [*Grumon* v. *Raymond*] at 44 (reporting on *Smith* v. *Bouchier*, 2 Stra. 993, in which "[t]he question arose upon a custom, that a plaintiff making oath that he has a personal action against any person with the precinct, and that he believes the defendant will not appear, but run away, the judge may award a warrant to arrest him, and detain him until the security is given for answering the complaint").

[70] "Substantive Origins", note 68 above, at 401, n 36.

[71] *Grumon* v. *Raymond*, note 69 above, at 45 (noting that in searches for stolen goods, "[t]here must be an oath by the applicant that he has had his goods stolen, and strongly suspects that they are concealed in such a place …"); *Entick* v. *Carrington*, note 41 above, at 817 (describing then-familiar cases of searches for stolen goods, in which "case the justice and the informer must proceed with great caution; there must be an oath that the party has had his good stolen, and his strong reason to believe they are concealed in such a place …").

searches purely on their own authority as well, but in doing so would risk exposing themselves to claims in trespass.[72] Warrants provided immunity against these actions.

Searches and seizures performed by minor functionaries and civilians raised significant concerns in eighteenth-century England because they threatened established social hierarchies by licensing civil servants to invade the privacy of the nobility. Those same worries underwrote resistance to professional police forces and founding-era critiques of general warrants and writs of assistance.[73] Unlike the particularized warrants issued by judicial officers based on probable cause imagined in the warrant clause, general warrants and writs of assistance provided broad, unfettered authority for bearers to search wherever they wanted, for whatever reason, with complete immunity from civil liability. These instruments were reviled by our eighteenth-century forebears because they invited arbitrary abuses of power.[74] But those threats did not come exclusively from agents of the state or only in the context of criminal actions. To the contrary, one of the most pernicious qualities of general warrants and writs of assistance was that they allowed for the delegation of search and seizure authority to minor functionaries and private persons. This is evident in the signal eighteenth-century cases challenging general warrants and writs of assistance.

The philosophical lineage of the Fourth Amendment traces to three eighteenth-century cases involving general warrants and writs of assistance that "were not only well known to the men who wrote and ratified the Bill of Rights, but famous through the colonial population."[75]

[72] *Entick* v. *Carrington*, note 41 above, at 817 (the common law "holds the property of every man so sacred, that no man can set his foot upon his neighbor's close without his leave; if he does he is a trespasser, though he does no damage at all; if he will tread upon his neighbor's ground, he must justify it by law").

[73] *Wilkes* v. *Wood*, note 41 above, at 497 (noting that Wood, a secretary to Secretary of State Lord Halifax, was "the prime actor in the whole affair"); William Cuddihy, *The Fourth Amendment: Origins and Original Meaning* (Oxford, UK: Oxford University Press, 2009) [*Origins and Original Meaning*] at 439–440 and 446–452 (discussing the conditions that led to the General Warrant cases and the British rejection of general warrants).

[74] *Entick* v. *Carrington*, note 41 above, at 817 ("we can safely say there is no law in this country to justify the defendants in what they have done; if there was, it would destroy all the comforts of society").

[75] "Substantive Origins", note 68 above, at 396–397. See also *Origins and Original Meaning*, note 73 above, at 39–87; Telford Taylor, *Two Studies in Constitutional Interpretation* (Columbus, OH: Ohio State University Press, 1969) at 24–44; Nelson B. Lasson, *The History and Development of the Fourth Amendment to the United States Constitution*

The first two, *Wilkes* v. *Wood*[76] and *Entick* v. *Carrington*,[77] dealt with efforts to persecute English pamphleteers responsible for writing and printing publications critical of King George III and his policies. In support of cynical efforts to silence these critics, one of the king's secretaries of state, Lord Halifax, issued general warrants licensing his "messengers" to search homes and businesses and to seize private papers. After their premises were searched and their papers seized, Wilkes and Entick sued Halifax and his agents in trespass, winning large jury awards. The defendants claimed immunity, citing the general warrants issued by Halifax. In several sweeping decisions written in soaring prose, Chief Judge Pratt – later Lord Camden – rejected those efforts, holding that general warrants were contrary to the common law.[78]

The third case providing historical grounding for the Fourth Amendment is *Paxton's Case*.[79] This was one among a group of suits brought by colonial merchants challenging the use of writs of assistance to enforce British customs laws in the American colonies. The colonists were ably represented by former Advocate General of the Admiralty James Otis, who left his post in protest when asked to defend writs of assistance. In an hours-long oration, Otis condemned writs of assistance as "the worst instrument of arbitrary power, the most destructive of English liberty and the fundamental principles of law that ever was found in an English law book."[80] He ultimately lost the case; but colonial fury over the abuse of search and seizure powers played a critical role in fomenting the American Revolution.[81]

(Baltimore, MD: Johns Hopkins University Press, 1937) at 13–78; Tracey Maclin, "The Central Meaning of the Fourth Amendment" (1993) 35:1 *William & Mary Law Review* 197 at 223–228. But see *Constitution and Criminal Procedure*, note 66 above, at 11 (allowing that the general warrants cases were "familiar to every schoolboy in America," but contending that the writs of assistance case was "almost unnoticed in debates over the federal Constitution and Bill of Rights").

76 *Wilkes* v. *Wood*, note 41 above.

77 *Entick* v. *Carrington*, note 41 above.

78 *Wilkes* v. *Wood*, note 41 above, at 498; *Entick* v. *Carrington*, note 41 above, at 817.

79 "In Opposition", note 68 above, at 27–37.

80 Ibid. at 28.

81 Mark Graber, "Seeing, Seizing, and Searching Like a State: Constitutional Developments from the Seventeenth Century to the End of the Nineteenth Century" in David Gray & Stephen Henderson (eds.), *The Cambridge Handbook of Surveillance Law* (Cambridge, UK: Cambridge University Press, 2017) 395 ["Seeing, Seizing, and Searching"] at 405–407.

Outrage over general warrants and writs of assistance was evident during the American constitutional movement.[82] Courts condemned them;[83] state constitutions banned them,[84] and states cited the absence of a federal prohibition on general warrants as grounds for reservation during the ratification debates.[85] In order to quiet these concerns, proponents of the Constitution agreed that the First Congress would draft and pass an amendment guaranteeing security from threats posed by unfettered search and seizure powers. The Fourth Amendment fulfills that promise.

All of this goes to show that we can look to founding-era experiences with, and objections to, general warrants and writs of assistance to inform our understandings of the Fourth Amendment. That record shows that the Fourth Amendment should not be read as applying exclusively to government officials. In their critiques of general warrants and writs of assistance, founding-era courts and commentators often highlighted the fact that they provided for the delegation of search and seizure powers to civilian functionaries. For example, the court in *Wilkes* argued that: "If such a power [to issue general warrants] is truly invested in a secretary of state, and he can delegate this power, it certainly may affect the person and property of every main this kingdom, and is totally subversive of the liberty of the subject."[86] James Otis railed that "by this writ [of assistance], not only deputies, etc., but even their menial servants, are allowed to lord it over us."[87] "It is a power," he continued, "that places the liberty of every

[82] See "Seeing, Seizing, and Searching", note 81 above, at 405–407; Bernard Bailyn, *The Ideological Origins of the American Revolution* (Cambridge, MA: Harvard University Press, 1967) at 117.

[83] *Frisbie* v. *Butler*, 1 Kirby 213 (Conn. 1787); *Grumon* v. *Raymond*, note 69 above, at 42–44 ("a warrant to search all suspected places, stores, shops and barns in [town]" because the discretion granted the officers "would open a door for the gratification of the most malignant passions").

[84] Massachusetts Constitution, US, Declaration of Rights (1780), Art. XIV; Vermont Constitution, US, Declaration of Rights (1786), Art. XII; New Hampshire Constitution, US, Bill of Rights (1784), Art. XIX; North Carolina Constitution, US, Declaration of Rights (1776), Art. XI; Maryland Constitution, US, Declaration of Rights (1776), Art. XXIII; Pennsylvania Constitution, US, Declaration of Rights (1776), Art. X; Delaware Constitution, US, Declaration of Rights (1776), Art. XVII; Virginia Constitution, US, Declaration of Rights (1776), Art. X.

[85] Department of State, *Documentary History of the Constitution of the United States of America* (Washington, DC: Department of State, 1894) at 193, 268, and 379 (reproducing reservations filed by New York, North Carolina, and Virginia).

[86] *Wilkes* v. *Wood*, note 41 above, at 498.

[87] "In Opposition", note 68 above, at 30–32.

man in the hands of every petty officer." "What is this," he lamented, "but to have the curse of Canaan with a witness on us; to be the servant of servants, the most despicable of God's creation?" The extent of that servitude, he explained, was virtually without limit, so that "Customhouse officers [and] [t]heir menial servants may enter, may break locks, bars, and everything in their way; and whether they break through malice or revenge, no man, no court, can inquire." Because a writ of assistance "is directed to every subject in the king's dominions," he concluded: "Everyone with this writ, may be a tyrant."

To be sure, many of the antagonists in these cases were state agents, if only of minor rank, or were acting at the direction of state agents. But the existence of general warrants and writs of assistance allowed both private citizens and government officials to threaten home and hearth. Otis explained why in his oration, quoting language common to writs of assistance that allowed "any person or persons authorized,"[88] including "all officers and Subjects," to conduct searches and seizures.[89] That inclusion of "persons" and "Subjects" reflected the fact that writs of assistance and general warrants were issued not just in cases of customs and tax enforcement, but also to assist private litigants in civil actions[90] or even to vindicate private animosities. Otis explained the consequences: "What a scene does this open! Every man prompted by revenge, ill humor, or wantonness, to inspect the inside of his neighbor's house, may get a writ of assistance. Others will ask it from self-defense; one arbitrary exertion will provoke another, until society be involved in tumult and blood."[91]

Anticipating a charge of dramatization, Otis offered this anecdote:[92]

> This wanton exercise of this power is not a chimerical suggestion of a heated brain. I will mention some facts. [Mr. Ware] had one of these writs … Mr. Justice Walley had called this same Mr. Ware before him, by a constable, to answer for a breach of the Sabbath-day Acts, or that of profane swearing. As soon as he had finished, Mr. Ware asked him if he had done. He replied, "Yes." "Well then," said Mr. Ware, "I will show you a

88 Ibid. at 32.

89 Philip B. Kurland & Ralph Lerner (eds.), *The Founders' Constitution*, 5th ed. (Chicago, IL: University of Chicago Press, 2000) at 226 (quoting from the text of the writ at issue in *Paxton*).

90 Ibid. (noting "writs [of assistance] issued by King Edward I. to the Barons of the Exchequer, commanding them to aid a particular creditor to obtain a preference over other creditors …").

91 "In Opposition", note 68 above, at 32.

92 Ibid.

> little of my power. I command you to permit me to search your house for uncustomed goods" – and went on to search the house from the garret to the cellar; and then served the constable in the same manner!

So, at the heart of this speech marking the birth of the American Revolution, we see Otis decrying general warrants and writs of assistance because they protected private lawlessness. That is hard to square with the contemporary state agency requirement.

The facts in *Wilkes* and *Entick* provide additional evidence of the potential for general warrants and writs of assistance to vindicate private interests and facilitate abuses of power. The searches in these cases aimed to discover evidence of libel against the king. In fact, the court in *Entick* characterized the effort as "the first instance of an attempt to prove a modern practice of a private office to make and execute warrants to enter a man's house, search for and take away all his books and paper in the first instance ...."[93] The *Entick* Court went on to suggest that allowing for the issuance of general warrants in search of libels would pose a threat to the security of everyone in their homes because simple possession of potentially libelous publications was so common.[94]

So, neither the text nor history of the Fourth Amendment appear to support a state agency requirement, at least not in its current form. That is evidenced by the fact that a strict state agency requirement appears to exclude from Fourth Amendment regulation some of the searches and seizures cited as *bêtes noires* in the general warrants and writs of assistance cases. Certainly, nothing in the text suggests that state agents are the only ones capable of threatening the security of the people against unreasonable searches and seizures. Moreover, eighteenth-century criticisms of search and seizure powers indicate that the founding generation was concerned about arbitrary searches performed by a range of actors. Given that history, there is good reason to conclude that the Fourth Amendment governs the conduct of private entities to the extent they pose a threat to collective interests, including privacy as a public good. Fortunately, the Court appears to be developing some new sympathies that line up with these ancient truths.

[93] *Entick* v. *Carrington*, note 41 above, at 818.

[94] One might object to this historical analysis citing *Shelley* v. *Kraemer*, 334 U.S. 1 (1948), the landmark case prohibiting judicial enforcement of racially restrictive covenants, as grounds for concluding that private agents acting in the shadow of judicial sanction are state agents. Of course, that conclusion does not follow. As the Court noted in *Shelley* v. *Kraemer*, its holding bore on the "judicial enforcement of [racially restrictive covenants]," not the validity "of the private agreements as such."

In addition to sparking a potential revolution in the rules governing Fourth Amendment standing, the *Carpenter* Court also appears to have introduced some complications to the state agency requirement. To start, the Court is never clear about when, exactly, the search occurred in *Carpenter* and who did it. At one point, the Court states that the "Government's acquisition of the cell-site records was a search within the meaning of the Fourth Amendment."[95] That would be in keeping with the state agency requirement. Elsewhere, the Court holds that the "location information obtained from Carpenter's wireless carriers was the product of a search,"[96] suggesting that his cellular service provider performed the search when it gathered, aggregated, and stored the CSLI. That is intriguing in the present context.

The *Carpenter* Court does not explain its suggestion that cellular service providers engage in a "search" for purposes of the Fourth Amendment when they create CSLI records. This is an omission that Justice Alito, writing in dissent, finds worrisome, pointing out that: "The Fourth Amendment … does not apply to private actors." Again, the Court offers no direct response, which may leave us to wonder whether its suggestion that gathering CSLI is a search was a slip of the pen. There are good reasons for thinking this is not the case. Foremost, *Carpenter* is a landmark decision, and Chief Justice Roberts has a well-deserved reputation for care and precision in his writing. Then there is the fact that what cellular service providers do when gathering CSLI can quite naturally be described as a "search." After all, they are looking for and trying to find an "effect" (the phone) and, by extension, a "person" (the user).[97] By contrast, it is hard to describe the simple act of acquiring records as a "search," although looking through or otherwise analyzing them certainly is. And then there is the fact that the acquisition was done by the familiar process of subpoena. As Justice Samuel Alito points out at length in his dissenting opinion, treating acquisition of documents by subpoena as a "search" would bring a whole host of familiar discovery processes within the compass of the Fourth Amendment.[98] By contrast, treating the aggregation of CSLI as the search would leave that doctrine untouched. For all these reasons, the best, most coherent, and least disruptive option

95 *Carpenter* v. *United States*, note 30 above, at 2220.

96 Ibid. at 2217.

97 *Kyllo* v. *United States*, 533 U.S. 27 (2001) at 32, n. 1: "When the Fourth Amendment was adopted, as now, to 'search' meant '[t]o look over or through for the purpose of finding something; to explore; to examine by inspection …'"

98 *Carpenter* v. *United States*, note 30 above, at 2246–2250.

available to the Court may have been holding that the cellular service provider conducted the search at issue in *Carpenter*.

Expanding the scope of Fourth Amendment regulations to searches conducted by private actors would provide invaluable protections for human–robot interactions and protections from robot surveillants. As Justice Alito points out in his *Carpenter* dissent, many of the most significant contemporary threats to privacy come from technology companies and parties who have access to us and our lives through our robot collaborators or deploy and use robots as part of their businesses. This gives them extraordinary power. We have certainly seen the potential these companies hold to manipulate, influence, and disrupt civil society and democratic institutions – just consider the autonomous decisions made by social media algorithms when curating content. In many ways, these companies and their robots are more powerful than states and exercise greater degrees of control. There can be no doubt that holding them to the basic standards of reasonableness commanded by the Fourth Amendment would substantially enhance individual and collective security, both in our engagements with robots and against searches performed by robots.

VI Conclusion

This chapter has shown that the Fourth Amendment's capacity to fulfill its promise is limited by two established doctrines, individual standing and the state agency requirement. Together, these rules limit the ability of the Fourth Amendment to normalize, protect, and regulate human–robot interactions. Fortunately, the text and history of the Fourth Amendment provide grounds for a broader reading that recognizes collective interests, guarding privacy as a public good against threats posed by both state and private agents. More fortunately still, the modern Supreme Court has suggested that it may be willing to reconsider its views on standing and state action as it struggles to contend with new challenges posed by robot–human interactions. As they move forward, the Justices would be well-advised to look backward, drawing insight and wisdom from the text and animating history of the Fourth Amendment.

PART III

Human–Robot Interactions and Legal Narrative

12

Narrative Approaches to Human–Robot Interaction and the Law

HELENA WHALEN-BRIDGE

How should we understand human–robot interaction? Are robots tools mindlessly following their programming, or are they actors with agency, as Frode Pederson queries in Chapter 13? Are robots an inevitability we should just accept, or does regulation have a role to play, as Helena Whalen-Bridge considers in Chapter 14? More broadly, how do we generate concepts to understand human–robot interactions in a way that adequately incorporates knowledge from different disciplines, as Jeanne Gaakeer investigates in Chapter 15? These questions suggest that we must consider subject matter beyond substantive law and procedure if we wish to understand robots and our place in the world with them – even if the focus is law. This is the central challenge addressed in Part III, "Human–Robot Interactions and Legal Narrative."

Narrative form is ubiquitous. It helps us understand and respond to daily events,[1] and it is now incorporated into many fields of knowledge,[2] including the sciences.[3] Narrative can be simply defined as the representation of events,[4] and as such it is also present in legal cases. Narrative is in fact reflected throughout the process of dispute resolution, appearing in witness testimony,[5] judicial fact-finding,[6] and even

[1] For the beginnings of this research, see Willam Labov & Joshua Waletzky, "Narrative Analysis" in June Helm (ed.), *Essays on the Verbal and Visual Arts* (Seattle, WA: University of Washington Press, 1967) 12.

[2] See Cristopher Nash, *Narrative in Culture: The Uses of Storytelling in the Sciences, Philosophy, and Literature* (London, UK: Routledge, 1990).

[3] See e.g. narrative-based medicine, in George Zaharias, "What Is Narrative-Based Medicine?" (2018) 64:3 *Canada Family Physician* 176.

[4] See Gerald Prince, *Dictionary of Narratology*, rev. ed. (Lincoln, NE: University of Nebraska Press; Chesham, UK: Combined Academic, 2003) at 58–61.

[5] See Line Norman Hjorth, "Underlying Narratives in Courtroom Exchanges" in Frode Helmich Pedersen, Espen Ingebrigtsen, & Werner Gephart (eds.), *Narratives in the Criminal Process* (Frankfurt am Main, Germany: Vittorio Klostermann, 2021) 139.

[6] For a variety of approaches to judicial narrative, see Simon Stern, "Narrative in the Legal Text: Judicial Opinions and Their Narratives" in Michael Hanne & Robert Weisberg

the structure of law.[7] This legal ubiquity suggests that narrative should have a place in discussions of substantive law and procedure,[8] but it is frequently missing, perhaps because, as Peter Brooks has observed, an explicit narratology for law might muffle law's majesty.[9]

If legal narrative should be included in analysis of the law generally, it certainly has a place when the law struggles to address a new issue or problem, because legal change may require the reconsideration of old narratives and the construction of new ones. Human–robot interaction is one such emerging field, as evidenced by the questions posed in Parts I and II that we never had to ask before, e.g. whether automated vehicles (AVs) should be liable for vehicular accidents, and whether robots should testify against their human drivers.

Earlier research has explored robot and artificial intelligence (AI) metaphors[10] and narratives to a degree, inside and outside the legal context. Chen Meng Lam has examined the use of AI to generate factual narratives in legal disputes in the future, and while these AI narratives would be highly evidence-based, such a system would suffer from an inability to explain precisely where and how conclusions were reached.[11] In a series of cases regarding accidents with AVs, Helena Whalen-Bridge

(eds.), *Narrative and Metaphor in the Law* (Cambridge, UK & New York, NY: Cambridge University Press, 2018) 121; Paul W. Kahn, *Making the Case: The Art of the Judicial Opinion* (New Haven, CT: Yale University Press, 2016); Sanford Levison, "The Rhetoric of the Judicial Opinion" in Peter Brooks & Paul Gewirtz (eds.), *Law's Stories: Narrative and Rhetoric in the Law* (New Haven, CT & London, UK: Yale University Press, 1996) 187; and Pierre N. Leval, "Judicial Opinions as Literature" in Peter Brooks & Paul Gewirtz (eds.), *Law's Stories: Narrative and Rhetoric in the Law* (New Haven, CT & London, UK: Yale University Press, 1996) 206.

7 See Maksymilian Del Mar, "Exemplarity and Narrativity in the Common Law Tradition" (2013) 25:3 *Law and Literature* 390; and Andrew Benjamin Bricker, "Is Narrative Essential to the Law? Precedent, Case Law and Judicial Emplotment" (2016) 15:2 *Law, Culture and the Humanities* 319; for Ronald Dworkin's characterization of the common law as a chain novel, see Ronald Dworkin, *Law's Empire* (Cambridge, MA: Harvard University Press, 1986) at 228–234.

8 See e.g. Anne E. Ralph, "Narrative-Erasing Procedure" (2018) 18:2 *Nevada Law Journal* Article 11.

9 Peter Brooks, "Narrative Transactions: Does the Law Need a Narratology?" (2006) 18:1 *Yale Journal of Law and Humanities* 1 at 28; see also Peter Brooks, *Reading for the Plot*, 1st ed. (New York, NY: A. A. Knopf, 1984) at 27–28.

10 See Ryan Calo, "Robots as Legal Metaphors" (2016) 30:1 *Harvard Journal of Law and Technology* 209 (examining judicial use of the robot metaphor).

11 Chen Meng Lam, "Using Artificial Intelligence in Narratives in the Criminal Process" in Frode Helmich Pedersen, Espen Ingebrigtsen, & Werner Gephart (eds.), *Narratives in the Criminal Process* (Frankfurt am Main, Germany: Vittorio Klostermann, 2021) 357.

identified a narrative of fear concerning the havoc that could be created if robots were to function independently of human control or supervision, as well as narratives concerning the superior and inferior abilities of humans and robots.[12] A narrative of human superiority would support the view that any driver must always remain attentive to the road, regardless of the functions of a driving aid, and this narrative may help explain why courts in particular cases imposed criminal liability on the driver for what were, in fact, robot malfunctions.[13] Chris Tennant and Jack Stilgoe have examined the narratives used to promote autonomous vehicles among developers, researchers, and other stakeholders, and they observed that while there is a dominant narrative of autonomy in which self-driving cars will replace error-prone humans, there was also some recognition that these vehicles are "attached and enmeshed in social and technological complexities."[14] Sabine Payr's investigation of science fiction literature and films about robots revealed a prevailing narrative of robots as unproblematic sidekicks, but even though the narratives purportedly focused on robots, the dominant theme was human identity.[15] Payr noted that there was a lack of productive narratives about emerging, more complex human–robot relationships, and Payr's study, as well as the work of Whalen-Bridge, and Tennant and Stilgoe, underscore the need for the volume's focus on human–robot interaction.

The three chapters in Part III assist to shed light on human–robot interactions. They also reflect the variety of research in narrative generally,[16] regarding both methodology and substantive focus. Examining a series of Norwegian cases regarding a trading robot, Frode Pederson's chapter considers competing narratives regarding the characterization of robots, as either exercising choice or merely following directions. Pederson demonstrates that although the narratives contain

[12] Helena Whalen-Bridge, "Constructing the Human–Robot Relationship: Stories of Ability and Fear in Cases of Criminal Liability for Driving Aids in Automobiles" in Frode Helmich Pedersen, Espen Ingebrigtsen, & Werner Gephart (eds.), *Narratives in the Criminal Process* (Frankfurt am Main, Germany: Vittorio Klostermann, 2021) 325.

[13] See also Madeleine Clare Elish & Tim Hwang, "Praise the Machine! Punish the Human! The Contradictory History of Accountability in Automated Aviation" (2015) Intelligence and Autonomy Initiative, Working Paper #1 V2.

[14] Chris Tennant & Jack Stilgoe, "The Attachments of 'Autonomous' Vehicles" (2021) 51:6 *Social Studies of Science* 1.

[15] Sabine Payr, "In Search of a Narrative for Human–Robot Relationships" (2019) 50:3 *Cybernetics and Systems* 281.

[16] See James A. Holstein & Jaber Gubrium (eds.), *Varieties of Narrative Analysis* (Los Angeles, CA: Sage, 2012).

contradictions, the different narratives chosen by the respective courts support different interpretations of the law. Taking a more empirical approach, Helena Whalen-Bridge examines the use of narratives in public arguments regarding AVs by tracing narrative themes and conflicts in Singapore newspaper coverage. She observes that the narratives of government and commercial entities were similarly upbeat and complementary, but they differed in that commercial entities asserted the narrative that AVs were inevitable, while government entities did not. Whalen-Bridge suggests, however, that the governmental rejection of inevitability does not dictate a particular regulatory approach and is consistent with either a light-touch or stricter styles of regulation. Jeanne Gaakeer's chapter widens the focus, making the important argument that automated driving systems require a "hermeneutics of the situation." Gaakeer suggests ways in which narrative and philosophical traditions necessarily inform the required interdisciplinary framework to guide factual and legal interpretation for automated driving systems, and she highlights the dangers of approaches which fail to heed lessons from other disciplines such as law, ethics, and technology.

The importance of narrative analysis to the study of human–robot interactions is also reflected in the appearance of narrative in chapters that do not have narrative as their primary focus. Regarding legal procedure, Sara Sun Beale and Hayley Lawrence observe in Chapter 6 that an important feature of human–robot interaction is the human tendency to anthropomorphize robots, which can generate misleading impressions or create the potential for manipulation when robots are given more of a backstory or designed to evoke a more trustworthy and believable character. Bart Custers and Lonneke Stevens conclude Chapter 10 on the point that even though the use of digital evidence is set to increase in the coming years, humans still seek to understand evidence by means of stories. Regarding the substantive law, Janneke de Snaijer examines the liability of medical professionals for remote-control and independent surgical robots in Chapter 3, but not the more advanced, self-learning robots which are on the horizon. These chapters indicate that the story of human–robot interaction is many stories, a number of which remain to be told.

MAMA K©

13

The Case of the Stupid Robot

FRODE HELMICH PEDERSEN*

I Narratives about the Human–Robot Relationship

Humans have long been fascinated by the notion of intelligent machines. The fascination is closely linked to the ancient dream that men will be able to rival God and create a sentient being. This theme is reflected in the story of Pygmalion, most famously told by the Roman poet Ovid and later iterated in numerous variations, where a master sculptor brings his sculpture to life. This kind of creation story has always been associated with the sin of hubris, where men are punished for challenging the authorities of the gods. Consequently, there is a long history of human anxiety connected with the notion of artificial sentience, as witnessed, e.g., in Mary Shelley's famous story of Frankenstein's monster from 1818, where the assembled being brought to life by Dr. Frankenstein becomes murderous after having been rejected by human society, bringing down a curse on his creator. The same anxiety can be traced through much twentieth-century science fiction, where intelligent robots often, for different reasons, are depicted as rebelling against their human creators and becoming a threat to humanity. A different strain of twentieth-century science fiction, often associated with the Russian-born American novelist Isaac Asimov and his positronic robots, portray robots as generally beneficial to mankind.[1]

Stories about the relationship between humans and machines are typically based on comparison and analogy. As humans, we see ourselves and our mental capacities mirrored or even replicated in the performance of so-called intelligent machines.[2] The stories of comparison can be divided into two categories. In the first, machines are seen as

* I would like to thank Helena Whalen-Bridge (NUS Law) for her insightful suggestions and helpful advice.

[1] Sabine Payr, "In Search of a Narrative for Human–Robot Relationships" (2019) 50:3 *Cybernetics and Systems* 281 at 282–287.

[2] See Chapter 6 in this volume.

ultimately superior to humans because of their greater computational capacities and lack of emotional instability. In the second, machines are seen as inferior to humans due to the rigid nature of their behavior and their inability to make spontaneous, meta-cognitive, or ethical judgments. Both of these narratives about the human–robot relationship may be present in the same story.

In some recent stories about the human–robot relationship, a new kind of anxiety is discernible, that of the human tendency to treat robots as mere tools. This treatment is increasingly shown as morally questionable, even outrightly wrong. The HBO series *Westworld* offers perhaps the clearest example of this anxiety. The humanoid robots are here initially depicted as all but innocent in their naïve devotion to their programming, whereas humans are depraved in their exploitation of the robots, which they rape and murder for their entertainment. When the robots rebel, the viewer gets the impression that the rebellion is justified, implying that the robots are ethically equal or even superior to humans. In this later development within popular narratives about the human–robot relationship, the ethical side of the comparison tends to remain disquietingly unresolved.

In this chapter, I will take a closer look at a Norwegian criminal case against two day-traders at the Oslo stock exchange who were accused of having manipulated a trading robot which had made a series of unfortunate trades at the Oslo stock exchange ("Robot Decision"). The Robot Decision is normally referred to in the singular, but it includes three different decisions from three instances of court, the first decision by the court of first instance, the Oslo District Court in 2010,[3] the second by the Court of Appeal (*Borgarting Lagmannsrett*) later the same year,[4] and the final and binding decision by the Norwegian Supreme Court in 2012.[5] As I will attempt to show, many aspects of the arguments and narratives that were put forward during the case explicitly or implicitly touch upon the same kind of dilemmas that we find in traditional Western stories about humans interacting with intelligent machines, and the way these dilemmas about the human–robot relationship are dealt with will to a large degree determine the outcome of the case.

[3] Oslo District Court, TOSLO-2010-94868 [TOSLO-2010-94868], available online in Norwegian: www.lovdata.no.

[4] Borgarting Court of Appeal, LB-2010-201611 [LB-2010-201611], available online in Norwegian: www.lovdata.no.

[5] Supreme Court of Norway, HR-2012-919-A–Rt-2012-686 [HR-2012-919-A], available online in Norwegian: www.lovdata.no.

The guiding hypothesis in my discussion of the Robot Decision is that any narrative will be affected by the presence of a robot when the robot is performing actions that are part of the narrative's sequence of events. Storytelling has traditionally been concerned primarily with representing human action,[6] which always involves certain assumptions about intention, motivation, rational choice, freedom of will, and goal-orientation. It is therefore not unreasonable to surmise that such assumptions are to some degree embedded in the narrative format itself. An action-performing robot causes perplexities in the narrative because we are unsure to what extent the robot can be reasonably said to possess the qualities that are required for being a real agent performing real actions. To the extent that we understand the robot to perform narrative acts, there will likely be a tendency, both on the part of the narrator and the receiver, to imply traits to these acts that are, strictly speaking, reserved for humans. In the following analysis of the Robot Decision, I will examine how and on what grounds the courts present their views on the way one should view the actions of the accused day-traders in relationship to the inept actions of the trading robot in light of the charges that were brought forward in the case. First, I will argue that the conflicting conclusions reached by the three instances of court are to varying degrees dependent on competing underlying narratives about the relationship between the trading robot and the human traders. Second, I will argue that the presence of the robot in the narrative about the facts of the case causes dilemmas and perplexities that are not exhaustively discussed in the courts' judgments and therefore never quite resolved. Third, I will argue that the present reading of the Robot Decision, with its focus on the case's narrative aspects, also uncovers unexamined assumptions about the notion of rationality in the stock market.

II Terminological Clarifications

The present examination of the Robot Decision is interdisciplinary in the sense that it is a narrative analysis, a legal commentary, and a reflection on the human–robot relationship. While the discussion should largely be understandable without theoretical knowledge in these fields, a few terminological clarifications are in order. Within the expanding field of

[6] See Aristotle, "Poetics" in Jonathan Barnes (ed.), *The Complete Works of Aristotle*, vol. 2: *The Revised Oxford Translation* (Princeton, NJ: Princeton University Press, 1984) 2316, 1448a 1 and 1450b 24–26.

interdisciplinary narrative studies, including Law and Narrative, there has been a tendency to use the term "narrative" rather loosely, referring to a whole range of phenomena, including general notions of how the world works and various arguments about concrete issues. In this chapter, I will mainly use the term "narrative" to refer to the verbal presentation of the facts of the case by the prosecution authorities, the defense, and the courts. In addition, I will use the term "underlying narrative" to refer to the narratives about the case that are implied or evoked by the arguments presented during the legal proceedings. The term "underlying narrative" was introduced in this specific sense by the literary scholar Line Norman Hjorth in the 2021 article "Underlying Narratives in Courtroom Exchanges."[7] As Hjorth explains, the underlying narrative is typically not spelled out, but it is nevertheless possible to reconstruct or perceive it, e.g., on the basis of cross-examination in the courtroom or arguments presented to or by the court.[8] Indeed, underlying narratives are often part and parcel of the parties' legal strategies and thus a crucial component in the kind of "narrative transactions" that take place in all legal proceedings.[9] The outcome of the case is entirely dependent upon which underlying narrative the court ends up accepting. One should note, however, that even the underlying narrative that wins the court's final acceptance will rarely be spelled out, it being a narrative of more general nature as opposed to the specific narrative about the facts of the case that courts normally concern themselves with. Therefore, an interpretation is required in order to give the underlying narrative a concrete formulation. In the case discussed in this chapter, it is possible to see the entire case as a contest between two underlying narratives: Is this a case about two small-time traders who take on the trading robot of a resourceful company and make a profit through their human ingenuity, or is it a story about two swindlers exploiting an essentially stupid robot's malfunction for their own gain?

With regard to terminology, I will in the following analysis not make use of the narratological distinction between story and discourse.[10] I will

7 Line Norman Hjorth, "Underlying Narratives in Courtroom Exchanges" in Frode Helmich Pedersen, Espen Ingebrigtsen, & Werner Gephart (eds.), *Narratives in the Criminal Process* (Frankfurt am Main, Germany: Vittorio Klostermann, 2021) 139 at 142.

8 Ibid.

9 Peter Brooks & Paul Gewirtz (eds.), *Law's Stories: Narrative and Rhetoric in the Law* (New Haven, CT: Yale University Press, 1996) at 9.

10 Dan Shen, "Story-Discourse Distinction" in David Herman, Manfred Jahn, & Marie-Laure Ryuan (eds.), *Routledge Encyclopedia of Narrative Theory* (London, UK & New York, NY: Routledge, 2008) at 566–568.

therefore occasionally use the word "story" in the non-technical sense for stylistic reasons, to mean a verbal representation of a series of events.[11] As regards the term "robot," I will use it interchangeably with "machine" in accordance with the usage in the written judgments in the case.

III The Case of the Stupid Robot

The Robot Decision concerned two day-traders at the Oslo Stock Exchange who had both, independently of each other, found and over a period of time exploited the same weakness in a trading robot belonging to a company called Timber Hill AG ("Timber Hill"). They were charged with several accounts of market manipulation. After having been convicted in the first instance Oslo District Court, both defendants were acquitted by the Court of Appeal. The Supreme Court upheld the decision of the Court of Appeal with a majority opinion of three judges against two dissenting votes. As can be ascertained from this brief account of the legal process in the case, there was significant disagreement among Norwegian judges as to how the case should be decided. My central argument in the following discussion is that legal decision-making in this case is animated by two different underlying narratives about the robot. In some of the arguments, which tend to work in favor of the defendants, the robot is seen as having a separate agency, as opposed to just being a tool in the hands of humans who have agency, whereas in other arguments, which tend to work in the opposite direction, the robot lacks agency, and is viewed as a tool bound by its programming in the hands of humans, who have agency.

IV The Factual Basis of the Charges

It is an undisputed fact of the case that the defendants' behavior was motivated by their realization that they were dealing with a trading robot. The robot belonged to Timber Hill, which had for several years specialized in automated trading. The two defendants had, independently of each other, discovered that the trading robot, which made all the trades on behalf of Timber Hill, responded mechanically to certain transactions. They figured out a way to exploit the robot's responses in order to profit from

11 In narrative theory, "story" refers to "the content plane of narrative as opposed to its expression plane or discourse." Gerald Prince, *A Dictionary of Narratology*, rev. ed. (Lincoln, NE: University of Nebraska Press, 2003) at 93.

them. A prerequisite for the defendants' trading strategy with the robot was that the transactions were made in illiquid stocks, or at least in stocks with a very low degree of liquidity. This allowed them to engage with the trading robot without the interference from other traders.

The defendants proceeded in the following way. First, they acquired a large block of the illiquid stock from the robot. The robot responded to this transaction by raising the price of this stock. The traders then went on to buy a small amount of the same stock at the new price, knowing that the robot would respond by further raising the price of the stock, irrespective of the volume of the transaction. This action was repeated several times until the price had become significantly higher than it had been when the traders acquired the larger block of stocks. They then sold the stocks back to the robot at the higher price. On occasion, they also did it the other way around, selling several smaller quantities of the illiquid stock to the robot in order to get it to lower the price, before they went on to acquire a large amount of the same stock. The actions of the defendants eventually triggered an alarm in a security system called SMARTS at the Oslo Stock Exchange, leading to an extraordinary trading break. The owner of the robot, the company Timber Hill, was informed of the irregular trading pattern, and they responded by correcting the imperfection in the robot's programming.

V The Legal Issue

The basic legal question in the Robot Decision was whether the two traders were guilty of market manipulation under the Norwegian Securities Trading Act (the "Statute"). The courts had to make a decision concerning the following two legal questions, based on the relevant provision in the Statute: whether the actions of the defendants had amounted to giving "incorrect or misleading signals as to the supply of, demand for or price of" the stocks that were traded,[12] or whether their transactions had secured "the price of one or several financial instruments at an abnormal or artificial level."[13]

12 Act on Securities Trading (Securities Trading Act), Norway, 2007, chapter 3, s. 3–8 (Market manipulation) (1), first alternative. Section 3–8 of the Statute was revoked in June 2019 and no English translation of the pre-amendment version of the Statute is available online. The Norwegian version of the pre-amendment Statute is available online: https://lovdata.no/dokument/LTI/lov/2007-06-29-75.

13 Securities Trading Act, ibid., at chapter 3, s. 3–8 (Market manipulation) (1), second alternative.

The prosecution claimed that the actions of the defendants amounted to market manipulation, since the purpose of their transactions was to trigger a change in the price, not to acquire the stocks. Therefore, the defendants had given misleading signals to the market, seeing as their transactions were designed to express an interest in the stocks that was not real. Furthermore, the prosecution claimed that the transactions were suited to disrupt the market's mechanisms for securing the correct price of the stock, which qualifies as market manipulation in the sense of the Statute, chapter 3, section 3–8.

The defense argued that the defendants' actions had not amounted to market manipulation, since all the trades had actually been made and therefore could not be regarded as misleading signals. And far from disrupting the market, the defendants' actions had ultimately contributed to its smooth running by effectively removing an inefficient player. Their actions should therefore be viewed as beneficial to the market.

VI The Decision of the Oslo District Court

In the judgment issued by the court of first instance, the Oslo District Court (*Oslo Tingrett*), the court started its decision by establishing that the defendants had acted willfully.[14] The court declared that there could be no doubt that the defendants knew how the robot would respond to their trades, and that they used this knowledge to make Timber Hill raise the price of the stock, allowing them to make a profit by essentially reversing the transactions when they sold the stock back to the robot. The court then gave an account of the defense's argument, where it was claimed that it would be unreasonable to regard the defendant's actions as market manipulation. The defense denied that the trades made by the defendants had caused the change in the price, since no legal causation could be established between the actions of the defendants and the changes in the price of the stock. It was the company Timber Hill, and not the defendants, that issued new trade orders with a different price.

The court countered this argument by pointing out that the purpose of the defendants' trades was the reaction of the trading robot, not to acquire the stocks, noting also that the defendants were "the active parties" in the transactions, seeking to produce a change in the price through their trades with the robot, who was, by implication, a mere passive tool. On this basis, the court held that legal causation was present between

[14] TOSLO-2010-94868, note 3 above.

the actions of the defendants and the changes in the price of the stock, concluding that the defendants had themselves caused the change in the price that they profited by. The court maintained that the purpose of the trades, i.e., to cause the change in the exchange rate, was not "legitimate" and that the defendants' actions toward the robot therefore amounted to giving "misleading signals about the supply of, demand and price for" the stocks in question under the statute. The court also found that the transactions initiated by the defendants secured the price of the traded stocks "at an abnormal or artificial level," thereby meeting the statutory requirement, if only for a very short period of time.

At the end of the deliberation, the court included a reflection on the human–robot relationship that should be quoted in full:[15]

> The defense has argued that the actions of the defendants cannot be viewed as "suited" to give false or misleading signals. The basis of this argument is that TMB [Timber Hill] must be treated like a human, and that a human would not have reacted so automatically and unintelligently without learning from its mistakes. The court remarks that the defendants are not charged with misleading TMB but with misleading the market *through* their trades with TMB. The defendants knew that they traded with a machine, their trading pattern was designed to mislead TMB and succeeded in this, with the consequence that the transactions gave incorrect and misleading signals to the market. The court is therefore of the opinion that the defendant's transactions – in this particular case – both gave and were "suited to give" misleading signals.

These concluding remarks suggest that the basis of the court's decision hinged more significantly on the implicit narrative of how the human–robot relationship should be understood, rather than what could be discerned from the analysis in the judgment and the existing legal commentary about the Statute. The commentary was sparse and primarily concerned with the types of actions that are punishable under the Statute, the main point being that, certain actions were not punishable even if they, strictly speaking, fit the description of the unlawful action. This is called *rettsstridsreservasjon* in Norwegian law, which necessarily involves an interpretation of the intention of the lawmakers.[16] As should be clear from the quoted portion of the judgment above, however, the basis of this interpretation was an underlying narrative about the robot as a mere malfunctioning tool in the hands of human traders. In the following

[15] Ibid. (author translation, emphasis added).
[16] Knut Bergo, *Børs- og Verdipapirrett* (Oslo, Norway: Cappelen Damm, 2021) at 514.

analysis of the Oslo District Court's written discussion of the case, I will attempt to highlight the significance and implications of the competing underlying narratives about the human–robot relationship that were at work during the hearings and in the court's deliberation.

VII Analysis of the Judgment of the Oslo District Court

In her influential book *Transparent Minds*, the narratologist Dorrit Cohn notes that with regard to factual as opposed to fictional stories, the narrator can never escape the epistemological premise that no human being can ever know with certainty what goes on in other people's minds.[17] Should a narrator of a factual story break with this premise and imply that he or she is in fact in possession of such a knowledge, the story becomes less plausible than it would otherwise have been. While it is true that judges routinely make judgments about states of mind without their narratives being therefore necessarily regarded as less than plausible, this does not, to my mind, significantly affect Cohn's point. First, these kinds of judgments are made on the basis of legal conventions and not on a presumption that judges are endowed with the ability to read people's minds. Second, they are presented as court findings about states of mind deduced from other story-elements, not as directly observable facts.

Cohn's narratological point is relevant for the understanding of the human–robot relationship. While it is an inescapable condition for all human interaction that our minds are not transparent, this constraint is not necessarily present in our interactions with robots. If we know how a robot is programmed, we know what goes on inside it. And even if our knowledge of AI programming is less than expert, we can still, in many cases, know with certainty how a machine will respond to certain human actions, based on our knowledge of the tasks it is programmed to perform. Cohn's epistemological boundary, that human minds are not transparent, is everywhere implied in the language that we use when describing human interaction, including legal language. The question is whether this language is so ingrained in the way we narrate factual stories that it will inevitably also seep into our descriptions about the human–robot relationship in ways that may not reflect the actual circumstances.

[17] Dorrit Cohn, *Transparent Minds: Narrative Modes for Presenting Consciousness in Fiction* (Princeton, NJ: Princeton University Press, 1978) at 3–5; see also Dorrit Cohn, "Signposts of Fictionality: A Narratological Perspective" (1990) 11:4 *Poetics Today* 775 at 775–804.

In order for the court to present a coherent argument in support of the decision to convict the defendants, several assumptions concerning the human–robot relationship must be in place. Going through the court's narrative step by step, we can begin by observing that in order to find the defendants guilty, the robot's responses to the traders' actions cannot be portrayed as independent acts; they must be viewed as a mechanical response to the actions of the traders, in line with the court's underlying narrative about the human–robot relationship in the case, i.e., that the robot is stupid and it was used by the traders in a way that violated the law. This underlying narrative connects with the notion of purpose, which the court ascribed to the actions of the traders, but not to the robot, whose actions must be viewed as having been accomplished without independent purpose. This approach, in turn, ties in with the distinction between active and passive, in which only the parties that were capable of acting with a purpose can be viewed as active, which means that the changes to the price made by the robot must be seen as mere reflexes, caused by the controlling actions of the real agents, the defendants. To the extent that these assumptions can be legitimately presupposed, the court can then reasonably go on to reach the legal conclusion, as it does, that the price offered by the robot immediately before the final transaction was "artificial," since it was not offered as a result of regular trading, but because of the traders' meddling with an imperfect machine, one that had no choice but to respond to the traders' actions as it did.

However, for the court to construct a coherent narrative about the case based on these assumptions, it must overcome a seeming paradox with regard to the notion of deception, which is a crucial element of the criminal charge. The court's narrative implied that the defendants had deceived the robot into thinking that the series of trades of small quantities of the illiquid stock were regular trades, whereas in fact they were just a means of getting the robot to increase the price of the stock. The reason why these transactions were not, in the eyes of the court, real trades is that the defendants could – contrary to what would have been the case in mutual human trading – predict with certainty how the robot would respond. The mind of the robot must then, in a certain sense, have been regarded as transparent, making it easy to deceive. Yet a stupid robot which was seen as a mere tool could not at the same time be said to possess the qualities of mind that are necessarily involved in being deceived, i.e., being misled into making an error of judgment. This is presumably why the court argued that the deception was directed at the market and not at Timber Hill via its robot. This factual finding does not seem immediately evident yet, since no evidence was presented that suggested that the market had been affected at all by the transactions, which, as we recall, were made in stocks that were all but illiquid. Another difficulty with finding that the market was deceived is that for the traders to deceive the market, surely, they would have had to deceive their robot trading partner first? Had it not been possible to deceive the robot trading partner, they would not have been able to manipulate the market. And this is indeed what the court goes on to find, that it was by misleading Timber Hill that the defendants sent misleading "signals" to the market.

At this point in the court's argument, it seems clear that the conflicts regarding the status of the robot within the underlying narrative create inconsistencies in the court's explicit narrative about the facts of the case. The paradox may be spelled out in the following way. On the one hand, the trading robot was seen as a mere tool, and as such not endowed with the capability of being misled. Its responses to the traders' actions were seen as mechanical reflexes, stemming from a glitch in its programming. This, in turn, made it possible to argue that the transactions were not real trades, but just a means to raise the price of the stock. On the other hand, in the court's narrative about the facts of the case, the robot was seen as the acting agent of Timber Hill, and as such endowed with the capability of being deceived by the traders. The deception necessarily involved an error of judgment intended by the deceivers: what seemed like one thing, trades, was in fact another thing, a means of raising the price of the stock. The machine mistook one for the other and was, therefore, by implication, engaged in an act of interpretation. This latter notion is precluded by the former notion of the robot as a mere mechanical tool. Nevertheless, both notions served as premises for the court's narrative about what happened in the case. And as noted above, the inconsistency cannot be resolved simply by concluding that the deception was directed at the market and not Timber Hill's trading robot.

Turning now to the court's report of the defense's narrative about the facts of the case, we notice that the key notion concerning the human–robot relationship is reversed. The underlying narrative informing the defense's argument was that Timber Hill's imperfect robot should be regarded as a regular human trader. The defense made this argument because a robot that can make its own decisions meant that the traders did not cause the market to be deceived – the robot did. This way of viewing the human–robot relationship does not, however, resolve the conflicts that are present in the court's narrative about the case. On the one hand, the defense's denial that legal causation has been established relied on viewing the robot's responses to the defendants' trades as proper acts, as opposed to just mechanical reflexes. This approach is consistent with the defense's underlying narrative that the robot is analogous to human traders. Normally, however, the requirement for something being an act is that it is based on a decision, meaning that the agent performing it could in principle have chosen to act differently.[18] Since this cannot be said to have been the case with the robot, the defense must instead argue that the robot's actions were caused by its imperfect programming. But seeing things in this way would imply that the robot is stupid, a mere tool, and therefore it cannot reasonably be viewed as if it were a human trader.

The conflicts concerning the status of the robot are therefore also present in the defense's narrative about the case. Even so, the defense's reasoning did convincingly support the claim that no legal causation is present in the case. If the ultimate cause of the robot's actions laid with its programming, for which the defendants bore no responsibility, there was a kind of black box between the actions of the traders and the actions of the robot which made it unreasonable to claim that the traders had caused the robot to do things. Viewed in this way, the defendants were blameless for the losses of Timber Hill, in the same way that they would have been blameless if Timber Hill had been using an incompetent human trader who was slow to learn from his or her mistakes.

VIII The Decision of the Court of Appeal

In the Norwegian justice system, the Court of Appeal conducts an entirely new hearing of all aspects of the case. In this case, the Court of Appeal agreed with the account of the facts of the case as they were presented by the first instance Oslo District Court, but there was one significant new aspect of the case that came to light during the appeal hearing. A witness from Timber Hill explained to the court that the company has employees who are tasked with overseeing the trades made by the machines. These employees were supposed to adjust the trading robot's algorithms when necessary. In the trades at issue in this case, none of the employees at Timber Hill had discovered the irregularities in the activities of the trading robot prior to the company being alerted to them by the Oslo Stock Exchange. The witness explained that these particular trades had probably "gone under the radar," since they involved a relatively small amount

[18] For a discussion of criminal law and the freedom to act, see Chapter 15 in this volume.

of money and were made in stocks that were all but illiquid. In the context of our analysis, we can surmise that the court was here exploring whether a human agency "behind" the machine could reasonably be established, such that one could view the machine as a mere tool in the hands of human beings such as Timber Hill employees, who could then be said to be responsible for the trades made by the machine.

This is a theme that runs through several of the automated vehicle verdicts discussed, among others, by Helena Whalen-Bridge.[19] The crucial question in many such cases is whether a driver is responsible for malfunctions in the automated driving devices of these cars in the same way a driver would be responsible for driving with defective brakes or wheels. In the cases Whalen-Bridge discusses, the courts are quite clear in their view that the driver is in fact responsible for the behavior of his or her vehicle, even when the autopilot system is doing the driving.[20] This is comparable to Norwegian verdicts in cases concerning collisions at sea, where various autopilot systems are involved. As far as I have been able to ascertain, the captain or helmsman is always, as a matter of course, seen as responsible for the ship's course and movements, regardless of any malfunctions in the autopilot system. Navigation systems are viewed as mere tools that should always be used in combination with watchful seamanship.[21]

In the first instance Robot Decision, the court leaned toward adopting an underlying narrative in which the responsibility for the malfunction of the robot was not placed on the Timber Hill owners, who used it to make trades on their behalf, but rather on the traders who exploited its imperfection. I cannot conclude with any certainty why this is so, but I suggest that it has more to do with overarching considerations about the legal consequences of conclusions on the legal issues rather than with any principled notion about the human–robot relationship.

The Court of Appeal agreed with many of the conclusions reached by the Oslo District Court. It concurred with the opinion that the actions of the traders were intentional, and that there was legal causation between the actions of the defendants and the changes to the price of the stock.

[19] Helena Whalen-Bridge, "Constructing the Human–Robot Relationship: Stories of Ability and Fear in Cases of Criminal Liability for Driving Aids in Automobiles" in Frode Helmich Pedersen, Espen Ingebrigtsen, & Werner Gephart (eds.), *Narratives in the Criminal Process* (Frankfurt am Main, Germany: Vittorio Klostermann, 2021) 325; see Chapter 15 in this volume.

[20] Ibid. at 352.

[21] See e.g. the Financial Complaints Board, FinKN-2012-104.

The Court of Appeal commented that even if it was Timber Hill who effectuated these changes, the defendants knew how the trading robot would respond to their actions, and that this response was the intended result of their trades. The Court of Appeal therefore agreed with the Oslo District Court that the defendants were the active parties in the trades.

At this junction, the reasoning of the Court of Appeal started to diverge from the one presented by the Oslo District Court. The difference of opinion mainly concerned two aspects of the facts of the case. First, the Court of Appeal took care to underline the fact that all the trades made by the defendants were real trades: "The defendants have in fact bought/sold the stocks in the number and at the prices that have been indicated. Their counterpart has received correct information about the trades that were made, both with respect to price and to volume."[22] The court went on to say that, while this is the case, there was also the extraordinary circumstance that "the defendants knew how the counterpart would react to their purchase and sale orders and used this knowledge to get a gain for themselves."[23] This was, however, as the court pointed out, only possible because the programming in Timber Hill's trading robot did not take the volumes of the trades into account. Compared to the reasoning of the Oslo District Court, the Court of Appeal placed much more emphasis on the robot's malfunction, for which the defendants were obviously not responsible.

Second, the Court of Appeal disagreed with the Oslo District Court with regard to the effect that the irregular trades may be said to have had on the market. The Court of Appeal referred to two expert witnesses working on behalf of the court, who both opined that it was Timber Hill's algorithm, and not the actions of the defendants, which caused an inefficiency in the market, by making the same mistake repeatedly over time. According to both expert witnesses, there was nothing unusual or dishonest in the behavior of the defendants. Far from being harmful to the market, their actions resulted in the discontinuation of Timber Hills' irrational behavior.

IX Analysis of the Judgment of the Court of Appeal

Turning now to its legal deliberations, the Court of Appeal stated that the only legal provision applicable to the case is the first alternative in chapter 3, section 3–8 in the Statute, which forbids traders to give

[22] LB-2010-201611, note 4 above (author translation).
[23] Ibid.

"incorrect and misleading signals as to the supply of, demand for or price" of the traded stocks. The Court of Appeal confessed to having had doubts about how to adjudicate this question on the following grounds. On the one hand, the Court of Appeal agreed with the Oslo District Court that the transactions made by the defendants between the first and last trade had no purpose other than bringing about a reaction on the part of Timber Hill's robot. In this sense, they could be said to have profited by an adjustment of the price that they had themselves caused. It would not be unreasonable, the court noted, to view "the sum" of the actions of the defendants in these transactions as misleading signals. On the other hand, the Court of Appeal found that one must take into consideration that all the trades made by the defendants were real.

In the Court of Appeal's reversal of the Oslo District Court's decision, the crucial argument was the following one: "The intended reaction from Timber Hill came about because the algorithm Timber Hill was using was not capable of correctly interpreting the information contained in each trade." This was, the Court of Appeal went on to point out, "a result of insufficient programming of the machine used by Timber Hill, in combination with the fact that the people in charge of overseeing the actions of the machines did not intervene in the trades made by the algorithm." In this finding, the performance of the trading robot was viewed in analogy with an inadequate performance of a human trader, in the sense that the responsibility was seen as lying with the trader who made the irrational trades. Since the trading robot who executed the transactions did not have a will of its own, the responsibility laid with both the programmers[24] and the employees who were tasked with overseeing the robot's performance.[25]

As Hayden White has suggested, there is an ethical aspect to any story.[26] Viewed in relation to the question of whether the robot should be seen as a mere tool or as an independent actor, the decision of the Court of Appeal can be seen as a correction of an ethical misjudgment in the first instance Oslo District Court's narrative about the case. The narrative of the Oslo District Court, which substantiated the court's view that the defendants were culpable, appears to have been informed in part by an ethical analogy between the robot's malfunction and human

[24] On programmer liability, see Chapter 2 in this volume.

[25] On corporate and employer criminal liability, see Chapter 4 in this volume.

[26] Hayden White, "The Value of Narrativity in the Representation of Reality" (1980) 7:1 *Critical Inquiry* 27 at 27.

impairment. The logic here seems to be that since it is ethically wrong to take advantage of a human being who is obviously not acting in accordance with his or her own best interest, it is also wrong to take advantage of a robot which is obviously not acting in the best interest of the people who use it to act on their behalf.

In the underlying narrative of the Court of Appeal, the ethical assumptions were different. The basic idea of a capitalist market is that everyone acts to the benefit of the market by acting in accordance with their own self-interest. When a trading company uses robots instead of human traders, it is their way of trying to maximize profits. When other traders discover a glitch in the robot, they are acting in the best interest of the market precisely by exploiting this glitch to their advantage, since this will eventually lead to the improvement of the robot, which will increase the efficiency of the market. According to this logic, it does not matter whether the cause of the inefficiency lies with the robot or with the people behind the robot. Neither does it matter whether the cause of the inefficiency is bad programming or human stupidity. The important thing is that the irregularity is eliminated through actions taken in the market. One may, of course, question the ethical soundness of this argument, relying rather heavily as it does on capitalist ideology and its tendency to view egotistical actions as ethically desirable. But the fact of the matter is that the use of trading robots has been increasing in recent years, and they are typically used by large and powerful companies which makes it harder for small-time traders to make a profit, especially on day-trading. It is therefore not so obvious that human traders would act ethically by reporting suboptimal performances of trading robots instead of exploiting them to their own benefit. No such fairmindedness would go in the other direction, as no existing trading robot would report a human trader who kept making stupid trades.

X The Decision of the Supreme Court

The majority vote of the Supreme Court ruled to uphold the decision of the Court of Appeal, acquitting the defendants of all charges.[27] The minority vote argued that the defendants should be convicted of market manipulation. Judge Webster, writing for the majority, discussed at length whether market manipulation had occurred in the case. As we have seen, a discussion of this kind incorporates underlying

[27] HR-2012-919-A, note 5 above.

narratives, which ultimately demands a clarification regarding the nature of the human–robot relationship.

Having gone through multiple sources regarding the legal issues at hand, Judge Webster explored the question of whether manipulation was present in the defendants' trading activity, or if it would be more appropriate to say that it was the robot's inept responses to the defendant's trades that caused the irregularity in the market. The question here is whether the trades made by the defendants could only have been misinterpreted by an imperfect robot or whether they could also have fooled a rational human trader. Judge Webster made the point that no trader would have been able to ascertain that all the trades made by the defendants were in fact made by the same trader. One would only be able to find out for certain that they were made through the same broker. Therefore, the increased trading activity in the specific stock could conceivably also have given a human trader the impression that the market demand for these stocks had suddenly increased. Judge Webster commented that "a trained eye" would have been required in order to see that the trades made by the defendants did not, in fact, reflect a real increase in market demand for this stock.[28] The implication is that the malfunction of the robot could be viewed in much the same way that one would view the inexperience of a human trader. In both cases, one would speak of a misinterpretation of the intention behind the trades. Nevertheless, the changes in the price of these stocks did not, according to Judge Webster, come as a result of a normal effect of supply and demand in the market, but as a result of the defendants exploiting the malfunction in the trading robot. Therefore, the changes in the price of the stock, resulting from the defendants' trading pattern, could justifiably be viewed as "irregular or artificial" under the statute, thereby fulfilling the legal requirement of market manipulation.[29]

Judge Webster's next point was that the market regularly accepts trading practices that would, strictly speaking, fall under the definition of market manipulation. An example would be cases where a trader did not want to disclose the real nature of his or her interest in a stock, and therefore only purchased small amounts of it in each trade, in order to avoid an increase in the price. Such trades were not punished, nor did the lawmakers intend them to be, according to Judge Webster, who thereby suggested that the trades made by the defendants were not necessarily so

[28] Ibid. at para. 38.
[29] Ibid. at para. 43.

different from the kind of trades that are made all the time. All traders respond to movements in the market. In this case, the traders responded to an inefficiency in Timber Hill's robot, which resulted in an "irrational adjustment of the price" of a certain stock as a response to a specific trading pattern.[30] Judge Webster commented that this might be viewed not as an act of manipulation on the part of the traders, but as a mere "reaction to an inefficiency in the market."[31] This was in line, she continued, with the market's ordinary way of functioning, where trades were based on predicting and adapting, to the best of one's ability, to the actions of other traders. She added that the whole case also had to be viewed in light of recent developments in stock markets, where big companies increasingly made use of computer technology in order to increase the efficiency of their trades. This business model was based on a calculation in which the benefits of using trading machines rather than human traders are presumed to make up for exactly the kind of glitches that may occur when rational players respond deftly to the actions of the trading robots. She concluded this line of thought with the comment that "there is good reason to hesitate over imposing penal sanctioned limitations on other investors' opportunities to adapt to the preprogrammed trading pattern" of companies such as Timber Hill.[32] Judge Webster's overall view, then, was that the market irregularities arising from these trades were a consequence of the robot's programming and not of manipulation on the part of the defendants. The defendants did not put out incorrect information, and they acted openly. Judge Webster therefore voted to reject the appeal and acquit both defendants, even if their actions fit the description of unlawful actions in the Statute.

Judge Tønder, representing the minority vote, disagreed with the majority vote, mainly on two points. First, he found that the defendants' transactions were dishonest and therefore illegitimate. He opposed the argument that the defendants had, through their actions, revealed a deficiency in the robot's programming and thereby contributed to the efficient running of the stock exchange: "What the defendants have done, is not only to reveal a weakness in the robot's programming but to exploit this weakness over time, through a series of transactions, until they were exposed."[33] The rightful course of action, on the part of the defendants,

30 Ibid. at para. 72.
31 Ibid.
32 Ibid. at para. 75.
33 Ibid. at para. 92 (author translation).

would have been to inform the Financial Supervisory Authority of the weakness in the robot and to request a clarification as to whether further trades with this robot would be in accordance with accepted practice.

Second, Judge Tønder resisted the view that the defendants are solely guilty of exploiting an inept actor in the market, which is not illegal. In other words, he did not accept placing human traders and a malfunctioning robot on equal terms. His argument was that the kinds of trades conducted by the defendants would have been quickly discontinued if their counterpart had been human, and that it was therefore only the imperfection in the programming of the robot that allowed this trading pattern to go on for months. Still, the central issue was not the malfunction of the robot, according to Judge Tønder, but the fact that the transactions of the defendants resulted in an artificial price of the traded stocks. It was this continuous artificiality of the price of the stock which was the central legal issue in the case, according to Judge Tønder, and responsibility for this laid exclusively with the defendants, who were, in his view, guilty of market manipulation.[34]

XI Analysis of the Supreme Court Decision

The judicial opinion of the Supreme Court presents us with two different underlying narratives about the case, where the differences in part result from divergent views about how to characterize the abilities of the robot and its role in human–robot interactions. The events of the case, as formulated by Judge Webster, could be narrated in the following way. A major trading company decided to use trading robots in order to optimize their profits. One of these robots had a glitch in its programming which was not discovered by the company's technicians. Two traders discovered, independently of each other, that a player in the market acted irrationally by increasing its purchase order for certain stocks irrespective of the volume of the trades. The traders responded rationally to this behavior, by using a trading pattern which triggered a response in the trading robot that allowed them to harvest a profit from the transactions. In this story, the blame for the inefficiency is laid on the company using the robot.

The underlying narrative of the minority vote could be formulated as follows. Two day-traders discovered a peculiar reaction by a player in the market and concluded that it must be a robot which was not working properly. Instead of alerting the Financial Supervision Authority, as they should have done, the traders decided to exploit the malfunctioning

[34] Ibid. at paras. 93–98.

robot in order to enrich themselves. By exploiting the glitch in the robot's programming, the traders were able to generate an artificial price of the stock, which falls under the definition of market manipulation. In this story, the blame is laid on the traders who are exploiting the robot.

From this, we can conclude that the underlying narrative that serves as a basis of the decision to acquit the defendants tends to view the robot as just another trader in the market, whose mistakes cannot be regarded as the responsibility of other traders, who are, on the contrary, entitled to respond to any movement in the market with their own self-interest in mind. The underlying narrative that supports a conviction, on the other hand, sees the robot as a mere instrument in the hands of human traders, and the glitch in the robot as a malfunction on par with any other computer malfunction in the stock exchange system. Viewed in this way, the trades that the defendants made with Timber Hill cannot be viewed as real trades, but must rather be seen as an exploitation of an obvious malfunction in the system, in the same way one would perhaps have seen it if someone discovered a slot machine at a casino that consistently gave a prize every second time it was used. Therefore, the trading pattern of Timber Hill's robot cannot be viewed as if they were just stupid actions by an inept trader, but should rather be seen as an error in the system which one has a duty to report.

XII Concluding Analysis

When we consider all the arguments and narratives that were presented in the Robot Decision, it does not seem possible to resolve once and for all how the role of the robot should best be viewed. The view of the robot as either a mere tool or as an independent actor must therefore be seen as a choice. What one chooses is not a small matter, since the two main possibilities, tool or trader, have different legal consequences.

Reviewing the narratives that were put forward in the case, as well as their basis in underlying narratives about the case's crucial aspects, we notice that they all tend to presuppose a normal situation, from which the circumstances of the case are a deviation. What characterizes the normal situation? Judged by the arguments discussed in the written judgments, it seems clear that the implied normal situation's most central feature is that the stock market is dominated by rational agents. When the deviation is described, the word "irrational" is invariably used, with the implication that "irrational" behavior in the stock market always undermines its smooth functioning. However, the notion of "irrationality," when used about the robot, differs from what would have been the case if it had been used about a human being. If we imagine an irrational human trader, who made a series of very bad decisions over time without being able to learn from his or her mistakes, the situation would surely have been very different from the one we have been dealing with here. For example, the actions of such a person would have been unlikely to cause an extraordinary stock market break. It is also hard to imagine that such actions would result in a criminal process against this person's trading counterparts. If such a person were acting on their own, they would probably have been allowed to go on trading until they had lost all their money. If the irrational person had been employed by a trading company, they would most likely have been discharged very quickly. Had it turned out that the irrational trades were a consequence of mental illness, the most likely scenario would have been that family members intervened to stop the trader's calamitous behavior.

This leads us to the question of how the irrationality of a human being differs from the irrationality of Timber Hill's robot. The main difference seems to lie in the predictability of the robot's irrational trades, a point which ties in with Dorrit Cohn's point on the non-transparency of minds mentioned above. Whereas an irrational human trader would most likely be less predictable than a rational trader, the irrational robot is entirely predictable, which is of course the only reason why the robot was vulnerable to the kind of exploitation that the defendants engaged in. This difference appears to affect the very notion of a "trade," i.e., under what conditions one may say that a trade has occurred. The underlying narrative that supports the conclusion that the two defendants should be convicted relies upon the view that their transactions cannot be viewed as real trades, but must instead be seen as a kind of system error on par with what would have been the case if there had been a malfunction in the stock exchange's own computer system. The narrative that underlies the acquittal of the defendants, on the other hand, is more inclined to view the transactions as real trades, where the responsibility for the actions of the robot lies with the company using it.

Exploring this question further, we may ask whether the noted difference between robotic and human irrationality must mean that there is also a difference between their rational actions in the market. This point connects, of course, with the wide-ranging philosophical debate concerning the question of whether machines can think.[35] For the purposes

[35] A foundational work in this debate is Alan Turing, "Computing Machinery and Intelligence" (1950) LIX:236 *Mind* 433.

of this chapter, it suffices to note that the actions of the trading robot differ from the activities of a human trader on two significant accounts. First, the machine's being is entirely dependent on its programming, precluding the notion of choices and judgment. Second, the machine has the ability to process much larger amounts of information a lot quicker and more accurately than would ever be possible for a human. The question is how these differences affect the normal functioning of the stock market. Ultimately, in the final stage of the Robot Decisions, the judgment of the Supreme Court adopted the underlying narrative that the trading robot is not an independent actor in the market, but a tool in the hands of the real traders at Timber Hill.

As regards the question of what constitutes a disruption of the stock market's normal functioning, it is perfectly possible to make the argument that the real disruption to markets occurred with the introduction of trading robots, and not with individual cases of malfunctioning robots. According to a 2012 article by the business journalist David Potts of the *Sydney Morning Herald*, automated trading has resulted in "wild price swings" on Wall Street.[36] Because of their rapid calculation capacities, and the privilege granted to them to skip the agency of the broker, robot traders are directly connected to the stock exchange system and can act on new information in the blink of an eye, making hundreds of trades in a millisecond. Because of this, Potts calls trading robots "the ultimate inside traders."[37] According to the stock market analyst Dale Gillham, trading robots "make the market much more volatile and unpredictable" because of their high-speed trading and their ability to strategically cancel transactions "a millisecond before the market opens."[38]

Is this not precisely the kind of situation that evokes the nightmare scenario about robots taking over the world because of their superior abilities? Potts alludes to these narratives at the outset of his article: "Robots don't have to take over the world when they've got sharemarkets in their clutches already."[39] Compared with the performance of trading robots, especially as they have been developed in the years after

[36] David Potts, "Share Wars: How the Robots Are Robbing You," *Sydney Morning Herald* (August 26, 2012) ["Share Wars"], www.smh.com.au/money/investing/share-wars-how-the-robots-are-robbing-you-20120825-24t4t.htm.

[37] Ibid.

[38] Dale Gillham, "What Is Robot Trading & Should You Be Worried?" *Wealth Within* (February 9, 2021), www.wealthwithin.com.au/learning-centre/investing-and-wealth-creation/what-is-robot-trading-and-should-you-be-worried.

[39] "Share Wars", note 36 above.

the Robot Decision, a human trader is slow and prone to make mistakes. No one would view such mistakes as irrational or disruptive to the market. Inept traders and their exploitation by superior traders are everyday phenomena in the stock market. As we have seen, robots can also make mistakes, but they differ from the kinds of mistakes made by humans, as witnessed by the case discussed in this chapter. The Robot Decision suggests that the problem has never been that bad or irrational trades have been exploited. The issue running through the entire case is how to deal with the kind of irrational trades that only a robot could make. This problem inevitably leads to the question of how one should deal with the kind of rational trades that only a robot could make. The analysis has highlighted that the issue at hand in the Robot Decision is symptomatic of much larger problems which are inherent to the use of trading robots. Trading robots behave very differently from human traders, both when they act rationally and when they act irrationally. The analysis of the judgments in the Robot Decision does not warrant the conclusion that anxiety about robots taking over the world has influenced the courts' adjudication. Still, the final decision of the Supreme Court does suggest an unwillingness to allow robots the freedom to use their superior computational skills to outperform human traders, while at the same time denying human traders the freedom to use their human ingenuity to exploit the kind of weaknesses that are only found in robots.

MAMA K©

14

Inevitable or Not?

Narrative Arguments Regarding Autonomous Vehicles in Singapore

HELENA WHALEN-BRIDGE*

I Introduction

The technology era we now inhabit encompasses the Internet of Things, in which everyday objects send and receive data without human intervention.[1] But despite this presence in daily life, evidence of strong negative reactions of people in communities with autonomous vehicles (AVs) suggests that concerns remain. Fatalities caused by self-driving cars have been reported.[2] In the United States, Uber's pilot self-driving cars were met with rude gestures and forced to stop by other drivers, who drove up close to their rear bumpers, and Google's autonomous-vehicle unit, Waymo, experienced similar issues in which people slashed vehicle tires and even pulled guns on safety drivers.[3] In Singapore, residents have concerns about safety, including the ability of vehicles to react and evaluate traffic situations and follow traffic rules.[4] Among academics, there are concerns regarding AV

* The author gratefully acknowledges generous support from Singapore Ministry of Education Academic Research Fund Tier 1 Grant R-241-000-185-11, and from the Swiss National Science Foundation. The author received extremely helpful feedback from fellow authors at two conferences, and excellent research support from Research Assistants Tristan Koh Ly Wey, Jared Sim Yu Hern, and Reesa Chua.

1 Hanna Rzeczycka & Mitja Kovac, "Autonomous Self-Driving Vehicles – The Advent of a New Legal Era?" (2019) 10:1 *King's Student Law Review* 30 at 30.

2 See Peter C. Baker, "Collision Course: Why Are Cars Killing More and More Pedestrians?" *The Guardian* (October 3, 2019); see Daisuke Wakabayashi, "Self-Driving Uber Car Kills Pedestrian in Arizona, Where Robots Roam," *The New York Times* (March 19, 2018), www.nytimes.com/2018/03/19/technology/uber-driverless-fatality.html.

3 Isobel Asher Hamilton, "Uber Says People Are Bullying Its Self-Driving Cars with Rude Gestures and Road Rage," *Business Insider* (June 13, 2019).

4 "Singaporeans Worried over Autonomous Vehicle Tests," *The Star* (October 25, 2019), www.thestar.com.my/news/regional/2019/10/25/singaporeans-worried-over-autonomous-vehicle-tests.

risks and unintended consequences.[5] This chapter considers the case of Singapore, which has been testing the use of AVs. Using surveys and newspaper reports, the chapter explores the rhetorical devices used to frame relevant discussion, focusing on the concepts of narrative and narrative argument. The chapter identifies the narratives used to assert the potential benefits AVs offer, as well as addresses the concerns and fears they raise, thereby justifying the presence of AVs on the streets.

Narrative is used as the central instrument of inquiry in the chapter because this form of discourse is a fundamental way in which reality is understood and constructed,[6] and because it plays a particular role in the public discourse examined in the chapter.[7] The definition of narrative is contested, but for purposes of this chapter, "narrative" is defined simply as a representation of an event.[8] Some definitions of narrative use additional or expanded elements,[9] but without delving into the issue of narrativity,[10] this chapter adopts a more minimalist definition of narrative in order to identify the narrative character of public discussion of AVs.

The narratives considered here take place in the context of public discussions of the merits and drawbacks of AVs, and can therefore be understood as narrative argument, i.e., arguments relying to some degree on narrative. Concepts underlying narrative argument can be traced back to ancient rhetoric,[11] but they were developed in more

[5] See e.g. Araz Taeihagh & Hazel Si Min Lim, "Governing Autonomous Vehicles: Emerging Responses for Safety, Liability, Privacy, Cybersecurity, and Industry Risks" (2019) 39:1 *Transport Reviews* 103 at 103–128.

[6] See Jerome Bruner, "The Narrative Construction of Reality" (1991) 18:1 *Critical Inquiry* 1 at 4.

[7] See Bruce W. Weal, "The Force of Narrative in the Public Sphere of Argument" (1985) 22:2 *Journal of the American Forensic Association* 104 (discussed below).

[8] See Gérard Genette, *Figures of Literary Discourse* (New York, NY: Columbia University Press, 1982) at 127; Gerald Prince, *A Dictionary of Narratology*, rev. ed. (Lincoln, NE: University of Nebraska Press, 2003) at 58; Horace Porter Abbott, *The Cambridge Introduction to Narrative*, 2nd rev. ed. (Cambridge, UK: Cambridge University Press, 2008) at 13; and more generally at 13–27; per Moshe Simon-Shoshan, an event is dynamic in that something happens or changes, and specific in that it presents change through the concrete and the specific; see Moshe Simon-Shoshan, *Stories of the Law: Narrative Discourse and the Construction of Authority in the Mishnah* (Oxford University Press, 2012) at 16. For discussion of the concepts of narrative, story, and discourse, see Chapter 15 in this volume.

[9] For an overview of different narrative definitions, see Marie-Laure Ryan, "Toward a Definition of Narrative" in David Herman (ed.), *The Cambridge Companion to Narrative* (Cambridge, UK: Cambridge University Press, 2007) 22 at 22–35.

[10] See ibid. at 28–31, and see 33 (if "defining narrative has any cognitive relevance, it is because the definition covers mental operations of a more fundamental nature than passing global judgments of narrativity").

[11] See Paula Olmos, "Narration as Argument," paper delivered at the Ontario Study of Augmentation Conference 10 (May 22, 2013), Ontario Society for the Study of Augmentation Conference Archive 123 ["Narration as Argument"] at 2–13.

modern times by Walter Fisher, who is credited with distinguishing between the rational world paradigm and the narrative world paradigm.[12] In the rational paradigm, humans are essentially rational beings, and the paradigm for human decision-making and communication is argument, understood as clear-cut, inferential structures.[13] The narrative paradigm presupposes that humans are storytelling creatures, and that the paradigm for human decision-making and communication is "good reasons," including narrative probability, an internally coherent story, and narrative fidelity, a story consistent with lived experience.[14] The narrative paradigm can be considered the synthesis of two traditional strands of rhetoric, the argumentative, persuasive theme, and the literary, esthetic theme,[15] which makes it well-suited to analysis of narrative arguments.

The narrative arguments explored in the chapter occur in the wider Singapore community, and they therefore comprise narratives in the public space.[16] Bruce Weal has suggested why narratives perform a useful function in the public sphere. First, stories proceed via the actions of characters, and stories display the values of those characters; in a conflict of positions, the fact that one character prevails is an argument for that character's values.[17] Second, narratives engage audience attitudes and understandings because the story form is more easily comprehended by most audiences compared to technical arguments.[18] This point echoes Fisher, who asserted that decisions of a public nature are subject to public narratives, which members of the public can participate in if they are sufficiently informed, because unlike expert subject matter, the public can assess narrative probability and fidelity.[19]

12 See Walter R. Fisher, "Toward a Logic of Good Reasons" (1978) 64:4 *Quarterly Journal of Speech* 376; Walter R. Fisher, "Narration as a Human Communication Paradigm: The Case of Public Moral Argument" (1984) 51:1 *Communication Monographs* 1 ["Communication Paradigm"]; and Walter R. Fisher, *Human Communication as Narration: Toward a Philosophy of Reason, Value, and Action* (Columbia, SC: University of South Carolina Press, 1989).

13 Ibid. at 4.

14 Ibid. at 6.

15 Ibid. at 2.

16 See James Hickling, "The Importance of Narrative in the Negotiation of Host Government Agreements for LNG Projects: The Case of British Columbia and Petronas" (2017) 10:4 *Journal of World Energy Law and Business* 293, although Hickling focuses on legal positioning in contract negotiation as a result of public space narratives.

17 Bruce W. Weal, "The Force of Narrative in the Public Sphere of Argument" (1985) 22:2 *Journal of the American Forensic Association* 104 at 105.

18 Ibid.

19 "Communication Paradigm", note 12 above, at 16, and generally at 11–16.

The field of narrative argument is a growing one with its own disagreements, e.g., the degree to which the traditional analysis of argument must accommodate narrative.[20] Paula Olmos has identified different categories of narrative argument, two of which are: (1) primary or core narratives, which assume that someone has been given the responsibility to give a plausible account of facts unknown or under discussion via narrative devices; and (2) secondary or digressive narrative, in which narratives are not the main event, but are related to a conclusion or claim, and their relevance is either fully expressed or left to the audience.[21] As explored below, narratives regarding AVs in Singapore are less about plausible versions of contested facts and more about contested views about how AVs function and how to evaluate the benefits and risks they pose; as such, AV narratives would fall within the category of secondary or digressive narratives.

I.A Methodology and Terminology

To explore narratives regarding AVs in Singapore, the chapter considers both research studies on public opinion in Singapore and newspaper coverage. The research studies help establish opinions and narratives within the public sphere, and while the studies appear to be commercially oriented and display some biases in favor of artificial intelligence (AI) and AVs, the studies in turn also help establish the narratives of commercially oriented entities.

After reviewing the studies, the chapter provides a detailed analysis of Singapore newspaper reports. Examining newspaper coverage is a common methodology in socio-legal research.[22] In this chapter, local newspapers form the narrative "topos" for analysis.[23]

[20] See Christopher Trindale, "Narratives and the Concept of Argument" in Paula Olmos (ed.), *Narration as Argument* (Cham, Switzerland: Springer, 2017) 11.

[21] "Narration as Argument", note 11 above, at 11–12; see also Paula Olmos, "Story Credibility in Narrative Arguments" in Frans Hendrik van Eemeren & Bart Garssen (eds.), *Reflections on Theoretical Issues in Argumentation Theory* (Cham, Switzerland: Springer, 2015) 155 at 156–157.

[22] See Steven Garber & Anthony G. Bower, "Newspaper Coverage of Automobile Product Liability Verdicts" (1999) 33:1 *Law and Society Review* 93; Lyn Hinds, "Three Strikes and You're Out in the West: A Study of Newspaper Coverage of Crime Control in Western Australia" (2005) 17:2 *Current Issues in Criminal Justice* 239; and Jianlin Chen, "Singapore's Culture War over Section 377A: Through the Lens of Public Choice and Multilingual Research" (2013) 38:1 *Law and Social Inquiry* 106.

[23] Zahr K. Said & Jessica Silbey, "Narrative Topoi in the Digital Age" (2018) 68:1 *Journal of Legal Education* 103.

The Factiva database was used to identify newspaper articles on AVs in Singapore from January 2014 to March 2021, using the Factiva search function that gathers articles related to AVs. This search produced an initial group of 67 newspaper articles in the relevant time frame. Different words were used for AVs in these articles, and these words arguably contain different orientations toward AV risks and benefits. For example, "driverless" vehicles might suggest a greater concern regarding vehicles, as the word emphasizes the lack of a driver and the associated risks of proceeding without a driver, while "autonomous" suggests that the vehicle can function autonomously without a driver. To determine chapter terminology regarding AVs, the frequency of terminology use was reviewed. Within the group of 67 articles, "autonomous" was used more frequently (59) than driverless (39), self-driving (50), and automated (5). The phrases "autonomous" and "driverless" both appeared first in 2014, but if "autonomous" and "automated" are combined, a phrase utilizing the root "auto" becomes even more clearly the preferred term (64). The chapter therefore adopts the phrase "autonomous vehicle" (AV), with occasional deviations to incorporate different usage in original texts, but with the understanding that the term autonomous vehicle may contain a pro-AV bias.

For purposes of performing narrative analysis, the chapter excluded publications based in jurisdictions outside of Singapore, as they appear less likely to reflect Singapore opinion. An exception was made for *IEEE Spectrum*, a magazine edited by the Institute of Electrical and Electronics Engineers, as it contained detail regarding commercial entities not available in local publications. The resulting 51 articles were analyzed qualitatively for narratives and narrative argument. Chapter analysis in the following sections is organized into three categories, depending on whether the article primarily represented the views of the public, government entities, or commercial entities. Articles were placed in one of these categories if more than 50 percent of the content comprised the opinions or activities of the public, commercial entities, or government entities.

II Research Studies and Surveys

Two relatively recent surveys contain information relevant to attitudes about AVs in Singapore. In 2019, the Boston Consulting Group (BCG) reported the results of a survey ("BCG Survey") of citizen perspectives on the use of AI in government, based on the responses of 14,000 internet[24] users in different jurisdictions, including Singapore.[25] The BCG Survey asked participants how comfortable they were if certain decisions were made by a computer rather than a human being, what concerns they had regarding the use of AI by governments, and how concerned they were regarding the impact of AI on the economy and jobs.[26] Overall, the findings indicated that citizens were most supportive of using AI for tasks such as transport, traffic optimization, and predictive maintenance, but citizens did not support the use of AI for sensitive decisions associated with the justice system, such as parole board and sentencing recommendations.[27]

Noting Singapore's "Smart Nation" and Digital Government Group, the BCG Survey characterized Singapore as a case study in how to promote the application of AI technologies across the government.[28] Characterizing Singapore as a positive AI case study also indicates the survey's pro-AI orientation to promote the use of AI in government. The BCG Survey's orientation is reflected in how questions were posed, e.g., "[w]hen is it acceptable to use 'black box' deep-learning models, where the logic used ... cannot possibly be explained or understood,"[29] as opposed to asking whether this kind of AI should be used at all. The BCG Survey's pro-AI orientation is also illustrated in its use of what the chapter calls the "inevitability narrative," the narrative that AI or AVs are inevitable and should just be accepted and managed. An opinion piece by the Partner and Managing Director of BCG, Singapore, while highlighting key points from the survey, asserted that the "AI genie is out of its bottle, and no amount of wishing it were otherwise will turn back the tide of AI innovation."[30] The inevitability narrative occurs primarily in the narratives of commercial entities, and it is analyzed in this Section II, as well as Sections III.A.4 and III.B.3.

A second study conducted by the insurance company American International Group ("AIG Survey") focused squarely on attitudes

[24] *The Citizens' Perspective on the Use of AI in Government* (Boston Consulting Group, 2019) at 3.

[25] Ibid. at 7, 8, 11–12.

[26] Ibid. at 3.

[27] Ibid.

[28] Ibid. at 12.

[29] Ibid. at 3.

[30] Michael Tan, "Trust, Transparency Must Form Pillars of Singapore's AI Success," *The Business Times* (May 10, 2019).

regarding AVs, and this study segregated data on respondents from the United States, the United Kingdom, and Singapore.[31] The answers of the Singapore respondents indicate that one in five adults self-identified as the current driver of a vehicle with automated assistance systems such as emergency breaking, lane departure avoidance, or features that make the vehicle capable of self-driving part of the time, and two-thirds of Singapore drivers said that autonomous features had a positive influence on their decision to purchase the car.[32] A total of 49 percent of Singapore adults who did not currently drive a vehicle with autonomous features said they thought they would buy, rent, share, or travel in a vehicle with those features, although 25 percent said they would not.[33]

Respondents were concerned about safety. As the AIG Survey put it, the "general public is especially concerned about safety."[34] Singapore respondents cited safer roads as the second-most appealing benefit for AVs, but there was divided opinion regarding sharing the road with driverless vehicles: 46 percent said they would be comfortable, and 29 percent said they would be uncomfortable.[35] Only 32 percent of Singapore drivers thought that driverless cars would be safer than the average driver, and when asked if driverless cars would be safer than their own driving, only 22 percent said yes.[36]

Security is a related concern, and adults in all three countries saw security as a "significant barrier" to AV adoption.[37] A total of 78 percent of Singaporean respondents expressed concern about hackers taking control of AVs, and 73 percent were concerned about the privacy of personal data such as where they travel and when.[38] A total of 47 percent of Singaporeans said their biggest concern about privacy would be a breach of personal information, such as credit card data stored in the car.[39] Another issue included the car overhearing private conversations (10 percent),[40] a concern not unheard of in Singapore, where taxis can

31 *The Future of Mobility and Shifting Risk* (American International Group, Inc., 2018) [AIG Survey].
32 Ibid. at 6.
33 Ibid. at 7.
34 Ibid. at 9.
35 Ibid.
36 Ibid. at 10.
37 Ibid. at 11.
38 Ibid.
39 Ibid.
40 Ibid.

audio-record customer conversations.[41] The AIG Survey noted that AVs are susceptible to "cracking," outsiders taking control of the car, and that sophisticated software could take control of a car, and cause it to sense that the car is located in the wrong place, or "see" something on the road that isn't there.[42] A "less immediate but equally real risk" would be less invasive hacking to gain access to information stored in the vehicle.[43]

Like the BCG Survey, the AIG Survey is pro-AV. The AIG Survey stated that AVs "promise the potential of greatly reducing the number of deaths attributable to automobiles (currently about 40,000 per year in the United States) and injuries from vehicle crashes. Over 90 percent of today's roadway deaths and injuries are due to human error."[44] These figures are accurate statistics, but the assertion assumes that AVs would not commit any "human errors," and that AVs would not commit any AV errors, errors that humans would not commit. The AIG Survey also asserted the inevitability narrative, stating that "[i]nevitably, the role of the traditional driver will decrease and the role of technologies will increase."[45]

III Newspaper Articles

The majority of Singapore newspaper articles addressed the views or activities of the government or commercial entities. Of the few articles to address public opinion, one welcomed the idea of AVs on Sentosa, a small island close of Singapore that has been developed as a tourist and entertainment destination, because AVs would be "hassle-free" and more convenient for families with children, could help with long queues, and could be "exciting."[46] One view endorsing AVs noted that during a morning commute in which the commuter was focused on his daily activities, "I don't want to speak to anyone. I would even prefer hailing a driverless car to work to hiring one with a driver."[47] However, some

41 See Low Youjin, "Drivers Welcome LTA's Move to Allow Audio Recording in Taxis, Private-Hire Cars from July 15," *Today* (July 2, 2019), www.todayonline.com/singapore/drivers-welcome-lta-move-allow-audio-recording-taxis-private-hire-cars-july-15.

42 AIG Survey, note 31 above, at 12.

43 Ibid.

44 Ibid. at 1.

45 Ibid.

46 Olivia Siong, "Sentosa to Trial Self-Driving Vehicles from Early-2016," *Channel News Asia* (October 13, 2015) ["Sentosa to Trial"].

47 Wong Pei Ting, "Grab Users in One-North Could Get Free Ride on Driverless Taxis," *Today* (September 24, 2016) ["Driverless Taxis"].

newspaper articles regarding public opinion indicated concerns and fears regarding AVs, e.g., safety issues needed to be "ironed out."[48] In the context of automated buses, a school bus driver asked whether "parents of young school children would trust driverless technology more than bus drivers and their sidekicks, the 'bus aunties.'"[49] There was also the concern regarding jobs for drivers, and that "job disruption for bus drivers may occur sooner than for taxi drivers."[50]

In contrast to the bright futures asserted in government and commercial narratives reviewed below, one expert noted that if he was "taking the bus on a daily basis, and the bus is leaving the bus bay, I can waive my hand and the driver can stop and open the door. With the driverless bus, I don't think this is going to happen. Even though Singapore has been very aggressive in promoting driverless technology, I do not know if this is the future society we'd like to have."[51]

III.A Government Entities

Government discussions of AVs assert narrative arguments regarding the role of the government in pushing for AV development, the reasons for this, and the activities involved in working together with commercial partners to support AV usage in Singapore. Narrative arguments also addressed liability regarding AVs and rules or guidelines, and the careful testing of AVs and restriction of their movement.

III.A.1 AV Benefits

The emphasis in Singapore is less on AVs for personal use and more on AVs for community use, an approach which makes sense given population density in the city-state, but which also increases the risk of injury if there is an accident. In 2015, the Ministry of Transport's (MoT) Permanent Secretary and Chairman of the Committee on Autonomous Road Transport for Singapore (CARTS) stated that it was not "the replacement of one driven car today by a driverless car tomorrow that excites us. What we're interested in is the introduction of new mobility and transportation concepts that can enhance commuter mobility, and

[48] Koh Swee Fang Valerie & Neo Chai Chin, "Self-Driving Buses Easier to Implement than Cars but Concerns Remain: Experts; Safety Issues, Livelihood of Drivers and Handling of Quirks of Bus Travel Yet to Be Ironed Out," *Today* (October 20, 2016) ["Concerns Remain"].

[49] Ibid.

[50] Ibid.

[51] Ibid.

the overall public transport experience, especially for the first- and last-mile travel."[52] One 2014 article asked readers to imagine a "completely car free town and residents taking 'personalized MRTs' in the form of driverless pods running underground from under their block to public transport nodes."[53] The reference to "personalized MRTs" would be an appealing concept to many Singaporeans. MRT stands for Mass Rapid Transit, and as this public transportation is crowded at commuting times, it is anything but personalized. If a mode of transportation like the MRT could be personalized and offer a way from the user's home to other public transportation, that would be a significant improvement. This article describes a utopian AV future: "In our dream town, its surface would be dominated by green and open spaces for residents … and free of the smoke, noise, congestion and safety concerns posed by vehicles today."[54] Regarding the trial of driverless buses, the Chief Technology Officer of the Land Transport Authority (LTA) noted that while most AV technology focuses on self-driving cars, "Singapore's need for high-capacity vehicles to address commuters' peak-hour demands presents an opportunity for companies … to develop autonomous buses …."[55]

Beyond the benefits of AVs to commuters such as better mobility as well as safe and less congested roads, the advantages of connected cars were discussed. For example, an opinion piece noted that by having "information on a smart car's performance, a carmaker can predict when the car requires maintenance," which prevents manufacturers from over-investing in maintenance labor and parts, but also "delights customers as it shortens the time taken for maintenance."[56] The real value of connected devices such as AVs lies in the insights provided by

[52] Valerie Koh, "Driverless Vehicles Slated for Use in Four Areas; Three Trials Announced, Starting in December at Gardens by the Bay," *Today* (October 13, 2015) ["Driverless Vehicles Slated"].

[53] Joy Fang, "Driverless Cars May Be Closer to Reality; LTA, A*STAR Will Spearhead Setting Up of Platform to Spur Autonomous Vehicle Technology," *Today* (August 28, 2014) ["Driverless Cars"].

[54] Ibid.; regarding benefits, see also Zhaki Abdullah, "Two Firms to Test Driverless Cars for Last Mile-Trips; Service Set to Start by 2018," *The Straits Times* (August 2, 2016) ["Test Driverless Cars"]; Valerie Koh, "First Driverless Bus Trial Launch as Early as 2018 in Jurong West," *Today* (October 20, 2016) ["Driverless Bus Trial"].

[55] "LTA Signs Deal with ST Kinetics to Develop, Trial Driverless Buses," *Channel News Asia* (April 10, 2017) ["LTA Signs Deal"].

[56] Wong Yoke Choo, "Opinion; Driving the Future of Singapore's Urban Mobility with Open Data," *The Business Times* (May 29, 2018).

"the data they generate."[57] This opinion piece presented a positive narrative and did not address potential concerns regarding AV data such as hacking and cybercrime.

III.A.2 Government Support for AVs

The government's supportive role for AVs is illustrated by a 2014 article, which noted that previous development of AVs had been done by disparate organizations.[58] This disorganized state of affairs was to be replaced by the Singapore Autonomous Vehicle Initiative (SAVI), in which the LTA and the Agency for Science, Technology and Research (A*STAR) would jointly oversee "the setting up of a technology platform to spur research and development as well as the testing of AV technology, applications and solutions."[59] CARTS was also formed to "chart the strategic direction and study opportunities for AVs ...."[60] Among the possibilities mentioned were transport networks such as driverless buses, or intra-town shuttles in future residential developments.[61] Fares were anticipated to be "competitive."[62]

The narrative that Singapore was pushing for AV development arises regularly, often via literal use of the word "push." For example, the launch of the self-driving vehicle (SDV) research center and circuit was "part of the Government's push towards a car-lite Singapore."[63] To "push the development of self-driving technology" in Singapore, the LTA installed equipment aimed at supporting and monitoring the testing of driverless vehicles at One-North in 2016.[64] It was noted in 2017 that a project to trial driverless trucks on the industrialized Jurong Island was "one of several involving autonomous vehicle technology initiatives in Singapore, as the country pushes ahead to roll out driverless vehicles."[65] The "push for an AV transport system in Singapore" is

57 Ibid.
58 "Driverless Cars", note 53 above.
59 Ibid.
60 Ibid.
61 Ibid.
62 "Test Driverless Cars", note 54 above.
63 Ibid.; see also Zhaki Abdullah, "Start-Up Puts Brakes on Self-Driving Trials after Accident," *The Straits Times* (October 21, 2016) ["Brakes on Self-Driving Trials"].
64 Zhaki Abdullah, "CCTVs, New Equipment, Introduced at One-North to Support Driverless Trials," *The Straits Times* (October 18, 2016).
65 "Singapore's First Driverless Truck Makes Debut at Jurong Island," *Channel News Asia* (October 24, 2017) ["Driverless Truck"].

part of the country's Smart Nations initiatives, intended to also impact matters such as electronic payments and digital identity.[66]

Part of the Singapore narrative regarding AVs in that it is either the first country to achieve certain kinds of AV success, or it is one of the more conducive countries for AVs. For example, Singapore is the first country to "actively incorporate AV into future town-planning."[67] It was noted in 2014 that Singapore has been on the "forefront in testing transport concepts and transport technologies over the past three decades."[68] Guests to the tourist attraction Gardens by the Bay in 2015 were able to "test out the first fully-operational self-driving vehicle in Asia during a 2-week trial."[69] AV testing at One-North in 2015 was "the first public road network in Singapore for the testing of driverless vehicles."[70] Driverless buses in Jurong West continued Singapore's "bid to take the lead in self-driving vehicles," the "first of its kind in Singapore."[71] It was noted in 2019 that Singapore was an early champion of AVs and was ranked "first among 20 countries for policy and legislation regarding self-driving vehicles in KPMG's Autonomous Vehicles Readiness Index."[72] In February 2019, it was noted that the Economic Development Board was setting its sights on Singapore to take "a leading role in developing and deploying autonomous vehicles and smart mobility systems."[73] In December 2019, it was observed that tests on driverless cars using a 5G network would be the first time this was done in Singapore.[74]

Why should Singapore play the role of AV advocate? AVs can assist Singapore to "radically transform land transportation in Singapore to address our two key constraints – land and manpower."[75]

66 Hariz Baharudin, "Singtel to Develop Cyber Security Solutions for Self-Driving Vehicles with International Partner," *The Straits Times* (January 28, 2019) ["Cyber Security Solutions"].

67 "Driverless Cars", note 53 above.

68 Ibid.

69 "MOT Wheels Out Self-Driving Vehicle Trials across the Island," *Channel News Asia* (October 12, 2015) ["Self-Driving Vehicle Trials"].

70 Ibid.

71 "Driverless Bus Trial", note 54 above.

72 Zhaki Abdullah, "Standards Drawn Up for Safe Use of Fully Autonomous Vehicles," *The Straits Times* (February 1, 2019) ["Standards Drawn Up"].

73 Seow Bei Yi, "Driverless Cars No More a Pipe Dream: EDB Sees Mobility as Next Area of Growth for Singapore in 2019," *The Straits Times* (February 14, 2019).

74 Tan Ee-Lyn, "Kick-Starting Tests for 5G Driverless Cars at Science Park," *The Straits Times* (December 2, 2019).

75 "Self-Driving Vehicle Trials", note 69 above; see also Adrian Lim, "Center for Self-Driving Vehicles Opens in Jurong West; 3 New Towns Identified as Test Areas," *The Straits Times* (November 22, 2017).

Characterization of Singapore as a small country with limited resources is a regular refrain in public discourse,[76] and it contributes to AV narratives as well. Singapore's focus on the use of AVs in public transportation would "reduce reliance on private vehicles," and allow the saved road space to be used for other purposes.[77]

Driverless technology can also alleviate manpower concerns.[78] The adoption of AVs in the United States has "caused a stir because of the number of drivers who could be put out of a job," but Singapore faces challenges in attracting drivers.[79] Driverless buses could address the shortage of local bus drivers,[80] and driverless trucks were trialled in part because efficient freight movement is "critical" to Singapore's port activity.[81]

III.A.3 Addressing Issues Posed by AVs

Newspaper reports also contained narratives responsive to issues and concerns regarding AVs, such as the testing and trialing of AVs, and rules regarding legal responsibility. It was noted in 2014 that the LTA was working on a framework to allow AVs that "meet safety standards to be tested on all public roads" in the following year.[82] This position asserts that only safe vehicles will be tested, thereby protecting the public. A 2015 article noted that the MoT had unveiled "a slew of ongoing and upcoming self-driving trials" in locations including One-North, Gardens by the Bay, Sentosa, and West Coast Road.[83] Visitors to the Gardens could test out the SDVs during a two-week trial, and after this trial "further tests will be done before the vehicles are deployed in the Gardens."[84] Tests for A*STAR's self-driving car were done in urban areas, with plans to "test it on highways and in parking scenarios in the future."[85] But to get on the road, AVs in trials had to adhere to the LTA's requirements and could not go outside

[76] See Singapore Ministry of Foreign Affairs, "Small States," www.mfa.gov.sg/SINGAPORES-FOREIGN-POLICY/International-Issues/Small-States; and Danson Cheong, "As a Small Country, Singapore Has to Be Friends with Everyone, but at Times It Needs to Advance Its Own Interests," *The Straits Times* (July 18, 2017).

[77] "Driverless Vehicles Slated", note 52 above.

[78] Ibid.; see also "Driverless Truck", note 65 above.

[79] "Driverless Vehicles Slated", note 52 above; see also "Test Driverless Cars", note 54 above.

[80] "Concerns Remain", note 48 above.

[81] "Singapore to Start Trials of Driverless Trucks for Port Transport," *Channel News Asia* (January 9, 2017) ["Port Transport"].

[82] "Driverless Cars", note 53 above.

[83] "Self-Driving Vehicle Trials", note 69 above.

[84] Ibid.

[85] "PM Lee Rides in A*STAR's Latest Self-Driving Car," *The Straits Times* (July 27, 2016) ["A*STAR's Latest"].

of the test area.[86] In some trials, an alert sounded if vehicles went outside of the test area.[87] It was noted in 2017 that driverless vehicles could ply a wider area, adding four times the previous area, but that those who "wish to conduct trials in mixed-use and residential estates in Dover and Buona Vista will need to demonstrate to LTA and Traffic Police that they are able to handle more dynamic traffic environments in autonomous mode."[88]

Trials for driverless buses were discussed together with a description of Nanyang Technological University's (NTU) Centre of Excellence for Testing and Research of Autonomous Vehicles, which replicated road conditions in Singapore such as a rain simulator and a flood zone.[89] The trial was supported by the Singapore Mass Rapid Transport (SMRT), which was to "play a key role in determining the road worthiness of autonomous vehicles on public roads."[90] Start-ups "from around the world" came to the purpose-built track that recreates an urban environment, to "test how autonomous vehicles cope" with those challenges.[91] One vehicle's quirky design, which looked more like a "giant robotic bug," was intentional, because in order "for the public to know that this is different to conventional cars, it needs to be noticeably different on first impressions, and stand out in comparison to other cars."[92] The public may want to know that a vehicle is an AV as a matter of general knowledge, but the public may also need to know so that they can be on the lookout for potentially dangerous situations. Regarding the conducting of AV trials, the LTA stated in 2019 that it would "engage local grassroots and community leaders ahead of time if there were plans to conduct AV trials in their specific constituencies," and that "public safety will continue to be the top priority for all autonomous vehicle trials."[93] Further expansion of trials would be permitted "after the AVs pass stringent competency tests."[94]

86 "Driverless Taxis", note 47 above.

87 "Test Bed for Driverless Vehicles Ramped Up at One-North," *Channel News Asia* (October 18, 2016) ["Test Bed"].

88 Ng Huiwen, "Driverless Vehicle Routes Expand by 55km to NUS, Buona Vista and Dover," *The Straits Times* (June 23, 2017).

89 "Driverless Electric Buses to Be Tested from 2019 in Collaboration Between NTU, Volvo," *Channel News Asia* (January 11, 2018) ["Driverless Electric Buses"].

90 Nanyang Technological University, "'World's First' Autonomous Electric Buses to Hit Road in Singapore," *New Fortune Times* (March 5, 2019).

91 Zahra Jamshed, "Singapore Wants Self-Driving Cars to Help Its Aging Society," *Cable News Network* (February 26, 2019) ["Self-Driving Cars"].

92 Ibid.

93 "Self-Driving Vehicles to Be Tested on Roads in All of Western Singapore," *Business Times Singapore* (October 24, 2019).

94 Ibid.

Trials were sometimes reported to be conducted without passengers, thereby lowering risks to persons, e.g., in ComfortDelGro's trial of self-driving shuttle buses in 2018. During the initial stage of this trial, "the shuttle will not take any passengers."[95] Once the trial management team was satisfied that "the shuttle is ready for commuter trials, passengers will be able to start boarding the vehicle."[96] Trials were conducted for commercial vehicles as well, e.g., "the design and trials for autonomous truck platooning, which comprises a human-driven truck and one or more driverless vehicles, will be carried out over a three-year period ...."[97]

Newspaper reports of trials have at times also discussed the topic of safety drivers, which suggests that there are concerns that the AVs may not be sufficiently safe on their own. In the 2015 trials at the Gardens by the Bay, it was noted that "there will be a trained staff stationed in each vehicle to guide passengers and gather insights on commuter behavior, passenger feedback and the performance of the vehicle."[98] In Grab's "Robo-Car," which the public could book for free, a safety driver as well as a support engineer were present in the car "to observe system performance and ensure the passenger's comfort and safety."[99] The presence of two individuals beyond the passengers in the small space of a taxi indicate significant concerns about safety. The self-driving shuttle bus trials at the National University of Singapore (NUS) in 2018 also had a safety engineer on board.[100] In 2019, the creation of guidelines for fully AVs was announced, together with the statement that all AVs being tested in Singapore require a safety driver "who takes control of the vehicle if necessary."[101]

One of the challenges encountered by AVs in Singapore is driving in bad weather.[102] Singapore encounters periods of heavy wind and rain,[103] and in the 2016 partnership between Grab and nuTonomy, the plan was

95 "ComfortDelGro to Trial Self-Driving Shuttle Bus at NUS from March 2019," *Channel News Asia* (November 12, 2018) ["Self-Driving Shuttle Bus"].

96 Ibid.

97 Siti Nur Aisha Omar, "No Drivers Needed," *The New Paper* (October 13, 2015) ["No Drivers Needed"].

98 "Self-Driving Vehicle Trials", note 69 above.

99 "Driverless Taxis", note 47 above.

100 "Self-Driving Shuttle Bus", note 95 above.

101 "Standards Drawn Up", note 72 above.

102 See "Driverless Vehicles Slated", note 52 above; and "Sentosa to Trial", note 46 above; regarding the ability of AVs to navigate in heavy rain, see "LTA Signs Deal", note 55 above; and Christopher Tan, "ComfortDelGro's Self-Driving Shuttles to Start Picking Up Passengers at NUS," *The Straits Times* (July 29, 2019) ["Self-Driving Shuttles"].

103 "Sentosa to Trial", note 46 above.

to have a safety driver who would take over if it started to rain heavily.[104] The weather challenge was included in the LTA and the Jurong Town Council SDV research center and circuit, where driverless vehicles could be tested under traffic conditions.[105] Senior Minister for State for Transport Josephine Teo observed that the center and circuit could help Singapore develop standards and put SDVs on the roads.[106] The creation of the Singtel Cyber Security Institute was announced in 2019, a research center where researchers would be able to "put the solutions they have developed through rigorous testing and prototyping."[107]

The safety issues posed by AV navigation are also addressed in discussions of AV navigation mechanisms. AVs tested in Gardens by the Bay had laser technology to "scan the surroundings and register the position of the vehicle. It is able to detect obstacles, such as a person walking into its path."[108] Camera lenses are located at the front and back of the vehicle for video capture, sensor fusion can choose the best navigation techniques to suit various road conditions, and radio frequency identification can be placed at different locations in Gardens by the Bay to support navigation.[109] Proposed automated buses in 2017 would have radar and sonars to detect other vehicles and pedestrians.[110] The Prime Minister Lee Hsien Loong and Minister for Trade and Industry Mr. S. Iswaran "hitched a ride" in A*STAR's self-driving car, which used laser sensors and A*STAR's own algorithm "to ensure a safe driving experience."[111]

In a demonstration, this AV was shown to have the ability to detect traffic lights, stop lines, "and objects as small as a child. It is even able to function in complete darkness."[112] The use of the image of a child is significant, as one of the concerns regarding AVs is that if they do not detect pedestrians, they could hit them and cause injury. Children could be more vulnerable to injury from AVs compared to adults, a theme that arose above in connection with automated school buses. The presence of a child in narratives regarding AVs can therefore indicate fear, but children are also put to other uses in these narratives. The need for

104 "Driverless Taxis", note 47 above.
105 "Test Driverless Cars", note 54 above.
106 Ibid.
107 "Cyber Security Solutions", note 66 above.
108 "No Drivers Needed", note 97 above.
109 Ibid.
110 "LTA Signs Deal", note 55 above.
111 "A*STAR's Latest", note 85 above.
112 Ibid.

safeguards is contextualized in a more palatable manner via the observation that "[y]ou really don't want your five-year-old jumping into a self-driving car and then taking off to Disneyland."[113] This narrative acknowledges a fear regarding AVs, but inserts a happy, almost cartoon-like story of a mischievous child, with the happy ending of arriving safely at Disneyland.

III.A.4 Regulation and Liability

It was noted earlier on in Singapore's engagement with AVs that SAVI would "look into regulations required for the mass adoption of such vehicles, such as liability issues when accidents happen and infrastructure requirements."[114] In the context of constructing infrastructure, CCTVs were put into place along a test route, to identify challenges and because "footage can also serve as evidence in an investigation if an accident occurs."[115] When Grab introduced a self-driving "Robo-Car" for testing in 2016, users had to be above the age of 18 and sign a liability waiver before riding.[116] Legal and insurance experts opined in December 2016 that liability issues involving AV technology were unclear.[117] Then Dean of the NUS Faculty of Law Simon Chesterman noted that criminal law focused on the driver of the vehicle, and that the lack of a driver posed "a real regulatory challenge."[118]

An accident involving a self-driving car did occur in Singapore on October 18, 2016.[119] One of nuTonomy's self-driving cars hit a lorry in Biopolis Drive while on a test drive. The vehicle had two engineers on board, and one of them was behind the wheel as a safety driver.[120] The vehicle was driving at a low speed and changing lanes when the accident occurred.[121] No one was hurt,[122] but the right bumper of the

[113] Walter Sim, "Self-Driving Cars: Japan Start-Up Sets Up Research Lab in Singapore," *The Straits Times* (August 26, 2018) ["Japan Start-Up"].

[114] "Driverless Cars", note 53 above.

[115] "Test Bed", note 87 above.

[116] "Driverless Taxis", note 47 above.

[117] Zhaki Abdullah, "Driverless Vehicles Could Change Laws, Insurance Policies," *The Straits Times* (December 13, 2016) ["Change Laws"].

[118] Ibid.

[119] "Driverless Bus Trial", note 54 above.

[120] Adrian Lim & Chew Hui Min, "NuTonomy Resumes Driverless Car Trials in One-North, Says Software Glitch to Blame for Accident," *The Straits Times* (November 24, 2016) ["Software Glitch"].

[121] "Brakes on Self-Driving Trials", note 63 above.

[122] Ibid.

self-driving car was damaged and the lorry had a dent in the side.[123] The Traffic Police and LTA investigated the accident, and the company conducted its own investigation.[124] Following the accident, nuTonomy put its tests of driverless cars on hold, although tests by three other agencies, A*STAR, Delphi, and the Singapore-MIT Alliance for Research and Technology, continued.[125] Also following the accident, the Executive Director of the Energy Research Institute @ NTU said that his researchers would be spending more time identifying possible safety compromises and run simulations on the buses being trialed at NTU to ensure safety.[126]

Having investigated the accident, NuTonomy reported the following month that "an extremely rare combination of software anomalies" affected how the vehicle detected and responded to other nearby vehicles when changing lanes.[127] There was no discussion of why the two safety engineers were not able to prevent the accident. The company reported that it had made improvements to its software system to eliminate the anomalies responsible for the accident, and that extensive tests had been performed using computer simulations and private roads to ensure a safe operation moving forward.[128] The company also reported that it had resumed trials.[129]

The need for additional regulation has been acknowledged in Singapore, with changes to, e.g., the Road Traffic Act in 2017.[130] The changes included penalties for private-hire drivers operating without a proper license or adequate insurance.[131] Without identifying particular AV issues, it was stated that while AVs can enhance the efficiency and convenience of Singapore's land transport system, "the Government cannot take a 'completely laissez-faire approach.'"[132] Singapore would therefore adopt a "balanced, light-touch regulatory stance that protects the safety of passengers and other road users, and yet ensures that these technologies can flourish."[133]

[123] "Software Glitch", note 120 above.
[124] "Brakes on Self-Driving Trials", note 63 above.
[125] Ibid.
[126] "Driverless Bus Trial", note 54 above.
[127] "Software Glitch", note 120 above.
[128] Ibid.
[129] Ibid.
[130] Faris Mokhtar, "Laws Regulating Private Car Hires, AVs to Enhance Safety Passed," *Today* (February 8, 2017).
[131] Ibid.
[132] Ibid.
[133] Ibid.

Newspaper reports presented some competing narratives regarding the regulation of safety and risk. The Auto Insurance Head of AIG said that AVs could make the roads safer because of the large proportion of accidents caused by human error, and that other features such as collision avoidance systems have reduced accidents significantly.[134] However, NTUC (National Trades Union Congress) Income's general insurance and health general manager said that repair costs could be higher.[135] The creation of technical guidelines for AVs covering areas such as vehicle behavior and safety was announced in 2019, which came "after a year of discussions between representatives from the autonomous vehicle industry, government agencies, as well as research institutes and institutes of higher learning."[136] As noted by a professor at NUS's Advanced Robotics Centre, the guidelines were not rules, but they could be a basis for formulating regulations for AVs.[137] Permanent Secretary for Transport Loh Ngai Seng, Chairman of CARTS, said that he hoped that Technical Reference 68, a set of guidelines covering areas such as vehicle behavior and safety as well as cyber security, will "guide industry players in the safe and effective deployment of autonomous vehicles in Singapore."[138]

How might narrative arguments regarding AVs interact with Singapore's regulatory approach? Singapore has pushed for AV development, and given safety concerns, that would support a stricter approach with comprehensive regulation. However, a narrative that AVs are not inevitable, and that they would only be allowed if they pass rigorous testing etc., suggests that AVs do not need strict legal regulation, because testing and trial regimes ensure safe operation. Newspaper reports in fact suggest that government discussions of AVs did not assert that AV development was inevitable. Widespread use of AVs was characterized in 2015 as "possible in the next 10 years."[139] The study done on Sentosa would enable the venue to "decide whether the driverless vehicles will become a permanent feature after the trial," and the entire study on Sentosa should produce insights that "will also help authorities evaluate the possibility of deploying similar self-driving shuttle systems for intra-town in other parts of Singapore in the future."[140] The driverless

[134] "Change Laws", note 117 above.
[135] Ibid.
[136] "Standards Drawn Up", note 72 above.
[137] Ibid.
[138] Ibid.
[139] "Driverless Vehicles Slated", note 52 above.
[140] "Sentosa to Trial", note 46 above.

truck trials in 2017 took place in two phases, with the first phase conducted by companies in their respective countries, and "depending on those outcomes, MOT and PSA Corporation will then select one of the companies" for Phase Two, which would involve further local trials and development.[141] Regarding driverless electric buses slated for trial in 2018, the SMRT Chief Executive Officer (CEO) stated that AVs "are expected to be fielded in larger scale under the future land transport master plan," and that they would "leverage our extensive experience operating and maintaining buses to support the eventual deployment of autonomous vehicles safely on our roads," but that "if successful" the buses "will serve commuters in the coming years," and no timeline was provided.[142] Even when discussing progress in AV development, government discussions tended to conceive of the process in steps, e.g., regarding driverless trucks using a platoon approach with a human-driven lead truck with a convoy of driverless trucks, "it is timely that we move on to the next steps in developing truck platooning technology."[143]

III.B Commercial Entities

In the Singapore context, commercial entities have paired up with government entities to develop AVs, and their narratives revolve around commercial success, AV advantages, and AV inevitability.

III.B.1 Commercial Success

Highlighting the theme that AVs could provide seamless first and last mile connectivity for commuters, a joint venture between the government transportation entity SMRT Services and the company 2getthere Holding was announced on April 20, 2016.[144] The Singapore-based joint venture planned to market, install, operate, and maintain AV systems for customers in Singapore and the Asia-Pacific, and aimed to commercialize 2getthere's "third-generation Group Rapid Transit Vehicle system in Singapore by the end of the year."[145] It was announced in January 2017 that agreements were signed with two automotive

[141] "Port Transport", note 81 above.
[142] "Driverless Electric Buses", note 89 above.
[143] "Port Transport", note 81 above.
[144] "SMRT and 2getthere Partner to Bring Automated Vehicles to Singapore," *Channel News Asia* (April 20, 2016).
[145] Ibid.

companies, Scania and Toyota Tusho, to develop and test an autonomous truck platooning system,[146] and a partnership was formed in April 2017 between the LTA and ST Kinetics to develop and trial autonomous buses.[147]

Singapore newspapers gave significant coverage to the local start-up nuTonomy, which was expected to start limited commercial service by 2018.[148] The LTA signed agreements with nuTonomy, as well as the UK company Delphi Automotive Systems, to make AVs a reality.[149] Grab introduced a "Robo-Car" in 2016,[150] and announced its partnership with nuTonomy, the first company in the world to try out self-driving taxis in public, three days after raising $750 million in funding.[151]

III.B.2 AV Advantages

There was occasional coverage of commercial entities extolling the virtues of their products, and these narrative advertisements echo some of the advantages of AVs noted in government narratives. One 2018 article regarding an Audi AV asked, "What would you do with an extra hour of your life every day?"[152] If you're someone who loves to drive, "then autonomous driving might not be for you," but in Singapore, "we experience traffic jams daily," and AVs give the driver the choice to "clear … e-mails or spend time interacting with … friends and family."[153] This discussion assumes that the AV is at the most advanced level and does not require the attention of the driver: "Once all the conditions are met and the systems are engaged, it leaves the driver free to take hands off the wheel and do other things."[154]

III.B.3 Inevitability

The inevitability narrative favored by commercial entities makes a strong appearance in the research studies and surveys discussed at the beginning of the chapter, and inevitability also appears in newspaper

146 "Port Transport", note 81 above.
147 "LTA Signs Deal", note 55 above.
148 "Test Driverless Cars", note 54 above.
149 Ibid.
150 "Driverless Taxis", note 47 above.
151 Ibid.
152 Derryn Wong, "The Next Audi Limo Will Pay You Back in Time," *The Business Times* (January 13, 2018) ["Next Audi Limo"].
153 Ibid.
154 Ibid.

coverage of commercial entities. The CEO of MooVita, creator of AV MooAV, suggested that cars like MooAV "will become a common sight in Singapore."[155] The CEO of taxi company ComfortDelGro stated that the operational experience gained in AV trials would be invaluable "as we prepare for a future where autonomous vehicles … become an integral part of our daily commute."[156]

There are even instances of a commercial entity attributing inevitability to the Singapore government. For example, local start-up nuTonomy described how favorable the AV environment is in Singapore, stating that they see Singapore as "one of the best markets in the world for this technology … [Singapore wants] it to happen, and they're going to make sure it does."[157] However, this statement attributes an inevitability to the Singapore government which is not reflected in the government narratives analyzed above.

A related but slightly different narrative argument is raised in commercial entities' discussion of regulatory approaches. In a 2018 article, Audi acknowledged there are hurdles to overcome in AV development, because although autonomous driving is a reality, the question is "whether or not you'll be allowed to do it …."[158] The article noted two legislative barriers: "whether autonomous cars are allowed at all, and what drivers are allowed to do while the car drives itself."[159] Audi said it planned to seek approval from the LTA for its "Audi AI Traffic Jam Pilot."[160] Another 2018 article noted that the establishment of a Japanese start-up in Singapore was attributed to Singapore's "support in removing regulatory barriers and promoting testing."[161] Companies can build technology, but if the market does not accept it, or "the government does not allow us to introduce the car, then all it is is an interesting toy."[162] The commercial message here is that AVs are here, but short-sighted regulation could impede consumer access to it. In particular, the toy image suggests that imprudent regulation could trivialize a major development, one that has already arrived.

155 "Self-Driving Cars", note 91 above.

156 "Self-Driving Shuttles", note 102 above.

157 Evan Ackerman, "NuTonomy to Launch World's First Fully Autonomous Taxi Service in Singapore This Year," *IEEE Spectrum* (April 4, 2016).

158 "Next Audi Limo", note 152 above.

159 Ibid.

160 Ibid.

161 "Japan Start-Up", note 113 above.

162 Ibid.

IV Conclusion

The chapter has argued that research surveys and newspaper articles suggest a distinct group of narrative arguments regarding AVs in Singapore. Public opinion included some views that AVs would bring positive outcomes, such as convenience and task completion without the need to interact with a human, but concern and fear were also expressed, primarily about the safety of AVs with some discussion of job loss. Government and commercial entities expressed reassuring narratives, such as those emphasizing AV testing and controlled pilot projects. The Singapore government was portrayed, by itself and by its commercial partners, as pushing for AV development, to, among other reasons, address the Singapore need to deal with resources in short supply, such as truck drivers and land space.

Narratives of government and commercial entities often complemented each other, and in newspaper articles, the government and commercial positions were regularly intertwined. These narratives were frequently upbeat, and when they addressed safety concerns, they did not necessarily acknowledge the reasons why there would be any concerns. There is, however, a difference between government and commercial narratives regarding AVs: commercial entities asserted an inevitability narrative, while government entities did not. According to the inevitability narrative, there is no stopping technological advances like AVs and their composite parts such as AI, so countries and the public should simply accept that and focus on managing the risks. This narrative argument conflicts at a fundamental level with a different narrative regarding how government and law function, that government officials are responsible for determining what technology can be used in their jurisdiction and implementing rules regarding it, including prohibitions if warranted. The government's rejection of the inevitability narrative supports a view of law and government in which government officials decide the degree and pace of AV development. However, Singapore has not adopted a strict regulatory approach, and has opted instead for light touch regulation. As a narrative argument, the rejection of inevitability does not dictate a particular regulatory approach, and is consistent with either light touch or strict regulation.

MAMAK©

15

"The Knowledge of Causes and the Secret Motions of Things"

The Interdisciplinary and Doctrinal Challenges of Automated Driving Systems and Criminal Law

JEANNE GAAKEER*

The end of our foundation is the knowledge of causes and the secret motions of things; and the enlarging of the bounds of human empire, to the effecting of all things possible.[1]

I Introduction

On October 15, 2001, a coach driver wanting to make a right turn stopped to give the right of way to a mother and her 5-year-old son on a bike crossing. After the mother had reached the other side of the crossing, she made a gesture to the driver. He accelerated and ran over the boy, who had fallen in the middle of the crossing. The boy died of his injuries. In court, the driver explained that the gesture made him assume that the boy had crossed safely. The Dutch lower, appellate, and Supreme Court found that his claim that he had based his understanding on the gesture was irrelevant, but this chapter asserts that the driver's hermeneutic (mis)understanding of the mini-narrative of the human gesture is quite relevant. Because Article 6 of the Dutch Road Traffic Act 1994, applicable to traffic accidents resulting in grave bodily injury or death, is based on *culpa lata*, i.e., behavior less careful than that of the average person, the presumption of innocence allows a defendant to plead not guilty based on his or her interpretation of another person's action. It appeared that the disastrous consequence of the boy's death occasioned application of a stricter standard, that of *culpa levis*, i.e., whether the defendant behaved

* I am grateful to Sabine Gless for including me in this exciting project.

1 Francis Bacon, *The New Atlantis* (USA: Project Gutenberg, 2008), www.gutenberg.org/files/2434/2434-h/2434-h.htm.

as the most careful person possible.[2] As Ferry de Jong suggests, when it comes to determining *culpa*, guilt, and *dolus*, intentionality, in any specific criminal case, a "hermeneutics of the situation"[3] is required to gauge whether or not *actus reus* and *mens rea* can be established. In this chapter, hermeneutics refers not only to the individual interpretations of actions or meaning, but also includes the criteria or framework used to produce such interpretations. A hermeneutics of the situation stresses the connection between this process of meaning-giving and the situation in which the process occurs.[4] This process is difficult enough in traffic accidents involving traditional cars, and it will become even more difficult if the car is a robot.

An autonomous vehicle is a robot, and a robot is understood here as "an engineered machine that senses, thinks, and acts."[5] In view of the increased use of automated vehicles, referred to in the chapter as Automated Driving Systems (ADS), the need for a hermeneutics of the situation has become even more acute. When ascertaining the degree of criminal fault when ADS are involved in traffic accidents, we have to face the unpleasant truths that so far legislation lags behind and current versions of legal codes may fall short. Criminal law concepts dealing with intent and causality therefore need a new, careful scrutiny, because ADS have their own hermeneutics, one which is not easily comprehensible to the driver. ADS hermeneutics are based on their programming, i.e., their algorithms, and this introduces novel understandings of what it means to act – hermeneutical as well as narratological.[6]

In addition to drivers of ADS, legislators may also find the logic of new technologies fuzzy. The question of hermeneutically understanding technology at the legislative level is outside the scope of this chapter, and limited space does not permit me to elaborate. It can be noted that any

[2] Dutch Supreme Court, Decision of January 17, 2006, ECLI:NL:HR:2006:AU3447. European judicial decisions that have a European Case Law Identifier (ECLI) can be accessed via the European e-justice portal, see European Union, "European e-justice," https://e-justice.europa.eu.

[3] Ferry de Jong, "The End of Doctrine? On the Symbolic Function of Doctrine in Substantive Criminal Law" (2011) 7:3 *Utrecht Law Review* 8 at 44, n. 141, referencing Antoine Mooij, *Intentionality, Desire and Responsibility: A Study in Phenomenology, Psychoanalysis and Law* (Leiden, Netherlands: Brill, 2010) at 39–45 ["End of Doctrine"].

[4] See Antoine Mooij, "*Psychiatry as a Human Science: Phenomenological, Hermeneutical and Lacanian Perspectives* (Leiden, Netherlands: Brill, 2012) at 156.

[5] For this understanding of robot, see Chapter 6 in this volume.

[6] Narratology refers to the theory and study of narrative as story and storytelling, while the latter is the narrative representation of human actions, events, and happenings.

legislative choice regarding ADS in criminal law will influence future criminal charges, which are themselves always already mini-narratives of forms of reprehensible human behaviour, *mala prohibita*.[7] Both future legislation and pending concrete cases are in need of an informed hermeneutics of the situation, disciplinary and factual, not least because hermeneutic misunderstanding may be an impediment to the right to a fair trial.

Many disciplines were already involved in the development and construction of ADS before jurists became involved. The difficulties of how to interpret and understand the disciplinary other may easily lead to miscommunication when artificial intelligence (AI) experts who are not jurists must deal with jurists who are not AI experts.[8] In addition to problems of translation between disciplines, responsibility gaps may occur, "circumstances in which a serious accident happens and nobody can be reasonably held responsible or accountable due to the unpredictability or opaqueness of the process leading to the accident," technological opaqueness included.[9] For example, in 2020, a former member of the EU Parliament, Marietje Schaake, had a conversation with an entrepreneur. The entrepreneur told her that one of his engineers working on the design of ADS had asked him who he would prefer to be killed in case of a collision involving an ADS, either a baby or an elderly person, because such options had to be built into the software.[10] This brings to mind the ethical-philosophical thought experiment called the "Weichenstellersfall" or trolley problem. A train runs out of control and will kill hundreds of people in a nearby train station unless it is diverted to a side track, but on that track there are five workmen who will be killed as a consequence. What should be done? Do you divert the train or not? Even more complicated is the problem's elaboration in the fat man example; what if you are on a bridge and the only way to stop the train is to kill a fat man next to you and

[7] For the idea of the criminal charge as a mini-narrative, see Jeanne Gaakeer, "The Criminal Charge: A Narratological Bow Tie?" in Monika Fludernik & Frank Schäfer (eds.), *Erzählen und Recht* (Narrative and Law), 12 Faktuales und Fiktionales Erzählen (Baden-Baden, Germany: Ergon, 2022) 129.

[8] AI is understood here to include "neural networks engaged in deep learning"; see Chapter 7 in this volume.

[9] Filippo Santoni de Sio, "Ethics and Self-Driving Cars: A White Paper on Responsible Innovation in Automated Driving Systems" (Delft University of Technology, 2016) ["White Paper"] commissioned by Rijkswaterstaat for the "knowledge agenda automated driving," at 20. The term "responsibility gap" was coined by Andreas Matthias in Andreas Matthias, "The Responsibility Gap: Ascribing Responsibility for the Actions of Learning Automata" (2004) 6:3 *Ethics and Information Technology* 175.

[10] Economy Section, "NRC Handelsblad" (February 7, 2020) at 8.

push his body on to the track to stop the train?[11] Translated to the topic of ADS, when there is imminent danger, the human driver and/or the ADS have to decide between two evils and choose to kill either one person or the other(s). Any human driver killing one individual in order to save the other(s) will be acting unlawfully, but would that also be acting culpably? Furthermore, if a democratic state under the rule of law can never weigh the life of one citizen against the other and prohibits any distinction on the basis of age, gender, and sex, why would we allow an engineer to do just that when programming an ADS? Understanding our fellow human beings and their actions is difficult enough, but understanding, let alone arguing with, an algorithm not of one's own design is even more so. Technological advances in driving may be intended to reduce the complexity of the human task of driving a vehicle in contemporary traffic – the technological narrative of progress – but may in fact complicate it if such innovation demands that the human be on the alert for any surprise in the form of an error in the algorithmic and/or computational system, causing the vehicle to deviate from its intended course. While research is being done on how human drivers understand and use specific types of ADS, the current human driver-passenger may be hermeneutically challenged. How and when does she recognize that she needs to resume control?

While criminal law does not solely represent the pursuit of moral aims, new AI technologies force us to consider ethical issues in relation to hermeneutical and narratological ones, and to grapple with the criminal liability of ADS. To this end, the chapter incorporates different interdisciplinary lenses, including narratology. The chapter is inspired by the epistemological claim on human knowledge and progress voiced in Francis Bacon's utopian narrative *The New Atlantis*, because the fundamental philosophical questions "What is it? What do you mean? How do you know?" apply in technological surroundings as much as in criminal law surroundings. The actors involved have to be able to clearly express their stories, paying careful attention not only to *what* they are saying and claiming, but also to *how* they tell their stories.[12] These ontological, hermeneutical, and methodological questions are therefore narratological questions as well.

11 Hans Welzel, "Zum Notstandsproblem" (1951) 63:1 *Zeitschrift für die gesamte Strafrechtswissenschaft* 47; Judith Jarvis Thomson, "The Trolley Problem" (1985) 94:6 *Yale Law Journal* 1395.

12 On the narratological distinction between narrative as story and as discourse, see Gerald Prince, *A Dictionary of Narratology*, rev. ed. (Lincoln, NE and London, UK: University of Nebraska Press, 2003), Discourse ("the expression plane of narrative as opposed to its content plan or story").

In Section II, this chapter addresses the interdisciplinary issues of integrating knowledge, translating between disciplines, and responsibility gaps, as a prolegomena for Section III, which focuses on criminal liability. In Section IV, the human–robot/ADS interaction is discussed, in the context of issues raised by the concept of *dolus eventualis*. To conclude, Section V returns to the need for a hermeneutics of the situation that adequately addresses ADS challenges.

II Interdisciplinary Observations on the Interrelation of Technology and Law

II.A Whose Department?

The legal implementation of technology is too important to leave to technologists alone. This chapter therefore turns to philosophical thought on technology, in part to prevent us from falling into the trap of Francis Bacon's *idola tribus*, i.e., our tendency to readily believe what we prefer to be true.[13] The *idola tribus* makes us see what our rationalizations allow. This approach is the easy way out when we do not yet fully understand the effects and consequences of new technologies, but the moment is not far away when ADS becomes fully capable of independent, unsupervised learning, and we should consider Samuel Butler's visionary point on the side-effect of machine-consciousness, i.e., "the extraordinary rapidity with which they are becoming something very different to what they are at present."[14] When that happens, who or what will be in control?

An epistemology based on algorithmic knowledge, while helpful in many applications to daily life, runs the risk of introducing forms of instrumentalism and reductionism. Behind such "substitutive automation" is the "neoliberal ideology … [in which] dominant evaluative modes are quantitative, algorithmic, and instrumentalist, focused on financialized rubrics of productivity."[15] The greater the complexity of the issue, the greater the risks posed by algorithmic knowledge. Scientific dealings in these modes of analysis often disregard the fact

[13] Joseph Devey (ed.), *The Physical and Metaphysical Works of Lord Bacon, Including The Advancement of Learning and Novum Organum* (London, UK: George Bell & Sons, 1901) at 209.

[14] Samuel Butler, *Erewhon* (Harmondsworth, UK: Penguin, 1954) at 164.

[15] Frank Pasquale, "Professional Judgment in an Era of Artificial Intelligence and Machine Learning" (2019) 46:1 *Boundary* 2 ["Professional Judgment"] at 1 and 2.

that a human being is the source of the data, both as the object of the algorithms used in technologies when data is gathered to run the device, and as the engineer and designer who decides what goes into the programming process. Human fallibility is often disregarded, but ontological perfection either of humans or technologies is not in and of this world. While both human and AI learn by iteration, their individual awareness of past and present danger is not identical, or should we say, identically programmed.

Some Dutch examples may illustrate the difficulties in relying exclusively on algorithmic knowledge. In 2018, the advanced braking system of a Volvo truck failed because the camera system did not recognize a stationary truck in front of it in the same lane.[16] In the subsequent crash into the back of another truck, the driver of the Volvo was crushed to death. In a 2017 case, the warning system of a 2014 model Tesla failed to respond to another vehicle that changed lanes, the Tesla did not reduce its speed in due time, and it hit the side of the other vehicle. The manufacturer admitted that the 2014 model worked well when it came to detecting vehicles right in front of the Tesla, but not when these vehicles made sudden moves.[17] But that is not an uncommon event in traffic, is it?

The examples show that data-driven machines run the risk of incorporating forms of "epistemological tyranny."[18] The human is reduced to the sum of its "dividual" parts, selectively used depending on its user's needs.[19] Our making sense of the relations between individuals and their machines is then reduced to connecting the dots. If manufacturers focus on the development of new technologies rather than on the legal frameworks within which their products are going to be handled, any opacity as far as product information is concerned can lead to someone, somewhere, avoiding compliance with the law. We should therefore probe the "*narrative* of computationalist supremacy."[20] The humanities can help provide guidance at the meta-level of juridical-technological

[16] Netherlands, Dutch Safety Board, *Wie Stuurt? Verkeersveiligheid en automatisering in het wegverkeer* (Who's Driving? Traffic Safety and Automation) (The Hague, Netherlands: Dutch Safety Board, 2019) at 24.

[17] Ibid. at 31–45.

[18] "Professional Judgment", note 15 above, at 15.

[19] Gilles Deleuze, "Postscript on Control Societies" in Thomas Levin, Ursula Frohne, & Peter Weibel (eds.), *CTRL [SPACE] Rhetorics of Surveillance from Bentham to Big Brother*, 1st ed. (Cambridge, MA: The MIT Press, 2002) 317 at 319.

[20] "Professional Judgment", note 15 above, at 30, n. 2 (emphasis in the original).

discourse, because behind any form of "algorithmic imperialism,"[21] there is also linguistic imperialism that prioritizes one language of expertise above the other.[22]

Under the influence of Enlightenment thought, the stereotypical or stock story of modern technology, its constitutive narrative, founded as it is in the natural sciences, has been the narrative of human progress.[23] Its darker side-effects have often been pushed into the background until something went seriously wrong. But it is a mistake to regard technology "as something neutral."[24] If we look upon technology as production only, we may be reduced to Deleuzian dividuals, ready to be ordered by others, be they machines or humans, both in technology and law; then "'[t]he will to mastery' will prevail and we have to wait and see who gets in control at the level of production."[25] While the heyday of legal positivism is behind us, its referential paradigm may well resurface, if for lack of information or understanding we all too readily accept at face value what is held before us as technology. The consequence may be uninformed and unethical applications of technology, without proper legal protection of the humans impacted by it.

This chapter does not promote Luddism. It does, however, highlight the risks involved in a positivist view of both law and technology, i.e., the value-free, unmediated application of any form of code, as opposed to the value-laden human enterprises that they are. As Lawrence Lessig put it, "Code is never found; it is only ever made, and only ever made by us."[26] Technology should not be put to use for the simple reason that it is available, and one risk of modern technologies is that if it can be done, somewhere, someone, at some point in time, will actually do it, whatever the consequences. This attitude is brilliantly and cynically

21 Ibid. at 16.

22 See James Boyd White, *Living Speech: Resisting the Empire of Force* (Princeton, NJ: Princeton University Press, 2006).

23 For the idea of constitutive narratives in relation to law, see Robert Cover, "Nomos and Narrative" (1983) 97:1 *Harvard Law Review* 4 ["Nomos and Narrative"] at 4–68.

24 Martin Heidegger, "The Question Concerning Technology" in Martin Heidegger, *The Question Concerning Technology and Other Essays*, translated by W. Lovitt (New York, NY: Harper & Row, 1977) 3 at 4. It should be noted that Heidegger's career was severely tainted by his association with the National Socialists during his rectorate of the University of Freiburg. Despite this controversial aspect, he is widely regarded as one of the greatest philosophers of hermeneutics.

25 Ibid. at 5.

26 Lawrence Lessig, *Code: And Other Laws of Cyberspace, Version 2.0* (New York, NY: Basic Books, 2006) at 6.

voiced in Tom Lehrer's 1965 song "Wernher von Braun": "'Once the rockets go up, who cares where they come down? That's not my department,' says Wernher von Braun."[27] Careful attention regarding the what, the how, and the why of ADS technology is required. The what of the algorithm, the logic of the if … then, does not coincide with the how of its juridical-technical implementation, let alone the how of its technical discourse. This is no small matter if we think of the if … then structure of the criminal charge in terms of punitive consequences for human behavior involving ADS, and the narratives a defendant would need to steer clear of criminal responsibility.

II.B The Need to Integrate Knowledge

Mono-disciplinary approaches reinforce scientific dichotomies that preclude the necessary risk assessments. They bring us back to the *Erklären-Verstehen* controversy, as it is called in the nineteenth-century German philosophical tradition, to the concept of restricting explanations to the natural sciences, because explanation (*Erklären*) could only pertain to facts, whereas the humanities could only attribute meaning or hermeneutic understanding (*Verstehen*). This dichotomy has had far-reaching implications for the epistemological differentiation of knowledge into separate academic disciplines, with each discipline developing its own language and methodology, outlook, goals, and concepts, and each discipline functioning in a different cultural and social context of knowledge production. The interdisciplinary approach advocated here can show that in all epistemological environments, "[d]isciplinary lenses inevitably inform perception."[28] An interdisciplinary approach also calls for an appreciation of the fact that any discipline's or field of expertise's narratives cannot be understood other than within their cultural and normative universe, the *nomos* of their origin and existence.[29]

To see the connection between ADS technology and narratology, we could ask what the new technologies' rhetoric, scripts, and stock stories have been so far, and specifically, what the main narrative thrust of technology is and what it means for the non-specialist addressee. Any field of knowledge "must always be on its guard lest it mistake its own linguistic

[27] Tom Lehrer, "That Was the Year That Was" (1965).

[28] Siri Hustvedt, *The Shaking Woman or the History of My Nerves* (London, UK: Picador, 2010) at 28.

[29] "Nomos and Narrative", note 23 above, at 4–68.

conventions for objective laws."[30] Debate is essential, and engineers and jurists alike need guidance regarding the production and reception of narratives in their respective fields. One such form of guidance is Benjamin Cardozo's claim that legal professionals need to develop a linguistic antenna sensitive to peculiarities beyond the level of the signifier, because the form and content, the how and the what of a text, are interconnected.[31] Concepts from narratology can assist to accomplish this task. All professionals benefit if they learn to differentiate between, first, narrative in the sense of story or *what* is told, and discourse of *how* it is told. For jurists working in criminal law, it is important, second, to realize that story comprises both events, understood here as either actions or happenings, and the characters that act themselves or get involved in happenings, and that all of this occurs in specific settings that influence meaning.

Precisely because disciplinary lenses influence us, translating between collaborating disciplines must be undertaken. To the legal theorist James Boyd White, interdisciplinarity is itself a form of translation. He claims that resolving the tensions between disciplines "always involves the establishment of a relation between two systems of language and of life, two discourses, each with its own distinctive purposes and methods, its own ways of constructing the social relations through which it works, and its own set of claims, silences, and meanings."[32] At the core of translation as a mode of thought, then, is the claim that we should be alert to the possibilities and limitations of any professional discourse. This point illuminates the possibilities and limitations of any disciplinary language of expertise, limitations tied to the context of claims of meaning, and to the cultural and social effects of specific language uses. Translation requires that we address the fundamental difference between the narrative and the analytical, between "the mind that tells a story, and the mind that gives reason" because "one finds its meaning in representations of events as they occur in time, in imagined experience; the other, in systematic or theoretical explanations, in the exposition of conceptual order or structure."[33] When

[30] Italo Calvino, "Two Interviews on Science and Literature" in *Italo Calvino, The Uses of Literature*, translated by P. Creagh (New York, NY: Harcourt Brace Jovanovich, 1987) at 45.

[31] See Benjamin Cardozo, "Law and Literature" (1925) 14 *Yale Review* 699.

[32] James Boyd White, "Establishing Relations between Law and Other Forms of Thought and Language" (2008) 1:3 *Erasmus Law Review* 1 at 9, www.elevenjournals.com/tijdschrift/ELR/2008/3/ELR_2210-2671_2008_001_003_002.pdf.

[33] James Boyd White, *The Legal Imagination: Studies in the Nature of Legal Thought and Expression* (Boston, MA: Little, Brown & Co., 1973) at 859.

transposed to the subject of conceptual thought, the need for attention to language and narrative becomes acute. What, to start with, is "a concept"? White found "concept" a problematic term, because the underlying premise is once again the referentiality of language, one that implies transparency of the semantic load of a concept in one disciplinary language and, following this, unproblematic translation of a concept into another. Such a view is imperialistic, based as it is on the supposition that the "conceptual world … is supposed to exist on a plane above and beyond language, which disappears when its task is done."[34]

One central example of translation in the context of human–ADS interactions is the concept of driver, currently presumed to be a human driver. In a present with current levels of ADS development, and in a future of full ADS automation, a legal concept of the driver based on a human is no longer appropriate. Feddes suggests that "the human is a passenger, the automation is the legal driver."[35] If this is correct, attribution of legal responsibility in human–ADS interactions would require ADS to be able to handle any situation that crops up.

A Dutch case on the concept of driver illustrates arguments regarding who the driver is in a human–ADS interaction. The driver of a 2017 Tesla Model X was fined €230 in an administrative sanction for using his mobile phone hands-on while driving.[36] Before the county court, he claimed that because the autopilot was activated, he could no longer be legally considered the driver, and therefore the acts of driving and using a hands-on phone did not constitute the simultaneous act prohibited in Article 61A of the Rules on Traffic Regulations and Traffic Signs 1990.[37] This narrative did not save the day. The county court found the defendant's appeal unfounded because Article 1 of the Road Traffic Act 1994 applied. The defendant had stated that while seated on the driver's chair with the autopilot activated, he regularly held the steering wheel, but he did this because the system disengages itself if the driver does not react

[34] James Boyd White, *Justice as Translation: An Essay in Cultural and Legal Criticism* (Chicago, IL: University of Chicago Press, 1990) at 31 and 36.

[35] Gerben Feddes, "Towards the Legal Admission of Connected Automated Vehicles," Paper EU-TP1330 delivered at the 25th ITS World Congress Copenhagen (September 17–21, 2018) 1 at 5.

[36] County Court Midden-Nederland, Decision of November 22, 2018, ECLI:NL:RBMNE:2018:5707 [ECLI:NL:RBMNE:2018:5707].

[37] Per the Rules on Traffic Regulations and Traffic Signs 1990 [Rules on Traffic], Art. 61A, the legal driver is: "A person driving a motor vehicle, moped, motor assisted bicycle or disabled person's vehicle equipped with an engine may not hold a mobile phone while driving."

after the three auditory warnings from the vehicle when it notices that the driver is not holding the wheel.[38] He was found to be the legal driver of the vehicle and not a passenger, in part because drivers are "all road users excepting pedestrians" according to Dutch law.[39] Like the Netherlands, many legal systems lack a codified definition of the term "driver," which leads courts to define the term in context.

The defendant's other argument in this case, that Dutch legislation should be amended to provide a definition, did not help the defendant either, because in criminal cases future-oriented contextual interpretation is prohibited. On appeal, the defendant introduced a new element to his narrative, that a driver using an autopilot is similar to and should be treated like a driving instructor. Since a driving instructor is not the actual driver, he or she is allowed to use a mobile phone hands-on. This narrative forced the Court of Appeal to elaborate on the doctrinal distinction made in the Road Traffic Act 1994 and the Traffic Rules and Signs Regulations 1990 between the actual driver and the legal driver. Article 61A of the Traffic Rules and Signs Regulations 1990, the regulations used for the administrative charge against the defendant, pertained to the actual driver, not to the instructor or examiner. Activating and using the autopilot, as the defendant had done, made the defendant the actual driver, as his vehicle was not a fully automated ADS. Per this reasoning, Article 61A applied. The Court of Appeal upheld the judgment.[40] Under this reasoning, there is nothing automatic in autopilots yet!

A final, comparative question regarding translation is whether the process of ADS construction reflects unconscious biases. Suppose an ADS is of US American design. Surely the designer had US American law at the back of his mind during construction? Does such a vehicle fully comply with the demands of civil-law European systems and the mindsets of European users? An interdisciplinary approach regarding technology and law compels us to think through incompatibilities, while at the same time urges us to integrate their disciplinary discourses as much as possible. Rather than continuing a "'black box' mentality,"[41] we should promote

38 ECLI:NL:RBMNE:2018:5707, note 36 above.

39 Rules on Traffic, note 37 above, s. 1.

40 Dutch Court of Appeal Arnhem-Leeuwarden, Decision of July 31, 2019, ECLI:NL:GHARL:2019:6122.

41 Luciano Floridi, Josh Cowls, Monica Beltrametti *et al.*, "AI4People – An Ethical Framework for a Good AI Society: Opportunities, Risks, Principles, and Recommendations" (2018) 28:4 *Minds & Machines* 689 at 692, "a 'black box' mentality, according to which AI systems for decision-making are seen as being beyond human understanding, and hence control."

"technologies of humility,"[42] to preclude technological languages from imposing their conceptual framework to the exclusion of other languages.

II.C Mind the Gap

As noted above, a responsibility gap arises when a serious accident happens but nobody can reasonably be held responsible. Responsibility gaps can arise because of the gaps between disciplinary fields. An example of minding the disciplinary gaps is Santoni de Sio's attention to ethical issues, in which he urges integration of different disciplines. He observed that the Dutch Ministry of Infrastructure and Environment divides ethical issues in ADS into three levels: the operational level concerning the programming of automated vehicles; the tactical level of road traffic regulations; and the strategic aspect of how to deal with the societal impact of ADS.[43] For ADS, integration "should be done in such a way that 'meaningful human control' over the behaviour of the system is always preserved."[44] The simple fact that a human is present is not in itself "a sufficient condition for being in control of an activity."[45] This is the case because of the complexity of all the causal relations and correlations involved, and because "meaningful" control is not equivalent to "direct" control, i.e., when the driver directly controls the ADS's full operation. Confusing meaningful and direct control can easily lead to either over-delegation, as when the driver of an ADS overestimates the vehicle, or under-delegation, where the driver overestimates his or her own driving capacities in an ADS context.[46] The need to clearly define the scope of the driver's actual freedom to act is also inextricably connected to the notion of volition in criminal law.

III Criminal Liability

III.A Freedom to Act?

Human autonomous agency is inextricably connected to consciousness and to the capacity for rational thought. With these come free will, manifesting in criminal law, first as the self-determination to deliberately do

[42] Ibo van de Poel, "An Ethical Framework for Evaluating Experimental Technology" (2016) 22:3 *Science & Engineering Ethics* 667 at 668, referencing Sheila Jasanoff, "Technologies of Humility: Citizen Participation in Governing Science" (2003) 41:3 *Minerva* 223.

[43] "White Paper", note 9 above, at 5.

[44] Ibid. at 8.

[45] Ibid. at 11.

[46] Ibid. at 14–15.

the right thing and abstain from what is wrong, e.g., *mala per se* such as murder, and *mala prohibita* or what the law prohibits, and second as the criterion for assigning legal personhood. When it comes to attributing criminal liability, the first requirement is *actus reus*, the voluntary act or omission to act that the law defines as prohibited. Historically, the free will necessary for a voluntary act has been defined in numerous ways. It can mean that man is free to decide to go either left or right, even if there is no specific reason to do either. One has freedom to act if one is able to do whatever one decides, the *liberum arbitrium indifferentiae*.[47] Free will can also be seen when one is free to decide not to act at all. This is the precursor and precondition of the legal freedom to act in that it presupposes the mental ability to decide whether or not to do this, that, or the other.[48] The fact that man is aware of the fact that he has a will is not deemed enough, because being conscious of something is not evidence of its existence.

What are the necessary and sufficient conditions of a voluntary act in the context of ADS, and what are the legal consequences of those conditions? The lack of free will is still widely regarded as the axe at the root of the criminal law tree. The question today in human–robot relations is whether or not free will and forms of technological determinism can be reconciled, theoretically and practically. Is free will compatible with empirically provable determinants of action? If so, then free will is perhaps compatible with machine-determined action, and therefore legal causality. The necessary condition for free will is that an actor, in doing what he did, could have decided otherwise. In the law, we normally start from the premise that free will is a postulate that goes for the majority of ordinary human beings opposed to an empirically provable fact, because statistically speaking that is usually the situation. This approach leads to the traditional position that those suffering from mental illness are not free, and hence not or only partly responsible. The law's beginning assumption of free will also leads to the impossibility of punishing those about whom one cannot say anything other than we do not know whether their will was hampered or not. Practically speaking, free will is established when a state of exception, e.g., insanity in humans, does not occur.

[47] Pierre Bayle, *Dictionnaire historique et philosophique*, vol. II (Amsterdam, Netherlands: Compagnie des Libraires, 1734) at 466.

[48] Julien Benda & Raymond Naves (eds.), *Voltaire Dictionnaire Philosophique* (Paris, France: Garnier, 1961) at 277, "Vous êtes libre de faire, quand vous avez le pouvoir de faire."

Two opposing views regarding the application of these ideas to ADS could be entertained. One is that if an ADS is an agent capable of learning in the sense of adapting its actions to new information, an ADS could be held criminally responsible, with or without attributing consciousness of the human type, because the algorithmic reasoning skills and autonomy of the ADS would suffice. Second, if charges are brought against the human driver, one could argue that an ADS provides a defense based on the state of exception approach to free will discussed above. The human driver does not know the mind of the ADS and cannot probe the technological sanity of an ADS, partly because the ADS is a device programmed to act in response to its environment, but not by the driver.

Both views are connected to the question of a possible form of legal personhood for AI, another condition for the imposition of legal responsibility. As a status conferred by law on humans and entities such as corporations, legal personhood is a construct. In everyday life, it is relatively easy to recognize a fellow human being if you meet one. We then recognize the rights and responsibilities of that independent unit, and we distinguish among different entities with legal personhood, e.g., between a toddler without and an adult with legal obligations. Things are already more difficult regarding artificial persons such as corporations, in terms of the information required to assess what the artificial person's rights and obligations are, and the inquiry becomes more fraught regarding ADS.[49] Another issue is that as a matter of legal doctrine, most countries have a closed system of legal personhood. Adding to it may not be as easy as, e.g., the European Parliament thought, when in 2017 it spoke about personhood in the form of an "electronic personality" for robots[50] without explaining which form it could or should take. The European Commission then declined granting such legal status to AI devices.[51]

[49] For a comparison of criminal responsibility for corporate entities and robots, see Chapter 4 in this volume.

[50] European Union, European Parliament, Civil Law Rules on Robotics: European Parliament Resolution of 16 February 2017 with Recommendations to the Commission on Civil Law Rules on Robotics, P8_TA(2017)0051 (EU: Official Journal of the European Union, 2018), para. 59(f).

[51] European Union, European Commission, Artificial Intelligence for Europe, COM(2018) 237 final (Brussels: European Commission), PE 621.926, s. 2.1.22.1.1, https://ec.europa.eu/transparency/documents-register/api/files/COM(2018)237_0/de00000000142394?rendition=false; see also European Union, European Commission, Communication from the Commission to the European Parliament, the European Council, the Council, the European Economic and Social Committee and the Committee of the Regions – Artificial Intelligence

The issues of legal personhood and voluntariness are related. Voluntariness of the *actus reus* of any criminal charge is an issue for ADS. We assume that humans have volition because they do most of the time, and so the law does not always explicitly address the question of human volition. However, voluntary participation in an action is intimately connected to the Enlightenment model of thought that has individual autonomy at its heart and informs our current understandings of law. The requirement for voluntariness therefore prompts the issue of legal personhood to return with a vengeance, because the *actus reus* of a criminal charge, as the outwardly visible activity subject to our human understanding and judgment, is understood to be one committed by a legally capable and responsible person, unless otherwise proved. In short, the basic proposition of criminal law is that if one has legal personhood, one can be held responsible, if there is sufficient evidence and if the *actus reus* is accompanied by *mens rea*, the guilty mind. Legal personhood and voluntariness are elements that therefore remain inevitably entangled in any discussion of criminal liability and ADS.

III.B Which Guilt and Whose Guilty Mind?

Mens rea, the requisite mental state that accompanies the *actus reus*, is required for criminal responsibility, and a precise articulation of *mens rea* is in turn required by substantive due process. But because criminal law regarding ADS is currently under-developed, we should be even more aware than usual of the doctrinal differences regarding *mens rea* terminology at different levels. In particular, when comparing legal systems, legal concepts applicable in common law settings cannot immediately be translated to civil law surroundings. In any discussion of *mens rea* and ADS, we are always dealing with contested definitions and fundamental differences involving the mental pictures that jurists have of their own civil law and common law concepts. Comparative research on ADS is needed, but seemingly similar concepts may be false friends.

Regarding culpability, the US American Model Penal Code[52] distinguishes between acting purposely, knowingly, recklessly, and

for Europe, COM(2018) 237 final (Brussels: Official Journal of the European Union, 2018); European Parliament, "Artificial Intelligence and Civil Liability," www.europarl.europa.eu/RegData/etudes/STUD/2020/621926/IPOL_STU(2020)621926_EN.pdf.

52 American Law Institute, Model Penal Code: Official Draft and Explanatory Notes. Complete Text of the Model Penal Code as Adopted at the 1962 Meeting of the American Law Institute at Washington DC, May 24, 1962 (Philadelphia, PA: The Institute, 1985), and subsequent revisions.

negligently, with negligence occurring when one fails to exercise the care that the average prudent person would exercise under the same conditions. Culpable criminal negligence in this framework is recklessness or carelessness that results in death or injury of another person, and it implies that the perpetrator had a thoughtless disregard of the consequences or an indifference to other people's safety. The inclusion of negligence in the Model Penal Code was controversial, because purpose, knowledge, and recklessness entail the conscious disregard of the risk of harm, i.e., subjective liability, whereas negligence does not, because the risk of harm is one that the actor ought to have been aware of, but was in fact not. Culpability as negligence is therefore often thought to result in objective, i.e., strict, liability. For many jurists, negligent criminal culpability sits uneasily with the requirement of "some mental posture toward the harm."[53] In the criminal law of England and Wales, "there is to be held a presumption … that some element of 'mens rea' will be required for conviction of any offense, unless it is excluded by clear statutory wording."[54] Various forms of *mens rea* found in statutory definitions and case law presume either: intention, direct or oblique, i.e., acting in the knowledge that a specific result will or is almost certain to occur; recklessness, either subjective, i.e., foreseen by the actor, or objective, i.e., the reasonable person threshold; or negligence, a deviation from the reasonable care standard of behavior. While recklessness resembles negligence, negligence does not coincide with recklessness.

In German criminal law, recklessness is not a separate concept. It finds a place within the concept of intention as the condition for criminal liability. Intention and negligence are the defining concepts. In this system, a negligence form of liability regarding ADS could be *dolus eventualis*, a concept which resembles the related common law concepts of recklessness and negligence, but which includes the belief that the harmful result would not occur. *Dolus eventualis*[55]

> affirms intention in cases in which the actor foresaw a possible but not inevitable result of her actions (the element of knowledge) and also approved of, or reconciled herself to, the possible occurrence of that result

[53] Kyron Huigens, "Virtue and Criminal Negligence" (1998) 1:2 *Buffalo Criminal Law Review* 431 at 431–432.

[54] Celia Wells & Oliver Quick (eds.), *Lacey, Wells and Quick Reconstructing Criminal Law: Text and Materials*, 4th ed. (Cambridge, UK: Cambridge University Press, 2010) at 107–108.

[55] Greg Taylor, "The Intention Debate in German Criminal Law" (2004) 17:3 *Ratio Juris* 346 ["Intention Debate"] at 348.

(the volitional or dispositional element). This is contrasted with cases in which the volitional element said to be essential to all forms of intention is missing because the actor earnestly relied on the non-occurrence of the result foreseen as possible.

Two examples may illustrate the difference between intention and negligence, and the role of *dolus eventualis*. An example of a missing volitional element was presented in a Dutch case of allegedly reckless driving. The defendant driver was driving at double the maximum speed, and the case involved a collision that killed the five passengers of the other car. The driver was charged with homicide. The Dutch Supreme Court judged him to be extremely negligent, but held that his act was not intentional as he had not consciously accepted the possible outcome of himself being killed by his own speeding, i.e., he relied on precisely the non-occurrence of an accident.[56] In a comparable German case, two persons were involved in an illegal street race which ended in an accident that killed the driver of another car who relied on the green light. The defendants were charged with murder, and the judicial debate focused on whether they had accepted the possible danger to themselves knowingly and willingly, and had been indifferent, "*gleichgültig*" as the *Bundesgericht* later called it, to the possible fate of others in case of an accident. The Berlin *Landesgericht* pronounced a life sentence, then the *Bundesgerichthof* revised the sentence on a technical matter, the *Landesgericht* then stuck to its earlier decision, and in the second revision the *Bundesgerichthof* confirmed the sentence.[57] The driver was convicted.

The dispositional element of *dolus eventualis* as indifference to what the law demands of us was developed by Karl Engisch in the 1930s, and it became the criterion to distinguish between intention and negligence.[58] In the 1980s, Wolfgang Frisch developed a risk-recognition theory. He thought of intention in terms of "an actor's realisation, at the time of acting, that a risk exists that the offence might occur, which risk the legal order regards as unacceptable."[59] Intentional action requires that the actor was aware of and deliberately created a public

[56] Dutch Supreme Court, October 15, 1996, ECLI:NL:HR:1996:ZD0139.

[57] See Urteil von 27.02.2017-(535 Ks) 251 Js 52/16 (8/16), Landesgericht Berlin; Bundesgerichtshof, March 1, 2018, ECLI:DE:BGH:2017:010317U4SR399.17.0; and Bundesgerichtshof, June 18, 2020, ECLI:DE:BGH:2020:180620U4STR482.19.0.

[58] "Intention Debate", note 55 above, at 355.

[59] Ibid. at 366.

wrong. Greg Taylor elaborated on Frisch's theory by means of an example in which a car driver overtaking another car on a blind corner either relies on the non-occurrence of an accident or is indifferent to the outcome. Taylor asserted that "[c]learly, by overtaking when it is not safe to do so, she creates a risk, and one which is legally unacceptable as well ... Rather, the legal system condemns her conduct as unacceptable because, and as soon as, it creates a situation of danger beyond the ordinary risks of the road; it does not wait to see whether anyone is actually killed as a result of it."[60]

What issues are raised if *dolus eventualis* is applied to human driver or ADS defendants? If the foreseeability of an *abstract* risk is what is legally unacceptable, the distinction between negligence and *dolus eventualis* blurs and there is a shift in the direction of strict liability for the human driver of an ordinary car as well as for the human driver of an ADS, or the ADS itself if we accept the consequences of its self-learning. In terms of evidence, it then becomes more difficult to distinguish between intention and the advertent negligence of the driver in the Dutch example above, on the one hand, versus *dolus eventualis*, on the other. The question will then be whether we make the doctrinal move from *culpa* to *dolus eventualis* and/or strict liability in accidents involving ADS.

IV AI and the Human: Whose Liability, Which Gap?

Societal views often differ strongly from legal decisions on the concepts of recklessness and negligence, precisely because the death of innocent people is involved. But when is an occurrence a deliberate act warranting characterization as intentional, and when is it merely an event that does not warrant criminal liability? The answer depends on the hermeneutic judicial act of evaluating facts and circumstances, and this major challenge arises in all ADS cases, not only because the information in the file may be sparse.

Identifying the *actus reus* and *mens rea* for purposes of determining wrongfulness and culpability in individual ADS cases also creates major challenges for legislators pondering policy. As Abbott and Sarch suggest, "punishing AI could send the message that AI is itself an actor on par with a human being," and "convicting AI of crimes requiring a

[60] Ibid. at 369–370.

mens rea like intent, knowledge, or recklessness would violate the *principle of legality*."[61] The authors develop answers to what they call the "Eligibility Challenge," i.e., what entities connected to ADS, including AI, are eligible for liability.[62] The simplest solution would be the doctrine of *respondeat superior*,[63] i.e., the human developers are responsible[64] if and when they foresee the risk that an AI will cause the death of a person, because that would be reckless homicide. The second solution is strict, no-fault liability of a defendant, and the third solution is to develop a framework for defining new *mens rea* terms for AI, which "could require an investigation of AI behavior at the programming level."[65] In court, judges could then be asked to further develop the relevant *mens rea*. However, the task of constructing a hermeneutics of the situation at the programming level would not immediately alleviate the judge's evidentiary job. The interdisciplinary challenges of translation noted in Section II would still be present, and they probably require additional technological expertise in order to gauge the narratives told in court by the parties involved.[66]

Issues are also raised by a focus on legal responsibility for AI, because per Mary Midgley, what "actually happens to us will surely still be determined by human choices. Not even the most admirable machines can make better choices than the people who are supposed to be programming them."[67] This issue arises even in inquiries into negligence and *dolus eventualis*, because while[68]

> humans may classify other drivers as cautious, reckless, good, and impatient, for example, driverless cars may eschew discrete categories … in favor of tracking the observed behavior of every single car ever encountered, with that data then uploaded and shared online – participating in the collective development of a profile for every car and driver far in excess of anything humanly or conceptually graspable.

[61] Ryan Abbott & Alex Sarch, "Punishing Artificial Intelligence: Legal Fiction or Science Fiction" (2019) 53:1 *UC Davis Law Review* 323 ["Punishing Artificial Intelligence"] at 348–349 (emphasis in the original).

[62] Ibid. at 355.

[63] Regarding corporate liability, see Chapter 4 in this volume.

[64] Regarding programmer liability, see Chapter 2 in this volume.

[65] "Punishing Artificial Intelligence", note 61 above, at 354.

[66] Regarding evidentiary issues raised by robot testimony, see Chapter 8 in this volume.

[67] Mary Midgley, *What Is Philosophy for?* (London, UK: Bloomsbury Academic, 2018) at 207–208.

[68] Brian Cantwell Smith, *The Promise of Artificial Intelligence: Reckoning and Judgment* (Cambridge, MA: The MIT Press, 2019) at 60.

This chapter argues that human agency matters at all levels of evaluating an ADS. Abbott and Sarch assert that[69]

> [o]ne conceivable way to argue that an AI (say, an autonomous vehicle) had the intention (purpose) to cause an outcome (to harm a pedestrian) would be to ask whether the AI was guiding its behavior so as to make this outcome more likely (relative to its background probability of occurring). Is the AI monitoring conditions around it to identify ways to make this outcome more likely? Is the AI then disposed to make these behavioral adjustments to make the outcome more likely (either as a goal in itself, or as a means to accomplishing another goal)? If so, then the AI plausibility may be said to have the purpose of causing that outcome.

However, humans create AI programmes. The potential to programme ADS in a certain way, and the decision of whether to do that or not, brings us back to the case of the trolley discussed in Section I, and it supports the position that human agency is relevant to evaluating ADS. Another way of considering the role of humans in ADS is provided by what Philippa Foot calls the "doctrine of the double effect," "the distinction between what a man foresees as a result of his voluntary action and what, in the strict sense, he intends"; in other words, he "intends in the strictest sense both those things that he aims at as ends and those that he aims at as means to his ends."[70] Per Foot, the thesis is that it is "sometimes permissible to bring about by oblique intention what one may not directly intend."[71] But can a human inside an ADS exercise free will when it comes to the vehicle's actions?

Could we turn the tables on an ADS, and say that in the current state-of-the-art there is always the abstract risk that such vehicles will swerve out of the control of its human driver, on account of its newly developed intent or other basis, and that because the human driver is unable to anticipate such actions in a preventable way,[72] the risk is agent-relative to the manufacturer-engineer-designer and should be allocated solely to them, i.e., Abbott and Sarch's first solution?[73] This would avoid the

69 "Punishing Artificial Intelligence", note 61 above, at 358.

70 Philippa Foot, "The Problem of Abortion and the Doctrine of the Double Effect" (1967) 5 *Oxford Review* 1 at 1.

71 Ibid. at 2.

72 Regarding the concept of trust in medical robots, see Chapter 3 in this volume.

73 For the terms "agent-relative" and "agent-independent," see Peter Westen, "The Ontological Problem of 'Risk' and 'Endangerment' in Criminal Law" in R. Antony Duff & Stuart Green (eds.), *Philosophical Foundations of Criminal Law* (Oxford Scholarship Online, 2011) 304 at 306.

question of whether ADS can act intentionally in criminal law, as the risk would be independent of the mental state of the human driver. Depending on the jurisdiction, it may also bring back questions of legal personhood regarding corporate entities.

If the focus of liability is on the manufacturer-engineer-designer, how should liability be understood if an ADS device containing algorithms thinks for itself and gains a certain autonomy? Mary Shelley's fictive monster constructed by Victor Frankenstein began to think for itself. How would a manufacturer-engineer-designer liability for future actions not included in its original programming be understood, e.g., when the machine learning is unsupervised? If we want to distribute risk evenly, we would probably need empirical research to do the math regarding the probability of harm in terms of percentages. For the legislator, the need for refined probabilities of risk could mean an increase in highly refined regulatory offenses. This approach would require a novel definition – or should we say concept? – of conduct, depending on whether there is any active role left for the human driver-passenger. In narratological terms, the driver finds herself in an inbuilt plot of a technological narrative from which she cannot escape; she cannot constrain the non-human actant other than by trying to take over the system when she sees something go wrong, and only if she sees it in time. Thinking about ADS in this way would mean that many advantages of the automatic part of automatic driving systems are done away with, and yet the driver still constantly faces the risk of a future criminal charge.

V Conclusion: The Outward and Inward Appearances of Intention

This chapter argues for the development of a hermeneutics of the situation to address the issues raised by ADS. As surveyed in the chapter, the issues are many. The *factum probandum* with regard to foresight and the dispositional element included in the concept of *dolus eventualis* are surrounded by challenges. In accidents involving ADS, the debates regarding what the evidence shows in concrete cases will be massive. How is one to decide that a specific human or non-human defendant's disposition suffices for a conviction? These legal determinations will require a careful distinction between the outward appearance, i.e., apparently careless driving, and the legal carelessness of the driver, i.e., his or her indifference to the outcome. The externally ascertainable aspects of any defendant's action must be taken into consideration in order to make a coherent finding on the elements "knowingly and willingly" of intent.

Some final examples illustrate the importance of the distinction between outward appearance and inward intent or carelessness. Intelligent Traffic Light Control systems can perceive traffic density by means of floating car data apps, which then decide who gets right of way; they are based on the algorithmic ideal of the traffic light talking back to the vehicle. Numerous cases of ADS spontaneously braking in situations where traffic did not require it have occurred, merely because the autopilot thought it recognized the location as one where it had braked earlier. This ADS response is literally a hermeneutics of the situation, but technically a fake negative, in which the human involved may suffer the consequences. In a 2019 Dutch criminal case, the defendant's vehicle had swerved from its lane and collided head-on with an oncoming car. Based on Article 6 of the Road Traffic Act, the defendant was subject to the primary charge of culpable behavior in that he caused a traffic accident by his recklessness, or at a minimum the subsidiary charge that he caused the accident by his considerably careless and/or inattentive behavior, and as a result a person was killed.[74] The defendant pleaded not guilty, arguing that the threshold test for recklessness and/or carelessness had not been met, as he had taken his eye off the road for only a few seconds because he had assumed that the Autosteer System of his Tesla was activated. This position was not given any weight by the court. The defendant was found guilty because his lawyer admitted his client had taken his eye off the road for four to five seconds, and this action was characterized as "considerable" inattentiveness.[75] In the well-known *Vasquez* case in the United States, an investigation by the National Transportation Board suggested that the driver had been visually distracted. Generally speaking, distraction is "a

[74] All Dutch laws can be found at www.Overheid.nl, "Law Bank," www.wetten.nl. In 2013, the then Dutch Ministry of Transport, Public Works and Water Management published an English translation of relevant sections of both codes. Article 6 reads: "All participants in traffic are forbidden to behave in such a way that a traffic accident attributable to them occurs in which another person is killed or sustains serious physical injury or physical injury such that temporary illness occurs or that person is prevented from engaging in normal activity." The translation "attributable to them" does not capture the essence of the Dutch text, which refers to the doctrinal *culpa* in the sense of fault rather than criminal intention, so what is meant is attribution in the sense of culpability.

[75] Dutch District Court Oost-Brabant, Decision of September 3, 2019, 01/860055-19, ECLI:NL:RBOBR:2019:5057.

typical effect of automation complacency,"[76] and it suggests the need for driver training. But in this case, the driver had presumably been gazing downward to the bottom of the center console for 34 percent of the time that the ADS was moving, 31.5 minutes, and about "6 seconds before the crash, she redirected her gaze downward, where it remained until about 1 second before the crash," so that there was no time to react and avoid the crash.[77] The driver had supposedly been streaming a television show on her mobile phone during the entire trip.[78] The vehicle "was designed to operate in autonomous mode only on pre-mapped, designated routes."[79] Did the fact that it was a test drive, and a short one at that, on a test road, make the driver behave irresponsibly by watching television while driving? Technical issues with regard to the vehicle and/or the company's instruction of its employees aside, any driver of a non-automatic vehicle who acts in this way will probably be held criminally responsible, at the very least for behaving negligently. The difference between a traditional driver and a human operator of an ADS has not made great differences in court verdicts yet, in part because inattentiveness attracts liability of some sort. It is, after all, always a human driver who sets the ADS into motion.

Precisely because it is a mental phenomenon, the general concept of intent, as Ferry de Jong contends, is "an essentially 'normative' phenomenon."[80] It "designates ... a criminally relevant manifestation of intentional directedness *between* a subject and the social-life world," so that "this intention externalizes itself in the action performed and is thereby rendered amenable to interpretation," which as a "rule-guided process consists of a pre-eminently *hermeneutic* activity: by way of outward indications, the internal world of intentions and perceptions ... is reconstructed."[81] If the liability of ADS is to be hermeneutically ascertained, compared to being explained by means of, e.g., statistical evidence on traffic accidents in specific locations that invite some people's dangerous

[76] See US, National Transport Safety Board, Highway Accident Report: Collision Between Vehicle Controlled by Developmental Automated Driving System and Pedestrian (Washington, DC: National Transport Safety Board, 2018) at section 1, www.ntsb.gov/investigations/AccidentReports/Reports/HAR1903.pdf.

[77] Ibid. at 18 and 43.

[78] Ibid. at 24.

[79] Ibid. at 8.

[80] Ferry de Jong, "Theorizing Criminal Intent: A Methodological Account" (2011) 7:1 *Utrecht Law Review* 1 at 1, https://utrechtlawreview.org/articles/10.18352/ulr.144.

[81] Ibid., emphasis in the original.

driving, a hermeneutics of the situation in at least two forms is required. First, in court surroundings, the situation would include the doctrinal, conceptual situation of a specific case, a "hermeneutics of the [legal] signification,"[82] a thorough investigation of the defendant's acts and omissions, and the situation of technology in the sense of the state-of-the-art of the vehicle involved. Second, on the meta-level, such hermeneutics would include a debate on the acceptance of various forms of criminal liability in relation to forms of legal personhood, its technological thresholds and machine autonomy, and societal views on the subject.

A hermeneutics of the situation for ADS is necessarily interdisciplinary. The humanities can contribute to the construction of a hermeneutics of the situation partly by means of narratological insights, because insight is needed into the analysis of narratives, both as story, the what, and discourse, the how, in the pre-trial phase and in court, as well as on the narrative structure of technological proposals and their underlying arguments. As long as technological devices are not fully predictable, explanation must be complemented by understanding. To the French philosopher Paul Ricoeur, "narrative is 'imitation of action' (*mimesis*),"[83] which means that "to say *what* an action is, is to say *why* it is done."[84] In legal surroundings, narratives of judgment therefore address intent and legal imputation. The humanities can also contribute to a hermeneutics of the situation because the technological context of ADS raises the ethics of programming. There is good reason to add a legal-hermeneutic methodology of understanding when deciding ADS cases, lest our technological "swerve" swerves out of control, and we gain no further knowledge of causes and the secret motions of things as Bacon urged us to.[85]

82 "End of Doctrine", note 3 above.

83 Charles Reagan, "Interview with Paul Ricoeur" in *Paul Ricoeur: His Life and His Work* (Chicago, IL: University of Chicago Press, 1996) 75.

84 Paul Ricoeur, *Oneself as Another*, translated by Kathleen Blamey (Chicago, IL: University of Chicago Press, 1995) at 63 (emphasis added).

85 Stephen Greenblatt, *The Swerve: How the Renaissance Began* (London, UK: Vintage Books, 2012) at 7, "swerve" being "an unexpected, unpredictable movement of matter," coined by Lucretius in Lucretius, *De Rerum Natura* (On the Nature of Things), translated by John Watson (London, UK: Bell & Daldy, 1870).

INDEX

For EU product safety concerns, contact us at Calle de José Abascal, 56–1°, 28003 Madrid, Spain or eugpsr@cambridge.org.

www.ingramcontent.com/pod-product-compliance
Ingram Content Group UK Ltd.
Pitfield, Milton Keynes, MK11 3LW, UK
UKHW022014021125
464591UK00021B/792

* 9 7 8 1 0 0 9 4 3 1 4 8 4 *